The French Monarchy and the Jews

University of Pennsylvania Press
MIDDLE AGES SERIES
Edited by EDWARD PETERS
Henry Charles Lea Professor
of Medieval History
University of Pennsylvania

A complete listing of the books in this series
appears at the back of this volume

The French Monarchy and the Jews

From Philip Augustus to the Last Capetians

William Chester Jordan

University of Pennsylvania Press
Philadelphia

Copyright © 1989 by the University of Pennsylvania Press
Printed in the United States of America

Library of Congress Cataloging-in-Publication Data

Jordan, William C.,
    The French monarchy and the Jews.
    (University of Pennsylvania Press Middle Ages series)
    Bibliography: p.
    Includes index.
    1. Jews—France—History. 2. France—History—Cape-
tians, 987–1328. 3. France—Ethnic relations. I. Title.
II. Series: Middle Ages.
DS135.F81J67   944'.004924   88–36269
ISBN 0–8122–8175–6

Publication of this volume assisted by a grant from the Committee on Research in the
Humanities and Social Sciences, Princeton University.

Contents

Maps

Preface

This book is a study of the formulation of the "Jewish policy" of the Capetian kings of France from Philip Augustus through the sons of Philip the Fair. It represents, too, an attempt to explore the largely negative impact of this policy on social relations between Jews and Christians. Anyone who has knowledge of the range of scholarship on this period, which stretches from the closing years of the twelfth century to the opening decades of the fourteenth, will recognize at once that I owe a great deal to previous work. But as also will be seen in the pages to follow, much if not most of what has been written about the subject is superficial, decontextualized, or downright incoherent. Many previous studies suffer from a loose application of all sorts of evidence from all sorts of periods and places to the situation in medieval France. I have tried to avoid this error and to be very careful about adducing data not strictly applicable to the problems and circumstances under discussion in the text. I have not, I hope, been inflexible on this point, but in general I have preferred to squeeze the sources we are sure about than to import conclusions extravagantly from the history of radically different political and social experiences. I have done so because the French story is so full of excitement and wonder in itself and because it is a story worth telling right.

I have incurred a great many personal debts. I owe my undergraduate and graduate students more than they know for having forced me to formulate my thoughts with relative simplicity and vigor and to make things clearer and more interesting to them and, I hope, to the reader. I am profoundly obliged also to Mark Cohen, Professor of Near Eastern Studies and Chairman of the Committee for Jewish Studies at Princeton University for insisting that even in a work with a political theme like mine the history of Jewish and Christian conflict ought not to confine itself to a sterile description of the authorities' program. A workshop of which Professor Cohen was a part and that met off and on over several years to discuss problems of teaching Jewish history (including its Christian interface) aided enormously in stimulating me to keep faithful to that advice. Every deviance is, therefore, my own choice and risk. In any case, I wish to thank the members of that workshop and its director, Professor Ivan Marcus of the Jewish Theological Seminary of New York, for their erudite and wonderfully lively discussions. Finally, I owe debts to a number of other colleagues and friends who listened to me work through small or large parts of the argument of the book; Dina Copelman, Paula Sanders, and David Abraham.

Part of the narrative was presented publicly before a seminar of the Near Eastern Studies Department of Princeton University some years ago and more recently at the University of Georgia and Columbia University. I was able to present longer portions to kind audiences thanks to the opportunity offered me of being the Morgan Lecturer at Dickinson College, Carlisle, Pennsylvania, in October 1985. I take the greatest pleasure in thanking the former president and the faculty of that institution, particularly Professor Neil Weissman, for the hospitality they afforded me. My own university, Princeton, contributed to my expenses for research, as well as to the publication costs of this volume, by grants from the Committee on Research in the Humanities and Social Sciences. I wish also to acknowledge the support of a Rockefeller Foundation Fellowship in the Humanities (1982–1983) that allowed me to work intensively in archives and libraries on both sides of the Atlantic.

Disclaimers are commonplace in prefaces, but they may be no less sincere for that. The support that I have received gave me the opportunity to read, think, and write at some leisure. Any errors that might exist despite this benevolence are my fault. Nonetheless, whatever is useful in this study is offered as a small token of my gratitude to the fact that there are places like American universities, indeed, universities like Princeton, where people of diverse social and racial backgrounds and confessions can still talk with scholarly forbearance, kindness, and generosity about some of the most painful episodes in the history of the Western experience. That we can do so may sometimes delude us into thinking that the world now is a better place than it is and its prospects more hopeful than they are. There is always the danger of wishful thinking. But what is the alternative, except the sin of despair?

William Chester Jordan
25 August 1988

Note on Currency: The medieval French monarchy accounted its resources in two types of money, *livres parisis* (pounds of Paris) and *livres tournois* (pounds of Tours). Four *livres parisis* (l.p.) were equivalent to five *livres tournois* (l.t.). The English pound sterling was worth about four times as much as a French *livre parisis*.

I

Philip Augustus and the Jews
1180–1223

1. The Jews of the Royal Domain

In 1182 AD, after a reign of not quite two years, Philip II Augustus, the king of the Franks, expelled the Jews from the royal domain, that part of the kingdom under his direct administration and jurisdiction. The effect of this order was limited by the fact that the cluster of lands and rights, including rights over Jews, that made up the royal domain was small.[1] Conceived of in terms of a modern map, the area of France in which most of Philip's rights and lands were concentrated made a more or less narrow strip of territory, not entirely uninterrupted, running from the Beauvaisis in the north to Bourges in the south. At no point was this strip much wider than one hundred kilometers, and it was sometimes far narrower. Even this conceptualization (indicated by the shading on the accompanying map) gives a false impression of royal authority, power, and influence. To say, for example, that the king's rights were concentrated in a particular region is not to say that his lordship was absolute in that region. Many lords enjoyed a wide array of rights in the same general area. Some of these were said to have been granted to them by previous kings—an allegation that would be of value to future rulers—but the exercise of non-royal authority in the shaded region that for simplicity may be called the royal domain was a stubborn fact of life.

Similarly, here and there outside the shaded region the king had a number of rights. Sometimes these seem in hindsight pregnant with possibilities for the story of the consolidation of royal authority: rights to protect certain monasteries and bishoprics are a case in point. Others may seem trivial to the unsuspecting observer, like the right to collect a toll or to be received hospitably. To contemporaries, however, these apparently trifling possessions often loomed larger than theoretical rights of protection whose exercise over churches in lands far distant from Paris was severely constrained by the limited military power of the twelfth-century monarchy.

To bring the question of influence into the picture makes it more complicated. Influence did not depend merely on real authority or gran-

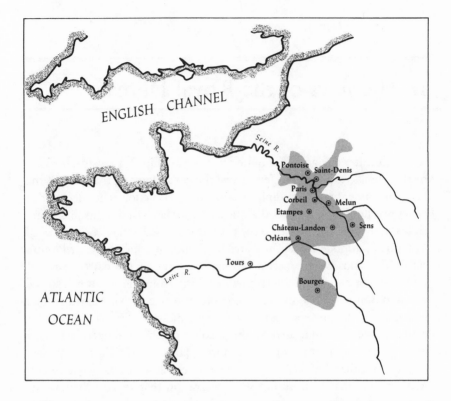

France: the royal domain, ca. 1180

diose pretensions to authority; and it was not necessarily correlated directly with military or economic power. In the twelfth century it often depended most on simple friendship. A great lord, such as the count of Champagne or the duke of Normandy, might do what or as the king of the Franks did simply because he liked the king of the Franks. To this extent royal policies were never necessarily limited to the domain per se in their application.

All this having been said, it remains true that the effect of Philip Augustus's order in 1182 to expel the Jews from the royal domain did not apply to and, despite whatever royal influence there was, was not enforced against very many Jews. Not that anyone knows precisely how many Christians or Jews were in the "domain." Sources that have been used to establish the demography of France before and after 1182 permit us to talk about an increase, more or less steady, in the total population, based on the extension of town walls, the creation of suburbs and new towns, and the progressive clearing of forests and morain and the draining of marshes for cultivating new land in the countryside. These sources do not permit us to come up with any wholly persuasive absolute figures, but they do suggest in gross terms that from the year 1000 to the year 1300, France (based on the modern map) enjoyed a tripling of population from about five million to about fifteen million.[2] The region that would have constituted the royal domain in 1179 (the year of Philip's accession) was by 1300 the most densely settled area in France; and every indication is that its relatively greater density was characteristic of the High Middle Ages. If this is so, and if the more informative sources for the period around 1300 have been interpreted correctly by economic historians, then the population density of this region was 50 to 70 inhabitants per square kilometer.[3] Again, if the shaded portions of our map can be roughly estimated at 25,000 square kilometers, then the population of that region in 1300 would have been 1,250,000 to 1,750,000. As the final manipulation (or sleight of hand), we must decrease this figure by some factor to account for population growth in the region from 1180 to 1300. If we halve it, we are talking about a population subject to Philip Augustus in 1180 in a range from six hundred thousand or so to almost nine hundred thousand.

These calculations are not intended to do any more than give a sense of the human resources at hand to the Capetian monarch. At best they provide "ball-park" figures. If a census document were miraculously to come to light and show that the domain in 1180 actually had only half a million (or a million) inhabitants, it should not surprise us. What is important, over all, is that although by either estimate the population is relatively substantial, it is only about one-tenth of the whole population of France (measured against any best estimate for the period). There were Jews among this number, but as we shall now see, not very many, because the Jewish population in France was concentrated largely to the east and south, far distant from the limits of the royal domain, in areas that few if any contemporary northerners would have called France.

In the royal domain per se, what was the nature of the Jewish population and settlement? Where and how were Jews living when Philip came to the throne? If we depend merely on the most explicit evidence, then the domain towns in which there were Jewish inhabitants were few in number: Bourges, Château-Landon, Corbeil, Etampes, Melun, Orléans, Paris, Pontoise, Sens, and Saint-Denis.[4] Yet there is one problem even with this short list: Saint-Denis. There is no doubt that there were Jews resident in the town. There is no doubt that the king's influence was extraordinary, thanks to the presence of the royal abbey of Saint-Denis. If one hesitates to talk about Saint-Denis as being quite like other towns in the royal domain, however, it is precisely because the royal abbey was so powerful in its own right and endowed with extensive privileges. More to the point, Philip Augustus's grandfather had ceded his rights over the Jews of the town and the castle to the abbot of Saint-Denis earlier in the century.[5]

If we remain wedded to explicit evidence even as our gaze leaves the shaded area of the map that represents the principal concentration of royal rights and lands, the references are meager and we can only speak circumspectly of Philip Augustus's possession of rights over Jews. At Tours there is some evidence of Capetian *dominium* over the Jews around the turn of the eleventh/twelfth century, but despite a temporary revocation this had been effectively ceded before 1180.[6]

Leaving direct and explicit evidence behind, the problems increase. It has generally been assumed that Jews must have been living in many places elsewhere in the domain. The justification for this view, besides extrapolating from the appalling paucity of royal documentation before 1180, is the occasional reference to Jews living in *and near* some named town. The most important such reference for our purposes is one which mentions the Jews of Troyes and the Jews of congregations nearby around the turn of the eleventh/twelfth century. To be sure, this reference concerns the county of Champagne where every scholar feels that Jewish settlement was denser than in the twelfth-century royal domain; but it has been marshalled to suggest the magnitude of the problem for the period before the thirteenth century.[7] Unfortunately it is not very satisfying to leave the matter at this. To say that there were probably more locations where Jews lived in the royal domain in 1180 than explicit documentation affirms is not saying much: were there a great many more or only a few?

Among the most problematic sources for Jewish settlement, but a source that is nonetheless somewhat suggestive, is toponymic material, location names like "Street of the Jews," "Street of the Jewry," or some such variant. The reservations are numerous. In the first place none of these local names—nor others much more indecisive—necessarily points to the historic existence of a Jewish community in the town where the name is or was found because the naming of streets is frequently eccentric. Second, presuming that a particular toponym does point to historic Jewish settlement, the earliest reference to the toponym provides only a terminus ad quem for the existence of the community. The long list of Jewish *rues* reported to the French version of *Notes & Queries* at the close of the nineteenth century illustrates this.[8] Luckily the list was assembled before fashion and embarrassment had effaced the very memory of some names.[9] Yet, as precious as these toponyms are in general, their value for determining positive patterns of medieval settlement is limited. At best they have stimulated researchers to look for Jewish settlement in places where they had not looked before or to re-examine the evidence from places where they thought no direct evidence of Jewish settlement had survived. Despite this spur to research, all too often the toponyms cannot be attested before the Renaissance or cannot be attested with certainty at all given the peculiarities of medieval Latin and Old French orthography.[10]

Finally in any town where there was a "Street of the Jews," modern presuppositions are hesitant to believe that there were two or more such streets. But medieval towns were not laid out so neatly. Explicit records of settlement, when they do survive, reveal that Jewish habitation in a town, even if concentrated, was not exclusive. Jews lived outside any single concentration (jewry), sometimes in isolated residences scattered about the town, sometimes in other concentrations.[11] The point is that speculation on the population of the Jews in individual towns and about the critical meaning of social space and liminality must be tentative only, indeed must be frequently distorted when based merely on the abstract notion of a single street or single well-defined cluster of streets being given over to Jewish residence.

Limited as the value of the information from toponyms is in making *positive* statements about Jewish residence, this information does contribute to our conception of the demography of the Jews in the royal domain. For, despite the fact that early modern France was peppered with towns bearing toponymic vestiges of the medieval Jewish presence, the sum of these toponyms adds virtually nothing to our picture of settlement in the royal domain of 1180 as derived from explicit contemporary documentary sources. That is to say, the street names sometimes confirm the explicit evidence of residence: for example, at Corbeil, Etampes, Melun, Paris, Pontoise, Tours.[12] But it adds only one other place, Mantes, unknown from other pre-1180 sources.[13] We should not conclude that the existing cartography of Jewish settlement in the royal domain of 1180 based on documentary evidence is nearly comprehensive, but that, however lacking in details, the extent of Jewish settlement was indeed very light in the traditional Capetian patrimony, much lighter than in most areas that make up the map of modern France.

If the density of Jewish settlement in the royal domain in 1180 was light, what there was of it can be fairly well described for the individual towns in which Jews lived.[14] In the first place, the population were not all native to the towns. Immigrants were a real and increasing concern to Jewish thinkers. Immigrants put pressure on productive resources and competed with established local Jewish merchants. Although in hindsight scholars view the eleventh and twelfth centuries as a period of significant expansion in urban and commercial life which could accommodate the crush of newcomers to those towns with the fastest growing economies, natives of the towns were less sanguine on this point.[15] Scholars have regarded the creation of one form of the *herem* (Jewish excommunication) as a device to deal with a heightened tempo of immigration that seemed to threaten native economic security and stable relations with Christians.[16]

The communities of Jews, at first glance, seem to have been deliberately situated at critical junctures in the towns either near a place of refuge or where there was a focus of commerce, like a market-place, caravan road, or river quai.[17] On the other hand, medieval towns, with not many exceptions, were quite small. Within the actual walls of the towns few urbanites lived at any considerable distance from a potential refuge or a space devoted to commerce. So it may be that what really occurred in the twelfth century was a strengthening of Jewish settlement at certain developing commercial points or, conversely, a tendency for commercial transactions themselves to become increasingly concentrated whenever several attractive nodes of carrying on commerce were juxtaposed: the cathedral, forges on a river bank, and a jewry; a castle, a cross-roads outside the walls, and a gateway to the town. Every entrepreneur would have wanted some sort of stall or business/residence there, but out of this generalized desire some clustering might also occur: butchers, drapers, parchmenters, Jews.[18]

The royal city about which most is known when Philip Augustus came to the throne is Paris. In the eleventh and twelfth centuries, together with the general increase in population of the region as a whole, the number of inhabitants of the city grew apace. It is presumed that the community of Jews in the city expanded commensurately. One scholarly guess suggests that in 1180 the whole city contained about one hundred thousand residents of whom five thousand were Jews.[19] This guess seems off the mark to me. Paris was certainly a city of one hundred thousand, perhaps considerably more, by 1250.[20] In 1180, so far as extrapolation from general trends and the indicative if not decisive archeological evidence suggest, we need a considerable corrective, probably a reduction to sixty thousand or so, which would nonetheless make Paris a very substantial city by medieval standards and a pillar of the king's economic influence and fiscal resources.[21]

Roblin, who estimated the high number of Parisians and Parisian Jews mentioned above, was on firmer ground when he focussed on the Ile de la Cité itself. For this, the very center of Capetian authority in Paris and increasingly in the realm, he estimated one thousand Jews among five thousand total inhabitants. Archeological and some documentary evidence shows that there was at least one large jewry (perhaps another concentration as well) on the island, which seems to have had a sufficient number of residences to easily match or exceed those in any Jewish neighborhood on the banks of the Seine. Given the amount of royal and ecclesiastical property on the Ile de la Cité and the nature of domestic architecture, the jewry (or jewries) might well have sheltered 20% of the total population of the island (as compared to a ratio of Jews to Christians in the city at large of 3% or 5% if Roblin's sense of the relative size of the two communities is more dependable than his absolute figures). Even if, to adduce the last caveat, not all the people living in the Ile de la Cité jewries were Jews, there is enough evidence to suggest that most of them were and that a large number of Jewish residences were scattered about the tiny island.[22]

This peculiarly large concentration of Jews in one part of one city in a royal domain not otherwise densely settled by Jews helps to situate Philip Augustus's perception of them. His contemporary biographer, Rigord, ultimately a monk of Saint-Denis, paints a picture that is completely receptive to the demographic sketch given above, even if he puts his own emphasis on the moral conclusions to be taken from the picture. He reports the general feeling that the domains of the French king had not historically been a center of Jewish settlement; but for a long time, owing to the relative favor of the French (read especially, Louis VII, Philip Augustus's father), they began to enter these domains in large numbers. Owing to the commercial possibilities of a rapidly growing Paris, they came mainly to that city in preference to all others in the domain. Rigord waxes hot about the Jews controlling half of Paris before Philip Augustus expelled them.[23] On this point he exaggerates, but like most exaggerations his was meant to attain a certain plausibility among the readers of his text:[24] since the Jewish presence on the Ile de la Cité was substantial and everybody knew it, everybody, or so Rigord hoped, would rightly praise the king who had removed the offense.

It is a giant's leap from a monk's feeling expressed after the fact to the expulsion by the king, a very radical act and, in the context of the period of lenience or relative favor that preceded it, a striking departure from Capetian policy. There is more behind this turn of events than a mere perception that there were a lot of wealthy Jews who lived, worked, and worshipped near the royal palace and the cathedral of Paris on the Ile de la Cité. What, then, were the additional factors that impelled Philip Augustus to move so decisively against the Jews?

To answer the question posed in the last paragraph requires both some sense of the general and partly longstanding attitudes (positive and negative) of Jews and Christians towards each other in the 1170s and 1180s and a close look at the immediate environment and sensibilities of the king during this period. To an extent the discussion must shift back and forth between trying to identify typical casts of mind and trying to explain why Philip might have shared or departed from prevalent attitudes. We begin with the enormously complicated question of mutual perceptions, and more particularly with how the religious leadership of the two confessions saw each other.[25] The aim is not to explain the political and social relations of Jews and Christians by reference to elitist predilections or to reduce individual behavior like the king's to an aping of an elitist program.[26] Quite the contrary, it is to demonstrate that in the grammar of perception there were categories from which any person might draw to find justification for his own views and actions or to fashion straw men against which he could assert them. Until and unless we understand these categories, we are not likely to achieve a vivid understanding of modifications in personal or collective behavior and attitudes in Philip's time.

Jews, Christian intellectuals would say in the Middle Ages, were alien; Jews insisted on the distinction between themselves (brothers) and others (strangers). Christians would have liked to think of themselves as a people for whom the category of "stranger" would grow steadily smaller as their universalist religion spiritually conquered the faithless. The twelfth century, the aftermath of the great massacres of Jews in the Christian self-confidence and crusader enthusiasm of 1096, put a critical value on these attitudes.[27] To Jews, it compellingly reaffirmed that social relations, notwithstanding certain positive features, were essentially precarious. This was a widely shared opinion even though the massacres of the late eleventh century had occurred in the Rhineland and there had been surprisingly little violence in what we would call France.[28] The Rhenish incidents set the tone for the century to come, since French and German Jews (and the few thousand English for that matter) were part of a single north European culture.[29]

The problematizing effect of the legacy of the massacres can be seen in what is usually alleged to be a continuing positive sign of social inter-course, namely the contacts of Christian and Jewish intellectuals, especially in Paris, on matters of the Bible and exegesis. Beryl Smalley rightly indi-cated in her classic book on the study of the Bible that the Augustinian canons of Saint-Victor on the Left Bank of Paris pursued these contacts in the twelfth century.[30] Since Smalley's work, scholar after scholar has con-structed a weighted picture of largely disinterested discussions between Christians and Jews, a distorting picture of symbiosis if once we think about the constraints on discussion.[31] Some friendship, some respect for cleverness there must have been on both sides, but also a great deal of shaking of heads in pity at the blindness of the other.[32] Our imagination of the tone of the conversations must ultimately be confirmed from the enormous amount of evidence on the exegetical techniques and content of the two traditions. On these points, because of the sheer mass of the data, we can be fairly certain.

In the first place, obviously controversial biblical texts were avoided. Presumably, however, non-controversial texts could have permitted "peaceful" discussions.[33] The problem is in defining a non-controversial Old Testament text. Some passages of the Old Testament—the long gen-erational and tribal lists, etc.—were non-controversial, but afforded little opportunity for discussion. Beyond these rather innocuous passages, very little of the Old Testament was neutral. All of the more or less explicit messiological passages should have been avoided for obvious reasons. A number of other passages that Jews did not regard as messiological were accepted as such by Christians, thus further limiting the number of so-called safe texts.[34] I do not mean that all Christians *did* avoid discussing such texts with Jews or resisted Jewish interpretations. Andrew of Saint Victor (d. 1175) was certainly sympathetic, but his "excessive" sympathy for the Jewish interpretation was to be roundly criticized and resented even though the data he accumulated would be used by future generations of exegetes.[35]

A good example of Christian attitudes emerges from a study of the exegesis of the biblical story of Dinah, the daughter of Jacob the

Patriarch.[36] It illustrates both how the technique and content of exegesis differed markedly between Jews and Christians and how these differences turned what might appear to have been a safe story for discussion into the material, upon reflection, for a hardening of attitudes.

The story itself is a thrilling one. While Jacob the Patriarch camped in the land of the pagan Hivites, a Hivite prince abducted Dinah as she went out to visit the Hivite women. The brutal act of rape that followed the abduction culminated in the prince's consuming passion for Dinah, whom thereafter he wished to marry. He pressed his suit with her father and brothers, promising under the prompting of two of the brothers, Simeon and Levi, to bind his people to the Hebrews ("become a single nation") by undergoing circumcision. Ultimately the circumcision of the Hivites was accomplished, but the operations left the adult males weak and feverish. In this state they were slaughtered by the sons of Jacob: They "killed all the males . . . , and pillaged the town because their sister had been dishonored. They took away their flocks, cattle, donkeys, and whatever there was in the town and in the countryside. They carried off all their riches, all their little children and their wives, and looted everything to be found in their houses." Jacob rebuked them for their enormities; but they rebuked their father in their turn, "Is our sister to be treated like a whore?"

How did exegetes in the two traditions approach the story?[37] Without exception Jewish interpreters denigrated the validity of the circumcision of the Hivites ("their hearts and minds were uncircumcised"), and they lauded the rescue of Dinah by her brothers.[38] These exegetes differed on details, differences sometimes closely correlatable to their changing perceptions of the threat posed by outsiders (pagans) in their own time. The great eleventh-century commentator in northern France, Rabbi Solomon ben Isaac (Rashi) of Troyes, apparently writing before the Rhenish massacres in the First Crusade, argued that the rescue was justified but that the intensity of the retribution was wrong. Subtle turns of phrases or complementary biblical texts that referred to the massacre were marshalled in defense of this interpretation.[39] After the experiences of the Rhenish massacres and other violent anti-Jewish incidents of the century to come, however, there emerged or, rather, re-emerged significantly more favorable judgements of the brothers. These judgements sometimes had their roots in remote periods when Jewish-Gentile relations had been equally deleterious. What re-emerged in the minority culture of the Jews of twelfth- and thirteenth-century Europe were "fantasies" of vengeance in which Jewish exegete after exegete found textual reasons, though these differed from rabbi to rabbi, to laud the violence, relish the retribution, and defend the massacre of the Hivites as God's work.[40]

On the Christian side, on the other hand, the story of Dinah meant something quite different: the prince of the Hivites had committed an immoral and disgusting act in raping a girl and robbing her of her virginity. To the extent that there was a variety of meanings in every text,[41] one could interpret (and there would always be a tradition of interpreting) the vengeance that was exacted for this crime as a trope of an epic battle of virtue overcoming vice.[42] Nonetheless, the deeper, traditional signification was typological, and quintessentially anti-Jewish. Any good Christian scholar would have told a Jew that the story was a foreshadowing of the coming of the church, the gathering of the nations into one mystical body. That is to say, all who knew of the rape rightly desired the wickedness to be punished. But the prince had fallen in love, and this was the first step toward his redemption. He was striving to undo his evil. It might have been possible, so Christian commentators suggested and our interlocutor would have noted, to bring his people into honorable union with Israel. His agreement to be circumcised along with his whole people was nothing less than a critical first step in this journey. Unfortunately, the brothers of Dinah could not overcome their thirst for vengeance sufficiently to see that there was a better way than violence and slaughter. To repeat, the story was a foreshadowing of the gathering of the nations under the banner of love in the church of Christ.[43]

A discussion of this story had its academic possibilities: how to probe intentionality in the circumcision; whether the desire of the Hivite "prince" for Dinah grew into genuine love or only into a modified form of lust. These and other points were debatable on literary-grammatical grounds. One could argue about the prince's emotions on the basis of the various contexts of phrases expressing love in the Bible; one could consider other biblical passages about circumcision and its efficacy. But debatable as the meaning of this whole story and of its individual parts may have been, given all the tools of rabbinic exegesis and emerging scholastic method, discussion offered no harmonious resolution, because the hermeneutic cleavage was too deep. Christian typology subordinated the details of the tale to a vision of salvational history in a way similar to that prompted by rabbinic concern for the preservation of unpolluted worship for the one God. The discussion would have been friendly; the afterthoughts less so, because Christian frustration with the Jews' resistance to union in the story would inevitably have been translated into the latter's contemporary resistance to the "Truth."

We can know that the story of Dinah was one of those non- messiological texts selected for discussion that yet revealed the depth of religious conflict when addressed in any detail. This is because one of the greatest of those Victorine canons in twelfth-century Paris, whose activity has been the focus of scholarship on Jewish-Christian contact on the Bible to date, firmly held to the typological opinion in the face of Jewish views, especially that the circumcision was without merit. Richard of Saint Victor (d. 1173), to whom I refer, laments in the *Benjamin minor*, one of his exegetical masterpieces that incorporates many of the Jewish interpretations he learned,

> Oh how much better it would have been had the men, although circumcised [as the Jews say] not so much for God as for Dinah, been led to the true worship of God little by little than destroyed by unexpected and sudden death.[44]

It is not so much that Richard refused to admit the validity of the Jewish interpretation. It is that for him (and on this he is more representative than his contemporary Andrew whose "judaizing" he condemned) their interpretation was incomplete, unfulfilled. As open as he might be to their truth, his words seem to intensify on the page when he comes to contrast "theirs" to "his."[45]

It is no objection to what has been written above that the example of Dinah is unfair, as if any medieval exegete would have recognized the potential ambivalence of the story and therefore would not have selected it for "pacific" discussion. It clearly was selected, and in any case this argument puts too low an estimate on the creative power of the human imagination. To cast one's eyes over the pages of scripture and to think that one has discovered an interesting but non-controversial text that Christians and Jews might discuss is, in the medieval context, probably delusive. The depth of the hermeneutical commitment on both sides was so great, so pervasive, that it can only be supposed that these encounters largely turned into confirmations of the extraordinary distance that, to contemporaries, separated the two confessions.

Scholarly monks like the Victorines of Paris had desired to consult the Jews in the first place because their own knowledge of Hebrew was limited.[46] Some Jews, on the other hand, because of the need to be familiar with certain Christological arguments and because of genuine interest in Christian scholarship, mastered the academic language of the monks, Latin.[47] The degree of this interchange must not be exaggerated; after all, we are looking at northern France. This was not a land, like Spain, Provence, or Sicily, where Jews and Christians were actively engaged in the translation and processing of philosophical and scientific texts for wider consumption.[48] Aspects of this sort of activity would eventually penetrate the north and help transform the nature of education; but the Ile de France on the eve of the reign of Philip Augustus was not a center of translation.[49] Few Jews, even among the polemicists, knew or were comfortable with Latin; still fewer Christians knew Hebrew.

Lore about the two languages, therefore, constitutes a rather interesting indicator of the ambivalent attitudes of Christians and Jews. In the first place, Christian scholars had great respect for Hebrew as an artifact, in a way that no Jew could have regarded Latin, for to savants of both religions Hebrew was the original language of Eden. It was the language spoken by the angels, had been the language reserved for the chosen of God after the Tower of Babel, and would be the preferred speech of those who went to heaven.[50] It was the language that literally opened the door to salvation: a northern twelfth-century church, for example, has contemporary messianic formulas inscribed in Hebrew on the portals.[51] Latin fared less well. It (or its liturgical variety) was indeed progressively achieving a sacrosanct status among Christians.[52] But it was just another language to educated Jews, no more, no less. Or maybe less: because it had long been the language of the oppressor (pagan Roman and Christian), peoples of "strange speech," it was sometimes regarded as peculiarly appropriate for a kind of derogation that sloped into mysticism.[53] Among Jewish demons of popular lore, non-Hebrew names, including Latin ones, had long been common; incantations and charms continued to evoke these in the twelfth century.[54] The twelfth century added little to the accumulated fund of this lore, except for the earliest Jewish attempt, so far as I know, to trace the origin of the name of the angel Metatron of Hebrew folk belief to a Latin *metator*, "Measurer" or "Surveyor". This occurs in a Rhenish text of about 1200.[55] The man who confected the etymology was one of that small group of Rhenish *hasidim*, "pious ones," who were unhappy with the compromises that the political leaders of the Rhenish communities had had to make in order to achieve a new and stable equilibrium with Christians after the breakdown of the First Crusade; or, better, were unhappy with the resumption of particular kinds of social relations that followed in the wake of these compromises.[56] Since Metatron was the most potent, protean, and frightening of the angels in Jewish lore, a measurer of fates, of men, and of souls, a Death Angel waiting to judge and to destroy, this new "etymology" may be of some significance,[57] but there is no purpose in belaboring the point.

The evidence on the other side is weightier but sketchy. Christian scholars might praise Hebrew and recognize it as a holy language, the language of God's first intimacy with humankind, but this very mystical appreciation degenerated at times into a kind of fear and necromantic estimate of Hebrew. It was the language of magic.[58] Much of this was fed by the sheer strangeness of its appearance: the Hebrew signs, for example, that Christians of many walks of life saw fashioned by Jewish merchants and moneylenders on the parchment records of debts.[59] In England, where the evidence is so rich and may reflect the French situation, angry mobs might destroy the deeds if they could get their hands on them. They did so in ways that, it has been intimated, bespeak not only a concern for their financial content (proof of Christians' indebtedness), but for their form. The perpetrators of the York massacre of 1190 consigned the deeds *flammis sollemnibus*, a curious liturgical rendering that Cecil Roth thought referred to the mob's burning of the covenants with fires lit from lights on the high altar of York Minster. Possibly.[60] Possibly, too, Christians suspected, through converts or informers, that the covenants contained slurs against the faith of Christ: Stein in fact tried to show that the English records did. How many of these punning slurs were really unintended errors is unknown,[61] but the deeds do occasionally refer to Christians as pagans; to clerics as "shorn ones"; to the date of Christmas as *nittel* (Latin *dies natalis*), but "with a [Hebrew] tav, . . . a reference," according to Stein, "to Jesus' death by hanging" and therefore to Deuteronomy 21:23 and the hanged one as "accursed of God." For All Saints Day the deeds are said to have punned and talked of All Slaves Day (*kadosh*, saint, being replaced by *kadhesh*, temple slave). The Christians' Saint Michael Archangel was rather the demonic 'ikkel, the "crooked" one in the fantasies of retribution attributed by Stein to the Hebrew deeds.[62]

Jews and Christians, to put the matter another way, spoke among themselves and to each other in their daily discourse in the same vernacular language,[63] but the languages that in formulaic cadences expressed the most sublime longings in their religions and enrolled their formal records were remote from the everyday speech of ordinary people and were not appreciated in the same way across confessional lines. What this did was to make the acts of worship and devotion of each religion, insofar as they were visible or audible to the adherents of the other, strange and forbidding. The theme that runs through so much ecclesiastical legislation against loud chanting by Jews in synagogue or actions in procession to burials reflects this attitude.[64] To the Christians—to ordinary Christians—the cultic signs were wrong, the sounds were wrong; and since in general they were told over and over again that the religion of the Jews was wrong (the irreducible message of the rather more subtle relationship between Judaism and Christianity that Christian theologians articulated), they were open to the possibility of a great inversion being at the center of Judaism. Perhaps ultimately this is why the charge of Deicide had such potency.[65]

In any case it helps to explain why the Jews as a whole could be conceived of as devilish. The inversion was a condition of Judaism; or, at least, some Christians advanced this view and advanced it with growing emphasis in the course of the twelfth century. The most remarkable consequence of this was the development of the idea of contemporary Jews as re-enactors of the crucifixion. This accusation, as is well known, began shortly after 1144 in England with the reports of a monk, Thomas of Monmouth, on the death of a boy named William around Eastertime in the city of Norwich. Thomas drew upon bits and pieces of lore and interpreted other bits and pieces of "evidence" which came to him to invent a fabulous tale of the crucifixion of the boy and the wonderful discovery of his body. With a singlemindedness of purpose he tried to popularize the cult of the boy, whom he regarded as a martyr. He had great difficulties in making headway—and his opposition and how he overcame it are fascinating stories in their own right—but his ultimate success in securing a modest cult of Saint William established the precedent.[66]

Other such accusations soon appeared in England; by the 1170s they were known on the continent and, more ominously, Frenchmen began to make them themselves, borrowing and progressively elaborating on the swirl of imputations at Norwich and by then also at Gloucester (1168).[67] The purity of William and of Harold of Gloucester was emphasized in the very fact of their being children. It was this purity that was said to offend the Jews. Regard for the watchfulness of adult Christians over their children required that the Jews act craftily (*subdole*) to obtain their victims.[68] We see this contrast between the innocent, pure, open, often tiny child and the secretive, devilish Jews repeated in nearly every future accusation, and there would be scores in the centuries to come.[69]

French cases, in or near the heartland of royal France (hints and reports of early ones from the 1160s and 1170s at Loches-sur-Indre, Pontoise, Epernay, Janville, Blois), are uneven in the quality of evidence that has survived.[70] But those of Pontoise and Blois offer some useful material. A tender association with the Virgin may be inferred from what were finally chosen as the feast days of these child saints: William of Norwich's was the eve of the Annunciation to the Virgin (24 March), Harold of Gloucester's was the twenty-fifth, the day of Annunciation itself. The French evidence shows that Richard of Pontoise (d. 1163), whose body was translated to the Church of the Holy Innocents at Paris and who is most commonly known as Richard of Paris, also had his feast day on the Annunciation of the Blessed Virgin. Robert of Bury, an English example that opened the decade of the 1180s, had his cult celebrated, too, on 25 March, Lady Day.[71]

Richard of Paris was a "gentle and pious boy." He was said to have been implored to deny the Christian faith, but he rather affirmed it, became a martyr to it, in the face of his tormentors[72] and happily (*feliciter*) accepted death.[73] He too, like his predecessors in these reputed child martyrdoms, became a miracle worker of renown.[74] The contemporary biographer of Philip Augustus, Rigord, makes plain that the young king knew of and trusted in Richard's and similar stories. Philip thought that the Jews of Paris did the same sorts of things to Christian boys as were narrated in these tales.[75]

The Blois accusation in 1171 of the murder of a youth (by crucifixion according to Robert of Torigni, d. 1186) provides different kinds of information.[76] Blois was not in the royal domain, but it was right on the "border"; and French royal "influence" on and concern with it was of importance.[77] The Blois incident, it has been pointed out, was the earliest in which the competent political authority, the count of Blois in this instance, not only seriously entertained the accusation but brought the powers of his government to bear against the Jews, this although no corpse was ever produced. The count may have had selfish reasons for doing so, among which was the desire to distance himself from his Jewish paramour. More to the point, the Jews mobilized their resources and worked hard to get other authorities to bring pressure against the count. They solicited his brother the count of Champagne, who took seriously plaints of a minority that was substantial in his domains. They called also on the king of the Franks, Philip Augustus's father, who interceded on their behalf, against the wishes of many people. Despite their best efforts thirty-two of the forty adults of the community were executed, and a number of others were temporarily imprisoned or forced to convert (later reversed).

Philip Augustus's evident acceptance of the charges of Jewish malice in the royal domain town of Pontoise and the celebration of the cult of Richard of Pontoise at Paris in his youth, coupled with the criticisms of his father's favor toward the Jews, provide the final links in the chain that led to his first forays against the Jews on his accession. There was to be—and we shall explore it—a rapid escalation of his program, fueled by other events that brought him from merely despoiling the Jews to expelling them.[78] But if the attitudes and events I have been describing had a profound effect on Philip and therefore on royal policy in his own time and as a precedent for the future, it also profoundly affected the Jews. What needs to be stressed and re-stressed is the perception of the precariousness of social relations. The Rhenish massacres, almost a century before, had radically challenged Jews everywhere in northern Jewry to rethink their notions of community. But if it was never possible to forget those events, new relations did evolve and even in the Rhineland achieved a certain stability. The leaders of Christendom defended the Jews' right to survive; and Saint Bernard himself, champion of the crusading impulse as he was, was a figure of respect among Jews precisely for his forthright refusal to countenance violence against them and his intervention against it.[79]

Similarly, social relations in northern France could not be immune from the general issues that deeply divided the mental world of Jews and Christians or from apprehension over incidents that revealed the uglier manifestations of this cleavage. But, once more, cautious attitudes did not preclude intellectual discussions, even if they gave them less the academic character than some scholars have thought; and incidents like the establishment of child cults remained isolated and not without resistance from authorities.

With the Blois incident, however, there did emerge the distinct belief that governments might swerve from the straight and narrow.[80] Bribery and cajolery could bring some political authorities around, but the shock of the destruction of a sizable and flourishing community at Blois with government support was great. Moving poetic laments express the despair: "why [Lord] did You hide Your face."[81] The existing method of communication among the three closely related parts of northern Jewry (English, French, and Rhenish), circular letters, so often used to convey internalist theological and legal judgements, were increasingly devoted to the more pressing problems of mobilizing these communities in defense of threatened Jews: informing them of their plight, suggesting ways of intervening, commending the abused to the succor of those who remained prosperous and unharmed.[82]

The pressures of the century vigorously animated the Jewish communities to construct a forbidding martyrocentric self-image, sometimes unnecessarily and derisively referred to as "lachrymose."[83] Rightly, the emphasis on origins has led scholars to lay stress on the impact of the Rhenish massacres as crucial. The Hebrew narratives of these events include liturgical centerpieces that praise the (holy) suicides of adults and the sacrifice of children—a re-enactment, in Ivan Marcus's view, of the Temple Cult: the unblemished lamb to the slaughter.[84] This emphasis in the narratives is repeated in the memorial poems of the events. They insist, in some of the most moving words ever written, that death is preferable to apostasy; and that knowledge of this truth has been successfully transferred from the elders to the children, who often express these profound sentiments in the poems.[85]

But everywhere, not just in the highly formal context of liturgical poetry, this martyrocentric image advanced. We may discover it, for example, on the gravemarkers from Jewish cemeteries. The cemeteries themselves, with their upright stones, were, to many Christians, dreadful places.[86] We know this because occasionally and under various circumstances they came into Christian ownership to be converted to other uses, in which case it was first necessary to remove the remains of the recent corpses.[87] There needed to be exorcisms—popular or otherwise—of the places after that.[88] The abandoned precincts were generally full of large grave markers, useful in building. Frightened workmen neither understood the Hebrew writing inscribed on the stones nor wanted to handle the stones themselves, but double wages might convince them to face up to their fears.[89]

Antiquaries and scholars have recovered and catalogued inscriptions on hundreds, perhaps thousands, of such gravemarkers from the Middle Ages, including the Paris of Philip Augustus.[90] In a sense these do have a specialness about them, though nothing much of the black arts or perfidy. The Hebrew was formulaic and poetic, a bit talismanic as well, for Jews were no more above "magic and superstition" than Christians.[91] Mostly like gravemarkers in many traditions, they simply proffered a most generous, even self-congratulatory interpretation of the life of the deceased, and the formulas wished the dead quiet repose in paradise or in the memories of living human beings.[92] More particularly, the markers stood as all too with God); and so forth.[98] Even living people insisted on this badge of honor. Hebrew deeds in England occasionally are signed or subscribed by men who add "son of the martyr" to their names.[99] Thus, the image of martyrdom served as a constant reminder of the fragility of social life and nurtured the spirit of resistance among the Jews to the overtures and threats of the Christians and reassured the Chosen People.

> Has the like of this
>   ever been seen or heard?
> Could anyone believe
>   such a stupefying sight.
> They lead their children
>   to the slaughter
>   as if to a beautiful
>   bridal canopy.
> After this, O Exalted and Triumphant Lord,
>   will You hold back?[100]

So exults a poem on the Rhenish massacres. A sentence in a memorial to the martyrs of Blois nearly a century later could serve as a refrain: "Is the Lord's arm so short that it cannot change my lot?"[101]

frequent witnesses to the way the legacy of martyrdom laid its bu
upon *successive* generations. For virtually no stones of the martyrs tl
selves have survived.[93] The killers tended to dispose of the martyrs' b
unceremoniously in common graves.[94] What survive are the recollec
of martyrdom among the descendants of the saints: exemplary signific;
expressed as a badge of honor. They are as liturgical in their own w
the great poems, and they were a recurring reminder of the blood-de
the present to the past.

> . . . R. Meir
> son of the martyr (*kadosh*, saint)
> Rabbi Iehiel
> Departed for the Garden of Eden
> The ninth year, the sixth day
> Parashat Vayishlah[95]

Like medieval Christian dating, with its references to festivals or da
which particular hymns were sung, the dating here is liturgical, the *pa*
being the portion of the Torah read in synagogue on Friday (the sixth
in the ninth year of the computation. The particular section menti
here was the one with the Hebrew incipit *vayishlah* (Genesis 32:4–36:
the modern reading). The key word, however, is *kadosh*, variously t
lated as holy one, saint, martyr. Instances with this martyrdom forr
stressing the implied burden/responsibility on more recent generat
can be repeated with relative ease: "Sagira the daughter of the *k*
Shemuel"; "the *kadosh* Issac, son of Shemuel the *kadosh*"; "Jacob sc
David the *kadosh*."[96] Or to cite one more in full,

> This is the tombstone of Rabbi
> Shemuel, son of the *kadosh* R. Joseph
> Who guided the schools (*chederim*)
> Many days in faith
> *Parasha Balak*[97]

The teacher, son of the martyr, had carried on and transmitted the 1
if in a different way, in this last example.

Other tombstones press this responsibility and burden even more
idly by recalling the nature of the martyrdom: *Harug al kidush ha-*
(slain for sanctification in God); *harug al yihud ha-Shem* (slain for u

2. Conflict, Abuse, and Expulsion: "That Wicked King"

The suspicions and enmity described in the last chapter were kept in bounds by the necessity among all people to earn their livelihood, raise children, worship, and deliver themselves, by play, from the pressures of daily life. Much of this activity even in small towns was carried on within small sub-groups. Later evidence could show us a close-knit Christian immigrant neighborhood or an occupational sub-group like goldsmiths in which endogamy was high, where the guild was a social club and also a quasi-confraternity under a patron saint that arranged the devotional life of its members.[1] The parallel with the Jews should be evident. Just as Christian sub-groups within larger communities achieved a level of semi-autonomy or clannishness, so too Jews constituted a distinct social not merely religious group. They had their butcher because of the rules of *kashrot*, their court and place of worship, their own leisure pursuits and patterns of endogamy.[2] Every town was comprised of a congeries of separated microcosms or distinctive networks of sociability.

Nonetheless, the words "separated" and "distinctive" rather than "separate" and "distinct" were used in the preceding paragraph because there was no absolute autonomy, no essential segregation, of any group in the north of Europe in the twelfth century. There were tendencies in that direction, focusing especially on lepers for both medical and ostensibly moral reasons.[3] These tendencies had not overwhelmed the Jews. There were no ghettos; there were few absolutely unbridgeable social distances. Rigord laments these facts and writes about their sinister consequences. But the data he provides, for all his bias, are quite revealing. He describes Christians in domestic service with Jews and Jews' activity as purveyors of credit.[4] The Jews had "fields, vineyards, granaries and winepresses" among their properties[5] and yet were not predominantly agriculturalists by the late twelfth century in the royal domain. Consequently, they bargained with Christian rustics at markets for grain and animals.[6] The rabbinic responsa from northern Jewry go to great lengths to classify what was and was not permitted with regard to this trafficking in goods; the very discussion of the matter establishes the wide variety of relationships.[7] A particular occupation in which Jews were prominent in the north and which, from time to time, brought them into intimate personal contact with Christians was that of medicine.[8] Beyond these formal occupational and commercial relationships—and the intellectual discussions earlier mentioned—there were of course normal social relations, either open and routine, such as conversation and children's play in the marketplace, at fairs, wells, and other social spaces open to both, or clandestine, especially sexual relations.

Despite the fact that an incident of any type might provoke an outbreak of social conflict, the problem facing an historian is where to separate those categories of voluntary social relations that by their very structure make conflict likely from those that do not. On the first side, one would prima facie put sexual relations, the reliance on Jews for medical care, and the market in distress loans. With regard to sexual matters—and this is obvious—one would have to say that however tender love and voluntary sexual relations might have been between individuals, community values on both sides vigorously opposed this activity.[9] Clandestine as such relationships usually were, falling out of love was a fact of life and could lead to spectacular problems. Recall the Blois incident of 1171 where this occurred at almost the highest level of the feudal aristocracy: the count of Blois fell out of love with the Jewess Polcelina. It is hard to know whether the fact of her previous sexual relationship with the count hardened his attitude toward the Jews. What is clear is that the resentment of Christians against her put inordinate pressure on him to act against them as a whole. Polcelina does not fare well in contemporary Jewish reports either: she was no new Esther. She was polluted, but her liaison had given her power; and power, until it faded, had made her cruel.[10]

Medical contacts, too, were ambiguous. The Jew was a repository of wisdom, both occult and "scientific," presuming that the distinction is an acceptable one. Medical practice, which largely depended on the administration of potions, always ran the risk of provoking the charge of poisoning. Twelfth-century conflations of medical practice and a knowledge of dark arts are well known.[11] Yet it remains true that few people in general turned to doctors (as opposed to wise men and women and to saints and relics), and fewer still among Christians turned to Jewish doctors. So, although there was, one might say, a systemic disposition toward being suspicious about any failure of a Jewish doctor to cure a Christian, this was, given prevailing contacts in northern France, a relatively minor and insubstantial theme in social relations per se.

To repeat, we are talking about voluntary relations, people seeking out or offering their services to others of the different religion. These acts are founded on some stratum of opinion that it is possible to enjoy friendly or at least not unfriendly contacts with people otherwise being denounced as perfidious or dangerous by polemicists of one side or the other. Ambivalence is implicit in all these relations. A wonderful example comes from the Jewish side, the report in a Rhenish hasidic text about the offer of a Christian woman to a Jewish woman whose son was ill.

> The son of a Jewish woman became ill. A Gentile woman came and said to her: "Give your son to drink upon this stone and he will be cured." The Jewish woman said: "What is the nature of this stone?" The Gentile woman said that the stone was brought from the pit [the storyteller's pejorative for the Holy Sepulchre] and it is part of the stone in which (Jesus) was buried, and indeed some Gentiles were given to drink and were cured. The Jewish woman said: "Because she said that it is of (Jesus), I do not wish my son to drink upon this stone": And this (is what is meant by) "With all thy soul . . . thou shalt love the Lord thy God."[12]

Few texts are as rich as the foregoing one. The naiveté of the Christian woman is supreme; or her duplicity is, if we believe that her ignorance of normative Jewish attitudes toward relics of Jesus was feigned. On the other side, the Jewish woman is both receptive and suspicious. She will not say, No, without first finding out what this "cure" is, that is to say, she entertains the possibility that she is being offered help as an altruistic or at least sympathetic gesture. But her ultimate refusal, which leads to the storyteller's moral, reveals not simply her adherence to Jewish values but also, I would suggest, a potential and probable stiffening of attitude: help from Christians, insofar as it is proffered at all, is likely to be wrapped in an ideology of condescension and missionizing. Her feelings in this regard would not likely have remained uniquely hers, for people always talk. She would have related this incident, perhaps with pride at her own faithfulness during her son's illness;[13] and the Christian woman would have talked, too, about how ungrateful the Jew was when all she herself had wanted to do was help. To understand the probable intensity of these feelings on both sides is not to exonerate the people who held them. Maybe a richer Christian catechism would have helped by cautioning Christians against trying to bring Jews into belief in devious ways when they were under stress. But if the Christian woman wanted to and really believed that she could help the child by the offer of the relic, what else was she supposed to do?

However much scandalous revelations about sexual relations or problematic encounters over healing might reverberate negatively on social relations, these matters pale before the importance that must be assigned to the market in distress loans. It is to that issue that we must now direct our attention, for Paris, as Rigord informs us, was a city with a strong network of credit, much of it in the hands of Jews and servicing not only the city proper but the smaller towns and villages in its hinterland. To Rigord it was all a plague of "usury," and it is one of the factors that, he says, most affected Philip Augustus's sensibilities in 1180, leading him to consult a famous hermit, Brother Bernard (well-known from governmental sources), who confirmed the king in his antipathy toward the Jews.[14]

As in the previous pages, the goal before us of trying to understand the actions of the 1180s means that we should be very careful though flexible about arguing back from later evidence and, whether later or not, from evidence from regions outside the royal domain in 1180.[15] The situation in the royal domain was not unique, but it was distinctive. One city, Paris—indeed one part of this city—dominated as a center of Jewish life; and the Jewish inhabitants of this center were many of them relatively recent immigrants. They had come because in the fast-growing commercial life of Paris good livings were waiting to be made and because lines of relatively long-distance trade in which Jews were already involved intersected increasingly in the city.

A broader shift in northern Europe (indeed, to a degree, in European culture) lay behind the developments in the Ile de France. Jews were progressively turning away from other pursuits, especially agricultural ones. This shift has been attributed to the Christian ethos of high medieval "feudalism" (as opposed to the rough-and-ready feudalism of immediate post-Carolingian times) and to the strict legal relationships accompanying the fief, especially the feudal oath. These relationships could not be accommodated to Jews, who were therefore constrained to give up their interests in land in inhospitable rural environments and become a much more urban and/or commercial minority than they might otherwise have become.[16] The concentration in *specific* aspects of commerce and trade was also stimulated, it is said, by the influence of churchmen on the attitudes and behavior of lay people in favor of increased separation between Christians and Jews. This pressure was mounting in the course of the twelfth century, but it was not decisive. We have already seen that in numerous areas people of the two confessions worked and associated with each other. Still, the pressure was there and growing: what was occurring by the late twelfth century was a slow but steady attrition of the Jewish presence in those commercial occupations or professions that were thought of by churchmen as inappropriate to them: wine merchandizing, for example, because of the possibility of "their wine" being used in the communion; meat marketing because of the sense of humiliation that some churchmen felt at Christians buying food from Jews that Jews themselves refused to eat (such as hind quarters).[17]

A final factor that may help account for this widely observed shift in the Jewish occupational profile is the evolution of guilds with their quasi-religious association. In these organizations there was usually no place for Jews. Since there was no place for them, and since the guilds tended to articulate an economic program that restricted to members only the commercial activities or trades that their guilds engaged in, Jews tended to be pushed out of these occupations.[18]

What was left? First of all, it is not accurate to think that all these trends had come to fruition by the 1180s or that there were no countervailing tendencies. Throughout the thirteenth century intelligent people in authority would still argue that the Jews ought to be allowed to carry on "honorable" trades, an idea that could imply a limit on the absolute application of the monopolist ideology of the guilds.[19] Moreover, the "ideal" programs of both radical churchmen and Christian merchants and artisans were far from determining social relationships: Jews continued to sell wine to Christians, to engage in the marketing of meat, to provide medical services, and so on.

It remains true nonetheless that many of these activities, in hindsight, were largely atavistic. More and more Jews began to earn more and more of their living from supplying credit.[20] To a degree this was an outgrowth of their involvement in commerce and trade in general. But the provision of credit, both in the productive sector of the economy and even more certainly on the consumer side (lending at interest for convenience and distress; pawnbroking) was not an "ordinary" occupation like merchandizing. Consideration of the borrowers, especially the lower class borrowers, establishes this. Everyone knows that in order to survive or to pay taxes or dues, people in a relatively primitive society who have little or no immediately disposable income in money will often need to beg or borrow. Since no medieval polity including the church ever succeeded in providing

the kind of charity (welfare) to meet the wants of the indigent or temporarily impecunious, the preferred tendency of people in want was to fall
back on family or friends or, where funds from these sources were un-
available, to turn to quasi-professional lenders, people who were in the
habit of making money by lending money.[21] Repeated borrowing from
the quasi-professionals (the local widow, the tavern-keeper, Jewish merchants) might dull the emotions, but resentments, rooted in the stress of
want, would be severe. Giving is charity; lending for greater return in
primitive economies, economies in which there is resistance to using the
language of commerce,[22] is perceived of as unfair or even morally wrong.
There may be some exceptions, but in general this seems to be true.[23] This
sense of moral betrayal or of the immorality of the transaction, as seen by
the borrower under stress, will be more vivid the closer the social ties
between the lender and borrower. The issue, after all, is not borrowing per
se but paying back more than is borrowed. It is still perceived as unworthy
and unseemly in many industrial societies for one close relative to lend
money to another at interest. Some people in the pre-modern past may
have risen above these sentiments and recognized the sometimes virtuous
impulse of the lender or the structural necessity of charging interest by a
person for whom the business of lending money was the principal enterprise on which his own family depended. But the weight of the evidence
leaves no doubt whatsoever that borrowing *at interest* (or pawning, which
amounts to the same thing) frequently engendered deep resentment, not
least among that underclass of irresponsible poor who were often turned
down for loans or who were never satisfied with what they received from
the cheap—though sometimes necessary or sentimentally precious—
objects (tools, utensils, clothing, bedding) that they pawned.[24]

For the lenders to be of an ethnic or religious minority like the Jews did
not necessarily exacerbate the tensions. I have already said that the resentment might well have been higher had an apparently grasping lender been
of the same social class, but the easy identification of the lender with a
distinct and already slighted social group in which many other members of
that social group engaged in the same occupation permitted a stereotype
of extraordinary potency. Here is where Rigord's picture becomes so
important: there were too many Jews; they owned too much. But he
spends even more time telling us that they squeezed townsmen and rustics
whom they serviced from Paris; they squeezed soldiers passing through.
They even managed to have Christians put in jail and their goods distrained for failure to pay debts. In other words, his stereotype of the Jewish

lender fits neatly with all the other characteristic features of Jewish social life that he denigrates. The image is of a swarm of Jewish "outsiders" (immigrants who have been attracted to Paris) sucking the life's blood of the Christian community to whom they should have been subjected, even taking in pawn holy vessels for which they had no respect.[25]

This inversion was permitted, of course, because those who were supposed to protect the community had developed a set of guidelines that tolerated this sort of activity. It was everywhere broadly hinted that they were bribed to do so;[26] for the radicals already were turning against the notion that lending at interest was permitted to Jews by religious law in their relations with strangers (Christians).[27] The more moderate discussants would have said rather that "usury" was impermissible and then would have argued about what usury (immoderate interest) was. But precisely because of the perceived inversion in the credit relationship, some leading churchmen were to forge beyond this moderate critique to declaim that no principle of Christian ethics in relation to the proper protection of Jews was violated by an absolute ban on their lending at interest.[28]

The extreme reluctance of lords to give effect to the more radical critique of Jewish lending at interest arose mostly from their view of Jews as an "exploitable" lordly possession. Churchmen in their role as moralists might advise them, but feudal lords (including prelates in this capacity) had jurisdiction and control over Jews. The twelfth century, as Gavin Langmuir has demonstrated, saw the formulation of a theory that being a Jew was a legal status in and of itself in feudal law; and increasingly the essence of that status for every Jew came to be his susceptibility to arbitrary taxation by the lord who exercised criminal justice over him. This was in practice a companion to the notion that a lord would arbitrate in *felonious* incidents among his Jews and between them and Christians. Contributions to the lord's coffers were the price of these forums for ajudication.[29] An obvious way for a lord to get at the (perceived) wealth of the Jews in moneylending was by taxing their outstanding loans, sometimes brutally called a *captio*, "taking." In the more formal language of a somewhat later period Jews would be said to be tallageable at the will of the lord; their chattels were theirs only at the lord's pleasure.[30]

To make the "takings" worthwhile, lords required relative stability for the Jews to prosper. They needed to allow or even foster lending at interest no matter how often radical churchmen denounced this as usury or how much some elements of the Christian population resented it as extortion. If the lord took a great deal of the Jews' wealth, therefore, he gave the Jews something in return—his peace. So long as the Jews were under his protection that peace was not to be impugned. As Philip Augustus's English counterpart, King John, once put it, referring to Jews, "If we were to give our peace to any dog, it ought to be kept inviolate."[31]

Philip Augustus lost little time in withdrawing his peace from the Jews of the royal domain. Fortified by the stories that he had heard even as a little boy about their perfidy, and undoubtedly upset by the studied unwillingness of his father to act against them, the fourteen- or fifteen-year-old monarch decided on a dramatic gesture, a Saturday raid on the synagogues.[32] Dating this raid, however, is a bit tricky. In keeping with Capetian convention, Philip had been crowned during his father's lifetime, on 1 November 1179; his father died on 19 September 1180. Traditionally, scholars have argued that the fourteen-year-old Philip began his actions against the Jews in February 1180 "even before" his father's death.[33] Their source is Rigord, who says that the raid occurred in February of the first year of Philip's reign after the coronation at Reims. If we are very strict about dating regnal years, therefore, it must have occurred in 1180 as the conventional wisdom has it.

The problem with this is that Rigord specifically dates the act to the XVI Kalends of March, which in 1180 would have been 14 February, a Thursday, not a Saturday. Consequently, most historians, tacitly following Rigord's editor, have emended "XVI" Kalends of March to "XIV" Kalends, which puts the attack on Saturday, 16 February 1180.[34] On the other hand this emendation would not be necessary if Rigord meant his reference to the first year of Philip's reign a little more loosely, because XVI Kalends of March 1181 (fifteen months after the coronation and five months after his father's death) would be a Saturday. Moreover, the only other authority who dates the raid, the English chronicler, Ralph de Diceto, places it in the year 1180, which means (given that the English usually dated the beginning of the year from Annunciation) that in our reckoning the year would be, again, 1181.[35] I believe this chronology—the raid in February 1181 not 1180, that is, after Philip's father died—makes more sense on the whole, even though there continue to be difficulties.[36]

Yet, however we date the raid, it was an extraordinary act reported not only by Rigord and Ralph but also by a Jewish source. The Latin records, already cited, tell us that the king ordered the Jews seized in their synagogues and their precious objects confiscated. The Hebrew source says that the king's guards (*shomrim*) in possession of keys ransacked the Jews' homes in search of artifacts of value,[37] an invasion that made a lasting impression according to Rigord, too, who lays stress on the reprehensibility of Jews having in their homes Christian holy objects in pawn.[38] The seizure of the synagogues' *objets de culte* was a form of ransom for the Christian vessels. The English chronicler adds the important information that the Jews were subsequently allowed to redeem their chattels for fifteen thousand marks.[39] If this figure is anywhere near accurate, it means that the financial value of the raid was equal to one and one-half times what Philip's government might expect in normal predictable revenue in an entire year.[40]

Where did the Jews' ransom come from? Since, in line with the more-or-less standard policies that were evolving among Christian princes, Jewish credit was a protected business, in which payment of debts was enforced by secular governments against Christian defaulters, Philip's men had some general knowledge of the network of credit in the royal domain.[41] The ransacking of homes undoubtedly permitted them to assess the extent of transactions from personal account books that, if in Hebrew, would have been translated by converts or collaborators. Whatever the root cause, the king cancelled all debts to the Jews while reserving to himself one-fifth of the sum—that is, presumably, of the principal—since he did this at Brother Bernard's advice and would not have wanted to profit from the "usury" of Jews.[42] There is no way to estimate even grossly the amount of this profit to the royal fisc except by suggesting that it formed part of the total fifteen thousand marks believed by Ralph de Diceto to be the ransom of the Jews. In other words, it is hard to see how the Jews could pay fifteen thousand marks at one sweep (for the ransom) and also provide a real additional windfall to the king from one-fifth of their outstanding debts, many of which must have been called in at the very moment Philip made known his willingness to accept a ransom.

Perhaps it was the rumor that the Jews of the royal domain town of Orléans had crucified a Christian child that provoked Philip not to stop at the bullying described above.[43] By April 1182 he had come to the opinion that the Jews would have to leave the royal domain. His thrust against them was somewhat less ruthless than the surprise sabbath attack on the synagogues. He accorded them time to make arrangements, the date of expulsion itself being set for 24 June. All attempts to dissuade him failed. He allowed the Jews to take with them the profits of the sale of the chattels that were still in their possession after the confiscatory measures of the first two years of his reign. But he seized the real property out of their hands without compensation.[44] Only to those who converted were the lands and houses restored.[45]

As usual the Paris evidence is the most comprehensive. The expulsion of Parisian Jews directly touched the lives of not less than two thousand people, perhaps somewhat more.[46] Their landed property—synagogues, cemeteries, baths, houses, granaries, vineyards, and appurtenances—could now be distributed at the king's pleasure.[47] Philip's plan, so far as he had one, is not hard to deduce from the surviving evidence. There is not much of this: we rarely know to whom the property was conveyed or how much was paid into the royal fisc to obtain it. Often we only read in later sources that such-and-such a place or building had once belonged to the Jews: "the house that used to be the Jews' bath" (*domus quae fuit stupe judeorum*), for example.[48]

Occasionally, however, better information is available. It shows that the king conveyed certain properties gratis to the church.[49] The synagogue of the Ile de la Cité was granted to the bishop of Paris, Maurice de Sully, who had it converted into the Christian church of the Madeleine.[50] Synagogues elsewhere in the royal domain—at Orléans and Etampes, to give the only concrete details available—are recorded as having been conveyed in a similar manner.[51]

With the other properties the king was usually more businesslike.[52] In Paris, on what is called today the rue de la Vielle-Draperie, Philip gave twenty-four confiscated houses to the drapers for an annual rent of one hundred pounds.[53] On the rue de la Pelleterie eighteen houses were conveyed to the pelters for seventy-three pounds annually.[54] The king let a small former Jewish vineyard near the church of Saint-Etienne-des-Grès of Paris for thirty shillings annual rent to a gold beater (*auri percussor*), another vineyard (charge unknown) to a royal official, and a house in Paris to a royal clerk for forty shillings (later reduced to twenty).[55] For Etampes and Bourges, there is also evidence of renting houses—in the first instance, to a royal clerk, in the latter, to one of the king's marshals (the tariff at Etampes is unknown, that at Bourges was seven pounds per year).[56] A few former Jewish houses were conveyed as outright gifts, possibly at Corbeil and certainly at Bourges (to loyal royal servants).[57] Some such conveyancing is probably behind a later charter for Sens.[58]

Information on the peregrinations of the Jews is more flimsy than that on property transfers. But, beyond the general lacuna of all evidence before 1200, there is a good reason for this. The disruption in life was unpleasant, but there had been time to prepare for the journey; and there were plenty of places to go that were close by. The Jews in the royal domain already had business and personal contacts in neighboring lordships; and since they migrated to those lordships with some resources, there was little resentment among the lords about the settlement of these Jews (whereas they might have been hesitant about accepting large numbers of absolutely destitute Jews into their domains). Again, because of the small numbers, the immigrants if dispersed widely would have caused few problems for the Jewish communities in which they took up residence.[59] There was no city that was so close to the royal domain, so welcoming, and so preeminent economically that the exiles flocked there. Rather we see, from the little evidence that we have, that immigrants trickled into Normandy and Maine to the west and southwest and, of course, to the east as well, where a wide scattering of Jewish communities existed in Champagne and Burgundy, though some scholars have rather exaggerated the impact.[60]

Did other barons follow suit and expel the Jews? Rigord in his enthusiasm talks of an expulsion from the *kingdom*. He means the royal domain.[61] The only case that has been made for a parallel expulsion touches the county of Chartres-Blois, in whose principal town, Blois, the terrible series of executions were carried out in 1171.[62] However, the evidence for an expulsion having taken place in the county as a whole in 1182 turns out to be a chimaera. A seventeenth-century scholar, Jean-Baptiste Souchet, whose massive history of Chartres was published in the nineteenth century, noted that a synagogue in the well-defined jewry of Chartres was converted at some period remote from his day into a hospital. Enormously hostile to the Jews and royalist to the core, Souchet rather cavalierly associated this conversion with Philip's expulsion.[63] Chédeville, citing Souchet, but without further evidence, therefore dates it "after 1179," perpetuating the myth that a relatively firm date can be given.[64] In truth, the Chartrain and Blésois were not affected by Philip's order.

Not only was Philip's order a dead letter with great secular lords, but ecclesiastical lords whom one might expect to have had an interest in showing their loyalty and friendship failed to adopt his program. Of course, the policy of the official church, with one or two exceptions, did not favor expulsion: Jews existed in Christian society to persist until the end of time and bear witness to Christian truth.[65] The existence of this "ideal" policy was not enough to inhibit ecclesiastical lords who wanted to do otherwise—in many matters they frequently defied official policies. But the need for a steady income, the kind of income that came from regularly taking the profits or some portion of the profits of the Jews, was an additional factor holding them back. An expulsion only sent Jews into other lordships where the new rulers began to profit from taxation of the settlers. For all these reasons, then, those churchmen who had *dominium* over Jews not only did not follow the lead of the king of the Franks in 1182, but may have especially welcomed the wanderers from his land.[66] This was true even in Tours and Saint-Denis itself, whose abbeys' *dominium* over Jews had been royal gifts and whose relations with the French monarchy were otherwise unalterably close.[67] The king's biographer, Rigord, does not particularly lament this fact because he had not yet become a monk of Saint-Denis; that was not to occur until after 1186. Moreover, he had already finished writing his discussion of Philip's early program against the Jews by the time he entered the monastery.[68] In any case the Jews of Saint-Denis who had been established there since at least 1111 with five families from Paris had become a prosperous little community with a jewry of good stone houses and close ties with the Lendit fair in the town. They continued to be instrumental to the credit needs of the abbey itself, and flourished—or so it appears—even at the height of the king's intolerance.[69]

Philip Augustus's lack of influence on his barons in regard to Jewish policy is symptomatic of his overall political insecurity. The world he knew was peopled with men and women determined to maintain or carve out new spheres of influence that threatened the fragile integrity of the royal domain. The press of events hardened him. The ins and outs of the confrontations between the young monarch and his rivals in the first decade or so of his reign need not be treated here; they have been described and discussed recently by Baldwin.[70] The theme that we are pursuing must however take cognizance of the fact that during this period Philip's fortunes varied. He was always unsure of the permanence of his work. And that insecurity undoubtedly affected his policies and the situation of the people most vulnerable to them.

In the mid-1180s Philip began to acquire dominion over certain lands to the north of the Ile de France—in Vermandois and Artois—which in the opening years of his reign were tenuously tied to the crown at best.[71] These lands were not particularly rich with Jewish settlement. One of the chief towns and a real economic center, Amiens, had no Jews.[72] But here and there in other towns and villages, a number of Jews lived and worked.[73] Whose Jews were these? As we have seen, a theory was being articulated about this matter. But we would do well to keep in mind that the general dominance over these northern lands by Philip did not mean that *all* the rights of government and *dominium* were in his hands. Besides the fact that many subordinate "lordships" continued to enjoy relative autonomy, the king's *dominium* was limited legally by the fact that it depended on the future escheat of these territories to him.[74] While he protected the whole and to a degree exploited certain towns from 1185 on, members of the family of the count of Flanders enjoyed legal possession of the region during their lifetimes; and it was not clear from 1185 to 1191 whether Philip could successfully enforce his residual claims. Only in 1192, after the death of the count of Flanders on crusade (the year before) and after arduous negotiations, were Vermandois and Artois recognized by most people as being permanently in the French orbit. Even after this date the historian has to be very precise, for many of Philip's rights still depended on whether the countess of Vermandois, a former sister-in-law of the late count of Flanders, were to remain childless. There was every expectation that she would, but she retained her interest in much of Vermandois until her death in 1213. Baldwin describes the king's *dominium* in Vermandois from 1191 to 1213 as a kind of "tutelage," on the basis, for example, of surviving evidence of Philip supervising the alms of the countess.[75] How far the tutelage went beyond this is unknown; and the question of the status of the Jews is an open one.

Undoubtedly, in the 1180s and 1190s the Jews of these northern lands were uncertain about what the governance of Philip would mean for them, should it become a reality. The principal event in his life that helped shape government in the future, his decision to lead a crusade, could not have reassured them. It bespoke a continued vitality of piety that might have awful consequences. In fact, as Baldwin has effectively demonstrated, the crusade of 1190 on which Philip embarked marked a decisive break with the advisers and pattern of governance of the past; many of the older counsellors and nobles died in the Holy War. Ultimately Philip was disappointed that the crusade did not live up to his own desires, especially that he was overshadowed by the English king, Richard the Lionhearted. Therefore he returned from the Holy Land relatively quickly, to the contempt of many other crusaders.[76] But he remained genuinely intense about his religious commitment, indeed genuinely fanatical, perhaps partly in compensation for his lackluster showing on the crusade. That fanaticism is demonstrated in his relations with the Jews.

Shortly after the king's return from crusade in 1191 to a royal domain more or less empty of Jews, there occurred the so-called "Bray" incident in a lordship nearby. A Jew was killed; other Jews succeeded in intervening and having his killer, a Christian, executed. The king himself then intervened—this in March 1192—since the Christian was one of his dependents and malfeasance of the local authority owing to bribes from the Jews was suspected: the Jews had paid off the countess in whose county the town was located. Philip exacted vengeance, surrounding the town, seizing a large number of Jews (eighty if the figures are accurate) and having them killed. Jewish children were allowed to flee.[77]

The best sources that alert us to the slaughter, Latin and Hebrew, do not tell us precisely which town is meant; and scholars have disputed the matter. Chazan and many others locate the incident in Champagne (Bray-sur-Seine), where there was a prosperous Jewish community.[78] This would mean that Philip overturned the justice of the countess of Champagne. It is very hard to accept this. The king was, as we know, already involved in difficult negotiations and machinations over securing his rights in Vermandois and Artois, where the competing interests of other lords had to be balanced. A brutal violation of a great lord's jurisdiction (even on the legal pretext of default of justice) would have been very provocative. The count of Champagne was still on crusade at the time, but his mother, the countess, to whom the Jews would have had to turn, was exercising his powers. One can imagine Philip acting the bullying overlord under these circumstances, but it means that he ignored the consequences of angering the extremely powerful Champenois nobility.

More likely, the town where the incident occurred was not Bray but Brie [-Comte-Robert], as Rigord's editor, Delaborde, long ago pointed out. The continuator of Rigord's biography makes this identification definite, and it is highly unlikely, despite Chazan's suggestion, that one writing only a handful of years after the event would get its location wrong.[79] Moreover, circumstantial evidence supports the identification with Brie.[80] The old count, Louis VII's brother, had died in 1188; his son and heir went on crusade with his cousin, Philip Augustus, but did not return with the king. His mother, the countess dowager, was therefore exercising authority and would have been the person to whom the Jews turned. Partly because of family reasons and partly because the fiefs were strategically located, the kings had intervened before.[81] Later in 1192 Philip continued to exercise a certain degree of "tutelage" over affairs in Brie. He certainly was concerned with the question of the proper distribution of alms from the town.[82] Perhaps one reason the countess had succumbed to a bribe in the first place was her own need for large sums that she was pouring into the building of the church of Saint-Yved of Braine; her heaviest donations came in her widowhood after 1188.[83]

Wherever the incident occurred, it seemed to make clear that the king had not changed very much in the decade since his coming to power. He was still wedded to the dramatic and impetuous gesture. Rigord talks about his failing to take counsel before he acted in Brie, of his moving with extraordinary swiftness to impose his will.[84] In the Hebrew remembrance Philip is "that wicked king," "that king steadfast in his wickedness from beginning to end."[85] What neither the few Vermandois and Artesian Jews who were then on the verge of coming under Philip's rule nor the thousands of other Jews who lived in neighboring lordships could have known was that the king was undergoing a great change of mind. Again, it is impossible to be certain about motivations. Some have suggested that the king just grew more politic with age; others that he realized his "mistake" in banishing a source of lucrative taxation; still others argue that political and matrimonial disputes with the church caused him to rethink the expulsion. Whatever the truth, a few years after the attack at Brie the king reopened the royal domain to Jews who wished to settle there.[86] Not even the adoring Rigord could hide his utter distaste for what the king had done.[87]

3. A New Beginning, 1198–1204

"Against his own edict," Rigord tells us, Philip Augustus permitted the return of the Jews to Paris. The king did not consult widely with his barons on the readmission. He merely announced in July 1198 his decision to allow the Jews' return.[1] Nothing has come to light to establish that this announcement was preceded by discussions with Jews, but this omission was of no importance politically. The king's failure to consult the barons of neighboring lordships did provoke a response. Despite what one or two scholars have written, the king expected the people or the descendants of the people whom he had exiled in 1182 to return freely in 1198. He did not accept the opinion that they had become the Jews of other lords in the interim, or rather that their residence in other seigneuries extinguished his rights or conferred on the lords of those seigneuries the authority to prohibit these Jews' resettlement in the royal domain.[2]

Neither were the Jews convinced that their freedom to transfer from one lordship to another could be fully limited by any single lord.[3] From July through September 1198 Jews did enter the royal domain. Some took up residence, but most were probably feeling out the new situation and established business outlets in the chief towns. By September a number of these businesses were flourishing, and the question of the taxability of the profits of the moneylending in which the Jews were engaged became a pressing one.[4] In September, therefore, on the complaint of Theobald the count palatine of Champagne, the king agreed that some sort of definite division of the Jews had to be made. The texts recording the agreement make the situation seem self-evident, because they ratify more detailed or clear oral understandings that the two great men reached at a meeting in Mantes in September. The gist of the agreement was that the king would recognize that certain Jews who had established business contacts in his lands since July were Jews of Theobald. That is, the king had no claim over their persons or the profits of their moneylending, either because they were not among the Jews (or descendants of the Jews) expelled from the royal domain in 1182 or because they had not actually taken up residence in his domains since July, but had only done business there. Other Jews, either expellees of 1182 and their descendants, or more likely only those among them who had chosen to take up residence again in the royal domain in 1198, were henceforth to be recognized as the king's Jews. From the moment of this agreement onward, the count would know and tax his Jews (they would not operate in the domain of the king); and the king would know and tax his Jews (they would not be active in the domains of the count).[5]

The count's government, as we can well imagine, had conceded by this agreement what for sixteen years had been a part of its tax base. The count himself, therefore, was paid for the concession. The king ordered his officials to take cognizance of all the debts owed the Jews that had been contracted in the royal domain before the agreement of September. Those debts owed to people who were to be regarded thereafter as the Jews of Champagne were to be repaid not to the Jews but *to the count*.[6] One supposes that this was not merely a compensation to the count for his willingness to allow some of the expellees of 1182 and their families to take up residence again in the royal domain and therefore effectively to transfer out of his lordship. Another justification for the action must have been to demonstrate to all "truly" Champenois Jews that they were "absolutely" under the power of the count, and that if they defied him they would be the losers.

The Christians in the royal domain who owed money to Jews now identified as Jews of the count of Champagne were to pay up within two years (the money, as indicated, to be transferred to the count).[7] Baldwin has noticed that two years after the initial two-year period, "Champenois" debts were still being collected.[8] This can only mean that some of the debtors in the royal domain found it difficult to pay up quite so quickly. This makes sense, because the first borrowers to whom the Jews would have offered credit in 1198 would not have been unknown rustics, but substantial and well-respected borrowers (even monastic and aristocratic) whose repayment of large loans might take more time than anyone at first supposed. Probably the count's and the king's men reached some sort of revised payment schedule to meet this problem, and this is what is reflected in royal fiscal records from a date slightly after the first two-year period for repayment had come to an end.

What the records for Philip and the count of Champagne have shown in a certain amount of detail is hinted at in another document touching

Normandy which, it seems, some Jews were leaving in order to take up residence or establish business in the re-opened royal domain. We know, for example, that in 1199, a few months after the French king's agreement with Champagne, the duke of Normandy issued a prohibition about his Jews leaving his domains.[9] Two points need to be made here. First, that the prohibition was needed implies that Philip and the duke had not succeeded in 1198 in reaching an agreement on this matter acceptable to both, though who was responsible is hard to say. We must remember that the duke of Normandy was Richard the Lionhearted, the king of England; and profound political problems separated the two men. Failure to agree on this issue was only one of many difficulties that were not successfully resolved, for Richard and Philip were slipping in and out of war all through 1198, and any number of attempts to bring peace were frustrated over and over again.[10] By the time Richard died in 1199, his successor, John, apparently thought his intransigence good, and issued the restrictive policy mentioned above. Second, what the duke declared for Normandy presumably reflects his attitude in all of his domains (England, Maine, Anjou, Touraine, Poitou, Aquitaine). Effectively, he barred legal migration of his Jews to the domain of Philip Augustus.

What all of this means is that very few Jews successfully returned to the royal domain in 1198, because the lordships with substantial Jewish populations bordering Philip's lands were in fact those of the Plantagenet ruler of England and the count of Champagne. Obviously there were any number of smaller lordships from which Jews might have emigrated. It is interesting in this respect that the effective preaching against usury by an itinerant priest, Foulques de Neuilly, in the 1190s had stimulated a few of these lesser lords, going beyond his recommendation merely to force restitution of Jewish usury, to expel their Jews. A contemporary chronicler, Robert of Auxerre, informs us that these Jews were admitted to the royal domain from 1198 and were "retained" by the king as his own Jews thereafter—to the evident consternation of Robert, who, like Rigord, lamented the king's reversal of the early policy of his reign.[11] Some of these immigrants were probably exiles of 1182. Still, because of the limited impact of the king's readmission on Champenois Jews and the minimal impact on Jews in the domain of the Plantagenets, resettlement, even with this immigration from a handful of smaller lordships, can only be regarded as modest.

Several questions need to be addressed about the resettlement and its aftermath. First, what was the status of the Jews who did return? Second, what was the nature, extent, and quality of their settlement? Third, what were Christian perceptions of the king and the Jews in the wake of readmission?

Opinions on the legal limits of migration and settlement of Jews were not fixed by the middle of the twelfth century. Yet, arguing back from Philip Augustus and Count Theobald of Champagne's agreement in 1198 over the proper *dominium* of Jews, from the refusal of Richard and John of England to enter into such an agreement with the king of the Franks, and from the "retention" of Jews immigrating to the royal domain at the same time from smaller lordships, it is clear that—whether everyone liked it or not—possession or seisin over Jews had to become a carefully delineated concept. Within three years after the agreement with Theobald, the count died, and Philip took the count's widow as his liege and her son in ward. The document that records this action dwells at some length on the status of the Jews. Mostly it refers to the series of protocols made earlier between Theobald and Philip. These were ratified.[12] The legal language is sharper here, however, because the document itself is more formal. "Seisin" is a key word. In a superficially obscure sentence, the king refers to Jews "of whom our land was seised of their bodies" who will be treated by the countess according to the "*census* and conventions made by her husband."[13]

The reference seems to be to the fact that some Jews, whom the count's men regarded as belonging to the count after the agreement of September 1198 and whose loans, made in the royal domain, were to be repaid to the count, had petitioned him to leave his lordship. The agreement of 1198 recognizes this possibility or the possibility that a Jew of one lord might do business in the domain of the other. Either king or count could with the consent of his counterpart permit these exceptions to the general rule.[14] It is fairly certain that not too much of this was expected or wanted. And one presumes that the exceptions were dearly bought. But a somewhat later arrangement involving a named Jew shows that such exceptions were envisioned in the conversations leading to the original agreement and were, though rare, sometimes permitted.[15] The status of the few Jews affected by these special agreements was therefore anomalous. The status of most royal Jews was relatively clear.

First, it was expected that their business would be lending money (and related matters, like moneychanging) and that the profits of that business would be subject to regular taxation.[16] To monitor their business, the government (or so slightly later, but pre-1204, evidence suggests) set up guidelines for the enregistering of debts, and must also have prescribed the legitimate rate of interest and announced what articles were permissible to pledge. Debts would be enregistered under special seals. That is, the Jews who lent money would have access to seals whereby they could authenticate their bonds. These seals, it seems, would be kept in the possession of local royal officials who would be available at appropriate times to authenticate the transactions for a price.[17] No doubt the bonds would be attested by the appropriate oaths (on the Torah for Jewish lenders; on the Gospels for Christian borrowers).[18]

Almost everything else we know about the government's guidelines post-dates 1204, the year of Philip's conquest of Normandy, and may not reflect his attitude between the readmission of the Jews in 1198 and the tremendous expansion of the royal domain from 1204 onward. Whether interest rates were very carefully prescribed seems doubtful. Probably there was talk about moderate interest, and only later did that phrase get defined with precision.[19] Probably there were *dicta* to the effect that certain groups of people ought to be treated with gentleness or forbearance, mimicking some ecclesiastical pronouncements: widows, crusaders, and so forth. But, if so, strict limitations on these matters date only from somewhat later, that is, after a number of problems had developed.[20]

Undoubtedly there were police regulations about what could be accepted in pledge; and we may not be wrong in arguing back from later evidence that local supervisors (*"prévôts* of the Jews") exercised their police powers to inhibit moneylenders from taking wet or blood-stained clothes in pawn.[21] They must, too, have seconded Jews' own realization of the dangers of dealing with hard-pressed churchmen who wanted to place holy objects—sacred books, patens, chalices, candlesticks—in their hands in return for loans.[22] The positive evidence of this is lacking. It is the future problems in these areas that suggest that whatever the content of admonitions, their value was limited by their imprecision. Furthermore, whatever reasonable limits were placed on distraining debtors' goods or persons for default (another obviously important aspect of the *prévôts'* work) were not successful, if later ordinances addressing the situation are a key.[23]

The allusion to enforcement brings us to the question of the nature, extent, and, most especially, quality of settlement after 1198 in the royal domain. Jews had been gone for sixteen years. In 1198 they were back. But back where? And what were the effects of the return on the settlements they entered? Baldwin, in analyzing the extant royal fiscal records for 1202/1203, showed that the total of all returns to royal income from the Jews

was very modest, perhaps 1% of total income.[24] This would include proceeds from the tariff on enregistering debts under the seal, rents on property leased to the Jews, and special taxes on certain products, like wine, and
on certain privileges (for example, to take the *esplees* or produce of land.)[25]
He attributes the modesty of the amount to the fact that the machinery for
the exploitation of the Jews was new and inefficient. But by 1202 Jews had
been resettled for nearly four years, and I do not see that the machinery of
government on this point had to be all that complicated anyway. It is more
likely that the financial return was modest because settlement was modest.
The Jews, those same fiscal records inform us, had taken up residence in a
few towns—Paris, Senlis, Sens, Orléans, Pontoise, Béthisy, Poissy, Montlhéry, and Mantes[26]; but if we go back to Rigord, we find identified for us
the main center of Jewish resettlement, Paris. Indeed, curiously, he talks
about the Jews being readmitted not to France (from which he had told us
they were exiled in 1182) but to Paris, for this is what impressed him.[27]

The return to Paris was not marked by the re-habitation of the former
jewries that were now occupied by Christians who had leased or been
given the confiscated properties. The Ile de la Cité, for example, seems to
have been forbidden to Jews; and another historic jewry on the right bank
was not re-occupied. For Christians these would long remain the "old
jewries."[28] A new locus developed on the right bank, the so-called "Juiverie de Saint-Bont," which included rue de Moussy, rue Neuve Saint-
Merry, rue du Renard, rue de la Tacherie and part of rue des Jardins (to
employ modern names). The Jews of this new jewry used one building as
a synagogue, and perhaps at some distance, as more immigrants trickled in,
a second. Whether a new cemetery was located here remains in dispute.
The fact that we can even speculate about this tells us that the major new
jewry was growing up near empty space, rather as an appendage to the city.
On the whole, Jews did not concentrate in an historic older section of the
city. There would soon be exceptions to this generality as the population
expanded from the freer migration that came in the wake of the rapid
expansion of the royal domain by conquest in 1204 and after. Ultimately
there would be small jewries on the left bank with appropriate communal
properties leased (not owned outright): synagogue, two small cemeteries,
a mill.[29]

Philip's permission to the Jews to resettle evoked a number of responses. Churchmen denounced it (or some did), not because official
church policy favored expulsion (we have seen that it did not), but because
it seemed to recreate problems. Robert of Auxerre and Rigord agree that

common opinion was strongly opposed to the readmission.[30] And the discussion above of Foulques de Neuilly's preaching and its success shows at least that some people were inclined in the direction that Rigord and Robert suggest. Philip himself is no simple character in this drama. It would be easy to assert that he had changed his mind and never looked back, but as we shall see he looked back time and again—and his erratic shifts always disturbed the fragile equilibrium that was being worked out in northern France between Jews and Christians.

The influence of the official church on all of this was also potentially disruptive. Though they never went the whole way toward urging expulsion or seriously endorsing violence, there came from the schools and from Rome ever more strident calls for separation. Schoolmen denounced the propensity of princes like Philip Augustus to sully themselves by enforcing the "usury" of Jews.[31] And emphatic declarations, echoing the earlier sentiments of Philip himself, were made about the heinous way in which crusaders, who desperately needed easy terms of credit, were being ruthlessly extorted by the Jews.[32] In 1198 the pope, Innocent III, forbad Christians to mingle with Jews who kept the usury exacted from crusaders. In 1205 he complained of the high rates of interest (usury upon usury) that were being charged. In 1208 he again vented his displeasure at princes permitting Jews to extort usury from Christians.[33]

The point is not that everything Innocent said was accepted sheepishly but that his voice and the voices of other interested bishops and schoolmen were a continuous chorus of criticism that could only be ignored by a considerable act of will. That chorus of criticism would not go away. Important barons, lay and ecclesiastical, became increasingly uncertain about their own permissive policies.[34] What was true of lords was true, too, of those Christians who themselves engaged in the business of lending at interest. We may aver that they simply accepted the onus of sin for the profits of filthy lucre, but the matter was not so simple. These Christian usurers hid behind a bewildering array of euphemisms not just to deceive their confessors.[35] At stressful times they were terribly frightened for having done so. Tales of preachers and collections of *exempla* from the turn of the twelfth/thirteenth century or thereabouts are full of images of the penitent usurer tearing himself away from his sinful past.[36] Again, the point is not that the *exempla* of the clergy testify to a mighty conversion of the usurers but that they do testify to a harsh, continuous criticism that would not let go.[37]

Part of the apprehension of Christian moneylenders, of course, was linked to that growing identification of their profession with Jews. To "judaize" in the Latin of the High Middle Ages, after all, did not usually mean to argue for more Old Testament ritual in Catholicism, let alone to convert to Judaism, a rare occurrence in any case except among re-converts.[38] It meant to act like an outsider, to regard others not as brothers but under a different set of rules that permitted forms of exploitation that were forbidden to the circle of brothers and friends.[39] To "judaize" meant to lend at interest.[40] It is not a pretty image. The avaricious moneylender may be depicted as an ape defecating the gold that is his inhuman, un-natural aliment or receiving his gold from the anus of a monster.[41]

To the lower levels of the social structure, among those who could hardly read the pronouncements of popes and bishops or of schoolmen and elitist moralists, this attitude about the Jews and usury progressively filtered down, and it made the backdrop for their relations with the Jews. They did not have to believe everything they heard, but they heard without cease sentiments like those just sketched. The "popular" work of Gautier de Coincy helps prove this.[42] Born in 1177 or 1178 in the northern French village, only eighty kilometers from Paris, from which his surname derives, Gautier became a monk in the Benedictine abbey of Saint-Médard of Soissons (from 1193), the prior of Vic-sur Aisne (from 1214), and the grand prior of Saint-Médard from 1233 until his death in 1236.[43] He would have been a small boy when Philip Augustus expelled the Jews. By the time he decided on a monastic career, he was in his mid-teens. Saint-Médard, where he chose to profess, was in Soissons, a town whose lord had not followed the king's lead in 1182 in expelling the Jews. This disjuncture, it is reasonable to suppose from Gautier's writings, had an impact on the young man. He seems also to have been upset by the readmission of Jews to the royal domain in 1198.

The Jewish community of Soissons which Gautier had the opportunity to observe was singularly tranquil, at least outwardly. But the existence of this community in the years between his profession of 1193 and the king's reversal in 1198, engendered Gautier's hostility. The royal domain was purified of Jews, yet right on the border of the domain, in Soissons, Jews lived and worked—doing what Jews increasingly did in the twelfth century, moneylending—protected and in peace. Within a few years after becoming prior of Vic-sur-Aisne (a town without any Jewish population), Gautier began to put together the large collection of vernacular miracle stories about the Virgin for which his name is mainly remembered. Drawing from Latin tales, he translated and adapted them to his own distinctive style.[44] One of his innovations was the elaboration of anti-Jewish leitmotivs into the miracles of Mary, whose fictive image henceforth in this sort of devotional literature is often set against the Jews.[45] The leitmotivs almost always touched on some repugnant or hardhearted act said to have been perpetrated by the Jews in order to put in jeopardy the faith of a Christian. The maleficent Jew in Gautier's hands is for the first time effectively integrated into *popular* literature, for these stories achieved enormous currency: the Jew as leeching usurer, the Jew as intermediary between Christian and Demon in the vending of a soul.[46] In a lyric poem that sums up Gautier's attitude toward the Jews, he wrote, "If I were king, I would have them all drowned in a well."[47]

The continued popularity of Gautier's stories and similar miracles of the Virgin owed much to Mary's own astounding devotion—one of the less subtle and more problematic aspects of the twelfth-century renaissance. Her devotion was exaggerated. The *reginarum imperatrix*, among other special titles for her, became something of a goddess or a kind of fourth person of the Holy Trinity. Increasingly an avatar rather than a mere saint (or even a great saint), she became a focus of worship, a tendency that affected even well-educated and otherwise careful churchmen.[48] This association of the gentle Virgin with the terrible Jew would have its sequel in the later thirteenth century.[49] There is little doubt that the work of Gautier de Coincy, informed by the erratic policies of the princes and responsive to the emotional seesaw that ordinary people endured under these circumstances, deeply colored social perceptions of Jews in the century to come.

We need not lay all the stress on Gautier. The point I am trying to make is that a fundamental negative shift in Christian attitudes toward the Jews occurred around 1200.[50] It cannot be coincidental that this took place at the same time as the incoherence of lordly policies became manifest and the inability of Christians to accept the dichotomy between the ideal of charity and the reality of usury became equally severe. To give one further illustration, the famous "bond of a pound of flesh" tale, made famous by Shakespeare, is medieval in origin. The earliest version (Latin, twelfth-century), however, does not make the unnatural usurer who seeks to be paid in human flesh, a Jew, but a rich serf. As such this and other stories in the cycle were even translated into Hebrew in the thirteenth century.[51] The thirteenth-century Christian French vernacular (popular) version of the tale, however, diverged from the original and recharacterized the usu-

rer as a Jew, a recharacterization that went on to overwhelm (if not completely exclude) all other formulations.[52] In sum, the climate of opinion in
the thirteenth century, as this and the earlier evidence indicate, began to
unfold full of menace. An unpredictable king had made a new choice, but
he was not unaffected by the criticism he endured or the tales he heard told
about the perfidious Jews. Whether Jews living in lordships anywhere else
in northern Europe were more confident is a moot point. (We shall address
it in due course.)[53] What is certain is that whatever the particular concerns
and worries of Jews in the royal domain from 1198 to 1202, the significance
of "their" problems was strictly limited by the fact that there were still
relatively few Jews living there in those years. Some of this was to change
after 1202 as Philip Augustus began that rapid series of conquests that
eventually brought vast territories and additional Jews under his authority.

In 1202, owing to an appeal in the French king's court against him that
went unanswered, John of England was deprived of the fiefs he held of
Philip Augustus in France. The judgement was more easily made than
enforced. We need not tell here the familiar story of how the king of
England came to be defeated in war over the next two years, losing first,
and most decisively, Normandy, but in the years to come also Maine,
Anjou, Touraine, and northern Poitou.[54] The first order of business in the
conquered province of Normandy from 1204 onward was pacification.
Philip Augustus had to make some arrangements with the Norman
population—nobles who stayed rather than go to England with John,
churchmen of the great abbeys and bishoprics, burghers of the greater
towns—offering to them confirmation of their status and resources in
return for loyalty. Again, this story has been well told by political and
administrative historians; and if at times they disagree on details, like the
financial contribution of Norman income to overall French royal income,
the range of disagreement is not usually very wide. The outlines of the
Norman occupation and of the integration of Normandy into the domain
are clear; and the success of the enterprise is as certain as any "fact" can be
in medieval history.[55]

The story of the gathering of the other lands is perhaps less well known,
but it has been studied diligently. Although the details are murkier and the
"success" of the monarchy in rapidly achieving the kind of loyalty to it that
it achieved in Normandy less complete, it may still be said that the broad

outlines of the administrative history of these lands and the principal patterns of development in ecclesiastical, feudal, and urban relations with the king are fairly uncontroversial.[56]

The same dichotomy between the relative quality of our knowledge about the general Norman situation and the situation of the other western provinces pertains to our understanding of the Jews, except here it is not a dichotomy between certainty and relative confidence. Rather we have only a few details about the Jews of Normandy in the first decade or so of Philip's rule and even fewer (and ill-understood) details for the Jews of the other conquered Plantagenet lands.[57] Our purpose, then, is to press this evidence as much as possible in order to write a coherent tale of Jewish-Christian relations.

By the time that Philip Augustus invaded Normandy, the royal domain had long outgrown its limits of 1180 by the addition of certain northern lands in Vermandois and Picardy. Not all of these lands were legally in the king's hand by 1202, but he had been exercising, as we have noticed before, a kind of tutelage over them from 1192 on.[58] The king had also added to the domain through reliefs in land of parts of several small fiefs. And the income from important wardships and other feudal rights seems to have strengthened his fiscal base.[59]

The territorial additions, though not all that large, did add to the population of the domain, and the natural growth rate of the native population in the generation from 1180 to 1202 also increased the human resources at Philip's disposal. Except, of course, for the expulsion of several thousand Jews in 1182, there do not seem to have been any strongly negative impacts on demographic growth. Although the readmission of the Jews in 1198 did little to compensate immediately for the original expulsion (we have seen that immigration was quite limited, a fact confirmed by fiscal records),[60] the expulsion of 1182 was in no sense a demographic catastrophe anyway. Whether we use the lower estimate of the population of the royal domain in 1180 (600,000) or the higher (900,000),[61] the exile of a few thousand Jews was easily compensated for in numbers in the years to come by the natural increase in the Christian population and the territorial growth of the domain. To be speculative for one last time about domain population, a reasonable estimate of it on the eve of the conquest of Normandy might be one million—perhaps slightly less if we start from the lower estimate of 600,000 for the small domain in 1180; perhaps somewhat more if we start from the higher figure of 900,000 for that year.

What was the population of Normandy? The same sort of guesswork has gone into scholars' estimates for Normandy as I have used for the royal domain. The value of these estimates lies not in precision but in the sense of the magnitude of comparison between the royal domain and Normandy. Nortier and Baldwin suggest that Normandy may have counted 1,500,000 inhabitants a generation after the conquest.[62] If we correct for a generation of natural growth (war did not upset the equilibrium of life in Normandy for any sustained length of time after 1204), it suggests that the population of Normandy and the royal domain were in the same order of magnitude on the eve of the conquest.

Every effort I have made to try to get at the relative size of the Jewish component of the Norman population around 1200 has proven, as will be shown, to be problematic. But we do know that the Jewish presence was not unimportant in terms of proceeds from taxation and patterns of settlement. Most authorities seem to concur that taxation of the Jews was heavy, more especially under John and around 1200. Besides frequent tallages of one thousand marks, there were also frequent fines and forced loans.[63] The very repetition of special taxation makes sense, in general, only if the Jewish communities were prosperous. On the whole, they seem to have been.[64] Normal times probably saw a divergence between the idealized ducal ordinances on the Jews and the reality of Jewish business life relatively small. Jews could live honestly in the duchy under the vigilant eyes of the duke's deputies. They enjoyed security of inheritance to their outstanding loans, could travel in relative freedom within the duchy, and were insulated by their special relationship to the duke from local harassment of a financial kind.[65]

It is certain that despite the temporary dislocations occasioned by Philip's conquest, the acquisition of Normandy brought a significant increase in the Jewish population of the royal lands. Unlike several Norman nobles who had property across the Channel, few Norman Jews had the kind of serious *financial* interests in England to induce them to go into exile with King John, and fewer still had sufficient loyalty to the English king, given the history of his recent exploitative taxation, to cast their lot with his.[66] What was terrible was that the severing of England from Normandy meant that Norman Jews could not travel to England and English Jews could not travel to Normandy. English Jewry therefore became an isolated outpost of at most about five thousand people, cut off from many close kin and from the intellectual and spiritual sustenance that they had had from the older, yet smaller Norman Jewry, for the English communities in fact were largely offshoots of Norman Jewry. Those communities had hardly existed before 1100, having been established in the wake of William the Conqueror's seizure of the English throne in 1066.[67] Now, scarcely more than one hundred years later and at a time when a rigorous denial of freedom of travel between lordships—let alone lordships at war—prevailed, they lost access to their historic patria.

The situation was, of course, quite similar for Norman Jews, barred from contacts with family and friends in England. Moreover, the Norman Jews faced a new and uncertain lordship. John was bad (he would behave even worse toward Jews in the years to come in England),[68] but Philip Augustus was equally if not more menacing. The man who arrested Jews on a Sabbath day in their synagogues throughout the royal domain in 1180 or 1181, the man who cancelled Jewish debts, confiscated Jews' homes and places of worship, the man who exiled Jews and even violated another lordship to destroy an entire Jewish community was not a man to be taken lightly. Although he was acting rather more solicitously in his lands after 1198, in the Jewish view he must still have been "that wicked king . . . steadfast in his wickedness from beginning to end," as, we will recall, a writer described him in remembrance of the outrage at Brie of 1192.[69]

The best evidence suggests that the Jews who faced this new lordship in Normandy resided in at least thirty-eight places on the eve of Philip's conquest, and immediately after. I have determined this number partly from the list of communities of northern Jews and of individual Jews assembled by Chazan. But I have only counted those places for which there is evidence of Jewish settlement before 1210. The reason for this is that 1210 marks a watershed when policies in both England and France would converge to disturb existing patterns of settlement.[70] In every case the evidence is firmly dated. Chazan's list then gives us thirty-three locations.[71] To this initial thirty-three I have added five locations not noticed by Chazan but based on Nahon's careful re-inventory of the Anglo-Norman documentary material that he published in 1975.[72] There may very well be a handful of other places that should be added to this list from references I have not noticed in the existing scholarship; and I am certain that some good cases might be made for adding one or two locations even where the date of the evidence, as is so often the case in rabbinic sources, is not precise.[73] But with the material presently at hand for Normandy, we can make some serious observations.

The first, obviously, is that thirty-eight is a very impressive number of communities that counted Jews among their inhabitants. Eighteen of these communities had Jewish clusters of population. In twenty cases the documentary record tells us only about one Jew or one taxable Jew at such-and-such a place.[74] It could be that some of these cases are in fact evidence of isolated residences, but probably the majority are comprised of settlements of a few families, it being a pure accident of documentary survival that the name of any Jew is known.

The size of these communities is a matter of some dispute. The rabbinic material collected by Gross is seductive. Words like "sages" or "elders" or phrases like "men well-known" suggest a flourishing set of schools and rabbinic institutions; and there may be a tendency to jump to the conclusion that Normandy was very rich in the Jewish population necessary to support this scholarly and religious enterprise.[75] No one will deny that the reputation of the Norman sages was high, but a Jewish school could be a very modest enterprise—the corner of a room in a private house—and the metaphorical "school" or following of certain sages was usually nothing more than the acceptance of the interpretations or techniques of interpretation of one teacher by a famous student.[76]

Most of the controversy has surrounded Rouen, the ecclesiastical capital of Normandy and the city from which many Jews came to England in the wake of William the Conqueror. This community suffered in a mob action in 1096, corresponding to the great First Crusade massacres in the Rhineland.[77] This fact casts doubt on the continued vitality of the community. Thanks to the research of Norman Golb, this doubt can be dispelled: the Jews of Rouen still constituted a thriving settlement in the later twelfth century. The discovery in 1976 of the remains of a twelfth-century Jewish communal building gave material proof to the random evidence of fiscal exploitation. This confirmation in turn reinforces the more-or-less independent ascriptions by Golb of a number of learned Hebrew works to Jewish savants of twelfth-century Rouen, works hitherto misattributed.[78]

What the material remnants of Jewish culture in Rouen testify to is, as mentioned before, clearly demonstrated in the taxation. Compared to that from English Jews, the return was low.[79] Yet, at one time in the decade before Philip's conquest of Normandy, Norman Jews had been told to make a contribution to the Anglo-Norman fisc of four thousand Angevin pounds.[80] It may be reasonable to suppose on the basis of this figure that Norman Jewry could produce a windfall for the duke at a good moment in the last decade of independence that was about one-seventh what the royal Jews produced for Philip Augustus in the ransom of 1180. But that ransom was one in which Philip's Jews were ruthlessly impoverished.[81] The Jews of Normandy (some of whom were those resettled exiles) were

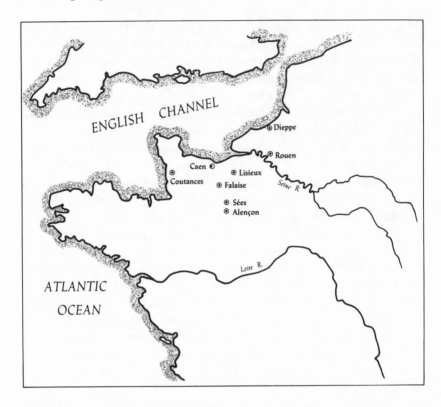

Normandy: Jewish settlement before 1210

never so completely "taken" by their lord before 1204, so the comparison is fraught with complications.[82] The most cautious conclusion will probably be the best: if the number of Jews in the royal domain in 1180 had been close to about five thousand, then the number in Normandy in 1204 was probably no more than two thousand, if that.[83]

The Jews of Normandy, then, were a distinctly small minority of this prosperous, largely rural province.[84] Because the level of urbanization of Normandy in 1200 was lower than that of the Ile de France in 1180, it is probably fair to say that this explains the relative lack of density of Jewish settlement in Normandy. The one difference which the Norman evidence suggests is the spread of Jews into villages; so far as the royal evidence informs us this spread had not occurred to the same extent in the royal domain prior to 1180.[85] The special attractiveness of Paris in the royal domain and of a few other cities—Orléans, Sens, Bourges—had conspired to make the Jews of the old royal domain urban dwellers almost exclusively. The exile of royal domain Jews in 1182 presumably sent these displaced "urban" Jews to nearby urban agglomerations by choice. Although, as we know, there was no one city that had the attractive power of Paris outside the royal domain, there were a number of towns on or near its "borders" that were about the same size as Orléans, Bourges, and Sens. Most of these would have been east or southwest of the royal domain. Only Rouen and perhaps one or two other real towns, like Falaise and Caen, would have served as magnets in Normandy for the refugees.[86]

Neither in the towns nor in the villages of Normandy were social relations between Christians and Jews free of the destructive episodes that characterized other parts of northern France and England in the twelfth and early thirteenth centuries. Probably in the first half of 1202, the Jews of the village of Silli-en-Gouffern were "massacred." We do not know how many Jews lived in this little village near Falaise. Two names have come down to us from a fine of 1195: Meir of Silli and his son, Davi. Their families would therefore have been killed in the "death of the Jews of Silli," for which one Gervais de Saint-Georges, though responsible all or in part, received a ducal pardon on 30 June 1202.[87] Nonetheless, the continuous pressure on Norman Jewry was less from criminal acts than from fiscal exploitation by Duke John. It may be somewhat naive, but one is inclined to think that the small settlements of Jews in the tiny hamlets of rural Normandy were much less targets of popular anger than the Jewish settlements in the cities elsewhere in northern Europe.

How the Jews of Normandy made their living in the generation before Philip's conquest is obscure. The ducal charter of 1201, which really echoes earlier pronouncements, appears to conceive of the Jews as a group engaging in some retailing and peddling (hence, the exemption from tolls and the freedom to travel within the duchy). It recognizes their activity as village moneylenders and pawnbrokers. It would not be surprising, however, if they did extensive gardening typical of the Norman agricultural regime or served as middlemen in the distribution and sale of agricultural surplus, since land was occasionally pledged to them.[88] It is doubtful, however, that many of the villagers were farmers in the full agricultural sense. The geographical spread of the villages for which we have evidence of Jewish settlement is wide, but not so wide that distinct patterns fail to appear. Leaving aside the problem of the bias of the surviving sources, the

Jews were not well-settled in the rugged regions, in the coastal fishermen's hamlets, or in the farming districts at large. The villages in which they lived were rather in the hinterland of the larger towns, suggesting that from time to time families of Jews had moved from towns to set up small moneylending/pawnbroking businesses in the villages nearby. The relative closeness of resettlement and the freedom of travel would have permitted these rural Jewish families to maintain a sense of social and religious community with the large number of Jews who continued to reside in the towns. In the immediate hinterland of Dieppe, on the northern tip of Normandy, there were Jews in Arques-la-Bataille, Auffay, Hodeng-en-Bosc, Longueville, and Veules-les-Roses. In the hinterland of Falaise, Jews lived in Argentan, Chambois, Exmes, Trun and, as recently as 1202, in the ill-fated Silli-en-Gouffern. Another such cluster was formed of the towns and villages of Sées, Alençon, Saint-Cénéri-le-Gerei, and Sainte-Scholasse-sur-Sarthe.[89] Spreading out from Rouen west and east were other villages of Jewish habitation, along the roads—as if peddlers who had once set up temporary shops now made permanent outposts in these hamlets.[90] Yet rugged eastern Normandy (east of Caen), large tracts of central Normandy, and most of the Atlantic coast were empty of Jews.[91]

Did Philip's war with John disrupt the pattern of social relations between Christians and Jews in these towns and villages? Wars—even the "off-again/on-again" skirmishes we call medieval wars—had significant repercussions on the non-combatant population: unpredictable fluctuations in prices, special taxes. Whether Philip's war with John had any particularly deleterious effect on Jews or Jewish and Christian relations is a hard question. Richardson says that the Jews "doubtless suffered severely."[92] That "doubtless" (otherwise rare in Richardson's book) gives away the fact that we are not likely to find a rich set of footnotes. It is known that during the war John had a tendency to release debtors from their debts if they guaranteed their loyalty and service to him; and it seems that this policy was widely practiced against the Jews of Normandy, whose loyalty was lost in the exchange.[93] There is evidence, too, of resort to the (forced) loan for fortifications.[94] If one pillages the magnificent book of Powicke on the loss of Normandy, one finds that at many places where Jews were settled—not just great towns—pitched battles or seiges of varying duration put the civilian population in danger: L'Aigle, Alençon, Arques-la-Bataille, Domfront, Gournay-en-Bray, Rouen, and Verneuil.[95] Philip, even after he conquered or received the peaceful surrender of towns and villages, constantly had to anticipate a Plantagenet counterattack, and his men seized

lands, dug fosses through non-combatants' property, and otherwise disrupted life. The records of these activities are complaints made sometimes
forty years later; but again they mention good-sized towns and little villages where there were Jews: Alençon, Falaise, and Verneuil; Exmes and
Sainte-Scholasse.[96] It is rare that these records provide any detail on how
the Jews were treated or behaved. There is perhaps one distant echo in a
complaint about the vill of L'Aigle, where for a brief period the Jews had
been run out. By the time of the complaint they had returned, but to the
petitioner's consternation.[97] The date of this incident was some years after
the conquest, but it may well go back to a problem or set of problems that
the French takeover had exacerbated.

The conclusion to all of this—and it is not insignificant—is that even
though the demographic profile of Norman Jewry shows a large proportion of Jews living in rural homesteads, Philip's war of conquest did not
pass them by. The villages they inhabited clustered around his preferred
targets. The suffering that the Jews endured in the war may or may not
have been significant, but the Jews themselves were immediately con-
fronted with the reality of occupation because they resided in areas
thought vital to holding the duchy and which the king therefore secured
tightly. The Jews knew the reputation of their new lord: he could be cruel
and he was susceptible to caprice. It remained to be seen whether he would
confirm this reputation in his future relations with them

4. The Machinery and Rhythm of Exploitation, 1204–1210

No lord who had *dominium* over Jews ever failed completely to exploit them, but the nature of the exploitation and its intensity, whatever its nature, varied from seigneurie to seigneurie. Philip Augustus was presented with a new group of Jews to govern (and exploit) after 1204, but their fates were embedded in a cluster of concerns about how he could best consolidate his hold on Normandy (and ultimately the other western fiefs) in the short term and over the long run as well. The modus vivendi that the king worked out with the Normans—both Christians and Jews—was not unchanging. Nor was the qualitative development of his relations with the Christians parallel over time with that of his relations with the Jews. The vulnerability of the Jews made them particularly susceptible to the king's shifting moods. In the early days there emerged a rather favorable working relationship between the Jews and the king in Normandy and subsequently in the other conquered western fiefs. This relationship was grounded in the king's standing policies toward the Jews of Francia proper and in his eagerness to represent himself as the defender of traditional local privileges in the conquered lands. By 1210, under significant pressures, this modus vivendi suffered enormous transformations and ultimately collapsed everywhere in the kingdom. This chapter addresses these developments.

The inhabitants of Normandy, who were daily expecting some indication of the conqueror's attitude toward the province, did not have to wait long.[1] Philip had concentrated many of his attacks on the towns, and it was understandable that he should direct his attention first to them. In an obvious bid for their support he issued charters that confirmed the franchises and privileges of several of these towns. Although these charters were not directly issued for the Jews, they would have given the first hint that the Jews' commercial livelihood might survive the conquest unimpaired, for the charters recognized that the occupation of moneylending was legitimate if not entirely savory. In 1204 both Falaise and Caen, towns that had Jewish communities, received this guarantee; and this or similar guarantees were soon bestowed on other towns where there were Jewish settlements.[2]

Meanwhile, the king received at Mantes the oaths and security of Jews who, in Baldwin's words "wishe[d] to remain permanent residents of the duchy."[3] The maker of the list of the Jews who chose to do so saw no need to record by name every Jew who made his pledge (he added, for example, "Et insuper alter alterum plegiavit" at the end), but specific information on fourteen Jews who came to Mantes is given. They swore on the scroll of the law (*super rotulum*) that they would not leave the king's domains. Their securities were comprised of part of the bonds (*carte*) in their possession which they handed over to the king's men in pledge. The total value of the bonds for the fourteen specified instances was 520 Angevin pounds. The individual amounts transferred varied from Jew to Jew: Jacob de Molins deposited bonds worth 160, two other Jews provided bonds worth only 10 pounds. The average was about 37 pounds. At least one woman is on the list, a certain Beleassez (Rachel)[4] who handed over 15 pounds worth of bonds to the king's men. Since there is so little evidence of Jews fleeing with John and since the list before us ends with the clause quoted above, it may be that the vast majority of Norman Jews were ultimately included in the formal pledge of "fidelity" without leaving much documentation behind.

We should remind ourselves that the bonds given as security did not represent disposable income for the Jews; they were a form of future potentially realizable income. But it must have been easy to think of them as part of the undifferentiated "wealth" of the Jews. *Baillis*, the great officials of provincial government, were being (or would soon be) paid yearly remunerations in excess of 50 or in some cases even 100 pounds.[5] Ordinary clerks would have received much less. *Carte*, then, worth 160 pounds coming from a single Jew must have struck the king's men, rightly or wrongly, as very substantial indeed. We do not know how many Jews pledged so much. The fourteen specified cases have only one set of bonds at 160 pounds and only two other sets valued at 50 pounds or more.[6] Even the smallest amount, 10 pounds, was a significant portion of the yearly income of a well-paid man and helped make an impression of the wealth of the Jews that was anything but sympathetic to them, rooted as it was in usury. The implications of these impressions will occupy us more fully later.

If Normandy was the first and principal concern of Philip Augustus, he and his men nonetheless progressively brought the other Plantagenet fiefs (Maine, Anjou, Touraine, and northern Poitou, around Poitiers) to the west and southwest of the Ile de France under control. Dynastic confrontations within the Plantagenet family had long disturbed these regions.[7] Some of this strife carried over to the Jews. Jewish community life had also frequently been punctuated by conflicts unrelated to internecine Plantagenet warfare. The documentary record is fragile, however, and nearly every incident is shrouded in mist. Some speculative reconstructions have been made of such incidents that supposedly occurred in Le Mans in 992, from 1138 to 1150, and around the year 1200.[8] These tentative attempts to uncover the conflicts in local society do not undermine the general, more positive impression of social and financial relations as they had been regulated by the Plantagenets: just as in Normandy, Jewish business, that part of it given over to moneylending, was protected by charter in 1201 but strictly subjected to the authority of the ruler.[9] Freedom of movement and exemption from tolls was characteristic of Jews' privileges, with few exceptions.[10]

As also in Normandy there was a kind of regional sensibility among the Jews themselves. The intellectual influence of the communities of Anjou and Poitiers is felt from Hebrew sources.[11] Brunschvicg long ago assembled evidence on the careers and works of Angevin Jewish theologians and poets before Capetian domination of Anjou.[12] A number of other scholars have remarked the evident flourishing of these and other communities on the borderlands of the Capetian conquest.[13]

Together, Maine, Anjou, Touraine, and the small strip of conquered Poitou were about the same geographical size as Normandy. What were the Jewish communities like? In the first place, Maine was by and large an underpopulated rural province. Its principal, in some ways its only, urban center was the capital Le Mans, which sat on a modest trade route from Paris to the Breton coast.[14] Except for those settled in Le Mans and in Mayenne, it cannot be said with certainty that there were any other Jews in the county before the year 1210.[15] Mayenne, in fact, was in some ways only a southern outpost of one of the clusters of Norman villages earlier identified.[16] The conclusion is not that Jewish settlement in Maine was restricted to these two locations, but that the apparent lightness of settlement in this distinctly rural region conforms with expectations derived from the general trend toward urban settlement in twelfth-century Jewish demography.

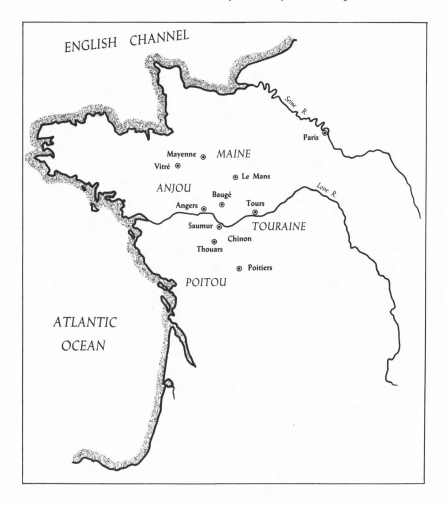

ENGLISH CHANNEL

Seine R.

Paris ◉

Mayenne ◉   MAINE
Vitré ◉
                    ◉ Le Mans
ANJOU   Baugé   Loire R.
Angers ◉   ◉   Tours
                                ◉
Saumur ◉   TOURAINE
         ◉ Chinon
Thouars

              ◉ Poitiers

POITOU

ATLANTIC

OCEAN

Western fiefs: Jewish settlement before 1210

Anjou (particularly from Angers southwards), Touraine, and northern
Poitou were much more heavily settled in general—and by Jews in
particular.[17] The Norman pattern reappears. Near a city, major market
town, or castle with a Jewish population (Angers, Saumur, Tours, Poitiers) there will be several villages in the immediate hinterland for which the
documentary record indicates Jewish settlement. Besides Angers, Saumur,
Tours, and Poitiers, therefore, we find evidence of Jewish settlement in the
Loire valley towns and villages of Baugé, Segré, Vitré, Thouars, Loches,

Chinon, Montcontour, Amboise, and Château-la-Vallière. Near Saumur the hamlet "Rue-Juif" and, near Baugé, that of "Juiverie" bespeak the Jewish presence in the region.[18]

Population figures are far from firm. From later thirteenth-century records, Blumenkranz estimated a population in 1269 of less than one thousand Jews in Anjou.[19] Two points need to be made about this figure. It reflects a depopulation of Jews in the rural north of Anjou around 1240, yet it also probably reflects some natural increase in the number of Jews in the clusters of towns and villages from Angers to Tours.[20] Nonetheless, if we take one thousand as a promising estimate of Angevin Jewish population in the early thirteenth century and we add roughly the same number for Touraine and around Poitiers, which was as densely settled by Jews as Anjou, we obtain a combined figure of two thousand.[21] The very low density of Jewish population in Maine should hardly lead us to augment that figure. So, if these seem to be reasonable considerations, it would mean that a similar number of Jews were living in Maine, Anjou, and Touraine, taken together, as were living in Normandy on the eve of Philip Augustus's conquest.

No comprehensive or satisfying profile of any individual Jewish settlement is presently possible. Still, some important features are recoverable in a composite reconstruction. The Jews in these areas, as elsewhere in the northern regions we have discussed, had small agricultural holdings in order to produce, for example, grapes for wine, and they had financial interests in rural property; but they were not farmers. They were primarily urban moneylenders and moneychangers living in their own semi-exclusive neighborhoods known for commerce by the time of Capetian domination.[22] The Le Mans evidence is good here. It shows us two vineyards in the possession of Jews of the city in the very early thirteenth century, held, I think, as small appurtenances of urban property.[23] Jews could evidently own property outright in Le Mans as late as 1192; evidence of renting in the town exists for the first decade of the thirteenth century.[24] The Jews possessed a synagogue and cemetery (and possibly a market and hospital).[25] In the second half of the twelfth century we encounter a Jew witnessing a charter in his capacity as a moneychanger.[26] The presence of Jews as witnesses (in this or similar capacities) in other twelfth-century charters from the western fiefs is well-attested: there is an instance for Tours dating from the mid-century; there is another for Château-la-Vallière in 1199.[27] In 1203 the evidence of Jewish moneylending in Le

Mans is explicit.[28] The Jews of Le Mans (or of Maine) were also servicing the credit needs of the rural hinterland at about the same time.[29]

The western fiefs of Maine, Anjou, and Touraine had been conquered almost as quickly as Normandy, but the king's troops also tried to penetrate deeply into Poitou with less success. Through 1206 the Poitevin resistance kept the southern flank of Anjou and Touraine unstable.[30] It is not to be expected, then, that settled relations between crown and Jews could develop quickly in this region. Nevertheless, from the moment he penetrated the western fiefs Philip made clear as he had in Normandy that he wanted it to be business as usual. In August 1204, while in Poitiers, and almost as an obiter dictum, the king affirmed the continued presence of Jews in Maine, Anjou, and Touraine by recognizing his intention in the future to take legitimate tallages and to inflict occasional special requests on them.[31] This was no *pactum* with the Jews, merely an acknowledgment that they would be exploited as they had been exploited in the past.

Strange to say, however, by 1206 business as usual was not quite the order of the day. In that year the king issued a charter for the Jews whose provisions react to their enhanced economic presence in the royal domain since 1198 and the impressions of Jewish success in moneylending in Normandy from the conquest on.[32] There was never any thought of destroying the Jewish moneylending business, but the king, even while confirming the privilege of Jews to continue in moneylending (warriors always need loans), made them a less desirable creditor from Christians' point of view. The charter for the Jews is not some sort of agreement with them or sop to them. It is a pronouncement made by the king and the Champenois (owing to his guardianship) *for the Jews*.[33] It is a royal response to Christians' complaints, and in every instance the king's response injured the Jews.

First of all Philip forbade the Jews to lend money at immoderate interest, greater than two pennies per pound per week. Moreover, Jews could not call in their loans within a year. That is, the debtors had a year minimum to pay their debts, unless the lender and debtor worked out a different schedule. Even if they did arrange a different schedule, the debtor could pay off his loan earlier without any penalty and despite any prior agreement to the contrary with the Jew (the Jew, as a result, losing expected interest).[34] There was a trade-off of sorts here, because royal officials had supervision over debts and they were not always available. Holding itinerant courts and seeing to the other voluminous business in their hands took time; so Philip ordered that a debtor's discharge of his debt earlier than agreed to had to be done at fixed times according to an otherwise undefined schedule to be established by the king's men.

Perhaps the king or his men deemed the various terms during the year when revenue was accounted the appropriate times for this official discharging of debts. I raise this possibility because the charter next goes into details on the use of the seal to enregister debts. Since the use of the seal was a supervisory as well as a fiscal tool for the government, officials very probably correlated the schedule for its use with other collections of revenue. The king commissioned new seals for each town where Jews lent money. One Christian was to have possession of the seal, another of the cast. A clerk was to write the bonds. The crown offered to reseal old debts, contracted under the old seals. Failure to reseal was a bar to further interest on the loan.[35] Another provision of the charter prohibited excessive penalty payments. People who could not make a scheduled payment to a Jew were to have their debt continue to generate the "normal" maximum interest, two pennies per pound per week, but nothing more than this. The provision indicates that there had been a tendency to inflict higher (or supplementary) penalties for delays in repayment even when the debtor was legitimately on pilgrimage or was a *fugitivus*, that is, under the special ban associated with the conquest.[36]

There follow then the police regulations about pawning and pledging of lands. The regulations foresee the option of pawning under bond, but pawning without seal would continue. Jews could not accept holy vessels or ornaments; they were not to accept bloodstained or damp clothing. With regard to the pledging of lands (by bond only), they could not take ecclesiastical lands as security in the royal domain or in Champagne. If they did so in defiance of these regulations, the transactions were void. These provisions complemented a regulation intended to get at clandestine agreements about lands and straight loans. Parties were to register every bond, and each would define the true extent of the transaction. The debtor was to receive no less and pay back no more than the legally registered bond required. To violate this provision annulled the transaction and put the debtor under the sanction (in mercy) of the royal court. Pawning seems to have been slightly different. As we noticed, the option remained open of pawning without bond. If bonds were employed, the government promised to adjudicate disputes only if the pledge had significant value—if it was made of gold or silver, or consisted of farm animals—or if it included clothes (perhaps going back to the police provisions already mentioned about bloodstained and damp clothing).

The charter ends with the details of the appointment of the two men to be in charge of the seal. And the document veritably cries out for openness and probity in the transactions. The fear of clandestine lending runs like an open sore through the charter. The keepers of the seal must swear on the gospels to do their work diligently. The clerk who writes the bonds is to provide security that he will carry out his task legitimately, for there seems to be much apprehension about bribery and other forms of corruption. The charter finally ends on an ominous note. It shall be in force only as long as the king and his Champenois co-subscribers care to keep it. This is no permanent arrangement with the Jews, no charter for generations to come. The king, if he wishes, will change his mind any time he cares to.

For about the next four years this set of regulations governed Jewish financial affairs. But little has survived from that period to inform us directly about how well it worked. That artisans fabricated new seals seems certain, but whether any examples of them, as opposed to the old seals, have survived is less certain (and what we might learn from them if they did survive is moot).[37] A later complaint about a royal official shows him, John the Warrior, enforcing a debt owed a Jew about 1207 and taking possession of the debtor's land until he paid up on an overdue loan in Normandy.[38] How the system of regulations was being applied in Champagne remains an open question, although later evidence, if carefully treated, might permit us to make a few comments.[39]

While the French were proceeding to elaborate the machinery of government in their newly enlarged kingdom, the English were determined to reconquer the western fiefs. John and his successor in the next half-century planned, schemed for, and always failed to make their great and triumphal return.[40] At times the planning reached a frenzy, and the frenzy carried over into a manic search for money to execute the plans. Of course, like all kings, the English monarchs, even though obsessed with the recovery of their ancient patrimony, had many matters competing for their attention. King John in the years after the initial disasters of 1202–1204 was faced with hostility from his own barons, a serious struggle with the pope, and Welsh and Irish insurgencies.[41] All of these matters required his action and his money. It is not surprising therefore that one of the expedients he employed to secure the money he needed was the tallaging of the Jews. But his ferocity cannot be explained by the desire for money alone.

Richardson, in a magnificent section of his book on the Jews of England, saw in the older generation of John's counsellors a restraint on the erratic and enigmatic king.[42] As these advisors died off or left government a nastier streak in John's personality was given full rein, to the lasting detriment of medieval English Jewry. What occurred according to Richardson was an escalation from traditional exploitation of the Jews to a much more vicious series of attacks. In 1205 there was a routine tallage, but in 1207 there was another, more comprehensive one based on information on the extent of all debts owed the Jews: the Jews themselves were to report their loans and the value of them to the central government. Possibly, administrators had misgivings about these returns and suspected chicanery, namely, that the Jews, fearing a potential seizure of their outstanding loans by the king, had provided incomplete information.[43] This provoked a second and much more ruthless inquiry in 1210, one which presumably revealed evidence of just the kind of falsehoods that officials had suspected: to carry out this investigation all Jews—or rich male Jews— throughout the kingdom were to be arrested and their accounts seized and audited. Those whom the crown regarded as flagrant liars were tortured to elicit information: their eyes were ripped out and they were starved.[44] Some were executed. In the course of these attacks many Jews did manage to escape, especially poorer ones; John may have been planning to exile these Jews anyway. The punitive tallage associated with the *captio* was supposed to bring in an enormous amount of money; some sources say as high as sixty-six thousand marks. But the greed exceeded the resources of the Jews. A great deal was paid, but, if Richardson is right, probably nothing quite like this sum.

We shall now see that the similarity between King John's evolving policies toward the Jews and the policies of Philip Augustus is unsettling, even uncanny. But why did the two programs duplicate each other so closely? Was Philip faced with a financial crisis of the same order as King John's?[45] What details can be put to the French experience?

We have to begin with the bonds of the Jews. Almost as soon as we begin to read about the return of the Jews to the royal domain in 1198, we read of their written transactions with Christian debtors. These documents, variously called *carte*, *littere*, or *conventiones*, were all supposed to be authenticated with seals in the possession of royal keepers whose duties were regulated by ordinance. Few of the seals,[46] and none of the straightforward and simple *littere*, have survived. But the reason is obvious. The sealed bonds themselves were in the possession of the Jews. When the debts were discharged the debtors made sure that the bonds were destroyed—in precisely the same way that IOUs are destroyed in informal modern practice. Two sealed bonds, noticed by Chazan, have been recovered; they are not ordinary bonds, however. Rather, they document the conveyance of real property or chattels real for the discharge of debts.[47] As surrogates for deeds, they were therefore retained.

In other words, Philip himself had access to very little precise information on the extent of Jewish lending, but as we learned in the last chapter, complaints about it were steady. Finally, bowing to this pressure, he decided to investigate more directly. His motivations are impossible to get at, but a case can be made *against* a severe fiscal crisis. To be sure, medieval kings always needed money. Nonetheless, Philip faced no serious threat from John for several years after the conquest.[48] The fiscal records themselves, meager as they are, show the king receiving huge amounts of money as special "gifts" in the period before and after the culmination of his Jewish policy in 1210, making the idea of an acute financial crisis even less persuasive. For example, the king received one thousand pounds in December 1209 from the bishop of Nevers for an agreement not to exploit his regalian rights over the bishopric in the future.[49] He received 7,500 pounds in May 1210 from a gift made by the count of Champagne, his ward, for support against a baron who was challenging his right to inherit; in December of the same year he received an additional 7,500 pounds from the Champenois.[50] The king expected an enormous windfall of 30,000 or even 50,000 pounds from the relief of Flanders a few months later.[51] Indeed, he had so much cash available in 1210 that he bought the town of Bray-sur-Somme easily in May for a little over 4,000 pounds; and he offered to advance 2,000 pounds to the burghers of Châlons from the surplus in his coffers at the same time.[52]

A much more likely motivation for the attack on the Jews was, as indicated, the growing perception of the "grip" of the Jews on Christians. In 1202 in Champagne the debts of one monastery had become so grievous that the house went into receivership.[53] Acts such as this often required the confirmation of lords.[54] What was true in Champagne had become true of the ecclesiastical institutions with which the king had an intimate relationship. La Charité-sur-Loire is a case in point. The king shared with the priory certain rights and powers defined in conventions of 1181 and 1203.[55] Moreover, the monks had stood by him in a difficult time in his struggle with Richard of England by guaranteeing in the name of the priory the king's subscription to the treaty of Gaillon in 1196, one of the many temporary truces in the long war between Philip and Richard.[56] La Charité was not a "regalian" house, but it was a faithful ally. It had briefly suffered the seizure of its lands by the English king after the breakdown of the treaty.[57]

In the fall of 1209 it became known to the king that La Charité was heavily in debt and that there was no way to overcome the situation except by selling off some of its properties.[58] The Hospitallers were willing to purchase them. The extent of the debt—owed to a single Jew (but a Jew possibly representing a consortium of Jewish creditors)—was extraordinary: eleven thousand pounds.[59] There was, the prior of La Charité stressed, no alternative. Unless the sale was ratified, "they could not free their church from the usury which was owed the Jews."[60]

Philip confirmed the sale, but in apparent reaction he authorized a special investigation into Jewish lending. He partly employed Jews to carry out the inquiry. We have a notice about five Jews "who made the assize on the other Jews." Their names were Elias of Sézanne, a Champenois by birth who had moved to the royal domain either in 1198 or later under a special convention between the count of Champagne and the king. He was then residing at the town of Echelles (*apud Scalas*; present *département*, Eure-et-Loir). Jacob the rabbi (*presbiter*) of Gonesse took part as well, and three other Jews: Morel de Yainville, Vivant Gabois, and Vivant de Melun.[61]

The results of the assize were unhappy for the Jews. The king's men became convinced—and in this they may have been influenced by rumors they had heard about what was going on in England—that the Jews were dissembling. A contemporary Scots chronicler explicitly sees profound similarities in John's and Philip's actions. The French king, persuaded of the Jews' ruthless usury, ordered their arrest.[62] Whether he did so, as the Scots chronicler states, in a subtle ruse that managed to have them all (and he means Jews all over the domain) taken into custody in one day is dubious.[63] His impression may arise from a too cavalier comparison with King John's viciousness, or it may arise from his knowledge of how Philip had opened his reign with the Sabbath synagogue attack two decades before.

What Philip Augustus intended to do at this stage is revealed to us in another contemporary or near contemporary record. The original of this record can be precisely located in 1210 on the basis of the most up-to-date evidence we have on the terms of administration served by the *baillis* mentioned in it. It is found in the *Registres* of Philip Augustus under the title "Investigation of the Debt of the Jews," and has been available to scholars for many years.[64] Philip had arrested the Jews (males only?), including those on whom he had depended for his investigation.[65] In order to get out of jail each Jew was supposed to redeem himself by ransom and necessarily have his debts called in to do so. As a Christian in Normandy complained thirty-seven years later: he had been forced—unjustly in his view—to pay a debt to Leo the Jew because "the said Jew owed it to king Philip of illustrious memory for his redemption when he was taken along with the other Jews in the time of the said king."[66] Because of the date of administration of the *bailli* mentioned in the document, Pierre du Thillai, we can be sure that the plaint refers to the thirteenth-century "taking" by Philip, not to his first attacks in the 1180s.[67] A number of other Christians would remember this *captio* of the Jews because of the effect on them of the calling in of debts.[68] Some could not pay up quickly, and there were still arrears of the "old debt of the Jews" a decade after the *captio*.[69]

We have here, then, evidence of an enormous transfer of debts in order for the Jews to obtain their freedom. The transfers, if all were carried out, would have been gargantuan in magnitude. The "Investigation" gives a total sum of more than 250,000 pounds. Collecting must have been difficult. I have alluded to arrears. Some of the Jews either could not pay or, rather, their debtors gave problems. Some debtors made special arrangements with Philip.[70] As the process unfolded, the king permitted the release of some Jews, but kept others in prison. We have the list of "Those Jews Who Will Remain in the Châtelet [Prison] at the Petit Pont" in Paris.[71] This list was so poorly edited in earlier versions that it was of very limited use to scholars.[72] There are twenty-six Jewish males from *Francia* and fifteen from Normandy. By collating the information on this list with the "Investigation," we discover that those kept in custody were among the richest Jews in the kingdom, as measured by the admittedly inadequate standard of outstanding debts.[73]

However, this state of affairs—the retention of some Jews in prison—did not last very long. It seems to have been decided, if I am interpreting two undated lists correctly, that all the Jews should be released so long as certain Jews became principal sureties for the payment of the "debt." Four Jews were chosen to stand surety for *Francia*; four others for Normandy.[74] Among these two groups one can identify two Jews—Morel de Falaise and Bonevie de Melun—who had been on the list to be kept in prison in the Châtelet until such time as the king had made up his mind how to proceed.

The attempt or plan to despoil the richest Jews (or all the Jews), it is said, led to widespread flight.[75] The atmosphere in Paris throughout the year was certainly hostile, and did not proceed only from the king. An ecclesiastical council that met in Paris in that year focussed on the problem of heresy. Although reports differ, there seems to be no question that the heretics attacked were the exact opposite of judaizers. They viewed the Old Testament with disdain, a burden from which to be delivered. But this fact hardly matters. It is the heightened atmosphere of the capital that is really important to us. This is nicely reflected in Guillaume Le Breton's continuation of Rigord's biography of Philip Augustus. The monarch emerges as *rex christianissimus et catholicus*, receiving the erring defrocked priests condemned into his hand for execution of the sentence of burning. The women and other *simplices* led astray by these purveyors of venomous doctrine were spared.[76] Our Scots chronicler, who also knew of the council and its work, recognized the signs of the times. Everything was of a piece to him. Judaizers or no, there was something elegant and exquisite for him as there must have been for others in the neat coincidence of a twin persecution of the Jews and the heretics of the city of Paris.[77]

As "there must have been," I wrote above, for at this council or possibly at a synod held in northern France slightly later under the presidency of Robert de Curçon, an influential cleric and close associate of the pope, the clergy spelled out their concerns in some detail and in picturesque language. Again the conflation of object groups is manifest. The churchmen repeated old injunctions against Christians working for Jews, laying stress on the vulnerability of females (midwives and nurses) to be led astray. Here they were extrapolating from the perceived influence of the heretics. But they added to this a concern for usurers who metaphorically raised up "financial" synagogues to their wickedness by training their children in schools "for writing the debts of their fathers acquired by usury."[78]

We have already learned that King John's attacks had sent many of his poorer Jews into exile. Where they went is difficult to determine. English Jews, it seems likely, would have been quite aware, if only by rumor, of the increasing harshness of Philip Augustus's policies since 1198—more and more restrictions on moneylending and collection of up-to-date information on debts—policies precisely like those of King John. If they knew also of Philip's arrests, it is not conceivable that they sought refuge in the French king's lands. The closest areas where they might be received fraternally by their coreligionists were slightly north of Normandy in the domains of the count of Saint-Pol, for example, where there were some small Jewish communities, and in Brittany, which, though subject to French influence, was not a conquered province.[79]

Any Jews in the French royal domain who chose to flee when the winds of royal policy turned cold in 1210 had even fewer alternatives. The entire royal domain was increasingly like a prison. Escape to England was impossible because of the deterioration of the English situation. Flanders was under royal tutelage until 1212 and had virtually no Jews living there and therefore no one on the spot and with influence to intervene with the count or with the prosperous towns to secure refuge for immigrants.[80] That other northern lord with modest domains, the count of Saint-Pol, entered into an agreement in May 1210 not to accept royal Jews into his domain.[81] With Champagne, Philip was already in agreement not to permit Jews to transfer allegiances. Significantly, the agreement was renewed in May 1210.[82] Adjacent northern lands Philip bought outright in May 1210.[83] These facts mean that the entire north and most of the east were completely cut off for Jewish migration. The band of lordships to the south of the royal domain was less cohesive. But we should recall that many of these lordships had excluded Jews around the turn of the century; it was not likely they would welcome refugees.[84] With one of these lordships, the county of Nevers, the king concluded still another agreement forbidding Jews to transfer allegiance; it too dates from May 1210.[85] Brittany was nearly the only refuge open to both French and English Jews unless they chose to try to escape to far more distant regions, even Palestine.[86]

The arrests and attempted closing of the kingdom were not the final acts in this drama. I have already mentioned the process of redemption. But even the redemption might have been viewed as the prelude to something more decisive. There is a quite curious charter that has survived from 1210 that can be roughly dated between April and October of that year, so that it is contemporary with the sudden taking of the Jews into custody.[87] Philip, for his soul and the souls of his ancestors, granted to the Hospitallers of Melun a set of properties on which they were supposed to build a chapel. He requested, however, that the churchmen refrain from undertaking the construction.[88] The reason is not explained. But it is noted that the properties were contiguous to the *scola Judeorum* (the synagogue). Of the many plausible explanations for the request not to build, one is that the king intended to expel the Jews after arresting and despoiling them and, in line with policy in 1182, turn over their synagogues (at least those leased from him) to the church. In this reconstruction of intentions, the *synagoga* of Melun would have become the chapel of the Hospitallers of Melun. Yet, however close Philip came to an expulsion—and Baldwin seems to think he came quite close—he soon changed his mind. The bullying stopped; the pressure came off.[89]

For the Jews who migrated in anticipation of expulsion or to avoid the *captio*, Brittany was the only close haven. The province had been a locus of political conflict between Philip Augustus and John of England almost from the moment of John's accession. It became a particular locus of contention as the French conquest of Normandy and the other western Plantagenet fiefs gained momentum. But neither Philip nor John managed to secure Brittany in the first decade of the thirteenth century or seriously committed the necessary resources to do so. It was not until Philip succeeded in arranging a marriage between the putative heiress to Brittany and his cousin Peter of Dreux (the infamous Peter Mauclerc) that his influence in the duchy increased. Even then, that is, after 1212, Peter proved a formidable lord in his own right, independent and difficult.[90]

If Brittany was one of the few places of relative sanctuary nearby for those who tried to escape the attacks of Philip (and John), it was, nonetheless, an odd and bewildering sanctuary. Brittany was first and foremost a land of coastal fishing villages, sparse internal population scattered about isolated villages, and hills so rugged that they seemed more like mountains. The religious establishment was firm but scattered as well, with monastic outposts in bleak and stony holds and hermits leading lives of solitary devotion in caves and fastnesses. The bishoprics were located in towns that were very small; even Nantes on the Loire border with Poitou was small. The internal rivers of Britanny were largely unnavigable and therefore not conducive to trade. That there were many Jews in this region before 1210 is doubtful. There is no evidence that there were, and given general tendencies in Jewish settlement, there is no reason to suppose that there were.[91] So, while the lack of strong authority in 1210 and the nearness of Brittany to French and English royal lands made it an acceptable destination for escaping Jews, it was not a very attractive one.

Perhaps in the early days of this migration Brittany was conceived of as nothing more than a way-station on the roads to more hospitable lands in southern Europe. As it turned out, some Jews stayed and found places in a few of the towns and larger villages as moneylenders. As early as 1222 there is evidence of that careful attention to jurisdiction over Jews in Brittany that characterized the turn of the century elsewhere in northern France. The jurisdiction of the bishop of Nantes over Jews in his domains was recognized in that year, for example, in the notice of an agreement that has survived between the bishop and Peter of Dreux.[92] By 1235 the evidence is strong not only of the business of moneylending, but of the wider activity of Jews in certain aspects of Breton financial culture. Peter of Dreux used the service of at least one Jew in the financial administration of his lordship.[93]

With the growing role of the Jews went a certain sophistication in the control of them. We read of the existence of a seneschal of the Jews of the bishop of Nantes in 1235 and of the seals of Jews.[94] It is not necessary to overstress the extent of organization or to exaggerate its importance. The evidence after all only points to small numbers of Jews at Nantes, Ancenis, Fougères, Clisson, Dol, Guérande, and Lamballe.[95] Yet these small numbers of Jews in only a handful of communities provoked a wave of resentment that is quite astounding.

De La Borderie called it one of the "most regrettable excesses" of Breton history when around Easter of 1236, during the preaching of a crusade, a wave of anti-Jewish violence swept Brittany and spread into the neighboring rural areas of Anjou and Poitou.[96] We can argue back from later restrictions on usury and an order of expulsion to the background for the attacks.[97] First there is no doubt that the network of credit achieved in the first generation of settlement was perceived as relatively extensive and that the property pledged with Jews included lands and movables. It is also certain that the clergy played a decisive negative role here, for the decree of expulsion (1240) provided for the excommunication of the lord (the son of Peter Mauclerc) if he were ever to rescind his order of expulsion. The insistence on this provision must mean that secular lords or ecclesiastical lords, in their feudal capacity, despite their ultimate support for the policy of expulsion, were ambivalent about the Jews. The reason for their ambivalence is obvious; they made money from them. The lord of Fougères, like the bishop of Nantes, had jurisdiction, which meant taxability as well, over his Jews.[98] Peter Mauclerc's son acknowledged in the expulsion order that properties once pledged to the Jews in one way or another had come into his hands and had been sold by order of his court, presumably to reimburse the Jews for bad debts. But it is not to be supposed that the right to employ this mechanism was given to the Jews gratis.

Nonetheless the Jewish presence was recent and weak. The violence against them in 1236 was both an affront to the public order to which all lords paid lip service and an unwelcome reminder to churchmen of the pervasiveness of "extortion" of Christians, as they perceived it, by Jews.

The depth of the reaction against the Jews may be measured by a clause in the order of expulsion that put an end to any investigations into the deaths of Jews in 1236. It was as if in 1240 Brittany would begin with a *tabula rasa*. The Jews who had entered Brittany in 1210 never successfully integrated themselves into the local society. They were always conceived as strangers involved in a business that was both extortionate and perverse. It would be better for everyone, or so the baronage of Brittany eventually came to feel, if the Jews simply left. As part of the expulsion order, all debts were therefore cancelled, bringing to an end a thirty-year episode in Breton history. No chronicler tells us where the Jews went.

The fate of Breton Jewry underscores the fact that the choices available to Jews who endured the crisis of 1210 were all pervaded with uncertainty for the future, uncertainty reinforced by information and rumors that passed back and forth across the political boundaries of France. Not every Jew who remained in the royal domain knew the full extent of the king's moves against Jewry in 1210 or came to know the fate of Jews who fled. But the royal investigation, the arrests, the snatching away of debts, and the precariousness of coreligionists who fled to places like Brittany which had no Jews to welcome them would have been facts more or less available to everyone. Out of this uncertainty (and supported by the successful emigration of some Jews to Palestine) emerged a persistent medieval Zionism that began to characterize Jewish thought in the thirteenth century. That is to say, it characterized it until that dream too was shattered by reports of the Muslim reconquest and the bloodbath of Acre late in the century.[99] In that unfortunate city, the Muslims regarded the immigrant Jews as supporters of the recently defeated European Christians and they exacted a horrifying vengeance:

> Respectable women who learned the sacred tongue ere they
>   learned to eat,
> Were bereaved of children whom they had borne in vain
> And for whom they had toiled to no purpose.
> Woe for innocent children who were attacked by vicious enemies.
> They destroyed the temple of the living God.
> Together with infants that knew not sin.[100]

5. The Last Years

From the point of view of Philip Augustus, the rounding up and punishing of the Jews that he authorized in 1210 was no unjustified deviation from his duty as lord and king to protect the Jews. A Christian king was also the doer of justice: Philip had punished the Jews in his capacity of chief judge of his kingdom because he had found them guilty of breaking his laws. Even if he had not acted after an investigation, he could have justified his "taking" of the Jews as a seigneurial privilege. Moreover, since he did not expel them, he expected that after the redemption by which they bought their release they would return, chastened and more circumspect, to the business of moneylending. For the first time, nonetheless, we get a hint that two voices were beginning to play on Philip's sentiments. There were the critics of royal policy. Radicals grew vehement in their condemnation of any princely support for the sinful business of usury.[1] Within a few years of his *captio* of the Jews Philip wrote to the pope to denounce some of this criticism, in particular the sermons of Robert de Curçon against usury in the Paris region. Robert was supposed to be preaching the crusade in France, but this member of Peter the Chanter's circle of reformers at Paris used the opportunity to attack usury as well—in all its aspects, not just its effects on crusaders and potential crusaders. Philip and Pope Innocent III had a bitter exchange of letters on the matter.[2]

No one could predict the outcome of this argument. No one knew what Philip felt or would come to feel about his toleration of the business of usury. As ecclesiastical pressures became heavier, the Jews of the royal domain had no alternative but to turn to the king for support. He had eviscerated their business, but he had not banned them from rebuilding it. Realizing their vulnerability in this difficult period, they sought stronger guarantees that new loans made by them to Christians would be enforced by the king's officials. We have an undated directive that refers to the difficulty that they had experienced in getting royal officers to enforce debts against defaultors. The king's reaction—an order to enforce—came either in response to a petition during the period of collection for the redemption payments circa 1210 or later after the Jews had resumed their business. In either case, he recognized that the grievance was legitimate.

This order to enforce that I have referred to is enrolled on the registers of Philip Augustus as a statute (*stabilimentum*) made for the Jews *de novo*. That *de novo* has been taken to mean that the statute was issued about the same time as another dated directive on the Jews with which it is associated in the registers. This is plausible; and since the dated—and more comprehensive—directive comes from 1219, it is possible that the undated statute is slightly earlier. It seems to me, however, that the undated statute owes much of its content to events in 1210 and immediately thereafter. If so, the phrase *de novo* ought to be taken as meaning "again" rather than "recently."[3] That is to say, the statute was issued once (perhaps soon after 1210) and again, near 1219, in the form we have.

The statute provided new, more restrictive limits to Jews' business while aiming at a firmer kind of control over the Jews, and it seems to be answering problems raised by the revelations of 1210. There is a provision that sealed bonds no longer be required for loans of less than three pounds, a good indication that local officials had been overburdened by the number of requests to seal bonds for small loans. The crown's interest was only in major lending, as the *captio* had earlier proved, a fact that explains other features of the undated directive. Like any modification it repeats several of the provisions of what it modifies, the ordinance of 1206.[4] What it adds is significant. Those appointed faithfully under oath to seal the bonds of the Jews were directed to keep copies or notes, *rescripta*, of the transactions, notes that could be used for the king's business (*ad opus nostrum*), suggesting that inquiries into Jewish lending would become routine. The special investigation of circa 1210 had thus pointed the way.

The directive also modified what could be agreed to by a Christian debtor and a Jewish lender. Each bond was to define a term or length of time within which the debt should be paid. This means that the amount of the bond was to include the legitimate interest payable within the agreed term. I do not think that the term had to be one year, as some scholars have written, or that no interest ran during the term specified in the bond, whether one year or not, as has also been argued.[5] Quite the contrary, the bonds (*conventiones prestitorum*) included a reckoning of the legitimate interest.

Legitimate interest was not in royal language usury. If the Christian failed to live up to the bond and discharge his debt in the prescribed term, a penalty was to be inflicted to the Jew's advantage as specified in the legislation of 1206: two pennies per pound of the outstanding debt per week. The new directive, unlike that of 1206, stipulated that this penalty could not run indefinitely, but could be inflicted only for one year. If the Christian still had not discharged his debt by the end of that year, the Jew had two options: either to call in the outstanding principal immediately by means of the coercive powers of local royal officials or to let the Christian have more time. Despite the desire to call in and recoup something on bad debts, one can imagine all sorts of reasons why a Jew might exercise the latter option—the desire to avoid the image of an oppressor, the desire not to discourage other Christians from borrowing from him, sympathy with the Christian's plight in some cases. No further interest, however, could be charged on the outstanding principal if this latter option were chosen, "because usury [in the sense of this penalty][6] ought not run beyond a year."

What was happening? It is crystal clear.[7] The king was reacting to the perception that had been growing in Christian circles that the Jews were grossly extending repayment schedules without relaxing the legal penalty permitted by the ordinance of 1206, to the impoverishment of the Christians. It was still felt that an agreement to pay interest, when bound by oath, was to be obeyed: better to pay interest than be a perjurer.[8] So, a defaulting Christian was to be punished; but under the new modification the punishment was limited to a year's extra interest on the outstanding debt. This was to be the limit of liability beyond the initial bond.

It makes sense that this directive was promulgated in the recent aftermath of 1210. The provision on *rescripta* is decisive in this regard. But it also seems certain that in the atmosphere of late 1210 and 1211, as Jews' debts were called in and generated the sorts of complaints still remembered forty years later, royal officials were hesitant to enforce any new loans made by Jews. Their hesitancy, I believe, led to the eventual reissue of the directive with an extra clause, one which responds to the complaint of Jews about the reluctance to enforce their bonds against dilatory debtors or defaultors. The directive *de novo*, as we have it, orders royal officials to stop dragging their feet. They are to heed every Jew who requests immediate payment after the one-year extension provided by the directive; they are to do so presumably by distraints of debtors' property or of their persons. The directive *de novo* ends with a characteristic feature of an ordinance renewed: the king of France indicated that he did not wish to hear about these matters ever again. It was a warning directed to the reluctant executors of his will; but their very reluctance and the Jews' formal or informal petition tell us much. The level of tension was high and the criticisms of the king's policy, of his wilful support of Jewish usury, were vocal and were continuing without cease.

It is not possible to obtain a nuanced picture of Jewish and Christian relations in the aftermath of 1210, not even of financial relations. For example, none of the *rescripta* seem to have survived. This misfortune is explicable. The *rescripta* or copies of the bonds were prepared for the king's business. When the *prévôts* of the Jews were asked for the *rescripta*, they either carried them to Paris or turned them over to the *baillis* so that these officials could take them there.[9] The failure of the *rescripta* to survive, therefore, is no more peculiar than the failure of the vast majority of financial records of the central government in Paris to have survived the Middle Ages or early modern period. It is a result of the ceaseless human and natural disasters, especially fires, that imposed themselves on these once-voluminous records.[10]

We must also keep in mind that independent of the survival of records actually written, the Jews did not themselves produce or have very many records produced about them that would really inform us of the ordinary details of daily life. Nonetheless, as the few remarks on the criticisms and ordinances of Philip Augustus immediately after 1210 have already indicated, the "problem" of the Jews—this tiny minority[11]—continued to intrude itself into the king's consciousness; and it would be wise of us to look very carefully at what has survived in order to explain the persistent fragility of Philip's relations with the Jews in the years until his death. That is the essential goal of the present chapter.

The lucrative and continuing returns of the redemption of 1210 convinced the king, if he needed any further convincing, that however many of his rights he might be tempted for political or sentimental reasons to grant away as concessions, especially in the need to consolidate his conquests, it would be foolish to cede his authority over Jews and "usurers" in general. An agreement dated 1211 (probably July 1211) with the abbot and convent of La Sainte-Trinité of Fécamp exemplifies this attitude.[12] The king ceded capital pleas (pleas of the sword) to the religious but reserved to himself that aspect of Norman justice known as the holding of *recognitiones* as well as jurisdiction over usurers and Jews. Usurers (that is, Christian usurers) and Jews continued to be a tolerated and exploitable resource. Notorious or manifest Christian usurers could be exploited whenever they violated the secular rules laid down for commerce or, in

Norman custom, by the imposition of inheritance "taxes" when they died; the Jews could be exploited on any occasion the king was moved to do so.[13]

By 1214 we have good evidence that Jewish moneylending was flourishing. Apparently not long before December of that year the marriage was celebrated of Moses of Sens, the Jew who in 1210 had had the highest amount of outstanding debts, sixty thousand pounds, and who had stayed in prison until the king declared the precise details of the redemption.[14] His new wife was the widow of one Samuel of Bray-sur-Seine, that is, of a Champenois Jew. I do not know whether she was Champenoise herself. If she was, then her marriage to Moses was a marriage outside the lordship to which she belonged. If she was a royal Jew all along, then her first marriage had probably been a union of this type. In any case, such marital alliances between Jews of different lords were handled in the same way as those between serfs. Lords arranged to divide the seisin of the children or the property inherited by the children.[15]

The document that informs us of these matters in Moses's life is an exchange of houses between his new wife and the extremely influential royal counsellor Barthélemy de Roye which provided the latter with a residence in the town of Gonesse, where he was building up a compact estate, and provided Moses and his bride with a place in Paris.[16] Arranged at Corbeil, the exchange was laid under the solemn ban of the rabbi of Corbeil supported by the oaths of Moses and several other Jews: Héronel, Dieudonné, Leo *et alii plures judei*.[17] On the Christian side, owing to the prestige of Barthélemy, several *baillis* attested to the exchange at Melun in December 1214. They included Cadoc, Gilles de Versailles, Guillaume de La Chapelle, Geoffroy de La Chapelle, Adam Héron, and Thibaut Le Maigre.[18] This tiny snapshot of the marriage and property exchanges of Moses and his wife suggests that the inordinate pressure associated with the year 1210 was over; and that the Jews had picked up the pieces of their business in credit.

Whereas the enforcement of this business by the king and the occasional exploitation of usurers were principles of public policy in the decade after 1210, they remained principles under challenge. The preaching of Robert de Curçon already alluded to was supplemented in this regard by the publication of the decrees of the Fourth Lateran Council, 1215. The council had a wide-ranging list of concerns, many of which were not of much relevance to Jewish life under Capetian domination. Decisions about usury were pertinent, however. The church came down hard against "extortion" by "heavy and immoderate usury."[19] What was "heavy and immoderate" was undefined.[20] Philip Augustus must have felt (or could have argued) that his ordinances, by moderating the amount of interest and scaling down the duration of penalty payments, successfully met this injunction. Clearly, he would have been "hostile" to clerics' excommunication of Christians who enforced repayment of interest-bearing loans by his command. But the decrees of the council admonished princes to restrain their hostility against these clerics, good Christians, and direct it against the extortionate Jews.[21]

Over and over the decrees condemn the Jews, especially for any insults to Christ that were perceived to emanate from them. The decrees do not threaten wildly or with abandon. They promise just judgement for slurs. But the language is severe.[22] Since the council was also used as a forum to issue instructions on a new crusade, an atmosphere of crusader enthusiasm and contempt for the Jews and their usurious practices toward crusaders emerged in the wake of the publication of the relevant decrees.[23] The popes themselves quickly acknowledged this. Innocent III almost immediately modified those directives issued by the council that commanded differentiation in dress between Christians and Jews, recognizing that the enforcement of the decree without some measure of flexibility might literally target the Jews for angry mobs of crusaders. He further admonished those who took the cross not to harm a single Jew. His successor, Honorius III, reissued the bull of protection, *Sicut Judeis*, soon after.[24]

Philip Augustus meanwhile had more pressing matters on his mind. It became an open secret after 1212 that John of England was planning a two-pronged attack against the French. To meet this attack, the king and his son devoted the greater part of their energies and resources to military and diplomatic preparations.[25] The virulence of Philip's antagonism to ecclesiastical pressures with regard to usury partly reflects this new focus of his concerns. His profit from taking part of the usury which he allowed the Jews to collect was helping to finance his war effort. Here again one would desperately like to know how much of the redemption of 250,000 pounds actually made it into the royal coffers from 1210 on. Since a little was still being collected as late as 1221, it is impossible to be sure what proportion the king got before the fighting with King John began. But given Philip's "ordinary" resources in the second decade of the thirteenth century (revenues certainly below 200,000 pounds per year), this is more than a matter of trivial interest.[26]

As is well known, John's plans foundered in his own disaster at La

Roche-au-Moine and in the disaster of his allies at Bouvines (1214), a double catastrophe that sent him back to England to face a native rebellion and that cemented the French annexation of Normandy and the other western fiefs.[27] For Philip it was a vindication of everything he had seemed to live for, although his troubles were far from over. Until John died in 1216, there was danger from that quarter, and the role of Philip's son, Louis, in trying to capitalize on discontent with John in England by invading the country remained a difficult issue until Louis's "forced" withdrawal in 1217.[28]

The church continued to be ambivalent. Innocent III, in making plans for and holding the Fourth Lateran Council, had necessarily tried to smoothe out his relations with every powerful prince—and he had flip-flopped in his attitude toward John after 1212. When the English king submitted to the pope's will in that year in order to bring a long dispute over the appointment of an archbishop of Canterbury to an end, the pope became John's feudal lord, solicitous friend, and an intercessor for peace between him and Philip Augustus.[29] Robert de Curçon played a role in this, but he also continued to embitter Philip Augustus even after the peace offensives came to nothing and the French king had won the glorious victory at Bouvines.[30] Or so it seems, if we can impute feelings to the king from Guillaume Le Breton's harsh remarks about Robert's preaching in 1215, which in the chronicler's opinion attracted some of the worst kinds of people to the projected crusade.[31] In his fervor Robert antagonized not only the king but significant members of the French clergy, and the pope himself was peeved with his legate and had, as it were, to smooth over these disputes. For Philip the matter effectively came to a close at the end of 1215. Robert attended the Fourth Lateran Council and never returned; Pope Innocent's death in 1216 meant the effective end of Robert's legatine authority and, as Baldwin has written, Robert's "remaining years formed a disappointing epilogue."[32]

What Philip became as he approached the age of fifty was something of an elder statesmen. This was especially so after Bouvines and the deaths two years later of both King John and the pope. The role suited him. One ought not construct a picture of an aging prince whose work was done, finally turning to domestic pleasures like playing with his grandson, the future Saint Louis, on his knee. He did not live out the rest of his days in the warmth of a lighted hearth proffering open-hearted generosity to all who shared his table and his memories. But he did effect changes in some of his policies or, better, permitted himself the luxury of articulating sentiments he might earlier have expressed, save for the recurrent crises of his reign.

One of these changes was a change in policy toward the Jews. Complaints continued from some quarters about Jewish moneylending, but the end of Robert de Curçon's commission in France and the death of the pope took the nasty edge off these complaints. At an ecclesiastical council at Melun in 1216, held under the presidency of Philip's friend the archbishop of Sens, Pierre de Corbeil, it was decreed that any prior who received money from a Jew was to be stripped of his office.[33] The decision indicates that the same sort of pressure on ecclesiastical institutions that Philip had responded to in 1209 had re-emerged in France by 1216.[34] He must have been made aware of it.

Also in 1216, probably in March, Philip confirmed an agreement between his trusted auxiliary, Dreu de Mello, the lord of Loches, on the one hand, and the dean and chapter of the regalian see of Saint-Martin of Tours, on the other, about disputed rights in and around the towns of Loches and Ligueil.[35] It is fairly certain that Philip would have known the range of problems addressed in the agreement, because a few years before the confirmation, he had been present for the much more elaborate exchanges between Saint-Martin and another lord that had led to the church's securing Ligueil in the first place.[36] Moreover, it was Philip who had earlier granted Loches to Dreu as a reward for his help in the conquest of the western fiefs.[37] In 1216 the king discovered that one point of contention between Lord Dreu and Saint-Martin was Dreu's claim to lordship in Ligueil, a claim that appears to have included the right to permit Jewish settlement in the town. The compromise of March 1216 directs, however, that "no Jew can dwell" there, the ecclesiastics having made known their discomfort with this license.[38] To Philip this may have been represented as still another instance of the general "problem" posed by the Jews.

There is no reason to insist on this interpretation. What we need to recognize instead is the existence of a climate of opinion in which Philip would have been urged or reminded by people whom he trusted and whom he liked a great deal more than he did Robert de Curçon that as king he suffered in the eyes of Christians for permitting Jews to exploit his coreligionists. His friend the archbishop of Sens, for example, was not only protecting the religious in his ecclesiastical province from Jewish usury as he saw it, but he was also putting great, even inordinate pressure on the secular lordship of Champagne, where part of his ecclesiastical province lay, to restrict Jewish usury.[39] The pressure was so great that some Champenois Jews evidently began to seek new masters in lands whose lords were not party to non-retention conventions with the countess of Champagne. This would explain why the countess began to make such agreements with lords of the Auvergne to the southwest of Champagne around this time (1215, 1218).[40] In any case the countess complained around 1217 that the situation was unfair. Because Philip Augustus had been so firm against Robert de Curçon, the clergy of the royal domain had been inhibited from using their weapons fully against Christians who permitted Jewish usury. The countess argued that her lands were entitled to be treated in the same way, even if, one supposes, her definition of what was "heavy and immoderate" interest was also less strict than some churchmen wanted.[41] Ultimately (1219) the pope recognized the validity of her complaint about the double standard.[42]

A sure sign that the king was himself moving in the direction of mollifying ecclesiastical opinions was his changing relations with another churchman, the archbishop of Rouen, Robert Poulain. Disputes of many sorts affected Philip's relations with the Norman episcopate as he tried to exercise the full range of rights to which he thought he was entitled in the conquered province. In a series of agreements around 1218 with Archbishop Robert, the king brought an end to many of these disputes, whether over the nature of holding the Norman *recognitiones* or over usury and Jews.[43] In January of 1218 the king authorized his *baillis* to move against excommunicated Christian usurers in Normandy at the petition of the archbishop and episcopate of Normandy "as you [the *baillis*] used to do" (*sicut consuevistis*), thus reconciling a dispute generated from some sort of reluctance that he or they had shown before.[44] In exchange, in March of the same year (or the year before), the king's wide jurisdiction over a number of matters, including the pleas of the Jews at Dieppe in northern Normandy, was recognized.[45]

There is no need to consider this an era of "good feelings," but the king was more open to the church.[46] For example, he may never genuinely have intended to go on crusade, but in August of 1218 he *promised* to do so against the Albigensian heretics in Languedoc.[47] And his sensitivity to the religious issue, however encumbered with other political considerations, assuredly heightened his concern with opinions about his apparent unwillingness to restrict Jewish "exploitation" of Christians. This argument is circumstantial, to be sure. But what is not circumstantial is the publication of a new ordinance on the Jews in February 1219 that created the picture of a king closely concerned with the poor and with those whose impecuniousness jeopardized their patrimonies. The image of the mature king, elder statesman and friend of the weak, and the church, comfortable in his sense of himself, emerges beautifully from the ordinance, which rather loftily refers to itself as a "constitution."[48]

By convention the ordinance of 1219 is divided into eight parts.[49] All of them are intensely interesting not only because they respond to what must have been widely shared notions of the excesses of the Jews but also because they speak to the readiness of Philip to modify his earlier opinions. Thus, in the first section, the king with one breath attempted to undermine the market in distress loans. Earlier he had shown no interest in little loans; he had gone so far as to prohibit the sealing and enregistering of bonds that dealt with loans of less than three pounds in value.[50] In 1219, however, he commenced his ordinance with precisely these little loans in mind—and the ordinary people who contracted them. The king prohibited the Jews from making any loans in the future to any Christian who was a manual worker, such as—for he specifies the sort of occupations meant—"an agricultural laborer, a cobbler, a carpenter and so forth," if such a worker did not have sufficient land or movables for his sustenance.[51] The king is not talking about master craftsmen or stewards on agricultural estates. He is addressing the problem of drudges who were doing routine jobs and who had nothing to depend on if they got in over their heads. Such people, one supposes, had frequently over-committed themselves before and had either been jailed until friends or family paid their loans or had fled or stolen rather than face imprisonment.

Those men already in debt, a later section will provide, and who declared themselves or were declared to be people without property beyond the property in the labor of their own hands, were given a staggered three-year respite from repayment. This can only mean that if or since their loans were not registered already (because they were less than three pounds in value), they had soon to be recorded along with the declaration of insolvency. Conceivably very many of these loans were already generating the extra one-year interest penalty provided in an earlier statute.[52] For simplicity it is probably wise to think that no matter what the stage of repayment, the outstanding debts of these people were allowed to generate no further interest. Rather, the amount was divided into three equal parts, one each to be paid to the lenders during each of the years in the three-year respite. To assure that these arrangements would be carried out, each debtor was to provide a surety, that is, a person whose own property became liable to distraint by the king's men if the debtor failed to discharge the debt according to the new schedule.

The few words of the ordinance that we have been discussing thus far envisage a very complicated system of men and women coming forward and declaring themselves paupers, having this status verified, and arranging to find family or friends to guarantee renegotiated debts by putting their own property at risk. The ordinance envisaged but said nothing explicitly about how the *baillis* and *prévôts* were to find these people in order to get them to come forward, how they were supposed formally to declare them paupers, or how they were to assure that no loans were made to such people in the future. Inchoate as the system was, what came of these provisions was good propaganda (the king forthrightly showed his concern for the poor) and circumspect behavior from Jews apprehensive over potential complaints that they had exploited the poor.

There were, of course, any number of artisans and rustics who did have sufficient property to make them permitted recipients of Jewish loans. But the initial provision of the ordinance of 1219 directs also that all loans made to this group not run beyond a year at a maximum interest of the now usual two pennies per pound per week. Thought of in modern terms, a small loan of, say, $100 could not be repaid at higher than $143; and if repaid in less than a year it would cost the borrower less. Later medieval records from throughout Europe show consumption loans of this sort often being paid back in three months or so, a time frame that in the case of our hypothetical loan would mean a payback of $110 or $115, which seems very reasonable.[53] What Philip succeeded in doing, in other words, assuming he was obeyed, was in making the market in lending considerably less offensive and less volatile, for the imposition of penalty payments on dilatory debtors, which was the most denounced form of usury among ecclesiastics, was not confirmed by the new ordinance.

The second major section of the ordinance of 1219 addressed the problem of the indebtedness of religious houses and, with additional specifications from section three, the weakness of certain churchmen. No Jew was to lend money to any "monk or canon regular unless [the cleric] have the consent of his abbot and chapter and [unless the consent be expressed] by letters patent." The focus here, monastic and quasi-monastic institutions, arose from the long history of concern about the great religious houses falling into debt. Almost as an afterthought, however, the ordinance added that no loan ought to be made to any religious, in the sense of anyone in orders, without the consent of his supervisor expressed also in letters patent. It was reiterated from earlier ordinances and statutes that pawning or, rather, the accepting in pawn of any church ornament was forbidden to a Jew.

The provisions on pawning continue with the usual remarks that Jews ought not accept bloodstained or damp clothing in pledge, but they add that plowshares and plow teams and unwinnowed grain must not be received either.[54] Earlier, in 1206, the king had recognized that some of these objects were critically important. So, despite his general desire to avoid becoming involved in disputes over pawning (even under bond), he had added one provision in 1206, namely, that if questions arose about quite expensive or important items, his courts would entertain suits. The special items defined in the earlier ordinance included farm animals.[55] In other words, the king earlier had recognized the legitimacy of rustics pawning their work beasts and tools. The constitution of 1219 cut hard by absolutely forbidding the practice.

The additional reference to grain is a curiosity. It may respond in some vague way to fears that Jews, with their leverage in credit, could corner the grain market in small localities to their great profit and the Christians' disadvantage. Or at least there was sometimes expressed by Christian critics of usury the apprehension that usurers, whether Jewish or not, were people who would buy up grain and resell it at inflated prices. The practice was specifically stereotyped as Jewish in our period by the Champenois poet Guiot de Provins, writing between 1204 and 1209.[56] Nonetheless, there is a complication in the text of the ordinance of 1219.

The reference there is to unwinnowed grain, *bladum non ventilatum*.[57] If the concern was with cornering the grain market, then all grain would have become a prohibited pawn. The fact of the matter is that unwinnowed grain was susceptible to fraud and would have given rise to just the kind of disputes that any authority was desirous of avoiding. Simple fanning of unwinnowed grain would release some of the wheat. The farmer who pawned a sack of unwinnowed grain and then redeemed it was bound to suspect that the pawnbroker had secretly taken a portion and replaced it with chaff. Since the best (heaviest) grain was the most easily winnowed, an impecunious farmer, whether justified or not, would have felt doubly cheated. Farmers had similar fears about millers whom Jerome Blum labels "notoriously dishonest folk figure[s]."[58] It was probably to avoid disputes like this that the king's advisers prohibited the pawning of unwinnowed grain yet not grain or flour in general.

Except for these admittedly serious restrictions, pawning, as a later section of the ordinance makes plain, was otherwise completely uninhibited. Anyone could pawn anything with any Jew who was willing to take it. A knight could even pawn his horse (a nice topos). On this issue of pawning, the previous exceptions aside, the king declared that he would simply not interfere.

The ordinance of 1219 has been misunderstood in recent scholarship on another point. It has been said that "all loans" were to be repaid from some sort of "assigned income".[59] Not quite. What the ordinance does is provide that in lieu of a mere promise to repay at interest (the typical bond) a Jew who lent to a "knight, burgher or merchant" would have to accept an agreeable specified portion (*assignamentum*) — that is, a specified amount over a specified time — of the return from certain lands, tenements, or rents in the debtor's possession. This provision was conditional because the debtor needed prior approval from the lord from whom he held the property. Obviously, very large loans were the concern of the drafters of this section of the ordinance.

The ordinance recognized that the debtor, once having made the agreement, might "do violence" (*Et si debitor violenciam fecerit*) with regard to the specified portion. This means, in the most watered down terms, that he might "violate" the convention in any number of ways. But more vividly it foresees a debtor wasting a piece of property in the technical sense — cutting the timber, for example, to his profit so that the land became of little value to the Jew in the period of its assignment to him; deforcing a tenant so a rent could not be paid; taking part of the harvest without license; or the like. If he were to do so, the Jew was to have a remedy: complaint to the king's court would eventuate in the quashing of the *assignamentum* and the reversion to the form of a typical bond in which the original debt would be charged the legal rate of interest as penalty (usury), two pennies per pound per week. On very large loans this would have been a crushing burden, but one that was not significant enough in the king's eyes. The debtor who had violated the agreement had abused the good services of the royal administration and was therefore subjected to a fine as well.

The drafters of the ordinance made every effort to detail the workings of this system, since once again the focus of concern in these middle sections was genuinely large loans. The agreements between Jews and Christians in Normandy were the subject of specific clauses because of the Norman use of the jury of assize and recognition.[60] The agreements were to be made before a *bailli* in his assizes or almost equally formally, if the assizes were not in session, before a *bailli* and ten knights. The assizes acting as courts of record were to enroll the agreements for possible future warranting, and the *bailli* and his ten knights, if this forum had to be used, were also to make official records noting the amount of money lent and the specifications of the *assignamentum*. In the off chance that these agreements had to be made while a *bailli* was absent, they could be enrolled later in either of the two appropriate forums. The drafters foresaw that a Christian, once he had received his loan from a Jew, might demur at coming forward to register the details. They therefore provided the Jew with a remedy: if he brought good Christian witnesses before a *bailli* and established the veracity of his claim that he had lent the money on condition of receiving an *assignamentum* of land, tenements, or rents, the royal officer was to compel the debtor and sureties to appear and have the proper enrollments made in the proper forum.

Finally, the ordinance dealt with the problem of debts contracted before its promulgation. The very existence of the ordinance should alert us to the fact that there was a resevoir of antagonism to the Jews for calling upon Christian officials to enforce their debts. The express desire to insulate economically marginal Christians from Jewish "usury" responds to those ejaculations of anger against Jews who supposedly "exhausted" or "extorted" poor Christians. The ordinance of 1219 thus presents itself as a fresh start. Propertied debtors who still had outstanding loans contracted before the ordinance was in force were partakers of a very partial clemency. Their debts were not forgiven. (We will recall that not even the debts of the destitute were forgiven; they were rescheduled over an extended period instead.) Propertied debtors, however, were assured that in case of default on debts already contracted, neither they nor their sureties would be imprisoned or would have their property seized and sold by the king's men in order to discharge the debts. Instead, the royal officials would see to it that two-thirds of the income from the real property and chattels real of each defaulter and his surety would be assigned to the Jews until the debt was completely discharged. One-third would be reserved to the debtor and surety for their sustenance, and there would be no attempt to take away goods essential to their livelihood or reasonable comfort: draft animals, bedding, household tools.[61]

Despite what has sometimes been written, there is not one word in this ordinance that distraint of property or imprisonment for default is forbidden in the future. Quite to the contrary and, to repeat, the ordinance provides a fresh start. Those who defaulted in the future under the new and meticulously drafted rules were supposed to face the consequences. And they did. Chazan is wrong when he considers a seizure of property in 1222 (only three years after the ordinance) as a "disregard" of the law against future distraints on post-1219 debts, for the simple reason that there was no such law to be disregarded.[62] But there was a law to be strictly enforced: default was as punishable by distraint in 1222 as it had been continuously from the moment the Jews returned to the royal domain in 1198, the brief clemency granted by the ordinance of 1219 on old debts notwithstanding.

The effect of the constitution of February 1219 on Jewish and Christian relations turns out to be very difficult to measure. By the new regulations there were three areas of legitimate business between Jews and Christians. The first, pawning, as always in the pre-modern period, has left virtually no evidence precisely because it was legal. Pawns were either redeemed or not redeemed. If they were not redeemed, they were sold. None of these transactions generated the kind of documentation that was likely to survive. (Where pawning was illegal, on the other hand, special investigations might reveal interesting details.)[63] The second area of business was, of course, traditional loans based on sealed bonds. For the same reasons adduced earlier, these records have disappeared. That is to say, the bonds would have been destroyed upon payment of the loans and the *rescripta* of the bonds, which were transmitted to the central government, have gone the way of the vast majority of the other financial records of the crown.[64] The third—and final—area of legitimate commerce was credit based on the *assignamentum*. Details of this sort of business transaction, it is virtually certain, would be recoverable from the records—if the system of enregistering debts under the royal seal and of enrolling the *assignamenta* on the records of a court or *recognition* had endured for any reasonable length of time. As we shall see, however, the system did not survive. It died with Philip Augustus in 1223.[65]

There are, nonetheless, a few indications of the business relations among Christians and Jews after 1219 and the application of royal justice with regard to bad debts. For example, distraints of property to pay future bad debts were, it has been pointed out above, one continuing aspect of the provisions of Philip's program. So we find soon after the constitution on the Jews that when the king renewed a grant of liberty of trading along the Somme River, he included a "traditional" reserve clause, providing that goods offered for trade could be distrained for bad debts.[66] The relevance of this grant and what I have labeled its "traditional" reserve clause to the specific issue of Jewish lending might be doubted, except for the fact that it was first issued with the reservation in 1199, immediately after the readmission of the Jews to the royal domain, and it was first confirmed in 1210 when the king was calling in Jewish debts to his advantage.[67] That it should be issued again in late 1219 or early 1220, immediately after the constitution on the Jews, is suggestive. Equally germane to the general issue of the enforcement of Jewish debts after 1219 is an example of landed property being sold to pay a "debt that [a Christian] owed the Jews" in May 1221.[68]

The adjustment of Jewish moneylending to the new rules of 1219 thus seems to have been swift and the creation of new business similarly swift. The apparatus of the state continued to be available to enforce Jewish credit under the new system although not against those who might be called the most miserable persons. If there were any tampering with the new rules, it would have been stimulated by the growing awareness of reputed abuses in Champagne, the typical story of people—especially ecclesiastical institutions like the monastery of Saint-Loup—in debt over their heads.[69] The Champenois had subscribed to Phililp's ordinance on the Jews in 1206 but did not follow his lead in all of his modifications after that (or so the silence of the records suggests).[70] The effect on Philip of the revelation of Jewish "exploitation" of Christians in Champagne is therefore problematic. He quite likely felt in June 1222, when some particularly startling revelations were made, that his own 1219 reformulation of Jewish policy for the royal domain already protected Christians from these dangers.[71] If he did anything at all, it was to lower the rate of interest chargeable by Jews to Christians in the royal domain. Rightly, however, the act that purports to make this change—a decrease from two pennies per pound per week to two pennies per pound per month—has been considered to be of dubious authenticity. Dated 17 July 1222 and known in a sixteenth-century "copy," the decree conflates regulations from several centuries about coining and about debts, and the language of the decree, especially the phrase "usury upon usury," is papal and uncharacteristic of Philip.[72] If the king really issued such an ordinance in 1222, that ordinance was another step toward mollifying the most radical churchmen, but it stopped short of a royal withdrawal from enforcing Jewish debts.[73]

That withdrawal actually did occur in November 1223 under Philip's successor, Louis VIII, and it bespeaks the transition to a new phase in Christian and Jewish relations.[74] From 1223 through 1285, that is, under

Louis VIII, Blanche of Castile, Louis IX (Saint Louis), and even later, the crown attempted to free itself of the taint of supporting Jewish usury, and it articulated a policy, often refined but never even temporarily abandoned, of putting pressure on Jews to recognize how reprehensible the profession of usurer was. The abandonment of usury was conceived of as a first and critical step in progress toward the ultimate goal, conversion.[75] To this extent, the shift in Capetian policy mirrors a tendency recently described by David Berger in which, among churchmen, there was a renewed emphasis from about the year 1200 on missionizing to the Jews.[76]

In earlier work I have argued, as have many scholars before me, that this transformation in Capetian policy created a considerably less lenient environment than what had existed before, since royal France under Louis VII and Philip Augustus had been a land where in general the business of moneylending at least received qualified royal support.[77] Let me confess now that this argument misses the point. Leniency in business practice is not the issue. Predictability of social experience is. From the moment Philip Augustus came to the throne in 1179 almost to the very moment of his death in 1223, the Jews had been witnesses to and victims of the erratic policy of the king. I cannot explain all his attacks, let alone the striking reversals—the violation of the synagogues during worship; the exile; the massacre at Brie; the readmission; the bullying arrests followed by a period of evident disinterest; the studied indifference to "poor debtors" followed by overarching concern for them.[78] But I am convinced that this erraticism was hellish for those who had to endure it. They did endure it, of course; and there were times when they secured their livelihood with a regularity and support that gave a renewed sense of normalcy to life. But as soon as any climate of normalcy reemerged—or so it seems—it would always be shattered by the rage or moral posturing or greed of a king whose will, at least with respect to the Jews, had the force of law in the royal domain.

When Louis VIII became king and there was yet another rethinking of Jewish policy, Jews like Brun of Rouen, Morel of Falaise, Elie de Bray of Paris, and Moses of Sens, who had lived through so much, expected that their world would be turned upside down once again.[79] What they got was change, but change that lasted: for fifty years and more the most Christian kings, consumed by the desire to convert the Jews, put steady pressure on them to do so. The type of pressure might change; indeed, it got steadily heavier and more grinding. But each Jew knew what he was up against and knew—in a way that he had never known with Philip Augustus—that there were some excesses to which these rulers would not be party. This relative improvement, of course, had little meaning to Jews who had never suffered the political and economic aggression of Philip Augustus. For them—and I am speaking about the tens of thousands of Jews who entered the domain as a result of the annexation of the south after 1223—the severity of their new Capetian rulers was set against the widespread and cosmopolitan tolerance in southern (urban) life before the annexation. The new regime would seem hellish enough in its own right.

II

By Honest Labor:
The Transformation of
Royal Policy and
Its Application, 1223–1285

6. Louis VIII and the *Stabilimentum* of 1223

The wicked king, Philip II Augustus, died after a reign of nearly forty-four years on 14 July 1223. He left as his successor a mature and, it is generally acknowledged, extremely pious son, Louis VIII. Louis's consecration took place on 6 August 1223. For the next two months, after a triumphal entry into Paris following the coronation at Reims, he seems to have set himself to accomplish a great deal of routine business.[1] Much of this was the business of confirming the offices of important royal officials and, more critically, reaffirming truces on the disturbed Poitevin frontier that Philip Augustus had made with local barons.[2] He did not achieve all of this from Paris, but stayed on the move, touring the royal domain starting with the provinces conquered by his father. In September he traversed Normandy and the western fiefs. In October he toured the northern lands of Vermandois and Artois. Very late October and early November he spent in Paris only to resume the northern progress later in November and to continue it into the following month.[3] Here was a king, at least as Petit-Dutaillis interprets the documentary and chronicle record, who resolved to make the royal power manifest as quickly and as surely as possible. Here was a king who wanted the progress to impress his subjects with the vigor of royal authority. And he was successful. The opening months of the reign saw no anti-royal disturbances.[4]

The one parenthesis in this royal progress was the lengthy sojourn at Paris in late October and early November. I do not know why Louis chose to act in the way he did at that time, but the king issued an ordinance on the Jews. Perhaps he had learned in the first part of his progress of the depth of some of his subjects hostility to them. Perhaps—and this, I think, is more likely—critics of Philip's policies gently reminded him that it diminished the luster of the crown and the new king to support or encourage the practice of usury and therefore to support implicitly the exploitation of his Christian subjects. Perhaps, finally, he saw the imposition of a new restrictive policy against the Jews as a positive force in stimulating enthusiasm for his regime. Whatever the reason, in November the Jews of the royal domain became aware that they were once again the object of royal concern.

As with all the ordinances on the Jews this one seems to have been victimized by preconceived ideas about its meaning and by rather hasty readings. To start with, the most readily available printed edition of the ordinance takes the form of a subscription to it by certain lords. The tone is straightforward. It begins by explaining that the king had caused the statute (*stabilimentum*) to be made after having taken the advice and received the consent of his council—archbishops, bishops, counts, barons, and knights—some of whom had *dominium* over Jews and some of whom did not. Once the king formulated and received the approval of this body in the formal sense, he submitted the *stabilimentum* for subscription to a number of lords who were present in Paris. The council had met at All Saints 1223 (or so it will be shown) to receive the accounts of the *baillis* and to do justice, among other things. The formal *stabilimentum* on the Jews was prepared; and on 8 November 1223 the octave of All Saints, lords who had *dominium* over Jews and were willing to follow the king's lead in Jewish policy had their names subscribed. Twenty-six did so.[5]

There can be no uncertainty on this issue, despite what one or two other scholars have said, because two versions of the *stabilimentum* exist. The earlier, which does not have the list of subscribers, dates itself at All Saints rather than the octave of the feast. Moreover, the tenses change from the All Saints version to the better known octave of All Saints version. In the first, reference is made to the subscribers in the future perfect, that is, "those who will have sworn"; in the later version in the perfect, those "who have sworn" as of 8 November.[6]

If we needed any further proof of this sequence, the following seems decisive. The twenty-six subscribers could not have constituted the council that formulated the *stabilimentum* because among the twenty-six there were no archbishops and only one bishop (and he actually subscribed as a count). To be sure, it is unwise to insist that the lofty formula "archbishops, bishops, counts, barons and knights" used to describe the composition of the council must be taken at face value. Still, the idea that the archbishop of Reims, who was at Paris in November but is not among the twenty-six, failed to participate in the council that authorized the *stabilimentum* is odd.[7] The council was a solemn *curia* giving formal sanction to the will of the king with regard to his own Jews. Those lords who, like the king, had *dominium* over Jews were urged to follow his lead and subscribe to the *stabilimentum*. Twenty-six, many of whom had been at the council of All Saints, did so a week later (8 November). When at the end of the record of their doing so notice is given of the affixing of the seals, the language is precise. Subscription, we are told, was not made by archbishops, bishops, and so on but by "counts, barons and others aforenamed." The solemn curial formula was not employed for the subscribers because they did not constitute the *curia*.[8]

Finally, it will be recalled that the preamble to the version of 8 November mentions the fact that present at the (original) council had been some great men of who did not have *dominium* over Jews.[9] Even as thin as medieval evidence sometimes gets, it can be shown with great probability largely from independent sources that every one of the twenty-six subscribers of 8 November did have *dominium* over Jews. These matters are not trivial. Establishing the proper sequence is important because, as we shall see, the *stabilimentum* as authorized on 1 November was somewhat changed to meet the circumstances of barons before they subscribed on the eighth.[10]

The substance of the *stabilimentum* (both versions) is absolutely certain. The king began by directing that all existing debts owed to Jews as of the date of the statute were to cease to incur interest. He said *nothing* about future debts. Nothing at all.[11] Any bonds on which it was specified that interest was due after the date of the *stabilimentum* according to the original agreements between lenders and debtors would not be enforced by either the king's men or by concurring barons. Instead, the outstanding principal of the loans, and the outstanding principal alone, had to be repaid. Debtors were given three years to repay in nine equal installments beginning with a payment due at 2 February 1224 (Candlemas), another at Ascension 1224, and a third on 1 November 1224 (All Saints). This cycle was to be repeated in 1225 and 1226. The payments made by the debtors were to go not to the Jews but to the king and to the various lords who had *dominium* over Jewish creditors and had subscribed to the *stabilimentum*.[12] In a word, we are witnesses to another *captio*.

If we have any doubts whatsoever that this is evidence of a *captio*, they vanish as we examine the next clause. The king commanded that neither he nor any of his barons would receive and keep Jews belonging to other lords, a classic way of cutting off escape for Jews who tried to flee. Exercising his regalian privilege (or perhaps a regalian fiction), he insisted that this provision applied both to the twenty-six barons who had explicitly sworn to the *stabilimentum* and to those who had not.[13] Essentially the king was treating the reception of fugitive Jews by a lord as a species of *cas royaux* over which he had jurisdiction. Or so I would suggest. There is no need to press the specific analogy, but the sentiment is clear enough: the king was forbidding barons to accept fugitives, and he was implying that he did not need what until then had been a traditional requirement, namely, a baron's prior specific approval of the prohibition, in order for it to be enforced against him.

The next clause of the statute was an equally striking break with tradition. Since 1198, when Philip Augustus had readmitted Jews to the royal domain, they had had access to seals in various towns for the certification of their bonds. Each town with Jewish creditors had officials specifically instructed to seal Jewish loan contracts. At the discharge of any debt the sealed bond was presented and evidently destroyed. A Jew could also present a sealed bond for enforcement against a defaulter. This mode of authentication, it was believed, made disputes more easily resolvable. The royal government charged for the service. From time to time, as we have noticed, the government tinkered with the system of authentication by closer supervision of the sealers, by modifying the lower limit of bonds that required the seal, by providing alternative authentication on assize rolls or on recognition rolls in Normandy for specific kinds of loans. From time to time, also, there were serious doubts that the Jews were having all their contracts enrolled or sealed as they were supposed to; there were suspicions that they were lending to prohibited groups and at higher interest clandestinely. Despite misgivings about the system, these methods of authentication under the aegis of the crown, especially the sealing of bonds by local government officials, were continuous features of royal supervision of the Jews from 1198 until 1223.[14] In a terse sentence, Louis VIII's *stabilimentum* withdrew the seal: "Henceforth Jews will not have seals for the sealing of their debts."[15]

An entire structure was collapsing. From November until the first installment due to the king and the consenting lords from the outstanding principal of debts, 2 February 1224, every Jewish creditor was to furnish information on all his loans. The 1 November version of the statute explains how this provision ought to be understood (*sic est intelligendum*). It refers to the belief that the Jews engaged in fraud.[16] So, even though the royal government had good records of legal lending, it was authorizing a supplementary investigation to get at fraudulent lending. Since it is not likely that the twenty-six barons who subscribed to the *stabilimentum* were as well furnished with records about their Jews as the king was about his, I presume that their investigations aimed at a greater thoroughness. The only baron who might have had records of legal lending as good as the king's was the count of Champagne, for, as we have seen earlier, the Champenois imitated some features of royal administration of the Jews.[17] However, the count of Champagne was not one of the twenty-six who subscribed to the *stabilimentum* on 8 November. He had recently made an elaborate convention with his own Jews in return for an enormous annual return of money and did not intend to disturb these arrangements.[18]

The Jews who were covered by the *stabilimentum* and furnished the information on their lending were to do so by bringing forward their bonds, however they were authenticated.[19] The final substantive clause of the *stabilimentum* directed that no bonds or records of debts over five years old were to be enrolled.[20] Why five years? The answer is easy. The five-year period must date from the first installment of repayment scheduled for 2 February 1224. In other words, this means that the crown was modifying the payment of no debts that went further back than Philip Augustus's great constitution on the Jews of February 1219 (a document that we can now feel confident dates from 2 February 1219).[21] The sense of the *stabilimentum* of Louis VIII is that the legislation of Philip Augustus had effectively closed the book on any lending contracted prior to 2 February 1219 and that his own *stabilimentum* effectively closed the book on all Jewish lending in royal (and many baronial) lands since that time.

There is one complication. Louis VIII intended, if we follow the version of the *stabilimentum* of 1 November, to permit the Jews to collect on any *bad* debts that were supposed to have been paid within the five years before 2 February 1224 if in that period they had made known their desire to collect on them (and, implicitly, were not letting interest run indefinitely, contrary to Philip Augustus's constitution).[22] The impulse was a generous one, at least relatively speaking. Jews were not to be penalized for obeying Philip's laws, nor were the procrastination and reluctance of officials to enforce the legitimate complaints of Jews under those laws to be validated *ex post facto*. I do not know how many debts were affected by this clause: few, I suspect, but it is clear that the matter was irrelevant to the barons, that is, to people who had never adopted Phililp's legislation which had applied only to royal Jews. Therefore the version of 8 November—their version of the *stabilimentum*—did not include the clause. The records of the Exchequer of Normandy prove that in his own domains the king did enforce this provision: those bad debts of Jews that Jews had sought to have collected under the legitimate rules of the constitution of 1219 were remitted to them.[23] It was only the interest on active debts that was cancelled, with the principal remitted to the king and any barons who adopted the *stabilimentum* as their policy.

Three documents that were issued very quickly in the wake of Louis's *stabilimentum* of 1223 need to be mentioned before we try to assess the impact of this legislation. The first, also from November, is the renewal of a convention between the French king and the count of Champagne that neither would retain the other's Jews. King Louis's *stabilimentum* had made the grandiose claim that all lords who were vassals of the king of the Franks were obliged by his mere will to refuse to accept into their domains the Jews of any other lords without the consent of the lords from whose lands they came. This claim notwithstanding, the king sought and received in the same month a formal renewal of the principle from the count of Champagne, who had not subscribed to the *stabilimentum*.[24] Evidently the count did not resist on this point. After all, promises of this sort between him or his predecessors and the crown were by then a commonplace. What he did refuse to do was to acknowledge the overarching principle that the king could prohibit him by fiat from accepting refugee Jews from baronies with which he had not explicitly made such agreements.

The matter did not stay quite so unresolved, however. What we have is a second agreement dated December by which the count also promised not to accept the Jews of the twenty-six lords who had subscribed to the *stabilimentum*.[25] Should we regard this as a submission to the general principle that the king could somehow "legislate" about all Jews, his and his barons, on the issue of fugitives? The point was an enormously important one. Clearly, both sides were trying to define the legitimate boundaries of their authority. And both might well have gone away believing that they had won, Louis by regarding the count's second agreement as an acknowledgement of the principle on fugitives articulated in the *stabilimentum*, the count by regarding this very same agreement as proof that what the *stabilimentum* declared as law on fugitive Jews was only a pious wish that had no effect on any baron, or at least none on the count palatine of Champagne until and unless he personally accepted it.

The third record that was issued only days after the *stabilimentum* is more transparent than the king's protocols with the count of Champagne. It is a letter which the countess of Nevers wrote to the king to the effect that she adhered to the *stabilimentum* of 8 November.[26] It has sometimes been urged that this is further evidence that there was widespread resistance to the king's *stabilimentum*.[27] Quite the contrary. Most of the resistance, such as there was, necessarily concentrated on the assertion of royal authority over the fugitives who fled to the lands of lords who had not subscribed to the statute. Except for this controversial clause, the *stabilimentum* took the traditional form of a treaty that bound the contracting parties and only the contracting parties.

Any general dismay with the content of the treaty would have been expressed by simply not subscribing to it. The count of Champagne showed his dislike both on the narrow matter of fugitives and on the content of the treaty broadly construed. He insisted on and got a separate instrument to define the matter of fugitives; and he refused to subscribe to the general content of the treaty because he did not want to treat his Jews the way Louis VIII was going to treat those of the crown. Now, not one jot of this can be true about the countess of Nevers. As a matter of fact she had been in Paris on 8 November and had subscribed to the *stabilimentum* and affixed her seal at that time. She was then accompanied by a royal clerk back home to Nevers, where she made known her subscription to her own *curia*. The royal clerk returned to Paris with the confirmation.[28] This confirmation in letters patent was requested because the countess was acting formally only as the tutrix for her underage son.[29] The duchess of Burgundy also subscribed to the *stabilimentum* on 8 November. It would not be surprising if she too issued a confirmation a few weeks later after formally obtaining the assent of her *curia* since she was tutrix for her young son.[30] Only one other lord did not have full power to assent on 8 November but did so anyway. Robert of Dreux subscribed for his brother Peter of Dreux, the count of Brittany. Insofar as the later records demonstrate, Peter did not recognize the subscription as valid: though his name is subscribed to the *stabilimentum* of 1223, his seal was never affixed. He continued to treat his Jews as he was already treating them.[31]

The Jewish reaction to the departure in royal policy was typical but as it turned out completely unsuccessful. Let us look at the behavior of the Jews who lived under the *dominium* of the lord of Dampierre, one of the subscribers to the *stabilimentum* of 8 November. The lord of Dampierre held his fief from the count of Champagne and was engaged in the 1220s in a bitter dispute with him. The details of that dispute make a tale in themselves, but they are not entirely germane to our story.[32] Nonetheless the antagonism presented possibilities. Although after 1 November 1223 Jews of the royal domain would not have tried to escape to Champagne because of the long, continuous history of agreements stretching back to

1198 between the crown and the count to return fugitives, only two temporary agreements (both long lapsed) had ever existed on this matter between the lord of Dampierre and his overlord, the count. At least, this was the situation until the count of Champagne swore to Louis VIII in December that he would respect that part of the *stabilimentum* that required (or urged) all lords in the kingdom to return refugees from the king's lands or the lands of the twenty-six concurring barons (including the lord of Dampierre's).[33]

Before it was known that the count would make this concession, however, and capitalizing on the hostility between him and the lord of Dampierre, the male Jewish heads of families fled the Dampierre lands for towns in Champagne, leaving their wives and children behind. The Jews were well aware of the range of conflicts and emotions involved. They fled because their books would have been seized or their bodies held to ransom for the *captio* authorized by the *stabilimentum* to which the lord of Dampierre had agreed. Typically in the past there had not been any effort on the part of lords who undertook *captiones* to harm or imprison women and children. The mass arrests that have been described in earlier chapters always focussed on or were limited to men. The Jews who fled knew also that the lord of Dampierre was the vassal of the count of Champagne and that the count therefore had leverage over him and might be persuaded to make him moderate his policies. In other words, they were seeking the count's positive help and protection against the fiscal depredation of his vassal.[34] Perhaps other Jews of baronial lordships covered by the *stabilimentum* also tried to escape to the lands of the count of Champagne, but it would be hasty to assert this. Since not all of them lived in lordships that were held from the count, they could not have depended on his influence to be used to protect their wives and children from their lords' anger.

Even if the behavior of the Jews of the lordship of Dampierre cannot be generalized to that of the Jews of the royal domain or of the other lordships affected by the *stabilimentum*, it is revealing in its own right of the careful playing off of political forces that had become a trait in Jews' self-protection. Without a doubt money was offered the count of Champagne to protect Jewish interests in Dampierre. What the Jews could not have known was that the count and the lord of Dampierre were relatively close to a temporary or interim agreement on the serious issues over which they had been in conflict.[35] Perhaps the flight of the Dampierre Jews in November even helped precipitate this agreement; perhaps not. When the agreement came on 31 December 1223, it shattered all the Jews' hopes.

Part of the agreement gave the lord of Dampierre and his vassals, burghers, and serfs respite in the debts they owed his Jews. Another part had him give sureties to the count for his adherence to the agreement. The sureties consisted of the "Jewish wives and families of the (male) Jews who had come from (Dampierre) to the count's land." The lord of Dampierre reserved the right to take the women and children back at a specified time immediately prior to the expiration of the temporary truce established between him and the count. And he insisted that if he did so the temporary giving of the wives and children as sureties worked no prejudice to his rights over them. These reservations notwithstanding, he began to transfer the wives and children to the count.[36]

One might ask whether the "transfer" was more than a scriptorial convention, a mere change of jurisdiction. In fact, it appears that we are talking about a physical removal of the families. The agreement between the lord of Dampierre and the count of Champagne effectively erased any leverage that the Jews had enjoyed. They became extremely vulnerable; their vulnerability is documentable within a month or two of the agreement. The situation was this. The count of Champagne was deeply in debt to royal Jews. Indeed, he was a defaulter, and Louis VIII invoked the *stabilimentum* of 1 November against him, namely, that defaulters had to pay their debts to Jews. In February 1224 the king announced that he had arranged for the count to repay 10,500 pounds to two royal Jews in installments of 500 pounds every four months for seven years.[37] Perhaps we should read the long repayment period as Louis the arbiter's leniency. But at least the money was to be paid—*paid to the Jews*. Rumors began to fly that the count was avenging himself by undertaking a policy of torture and murder against the refugee Jews from Dampierre who were at his mercy in his lands. In reaction—and having nowhere else to turn—the Jews passed word to the lord of Dampierre, from whom the refugees had fled in the first place, begging him not to send their wives and families from his lands to Champagne.[38] Undoubtedly the conduit for these entreaties were royal or Champenois Jews; and there is certainly no doubt that they offered the lord of Dampierre money.

He held back just a little. The family of a particularly wealthy Jew named Cochin of Saint-Dizier he hesitated to turn over to the count.[39] Behind the scenes there were negotiations. At last (1 May 1224) the lord of Dampierre announced that the two sons of Cochin and their families would be turned over to the count of Champagne but only because of the count's assurance that he would neither mutilate nor kill them or any of the other Jews whose families were being or had been transferred. The count, instead, would exploit the Jews (force them to redeem themselves) in good faith; and the two great nobles would split the profits from the redemption down the middle. The count would also keep the now- impoverished Jews. What had been a temporary transfer in December became permanent in May; the Jews of Dampierre would be permitted to resume their business in Champagne after they had redeemed themselves by giving up all their existing wealth. (They could borrow from their Champenois coreligionists to start over again.) The lord of Dampierre lost Jews, but he got half the redemption and all the real property from which the fugitives' families had been evicted, proof positive that this was no mere clerical exchange. Naturally, any and all debts owed by the count or the lord of Dampierre to these Jews were cancelled.[40] Fiscal matters that might cause dispute on the execution of these conventions were placed under the jurisdiction of the count.[41]

In brief, the Jews of Dampierre, counting on the hostility of the count of Champagne toward their lord, his vassal, to work in their favor, had fled to Champagne to avoid a *captio*. Instead, they miscalculated and found themselves under the regime of a man who, if the rumors are true, stopped at neither mutilation nor the threat of murder to squeeze them dry. The lord of Dampierre, on the other hand, when appealed to contritely for his good offices, managed only to get a promise (or to say he got a promise) from the count that the latter had thought better of mutilating and murdering Jews. And with that effort he washed his hands of the matter, turned over innocent Jewish families to the count, and made a windfall himself from the seizure of their property. In this sordid affair, only Louis VIII gave the appearance of having any scruples at all by making the count of Champagne pay up on his defaulted debts to royal Jews consistent with the legislation of Philip Augustus, though, of course, it might plausibly be argued that he did this only to injure the count, not to be fair to the Jews.

The network of old agreements that bound several barons not to accept fugitive Jews and the general reinforcement of this principle by Louis's *stabilimentum* (which must have carried considerable weight with many lords less powerful than the count palatine of Champagne) combined to circumscribe the options of most Jews in the kingdom. They never fled their native lands and, thus, were "taken" as provided by the *stabilimentum*. In the royal domain itself there is good evidence, in addition to Louis's judgement on the count of Champagne to pay his debts to the Jews, that other Jews managed to receive the legitimate debts whose payment they had tried to enforce under the constitution of Philip Augustus.[42] So the *captio* was offset to a degree by the collection of bad debts, some of which may have been substantial. This meant that the Jews of the royal domain were not entirely impoverished by the taking. Their chattels remained intact, as well as their leaseholds. Nothing was taken from them on the basis of past usury. Bitter as the royal *captio* was, it was not remotely similar to the brutality and absolute despoliation experienced by the unfortunate emigrants from Dampierre in Champagne.

Neither among royal and baronial Jews covered by the *stabilimentum* nor among the refugees in Champagne was the *captio* intended to bring an end to Jewish moneylending per se. The important point with regard to the royal lands was that the government would no longer offer its good offices for the registering and enforcement of the debts. This distinction — permitting "usury" but withdrawing government enforcement — is nicely illustrated by a charter of August 1225 that the king issued to certain Christians who were "citizens" of the Italian town of Asti on the Lombard March. He permitted the Astigians to reside in Paris for a fee of fifty shillings per year per person. The charter was for five years and gave them free movement of their goods and freedom from additional levies. The Astigians were "Lombards" in the technical fiscal (if not geographical) sense, moneylenders and pawnbrokers. The charter regulates the length of time that objects pledged to them had to be retained before being sold, as a way to protect the interests of Christian borrowers.[43] The appropriate conclusion seems to be that while the crown continued to permit moneylending and pawning and continued to regard abuses of the business as falling within its jurisdiction, it would not directly encourage the business by providing offices where the deals were struck, authenticated, concluded, or enforced — whether the lenders were Christians or Jews.

Finally, it is impossible to measure the overall profitability of the *captio*, but one royal figure is available. At Candlemas (2 February) 1226, which would have been the date of the seventh installment of the nine granted by the *stabilimentum* to debtors to pay the king the outstanding principal of active debts, the king's men accounted for at least 8,682 pounds.[44] It is unwise to insist that every installment brought the crown the same amount. But if the size of this render is roughly similar to the returns at the previous six installments and the two to come, it would mean that the king was collecting about one-tenth to one-eighth of his total annual income from "Jewish debts" in the three years of his reign.[45] We shall later have to follow this thread of the story — the financial aspect — a little further to see why no simple answer to the question of how much money was obtained is really possible; this will lead us into the regency of Blanche of Castile in the reign of her son.[46] Before we make this transition, however, we need to address the major political accomplishment of Louis VIII, his wars of conquest.

7. Conquests in the South

The situation on the uneasy Poitevin frontier was changing radically in the course of the year 1224 while the Jews were being taken in France. Philip Augustus had possibly been considering an invasion before he died, but, if so, it was left to Louis VIII to carry it out. The Poitevin baronage had an unsavory reputation for changing sides and negotiating its support. There was no certainty that the barons of the region would favor the French if war with England became hot at the expiration of any of the several truces that circumscribed the fighting. When Louis VIII came to the throne, as we have seen, he spent some time immediately working out or renewing truces with certain of the important Poitevin barons whose neutrality he might need in a head-to-head confrontation with the English. The new French king was not averse to extending his truce with the English, but he continued to make overtures to other powerful uncommitted members of the Poitevin nobility, especially the Lusignans, for their support. Petit-Dutaillis brilliantly portrayed these matters in his classic book.[1] When war did break out again between England and France in mid-1224 at the end of a truce that the kings could not agree on extending, Louis had the promise of support of many local barons. Not all of them were eager to fulfill their promises; some posturing took place. But Louis's astuteness and determination won the day.

The conquest of Poitou was almost too easy. Niort capitulated following a two-day seige in July. Saint-Jean-d'Angély surrendered soon afterwards. La Rochelle surrendered after only a two-and-one-half week seige. It is true that the barons of the French host could not have anticipated the striking success against La Rochelle, a well-fortified port that might have been reinforced by sea from England or Gascony. It is true that the grumbling against undertaking the siege briefly became strident. Theobald of Champagne, the count palatine who was always self-important and rarely on friendly terms with his suzerain, was eager to abandon it. All the same, Louis held firm; and in a very short space his firmness was rewarded.

Petit-Dutaillis believed that the king, who sent his armies further into the southwest with considerable success (thus bringing Périgord, Quercy, and the Limousin under nominal control), was ultimately disappointed with his and his allies' campaigns. His armies were quite cautious. He wanted to conquer all that remained to the English king in the southwest; but he had no strong network of support or beneficent neutrality in Gascony. It is assuredly the case, too, that he came to the opinion that loyalty to the English king in Bordeaux, the key to the region, was exceptionally strong and that the interest of other allied lords in continuing in a hard fight was very limited. Never perhaps abandoning hope that all of the southwest would be his, he nonetheless turned his attention elsewhere.[2]

The English were just as happy that Louis did so. Losing Poitou and their hegemony over Périgord, Quercy, and the Limousin was sobering. They would have fought desperately if Louis's thrusts had continued, for the southwest was their last best hope. On the other hand, the time was not appropriate for them to try to recover what was already lost, since internal troubles in England in the minority of John's son Henry III were diverting a considerable part of the crown's resources. In 1225, the southwest therefore entered a short period of peace, with only occasional minor skirmishes on the new frontier.[3]

The Jews of the southwestern regions incorporated into the royal domain by Louis VIII were very unevenly distributed. The great towns of southern Poitou had Jewish settlements; and it has been persuasively argued that toponyms in the countryside establish that there was a denser settlement in southern Poitou than in Périgord and elsewhere on the frontier.[4] Indeed, Jewish settlement in Périgord, Quercy, and the Limousin was negligible.[5] In southern Poitou, on the other hand, not only were there substantial numbers of Jews, but talmudic and biblical studies were flourishing at the time of the Capetian conquest.[6]

Adjustment to Capetian domination for these communities was painless. The conquest had been swift and immediately successful in southern Poitou. It had taken more time and been a little less successful beyond the borders of Poitou, but these were regions with few Jews. There is no evidence of emigration from southern Poitou or the forcible movement of Jewish population within the province in the immediate aftermath of its conquest. Presumably, the *stabilimentum* of 1 November 1223 discussed in the preceding chapter took effect in the period of consolidation, but there was no reason formally to announce that it was to be applied because in theory southern Poitou, like all the Plantagenet domains, had been con-

Languedoc: selected Jewish settlements in the thirteenth century

sidered part of the Capetian holdings from the time of the judgement of Philip Augustus's court against John in 1202.[7]

The attitude of the crown's men in the new areas is less clear. In general, the conquest had gone so smoothly and the loyalty in southern Poitou to the Plantagenets turned out to be so weak that Louis VIII was willing to re-employ or confirm existing officials or at least men of the region as his own administrators.[8] Naturally their attitudes were influenced by a desire to appear loyal and obedient to their new overlord. They might show this in any number of ways—hostility to the circulation of sterling is a case in point. But the relative stability in administrative personnel would have been as reassuring to the native population, including Jews, as was, for example, the confirmation of liberties to a number of towns.[9]

The conquest of Poitou and its environs in the southwest was but a prelude to the really major achievement of Louis VIII, the conquest of Languedoc. To appreciate this accomplishment and its affect on the Jews, we need to go back in time to describe the constellation of forces in the region on the eve of the thirteenth century. Languedoc, or the Midi, as we might now call it, was comprised of a multitude of lordships—counties, viscounties, independent cities—in seemingly constant conflict.[10] The squabbling in this region was largely an aristocratic pastime affecting and even retarding but not decisively undermining the vitality of cultural life. From Aquitaine to the Provençal littoral, the lordly courts and the cities of the Midi were known for poetry and song, for a culture of warmth and beauty, of mannered elegance and satirical wit. Or so we may imagine.[11] The very fact that this region came under the hammer blows of northern French conquest in the thirteenth century and had a Capetian program of social and political organization imposed on it have caused sympathetic historians to look back nostalgically on the lost world of troubador sensibility.[12] Their wistfulness recalls that of English romantics lamenting the passing of the sturdy yeoman and the guileless rustic of their tiny island.

In truth the Capetians were not bugbears with fangs poised to rip the flesh of meridional culture. But they were different in ideological orientation from the lords of the south. In the late twelfth century they envisaged—and the vision was confirmed by Bouvines in the early thirteenth—that they had a mission, dearly beloved of God, to maintain and augment the integrity and authority of the French crown.[13] They might usually conceive of that authority effectively stopping at the Loire or in Auvergne; but legends, old promises, and the reality of political alliances intermittently made them look further south.[14] Still, they hardly comprehended the country they coveted, and in no aspect was this so much the case as with regard to the place of the Jews in the society of the Midi.

The Jews of the Midi had their traditional cultural ties with the Spanish, especially Catalonian, Jewry to the south and west and with Provençal and Italian Jewry to the east.[15] They shared this cultural coherence, if not unity, with any number of other social and economic groups. There was, for example, an intricately connected commercial network that linked the Mediterranean ports. In spite of bitter rivalries, business techniques, commercial language, forms of credit and exchange were extraordinarily similar from Barcelona to Genoa.[16] Or, another example: poetic genres were shared among the peoples of the entire Mediterranean south; and even though there were gross differences from one sub-region to another, the literary culture of the long northern shore of the western Mediterranean provided an unmistakable contrast to that of the north.[17]

The political frontiers of modern maps of southern Europe were permeable in more mundane ways. Thus Pyrenean shepherds regularly pastured their flocks at set intervals of the year in Catalonia or in Languedocian valleys far from their homes; they did so and had been doing so since time immemorial. They would continue to do so until the seventeenth century.[18] Meanwhile, whether in the Pyrenean villages from which they came or in Toulouse or other cities to which they repaired for recreation on their migrations, the migrants would have been adjudicated, if they broke the law, under almost the same "Roman" procedures. The characteristic features of these procedures set southern law apart from that of the feudal, customary north.[19] This coherence should not be over-stressed, whether we are talking about legal matters or anything else. As Gouron has recently shown, much of what has been written about the legal culture of the south is the sheerest nonsense. If there was anything like a distinctively Roman legal culture of the south, it did not date from time immemorial; it was only just emerging or re-emerging in the twelfth century, as the revolution in legal learning taking place at the Italian universities began slowly but surely to penetrate Languedoc and to shape the style of commercial instruments and the vocabulary of the law speakers at courts.[20] Despite this and similar reservations, the broader point remains accurate enough. A northerner—a man from Picardy or Normandy—if set down in the heart of Languedoc in the late twelfth century, would have felt all at sea. The language he heard would have been unintelligible, and if, perhaps, a friend translated for him, the northerner would have been all the more bewildered by the environment in which he found himself.[21]

Southern Jews and northern Jews, given these general circumstances, were largely indifferent to each other in the twelfth century. There was especially little sense that the northerners, the men of Tsarfat, could appreciate southern Jewish culture. An intellectual and spiritual canyon divided them.[22] We have already seen that northerners had their own internal squabbles (the *hasidim* against the accommodationists is the best-known example). But to southerners these distinctions seemed less telling than the general unity of Tsarfati culture, insofar as they knew anything about it. A century ago Weiss explored the contrast, locating it in the way northern Jewish thinkers delighted in the labyrinthine nature of talmudic lore and then promptly canonized their delight, while southerners, following or influenced by Arabic culture, extracted and developed rather more sophisticated philosophical (and mystical) systems from the treasury of accumulated Jewish learning. Weiss saw the thirteenth century—a time of further hardening of northern Christian attitudes toward Jews and therefore increased migration of northern Jews to the south—as the period when the battle over accommodationism penetrated southern Jewry. It was not that southerners stood fast against their newly arrived coreligionists. Most of them eventually perceived the general worsening situation and many admired the depth of pious northern learning. For these and other reasons one can see southern Jews co-opting northern conceits into their poetry and philosophical work. Nonetheless, the tension remained and divided Jews even as late as the fourteenth century.[23]

We know now that this interpretation is rather too simple. The intensity of the conflict had any number of socio-cultural components that need to be considered: the relative cosmopolitanism of the south versus the greater isolation and fragmentation of northern Jewry; the direct and repeated experience of massacre in the north as opposed to the south; the increasingly strong and resolute state in the north intruding into social relations between Jews and Christians in a firmly "nativist" way versus the imposition of an alien state apparatus on Christian nobles and bourgeois and on Jews as well in the south. All these and other factors enrich our picture. Where Weiss did not oversimplify is in the tone of the initial Jewish internal conflict. On first exposure, he seems to exaggerate the animosities; yet the more one probes, the more one recognizes the accuracy of his reading. It is as if the Jews of the south simply would not accept the analysis of Jewish-Christian relations that northerners articulated. It was too gloomy, too given over to a celebration of martyrdom, too much at variance with the social experiences of the south where tolerance prevailed.

At least three reasons for the relative tolerance of southern society in respect to the Jews have been put forward; and though it is not to the immediate purpose to dwell on these matters, it may be useful to state them briefly. First, it has been argued that the tolerance arose almost naturally from the fact that the Jewish communities of the Midi were an organic part of the cities and towns of the south. Jews had lived here since the period of Roman domination, and they had never lost the semblance of protection under Roman law. So baldly stated, of course, this explanation is superficial; yet, there is much to be said for it. Even if it glosses over substantive changes in Roman law in the later Empire and local variations in its application after the collapse of the Imperial administration, a case can be made that the wider sensibility to "alien" groups associated with Roman Imperial practice and idealized in Roman jurisprudence was a persistent legacy in southern life.[24]

A second explanation draws on the sense of self-confidence of southern Jewry itself, a sense cultivated by myths of service to Charlemagne and perpetuated by the highly elaborate and mannered literary culture of Jewish thinkers.[25] The reinforcement here was demographic. Thousands upon thousands of Jews lived in the south in the teeming maritime cities and towns and in the hinterlands of these commercial centers. A proper comparison of northern and southern Jewry would probably emphasize the similarity of Jewish life in the authentically rural parts and inland towns of Languedoc to life in the north and would argue that it was only the civilization of the strip of territory right along the littoral that markedly contrasted with that of English, north French, and Rhenish Jewry.[26]

A third explanation for the tolerance of southern life is political. The lack of a persistent, single-minded, and successful effort on the part of a southern dynasty to create a compact and institutionally coherent state is a case in point.[27] One of the traditional ideological rallying cries of such efforts is the demand for the isolation and degradation of aliens; and in the Christian Middle Ages, the Jews were an obvious target. Yet, no noble family ever quite managed this single-mindedness of purpose in the south; and as a consequence Jews in the south avoided some of the pressures of northern life, at least until the coming of the Capetians.

The other aspect of this political explanation of southern tolerance depends on the relative weakness of the church, the relative looseness of diocesan organization in the south, and the disharmony between native political leaders and high churchmen.[28] A few of the more important southern churches claimed to be under the protection of the Capetians. It flattered the Capetians to have them do so. It was originally no great threat to the freedom of the churches, which were far from the center of royal power, to seek the Capetian mantle; and it was one more device for keeping the local nobility at bay.[29] One can hardly imagine, despite recurrent troubles in the north between crown and church, that abbeys and bishoprics in the heartland of the Capetian patrimony would claim without serious challenge the protection of distant lords. What this reflected in the south was that there was rarely the kind of coordination of efforts between the highest political leaders and the church on matters of religious policy—whether toward the Jews or toward heretics, for that matter. The religious conscience of the south was articulated most eloquently and forcefully by outsiders: by preachers like Saint Bernard and Saint Dominic on special missions or by the papacy itself.[30]

It would be difficult to adjudicate among these three explanations. I have already indicated that something can be said for each one. And many other possible explanations have been suggested as well—ranging from the far too subtle to the certifiably insane. The lesson to take away from these speculations is, however, reasonably clear. Tolerance existed because of a balance of forces in social and political life. Tolerance was not a moral or even a cultural ideal so much as it was contingent on the continued existence of this balance. If at any time the balance were upset—as, for example, by a successful attempt to create a state or by the fashioning of a firm secular-ecclesiastical alliance with regard to "social discipline"—the Jews would be at risk. Countervailing tendencies would not dissolve under these new pressures. After all, the sheer fact of a huge Jewish population with its own strong sense of itself as a lobbying entity would confront moral, social, and political reformers. Moreover, shifts in alignment which might upset the balance of forces that sustained tolerance would provoke counter-challenges among some Christians, not in order to protect or salvage the Jewish position, but to preserve their own—with a result that the position of the Jews might persist in a relatively favorable equilibrium.

Several times I have had to refer to the size of the Jewish population of the Midi as a possible factor in the relative self-confidence of southern Jewry and its influence on political and social life. A number of aspects of the demographic situation must be taken into account here. First is the question of the gross population, Christian and Jewish, of the Midi. The best evidence, at least on the Christian side of this issue, comes from the early fourteenth century and relates to the number of hearths of the three *sénéchaussées* or administrative divisions of the south: Toulouse, Carcassonne-Béziers, and Beaucaire-Nîmes. Despite the fact that the French royal annexation after 1223 immediately brought into the kingdom only two of these areas, namely, those on the Mediterranean coast (Carcassonne-Béziers and Beaucaire-Nîmes), it is valuable to consider all three together, because in the 1240s the county of Toulouse came under Capetian cadet rule and was fully integrated into the kingdom by 1271 as a *sénéchaussée*.[31]

Opinions differ on how the records of hearths ought to be used to extrapolate to population, but most authorities seem to agree that a total Christian population of from 1,400,000 to 1,500,000 is safe.[32] This population in 1328 (the date of the figures) was unevenly distributed, the north being lightly, the coast heavily settled.[33] Equally to the point, there is not much evidence of steady growth from the early days of the thirteenth century so as to make correction downward to the population in 1200 an easy matter. Rather, slow increases in the mid-century were followed by quite rapid growth, particularly in cities and more especially in cities along the coast, in the late thirteenth and early fourteenth centuries.[34]

It is tempting, however, to imagine first that the low rate of increase of the middle thirteenth century was balanced by the rapid growth of the end of the century. If so, and if the sorts of extrapolation that were earlier used for the population of the north (and of Europe in general) may guide us, one would not be surprised if the territory covered by the three *sénéchaussées* had a population of about one million Christians around 1200.[35] Like the population in general, the population of the Jews was very unevenly distributed. Here comparative figures from data-rich regions can be of help. In Christian-dominated Castile, whose main centers of population were distant from the trading centers that constituted the maritime cities and where urban agglomerations were small and some rural areas were severely underpopulated, the best evidence gives a Jewish population of only about 0.4% of the total population in the thirteenth century.[36] In Aragon, part of which hugged the coast, on the other hand, the ratio was much higher, 2%; in Provence as well—in the early fourteenth century— the proportion of Jews to Christians was about 3%; and on the island of Majorca, a trading entrepot, it was 6%.[37] In the cities the ratios were higher. Whereas the overall proportion in Provence, as indicated, was about 3%, evidence from its towns shows ratios as high as 10%. And other cities and towns on the borders of Languedoc offer us Jewish populations of 10%, 15%, 28%, even 30% of total residents.[38]

It would be foolhardy, I think, to go further and try to give an overall figure for the number of Jews in the Midi in the year 1200 or thereabouts based on these comparative figures, let alone try to assess with any precision the numerical distribution of this population along the littoral and in the rural areas. All that needs to be said, if we can be led somewhat by the comparative Jewish and fourteenth-century Christian data, is that the density of Jewish settlement among the villages and petty seigneuries at any distance from the Mediterranean coast must have been virtually negligible.[39] Only a few inland cities, like Toulouse, were exceptional and also had networks of immediate hinterland villages with small Jewish settlements.[40] When at the end of the thirteenth and beginning of the fourteenth century additional data allow scholars to speculate on Jewish population in France in general so that figures like 70,000, 100,000, even 140,000 are bandied about, we should not conclude that any individual scholar is precisely right.[41] What is compelling is the relatively small range in recent scholarly estimates. If we were to take one of these figures as the crude standard—say, 70,000 Jews in royal France in 1300—what this would really mean on the basis of everything else we know is that the vast majority of these Jews lived along the Mediterranean coast in cities and seigneuries noted for their commercial, mercantile, and generally cosmopolitan culture. It was no different in 1200. We might want to reduce the overall figure slightly; we might want to correct for political and economic factors that altered the population profile of individual cities.[42] But the picture seems a reasonably clear one.

In the centers of population where Jews concentrated they owned and not merely rented property, and they engaged in a wide spectrum of occupations and interactions with Christians.[43] Ecclesiastical theories articulated in the late twelfth and first two decades of the thirteenth century notwithstanding, Jews were active in many ways that gave them authority over Christians.[44] An area usually emphasized and important symbolically is the role of Jews as financial agents for seigneurs.[45] Still, all the data that have been produced on this point for the Midi do not comprise very much; and no one has seriously argued that seigneurial administration was dominated by Jews. The important conclusion comes by way of contrast with the north, where illustrations of this sort of activity are rare in the extreme.

Insofar as the role of the Jew as a fiscal agent has wider significance for the Midi, it relates to the fact that the Jews who were called upon to take up these tasks were experienced in fiscal matters already. They became so by running businesses successfully and especially by engaging in the market in loans. The serial evidence on their role in credit is late and is associated with the registering of contracts by notaries in the wake of the penetration of Italian legal practices. Most of our notarial records only become good from the later thirteenth century. But as in the north there is sufficient evidence before the late thirteenth century to establish the existence of an extensive network of credit in and around the maritime cities of the south and the prominent role of the Jews in it.[46]

What differentiates the north from the south again is the fact that the Jews of the Midi were not exclusively tied to credit for their livelihoods before 1223. There were true Jewish agriculturalists or, rather, owners of estates.[47] Jews served as middlemen in grain and livestock marketing.[48] They routinely engaged in retailing of a wide variety of goods, including wine and meat.[49] Where patterns of occupation were not interrupted by Capetian restrictions, at least not before the evidence becomes abundant, we can also find them active in many other ways: as doctors, tailors, skinners, and leather merchants; bookbinders and illuminators; masons and dealers in old clothes, and so forth.[50] And in all of these areas they serviced Christians as well as themselves. Many of the details with regard to these matters we shall have to come back to.

An important related aspect of Jewish and Christian social contact along the Mediterranean, one that historians are beginning to address with great sophistication, is the interaction on matters of science and of learning in general. Although it is always possible to tell something like this story for the north—the "creative encounter" of Jewish and Christian biblicists—it takes very little time to discern that the comparison pales before the striking and profound contrasts.[51] Recent scholarship teaches us that contacts stimulated by intellectual curiosity were not only basically fruitful but long lasting in the Midi. Scholars of each confession praised the ability of their counterparts. To be sure, discourse was not free or liberal. Curious borrowings abound, for example, in various Jewish and Christian texts; but in religious texts per se such borrowings tend to be limited in number and restricted to relatively minor and non-doctrinal points.[52] Again, however, although sufficient evidence survives for the early period to establish the fact of fruitful scholarly interaction, it is not until well into the thirteenth century that the documentation becomes lavish. The fact that collaboration continued after "Capetian domination" does not mean that the Capetians consciously permitted this area of contact to develop and prosper. Quite to the contrary, the most fruitful dialog—typically in matters of astronomy and astrology, academic medicine, and philosophy—had to take place outside areas of Capetian domination, that is, in the anomalous enclave of Montpellier, which was part of the patrimony of the royal family of Aragon.[53]

I have described in the briefest outlines a society that may seem a little anachronistic. There is a danger of idealization in talking about the "cosmopolitan culture" of the Midi, more particularly about the maritime cities. But if by being brief I may have exaggerated the virtues and freedoms of the old regime, I am not certain that this is entirely misleading, because, just like some modern historians, "meridional patriots" (in the felicitous phrase of Dossat) began to idealize their own immediate past in the early thirteenth century.[54] It was not the tolerance of the Jews that they missed, it was the political autonomy, the freedom from close ecclesiastical scrutiny of matters of conscience, and finally the peace. Meridional culture, although it had always been strife-torn as a result of baronial rivalries, had seen nothing like the Albigensian Crusade, a combination of religious and political warfare and of inquisitorial repression in its wake that blurred the memory of pre-crusade strife and helped foster absurdly nostalgic sentiments and peculiarly mystical dreams of a world that had vanished and, it was desperately hoped, would return.[55]

By the mid-twelfth century it was thought by many people that the south of Gaul was a region permeated with heterodox beliefs. Scholars debate the range of heterodox opinions, the detailed nature of each, and the extent to which these opinions penetrated various strata of society. But it is unquestioned that high churchmen from throughout Western Europe came to see the Midi as a problem. Saint Bernard himself preached there against the "heretics"; and at the beginning of the thirteenth century Saint Dominic raised his voice against them. Sympathetic writers give the saints credit for stirring up fervor in the south, and perhaps in Europe generally, against heresy; but not even sympathizers believe that they accomplished much with the heretics themselves.[56]

Although it is acknowledged that there was a diversity of heterodox beliefs against which the saints struggled, learned opinion in the church of the time and subsequent scholarship have focussed on the so-called Cathar or Albigensian heretics as the principal foes of orthodoxy.[57] Dualist believers who saw the created world as the product of the evil demiurge, they abhorred the "things of this world," and the most rigorous among them—the perfect—practiced forms of extreme renunciation, including abstinence from sex. Here again, however, modern research would argue for varieties of belief among the Cathars, and it would stress also the relative leniency in personal behavior permitted to believers who did not aspire or claim to be "perfect."[58]

Keeping in mind the diversity, we can still recognize the general threat posed to the official church by Cathar beliefs. Catholicism, the Cathars believed, insofar as it reflected and incorporated the "ideals" of the world created by the demiurge ought to be rejected. The wealth, ostentation, and empty ceremonial of Catholicism, as perceived by Cathars, were offenses to the forces of light. There was, too, in Catharism a significant strain of docetism, the notion that Jesus only appeared to take on corporeal form in the incarnation; for him really to have done so would have meant bondage to the material world, a world of constructed evil, a world of suffering and of the hated cross.[59] It was not inevitable that the flourishing of these opinions—and many others accepted by some but rejected by other heretics—would provoke a religious war of Catholics against Cathars; but the situation was an extremely dangerous one. Nor was it softened in the least by the posture of local political authorities, which ran from ineffectual uncertainty to studied indifference to the urgent recommendations of the official church for confounding the heretics.[60]

For the Jews, the growing internal Christian dissension was full of danger, for the heightened sense of religious conflict would undoubtedly have ramifications on Jewish and Christian relations. Any precise connections between the *nature* of the Christian heretical beliefs and the content of Judaism, however, are tenuous at best. First of all, if we focus our attention on the general dualism of Catharism and its notion of the creator and his creation as evil, then the idea that Catharism learned from or contributed to orthodox rabbinic Judaism must appear ludicrous. But just as there were varieties of Catharism and varieties of heresy beyond Catharism in the Midi that *might* have picked up this or that notion from Judaism, there were also mystical varieties of Jewish religious experience, not entirely pleasing to the most rigorous rabbis, that *might* have accommodated some of the more mystical sensibilities, if not doctrines, of the Christian heretics.

The unrelieved tentativeness of the remarks in the preceding paragraph is a reflection of the scholarship on the subject. There have been wild opinions in the past, but the prevailing notions are these: Jews knew something, perhaps a great deal, of the nature of the Christian dispute. Some Christians—heretics or not—knew something about the internal content of contemporary Judaism. But the relation of Catharism to Judaism, even to the mystical kabbalistic strain of Judaism of the Midi that heavily allegorized the received texts and had a docetic tinge of its own, is doubtful at best. There were judaizing heresies in the Midi as there were occasionally elsewhere in Europe, but these were a minor element of the religious ferment in the south and of virtually no significance to the cluster of opinions identified by the Catholics as distinctively Cathar. More work needs to be done on these points, but it is only fair to add that I do not think the picture will ever change.[61]

For Jews of all sentiments Catharism was important not for what it contributed to the devotional language of Judaism (nothing) and not for what little, if anything, it learned from the varieties of Judaism. It was important because it helped provoke a crisis among Christians in which the position of Jews was jeopardized. The struggle against the Cathars was a watershed. Without ever necessarily taking seriously the possibility that Judaism stimulated Catharism, devout Catholics could denounce the leniency that they detected in religious life in general in the south, such as open debates with heretics as if their beliefs demanded respect. In tandem with this insistence on the isolation and degradation of heretics, they insisted on the subordination and segregation of Jews. The Midi thus became increasingly uncomfortable for the Jewish population as the struggle between Catholic and Cathar warmed.[62]

The crisis came in 1207. The most powerful of the barons of the Midi, Count Raymond VI of Toulouse, incurred excommunication for his failure, so typical of southern lords, to act against the heretics with the vigor the church desired. The papal legate who excommunicated the count knew the Midi well. A southerner himself, he must have been quite aware of the reasons for baronial reluctance.[63] Families were divided between Cathar and Catholic believers; some of the lesser nobility were Cathar; many Cathar perfect were regarded as holy men and women, living saints in their own right. The use of coercion against them in the sense of an organized program to force the miscreants to make their peace with the Catholic church would perhaps have provoked a civil war.[64] If the legate, Pierre de Castelnau, recognized the reasons for the reluctance of avowedly orthodox political leaders like Raymond VI to act, he still could not understand why they failed to overcome this reluctance and see their higher duty to Catholic unity and the Catholic faith. However personalities affected the confrontations between Pierre and Raymond, what was at issue was a high matter of policy. Pierre's excommunication of Raymond and his interdiction of Catholic services in the count's lands were a warning.[65] This warning would not have been the end of negotiations. Interdicts could go on for years. King John of England, for example, endured one for four years before capitulating to the pope, and he managed to come out of it relatively unscathed and with the pope as a genuine if cautious friend.[66] It was not the interdict of Raymond's lands but the assassination of Pierre de Castelnau on 14 January 1208 after words from the count—words later regarded by the Catholics as a veiled threat—that precipitated the Cathar war.[67]

An enormous number of books have been written on this wretched chapter in medieval history. A motley crusading army took shape in the east, slightly north of Languedoc proper, and with its expedition began the opening phase of a long and very bitter war. These forces, carrying the papal standard, were largely composed of northern Frenchmen fighting under many different captains. It took considerable time before command became more-or-less centralized under the northern French baron Simon de Montfort.[68] Especially difficult in all of this was the position of Catholic barons in Languedoc daily expecting the army. They felt some sympathy with the views of the official church but also had profound concern for the integrity of their territories. Raymond VI of Toulouse himself was in this position. He had despised the papal legate, but he insisted that he was not responsible for his murder and he also insisted (whether he was believed or not) that he was a loyal son of the church.[69]

It is not entirely odd, therefore, that as Raymond protested his innocence, he also made obeisance to the papacy and even offered to raise a crusading army in the west. Barons and towns—Catholic and Cathar—that might have supported him in a serious effort to oppose the separate northerners' army found his new role as a crusader against his own subjects somewhat puzzling and tried to resist the northerners on their own.[70] The great city of Béziers failed effectively to do so and was visited by a frenzy of religious and political terror (22 July 1209) that reminded publicists of the bloodbath of Jerusalem in the enthusiasm of the First Crusade.[71] Increasingly, thanks to the weakness of Raymond VI and the fall of other southern strongholds like Carcassonne, the Midi came under northern domination.[72]

Northern, not Capetian, domination. Capetian vassals were playing their part in the south, but although the thoroughly orthodox Philip Augustus permitted them to do so, his main concern in the first two decades of the thirteenth century was the winning and keeping of the Plantagenet lands of Normandy and the western fiefs north of the Loire.[73] Even when things temporarily went bad for the conquering northerners in the Midi after 1210, as local rebellion followed local rebellion, Philip remained aloof. Only terrorism practiced by the northerners against meridional diehards maintained the fragile ascendancy of Simon de Montfort.[74] Finally, in 1211, Raymond of Toulouse, unable to work out an acceptable modus vivendi with Simon and the new papal representative, renounced his role as a crusader and fully committed his resources to the task of expelling the northerners. His attitude provoked more acts of terrorism in the desperate game of control. What emerged was a war of sieges and blockades. A successful siege of a southern outpost by the northerners was not infrequently followed by a dramatic gesture determined to reinforce the image of Catholic power. In the event, Raymond's position steadily eroded.[75]

Catholic power in its alien northern guise was bound to antagonize other authorities, including especially the Aragonese who had lands in the Midi. By 1213, with the war still not quite successfully completed by Simon, the king of Aragon lost patience with those northerners who were carving out huge principalities on his border. Catholic though he was to the core, he allied himself with the defenders of the Midi and coordinated efforts with Raymond in order to overcome de Montfort. The strategy ended at the battle of Muret on 12 September 1213, where an outnumbered Simon smashed the forces against him and brought death to the king of Aragon himself.[76]

Although Raymond VI escaped, his star continued to fall. All around the south, even in Provence, Simon harried his supporters and imposed his will. Lingering resentments there were; outposts of steadfast resistance remained. But by 1215 the south seemed thoroughly under the domination of de Montfort; his position as de facto lord of the Midi seemed secure.[77] And what is more, the great Capetian victories against John of England and his allies in the north in 1214 gave an aura to specifically "French" achievements everywhere that was nothing less than arrogant.[78] In 1215, Philip Augustus's son, still Prince Louis, in a gesture of solidarity with Simon very briefly joined his crusade and helped complete what seemed to be de Montfort's definitive conquest of the Midi.[79] By May 1216 both the pope and the king of France had recognized Simon officially as the legitimate count of Toulouse and as lord of numerous other southern fiefs. There were a few unconquered fortresses, but time seemed to be Simon's, not Raymond's, friend. The old count was in exile in England with the even more unlucky King John.[80]

What went wrong in all of this? Theories abound. With the crusade apparently accomplished, most of the army returned home, leaving the conquered province undermanned.[81] Some scholars also point to Simon's personality as a problem: a charismatic commander, he was arrogant as a politician, offending his allies the more powerful he got. He certainly did not console the south.[82] His effort to impose the "Custom of Paris" as the law of the Midi proves as much.[83] Here was not a man like Philip Augustus who marched as a conqueror into Normandy with promises of continuity of institutions and of a good life to come.[84] Of course, the issues were more intense and personal in the south, the legacy of terror so heavy, and the war just so long, that it would have been hard for the most adept personality to soothe with mere promises. Everyone expected Raymond and his son, the young count, to return; few expected this to lead to a dramatic reversal. But in many ways the younger Raymond, to whom the old count had formally ceded his claims as a way to protect them, was a man around whom a more genuine loyalty might form. He carried none of the taint of political cowardice that some associated with his father. When father and son did reappear in the south in mid-1216, hostilities resumed.[85]

There was no immediate decline in Simon de Montfort's fortunes, but one incident after another (the failure to secure the eastern town of Beaucaire, an anti-French riot in Toulouse, and so forth) revealed his vulnerability and the widespread lack of loyalty to him.[86] Simon now became the harried lord in what was distressingly like a guerrilla campaign against his troops. While he was putting down a rising in the Provençal march, Toulouse went over to a rebel force led by the returned Raymond. A long and bitter siege ensued in 1218 when Simon went back west; and at a critical phase, as the northerners tried to retake the city, the great commander was felled. His death did not lead to a debacle, but a standoff; yet, to any serious observer it would have been plain that the Midi remained quite unconquered.[87]

Despite some brief if impressive support from Philip Augustus's son Louis, who had recently disengaged himself from an unsuccessful invasion of England, the situation was not turned around, but remained barely a stalemate.[88] Simon's son, Amaury de Montfort, took up his father's standard. What occurred in the years 1219 through 1223 was a progressive weakening of Amaury's hold. The legacy of bitterness undermined every effort he made, and he was scarcely as capable or as lucky a military commander as his father.[89] Meanwhile, the death of the old count Raymond in 1222 led to the "accession" of his son, who was popular, Catholic, and, in the event, might even have seemed to offer to orthodox southern prelates and the pope a better chance than the northern occupiers both of pacifying the south and of constraining the heretics in some way.[90] To be sure, the immediate effect of his ascendancy was to invigorate the heretics.[91] But this did not necessarily betoken his considered policy. More to the point, by January 1224 the south had completely slipped away from Amaury de Montfort, and with that erosion of power the baronial phase of the Albigensian crusade can be said to have come to an end. Amaury's defeat was total; he made a formal gesture of ceding his "rights" to his old ally, Prince Louis, now Louis VIII, king of the Franks.[92]

Saige judged that the effect of the Cathar war on the Jews was staggering inasmuch as they shared in and accepted the political culture of the Midi that was being challenged.[93] The direct effect of the military engagements is rather harder to assess. At a few places where there were major battles, sieges, or symbolic capitulations (and occupations by the northerners)—in places like Toulouse, Carcassonne, Narbonne, and Béziers—there were also significant Jewish settlements; but almost no information has come to light on the activity of Jews of these places in the war or as victims of it. Gross wrote that "the struggle against the Albigensians had unfortunate consequences for the Jews, for they suffered a great deal from the fanaticism" of the crusaders.[94] But a close reading of his massive book, especially of the entries on localities where major confrontations took place in the war (before the Capetian phase of the conquest), does not reveal a single documented instance of Jewish victimization, except perhaps at Béziers.

The case at Béziers bears some discussion. The war, of course, opened at Béziers in 1209 with a ferocity that set the tone for future events. The war would remain an extraordinarily vicious one in which those people perceived as enemies of the true faith would be burned whenever and however they were captured unless they immediately abjured Catharism. But the Béziers case is really the only case where the terror inflicted on the population was carried out by people whom the Latin sources call *ribaldi*, the undisciplined detritus around the organized army. Thus, the slaughter at Béziers was indiscriminate and all the more vicious. Nothing quite like Béziers occurred elsewhere during the war.[95]

The situation of the Jews in all of this was very peculiar. And it is hard to get a handle on the precise details. One reason Jews in general do not figure prominently in the tales of depraved slaughter and disfigurement that were done by both sides in the course of the war is that so few of the military encounters actually took place in the cities of the littoral itself. These cities, if they were invested, tended to capitulate without fighting; and the victors directed reprisals against carefully limited groups. The real war was a high country war with the French directing their attacks against castles perched on *montagnes*. Béziers therefore was exceptional in many ways. It was a real city, not just a fortified rock. It was a city on the littoral with a large Jewish population. And, instead of capitulating and giving up to the crusaders the leaders of the heretics and their most ardent defenders, the citizens engaged in pitched battle. The interesting thing is that before the sack of Béziers, even while the crusaders were still moving toward the town, the Trencavel viscount of the city entered and pleaded with its citizens to defend his patrimony against the northerners. He himself intended to retire to Carcassonne to defend it against the northerners as well. The people of Béziers were somewhat confused that he would leave them to their fate, but they were confident that they could withstand the crusaders. The viscount, however, took with him the Jews (or most of the Jews) and heretics (or their leaders) for safekeeping in Carcassonne. Although it seems certain that a number of the remaining Jews were killed in the subsequent sack, most others survived in Carcassonne. And no slaughter followed the later capitulation of that town. A few of these Jews never returned to Béziers, but emigrated to Aragon.[96]

Why the viscount took the Jews with him from Béziers at all is in dispute. Sumption has regarded the act as a mere response to their value as a "source of taxes and administrators."[97] This statement may not overemphasize their importance to the viscount's income, but it assuredly exaggerates the value of the Jews as a group in the administration of the viscount's fiefs. The Trencavel viscounts had sometimes employed Jews as reeves, but rather better proof than this is needed to sustain Sumption's assertion.[98] More likely is that the viscount acted out of genuine concern for the Jews and the heretics he took as well. Rumors undoubtedly reached him that the rallying cry of the crusaders included hatred of the Jews in their "easy" life in the south.[99] To take them to Carcassonne, which was "almost impregnable," was an anticipation of the likely behavior of the crusaders' army if it penetrated Béziers.[100] The deeper motivation for this act, at least as it touches the Jews, must go back to the historic relationship between the Jews and the family of the viscount. A generation before, one of the viscounts had been assassinated in a popular uprising in Béziers. In that crisis, the only group that had steadfastly remained loyal to the family (and endured suffering for it) was the Jews of the city.[101]

It is impossible, of course, to be certain about the motivations of the viscount, just as it is impossible to be certain how many Jews may have stayed behind to protect their property in Béziers and met their deaths in the sack of the city. It is nevertheless significant that almost nothing concrete has come to light on the destruction of Jewish communities in the first great phase of the war (1209–1223). Undoubtedly Jews suffered as Saige and Gross believed; undoubtedly the anti-Jewish theme in crusader propaganda made its impact. But the Albigensian crusade, so far as I can determine, did not become a war against the Jews. What it was was quite bad enough, a ruthless attempt to exterminate the Cathars. The use of the word *ruthless* does not reflect a liberal bias; it is appropriate for what one scholar has called the period of "the formation of a persecuting society." Specifically, the papal legate had no doubt that the fanatics, if overcome, would choose death by burning to immediate conversion; he was not a patient man willing to bring heretics to his faith by persuasion. He knew what he was about and intended to use terror to his purpose; and I have no doubt that he would have been pleased with the description of his policy as ruthless.[102]

The feeling that the southerners, against such ruthless determination, had made a comeback in 1223, that they had retaken their land, was euphoric—for Christians as certainly as for Jews of the Midi. Yet the wounds, even in the best of circumstances, would have taken a long, long time to heal. Time, however, was not on the southerners' side.

After some hesitation Louis VIII, to whom Amaury de Montfort had ceded his rights in Languedoc, decided to resume the Albigensian crusade in 1226. The hesitation arose from distrust of ecclesiastical policies. The official church had always been willing to seek support from any orthodox lord to thwart heresy in the south. Even so, churchmen knew that conquest would create political problems that might complicate the real war, the war against heresy, a war that would eventually have to be fought with the tools of intense persuasion over a long period of time. Consequently they were particularly intent on looking for native heroes, not northerners, who would carry the standard of orthodoxy unswervingly in behalf of the church.[103]

In the delicate negotiations with southerners on these matters gestures, tone of voice, facial expressions mattered. What always nagged churchmen was whether the other party could be believed. Raymond VII, from the time of the death of his father in 1222 and his own ascendancy in the south over Amaury de Montfort, pledged himself again and again as a friend of orthodoxy. And time and again rapprochement seemed possible and even imminent, but in the end (even long after the Albigensian Crusade was definitively over) he never succeeded in convincing the churchmen who counted that he was genuinely reliable. Perhaps, the one—and in some ways quite minor—factor that told against him was his earnest wish, constantly repeated, that his father's body be permitted burial in consecrated earth. There was something suspicious to clerics about this, how-

ever we may regard Raymond's filial piety. Some churchmen could not
tolerate or understand why a man who claimed to be ready and willing to
confound the heretics wanted to have the body of an excommunicate and
supporter of heretics, perhaps a heretic himself, buried in holy ground.[104]
This was just one of the small items that made rapprochement between
Raymond VII and the papacy difficult, ultimately impossible. And the
renewed vigor of the heretics in his lands, and the lands of other lords who
had recovered their seigneuries with Amaury de Montfort's departure,
compelled the pope to turn to northern Frenchmen once again.

Needless to say, the temporary uncertainty of the papacy about renewing the war, its willingness to negotiate with Raymond VII, and the fact
that that willingness threatened the legitimacy of the formal transfer of
Amaury de Montfort's rights to Louis VIII were all causes for coolness on
the part of the crown. For the king knew that if the count of Toulouse and
the pope reached an accord, royal claims to the "conquests" of Simon de
Montfort would be of little consequence. Even when the papacy came
around to the opinion that no such agreement was possible, the crown
remained rather cool. When the French knew that they were needed in the
struggle, they postured themselves. This is the kind of political history
beloved of people who relish "Byzantine" intrigue, the conversations of the
back room, the politics of oily deal makers. But these "conversations" never
fully defined the situation: Louis VIII was a pious man and Pope Honorius
III was an earnest and tormented personality who was not at all comfortable with the idea of war. Their advisers may have been out to make the
best deal for their own side (how much would the church contribute? who
would command the divisions of the army? how would spoils be divided?),
but the impulses of the two great men were not far apart. The faith was at
stake in the Midi; and the most Christian king, fresh from his victories in
the southwest, accepted the charge to lead the crusade in 1226.

Military history, like some forms of political history, occasionally seems
opaque to rational explanations of events. The south, which had fought
hard against the first great waves of crusaders, which was constantly seeth-
ing in the period of Simon de Montfort's dominance, and which, with
renewed vigor, had kicked out the invader in 1223, yielded with pusilla-
nimity in 1226. In beautiful prose, Jonathan Sumption has almost given
rhythmic cadences to the surrenders: the Occitanians were "weary of un-
ending war"; they wanted nothing to do with a "hopeless cause"; or, as he

quotes the supplication of the seigneur of Laurac not too far from Carcassonne, "We long to rest under your protective wings and live under your wise government," that is, the government of the king of the Franks.[105]

Much of this is retrospection. Occitanians must have been weary because they certainly did not fight. They must have viewed the cause as hopeless because they gave up quickly. They must have sincerely desired the protection of a king, for a king was infinitely superior to a baron; and the king of the Franks was the anointed of God.

On the spot the feeling among northerners was less confident. The one long seige was at Avignon where, though the northerners won in the end, the latent feeling that a hard war was before them came to the surface. Theobald of Champagne, as untrustworthy as he had been in the campaign in Poitou, deserted the army in disgust or in a personal pique. If the seige of Avignon had gone differently, other towns might well have fought. To be sure, the aura of a *royal* army in the south, an army led by a king to whom in some way every baron was supposed to be loyal ipso facto helped problematize the legitimacy of resistance; and many towns had offered their surrender long before the capitulation of the great city on the Rhône. But the failure of well-fortified Avignon to resist with success effectively assured that there would be a spate of new capitulations without any serious fighting. What developed was a progress through the Midi, in which there emerged throughout the region a profound sense of awe and fear of the majesty and power of the king and his army.

So long as the army marched and more and more towns capitulated, this sense of despair about resistance magnified itself. Raymond VII and many of his allies were still prepared to meet the royal menace if they had to, but perhaps only if they absolutely had to. Then, on 8 November 1226, the king died. The reaction that set in was almost like a sigh of relief. In the next two years there was indeed hard fighting against the commander who had been delegated to maintain the conquests. If it can be said that the commander despite some isolated defeats was successful on the whole, it may be that this was so because even among the most intransigent of the nobles of the region, including the count of Toulouse himself, there persisted a feeling that the Midi could not sustain itself against the crown. So compromise was necessary. The opportunity for compromise immediately presented itself because Louis VIII's heir was a minor and the regent, his mother Blanche of Castile, was detested in some quarters as a woman, in other quarters as a foreigner, and in still other quarters as both. All the same, a crisis at the top did not mean that the crown, whoever ultimately wore it, would abandon the south. The south was claimed *by right*, and the best thing to do was to exploit the situation and receive some promise that in the new order there would be a prominent place for the house of Raymond of Toulouse and the houses of his allies. In the event, the count almost waited too long. Blanche of Castile was proving so tough and determined that the opposition in the north was dissolving. And there is good reason to suspect that she was already actively planning to finish the job her husband had started in the south when Raymond sued for peace.

The peace of Paris, 1229, confirmed the possession of the Mediterranean littoral, along with great chunks of the hinterland, by the king of the Franks. The count of Toulouse was to retain his title and a large part of his county. Succession to the county after his death was to be through his daughter's heir. His daughter, however, was affianced and later married to the new Capetian king's younger brother Alfonse. Some of the allies of the count also struck bargains with the crown; others who were recalcitrant were dispossessed and, now without the support of the count of Toulouse, had little hope of recovering their seigneuries. Walls came down; fortresses were razed; deeply symbolic gestures of humility were effected; the extirpation of heresy was avowed. And finally, a huge country from the English Channel to the Mediterranean came into being under the direct rule of the king of the Franks. As sensitive as any ruler or rulers might be, the political joining of north and south was bound to be difficult, difficult for Christians and Jews alike.

8. The Regency and the Jews

An enormous challenge presented itself to the new monarch and his mother: to make the collection of widely disparate peoples and lands in Gaul into a unified whole. It is fashionable in our own day to denigrate their accomplishment, to talk and write about a France still divided by custom and popular culture and language until deep into the nineteenth century, when universal education and conscription finally turned "peasants into Frenchmen." No matter. What Blanche of Castile and Saint Louis accomplished was miraculous in its own right. Like many administrative historians, I admire the accomplishment, even while recognizing its limitations and how much was due to sheer luck. In fashioning, consciously or unconsciously, an ideology of the crown mystical that was an essential accompaniment of the administrative achievement, inordinate pressure was brought to bear on some groups of people and immoderate impulses in government were tolerated or encouraged. To study policy toward the Jews, its formulation, application, and effect, is to explore at once the essence of French state-building and, to some degree, the essence of state-building in the West as a whole where the majority of countries that have been successful have followed the French model.

I do not mean that the process was completed by the death of Saint Louis, that there were no regressions or new directions after his death, or that the study of Jewish policy incorporates every major thread in the medieval process of state-building. Still, certain distinctive features of Western state formation, without which we cannot understand later developments, emerged earliest and most characteristically in France: binding legislation in the absence of direct consent; governance through salaried non-noble officials who were not native to their locality of administration; the principle of the non-extinguishability of regalian right; the necessity of religious conformity within the polity; and so forth. Deviations from this model did exist. And some features of the model can be traced to Roman jurisprudence or the independent recovery of its spirit that had already begun in the twelfth century. Nevertheless, it is by no means an exaggeration to say that the blend of these elements was new in thirteenth-century France and became an example to most other princes.[1]

Active interference in the details of political and social life in the newly incorporated southern lands was muted after 1229. Part of the aim of government was to convince local elites that there would be continuity and respect for traditional privileges and ways of doing things.[2] An alien minority was in control of the highest offices of regional government—and when necessary this minority was supported by military force—but under normal conditions the French tried to avoid confrontations, except on the issue of heresy. Soon after the Treaty of Paris, a new institution was called into existence, the Inquisition. The friars who supervised and administered it, with the strong support of the crown, began the meticulous work of prying, identifying heretics and supporters of heretics, imposing penances, fines, confiscations, and death sentences. Always this kept the south in a state of tension: the chorus of complaints was continuous.[3] But Capetian interference in the south, in spite of the fact that there was genuine concern with heresy, tried as much as possible to confine itself to routine matters of governance. The primary goal was to avoid provoking a rebellion that could put the entire conquest at risk. It was not until the 1240s that more radical aspects of the policies of the crown began to affect wide dimensions of social life. The 1240s saw both the firming up of royal control, including the crushing of the last widespread armed dissent and the mobilization of the financial and human resources of the kingdom for a Holy War abroad.[4] Meanwhile, however, Capetian Jewish policy was played out in the north and underwent growth and change.[5]

The earliest evidence of Capetian Jewish policy in the reign of Saint Louis pertains to 1227 and 1228. These years saw a time-honored fiscal expedient, a *captio* of royal Jews, while the government was under considerable financial pressure from mounting the forces to thwart the actions of those who were challenging the regency. The documentary base on which any analysis of the situation in 1227–1228 must draw is not easy to deal with. First of all, the government no longer had good records of Jewish lending. Louis VIII's reforms—the suppression of the seal and the end of registering of debts—effectively cut the crown off from knowledge of the market in credit.[6] Moreover, his own *captio* in 1223, though limited in scope, effectively meant that the taking authorized by his son and the regent could only apply to debts contracted since 1223.[7] The new king (or his mother), probably on 24 June 1227, authorized the taking of all outstanding Jewish debts. The government clarified this order on 31 May 1228 in a directive that has come down to us in a somewhat awkward Latin.[8]

The directive of 1228 makes clear that the government had had problems in figuring out just how much was owed by Christians to Jews, and how much of that was interest. Not wanting to benefit from the "usury" per se, it demanded to know what amount of each debt was principal (*catallum*, strangely, in the surviving text).[9] It allowed the calling of witnesses on both sides if necessary to make these determinations whenever the debtor's copy of a bond differed from the Jew's, that is, whenever they did not agree (*non compareant*). To avoid such possibilities in the future and in obvious recognition of the unhappy lack of information that had resulted from Louis VIII's reforms, the directive also commanded that bonds would henceforth be made in triplicate, one for the creditor, one for the debtor, one for the crown.

The directive of 31 May 1228 reaffirmed the general parameters of Louis VIII's reforms despite the registering that was now being required. It also limited the debts that were "taken" by the crown to those that were active when the *captio* was first ordered on 24 June 1227. And officials continued the difficult and laborious process of finding the debtors and assessing them on the basis of the outstanding principal they owed (which they had now to pay to the crown). In those cases where the debtors were too poor to pay up immediately or where the debts were large, the officials made special arrangements, including, it would seem, pardons, respites, and installments, sometimes over several years. Two long and very informative sets of rolls relating to the collection of debts and the special arrangements have survived but, being misdated, have never seriously been studied.[10]

These texts are published in abbreviated form in the so-called *Layettes* or printed version of the royal archives with the misleading date, "about 1233," because of certain gross similarities that the editor noticed between them and a dated document reflecting the enforcement of a different, later ordinance.[11] Extremely large parts of the rolls were suppressed by the editor because he deemed them of little importance—just the names of common people. In the printed version he supplied about thirty names of elite debtors; the documents actually contain information on about seven hundred debtors of all social classes. What the records show repeatedly is the great difficulty of getting Christians to pay up. One refrain in the records is *nichil*, meaning that "nothing" had to that time been recovered by the crown from the debt enrolled. An alternative refrain is *isti non soluerunt* or *pagaverunt*; "these [debtors] have not paid up." And one of the texts ends with a list of *debita fugitivorum*. Yet, on the whole, more debts appear to have been remitted to the crown than were not; and the sums, even if paid in several installments, were occasionally very large (though this would not necessarily be evident from the abbreviated published version of the records).[12]

Some of the creditors had large numbers of outstanding debts that came now to be paid to the crown. It was not strange for a single person to be owed by thirty different people or more. On the other hand, many of the Jews appear to have had only one or two loans outstanding at the time of the *captio*.[13] The debtors to whom these loans were extended came from a wide variety of backgrounds. The editor of the *Layettes*, as indicated, was solely interested in the knights or the occasional high churchman. In fact, many other clerics were beholden to the Jews, and the social range of the debtors (as suggested by their surnames) was wide: village mayor (*maior*), woodworker (*carpentarius*), baker (*fornarius*), miller (*molendinarius*), smith (*faber*).[14]

The documents are too fragmentary to allow a determination of the full return to the crown of the *captio*. They appear to provide data only for a handful of places. So we must imagine many times more than the seven hundred debtors to the Jews represented in these lists becoming debtors to the crown. It is only fair to add that with a few exceptions the loans were modest; some indeed were in kind. The individual creditors (even if they had loans out to twenty-five or thirty people) were not of the financial stature of the Jewish creditors of Philip Augustus's day (say, 1210). *Captiones* had come too often since his time and with too great effect to permit the building up of truly colossal fortunes.[15]

From the time that the *captio* detailed in these documents was first authorized (24 June 1227) until the directive of 21 May 1228, Jews had continued to lend money. The clarifying directive, as was pointed out earlier, reaffirmed that the only debts that the king would take were those active in June of the year before. The directive very explicitly notices that new debts (post-June 1227 to the end of May 1228) were to be repaid not to the king but *to the Jews*. It provided, however, that Christians did not have to pay any usury on these debts. (Usury was not defined.) Future debts, those contracted after the date of the directive (after 31 May 1228), also could not charge "usury." Again, usury was left undefined.[16]

The famous ordinance of Melun of December 1230 faced up to the definitional problem.[17] This ordinance is more comprehensive and more thoughtful than the earlier governmental pronouncements. It comes at the end of the crown's successful campaign to thwart those who wanted to undo the regency, and is imperious, even imperial, in tone. The ordinance commands Christians to pay their debts, but never to pay usury. And usury is said to be "anything beyond the principal."[18] To start with a clean slate, the ordinance commanded the Jews to yield up their records as soon as possible, no later than the coming All Saints 1231 if they wanted to collect anything at all of their loans. Debtors were given three installments of equal size to liquidate the obligations recorded in these records (All Saints 1231, 1232, and 1233). Everywhere, *throughout the kingdom*, these requirements were imposed.

Again we have a detailed relic of the enforcement of the ordinance, in this case a record of the Jews' registration of their debts; and this tells us that the installments of one-third were discharged.[19] In the abbreviated published version a handful of the named elite debtors to the Jews is printed.[20] In fact, fragmentary and partial as the record is, it has approximately 185 named debtors. The social profile of these borrowers and the size of the outstanding loans remain more or less the same as they were in the time of the *captio*. We find woodworkers, cobblers, clothiers, and masons as well as merchants, priests, and villeins.[21] Consumption loans are at issue—sometimes evidently in the form of loans in kind.[22] There are few big lenders in the sense of lenders with many clients (one has forty-nine, another thirty-five, a third twenty-eight); most of the Jews are the owners of small businesses as measured by the number of outstanding debts, and this is understandable given the lack of disposable capital in their hands following the recent *captio*.[23]

The ordinance went further than merely to arrange for the repayment of debts. It effectively universalized the principle that every Jew had only one lord, that that lord alone had rights of exploitation at will over him, and that any attempt on the part of one lord to seduce the Jews of another into his lordship could be met by legal action enforceable by the king with the common counsel of his barons. The legislation (the word is not too strong for an ordinance that has long been considered the first piece of real legislation in Gaul since the Carolingians)[24] further provided that a Jew could be brought back under the *dominium* of his lord at any time on any occasion. Lords who resisted any or all of the provisions of the ordinance were denounced as "rebels" and were warned that they were liable to military coercion. All of this was seconded by the barons whether they liked it or not.

It will be immediately apparent that this expression of royal policy does not differ much in its hopes from the *stabilimentum* of Louis VIII of seven years before.[25] But it does differ in its voice. The king is no longer entreating his barons; he is commanding them. He does not feel the need to negotiate a separate instrument of baronial agreement (that is, separate from the ordinance for the royal domain); he does not feel required to negotiate special supplementary agreements with other individual lords, not even the count palatine of Champagne.

What has happened in the intervening seven years? In the first place, the royal success in holding the south after Louis VIII's death had given new emphasis to the crown's superiority.[26] In the second place, the intrigues of the first days of Saint Louis's reign that had tried to displace his mother from the regency had ended with decisive victories for the crown. All of the efforts to wrest from the crown the kind of concessions that would have rendered it impotent had failed.[27] Moreover, the count palatine of Champagne, who might otherwise have raised objections to the crown's imperious declarations, was himself desperately in need of support from the regent and her son in 1230. He was engaged in a terrible war with feudatories of the eastern provinces.[28] He therefore got no separate deal in 1230 as he had in 1223, but was obliged to subscribe with the other barons to the general order.[29]

Important as these features of the ordinance of Melun are, one incidental phrase has received more attention than others: *tanquam proprium servum*. Each lord is informed that he may seize any fugitive Jew and bring him back under his *dominium* "like his own serf." This was a mere analogy meant to evoke the way a fugitive serf could be challenged in his residence; but it was only an analogy, for unlike the serf who with open and unchallenged residence in a franchise for a year and a day could achieve his freedom, the Jew was provided with no such saving clause. Indeed, the opposite was stated as normative—no matter where (that is, in any franchise) or how long the fugitive had lived there, the Jew could be taken.[30]

While the legislation of Melun was reverberating throughout the political nation, the *captio* of 1227 was still bringing money into the royal coffers owing to the long schedules given to some debtors to pay the king and, of course, owing to disputes about what was and was not principal in these old debts. In 1234, the government decided to simplify the process.[31] The face-value of any bond was reduced by one-third; that was assumed to be the interest or usury. If the debtor had already paid the king and was available to receive a reimbursement, the one-third was remitted to him. If the debtor had not yet paid the king, his outstanding obligation was reduced by one-third. Those people who could not be located, yet who deserved the return of one-third of the sum paid to the king, remained a problem. In 1237 Louis received permission from the pope to purify, as it were, this usurious profit of his by donating it to the support of the hard-pressed Latin Empire of Constantinople, the first of his many efforts to aid that state financially.[32]

The king, who was in his twenty-first year in 1234, and his mother both felt that in carrying out the *captio* their officials had been harsh, not toward the Jews but toward Christian debtors in forcing them to pay the crown by use of imprisonment and by distraint of their real property. This was forbidden in the future. Finally, the king addressed pawning. Already the Jews were barred from making money from direct lending. Obviously, usurious lending did continue clandestinely, with or without the collusion of bribed local officials. (There are strong warnings to the *baillis* about corruption in these matters in the order of 1234, with the threat of confiscation of their own property.) But for any Jews who actually obeyed the laws, it made no sense to lend money outright because, interest being unchargeable, moneylending produced no income. Pawning, however, remained an income-producing activity, even in the absence of the weekly interest payments that had once been normal while the chattels waited to be redeemed. Presumably, after all, a great many chattels were never redeemed and could be sold at higher prices than they had been pledged for. The king was hesitant here. All he did was to authorize that good men were to observe the pawning: they were to be guarantors, to insure against the imposition of the older form of weekly usury. Failure to solicit worthy guarantors would put the Jewish pawnbroker at risk of forfeiture of the pledge (*catalum*).[33]

What the evidence shows is that the situation in 1234 was tense without being absolutely critical. Many Jews were failing to obey the laws that stripped them of their livelihood. The royal accounts for Ascension 1234 record exactions from Jews in Châtellerault and Montcontour in Anjou, from others in Tours and in the environs of La Rochelle.[34] The round sums involved, 20 pounds (l.), 120 l., 200 l., and the fact that none of the Jews who paid are cited by name, suggests that there was some sort of levy on these communities which may have been related to the illegal continuation of the market in interest-bearing loans. At least, a court case from thirteen years later brought by a Christian widow near Châtellerault seems to suggest this. She argued that the Jews had once come to court to collect on a debt from her. She called it usury, but also alleged that she and her husband had actually never received anything from the Jews. Nonetheless, the court of the *bailli* of Châtellerault in the 1230s enforced the repayment of the debt. She asked, in 1247, for this decision to be overturned, and she requested reimbursement both for the money the *bailli* forced her to give to the Jews (evidently four pounds) and for her earlier court costs.[35]

The point of this example is to show that a few disgruntled Christians were making it plain in the 1230s that despite the prohibitions they thought that the Jews were still exacting usury and that it was being enforced by the king's men. The Ascension Account of 1234 emerges therefore as a record of the government's resort to wholesale fining in an effort to suppress the business. And the order of the same year about reducing the face-value of bonds by one-third was another attempt to undermine what was widely perceived to be a market in usurious loans. Finally the threatening tone of that order to the *baillis* was yet another response to the popular impression that the king's men sometimes colluded with Jews in the business.

There is no doubt about what the government intended with all this pressure. The hope, even expectation, was that the Jews would take up and limit themselves to more honorable occupations. This is implicit in some evidence that has survived for Normandy in 1235.[36] Generations of historians (including myself) have long regarded this Norman evidence as the first explicit outlawing of *charging* usury by Jews, whereas all the legislation before (from 1228 on and especially from 1230 when usury was explicitly defined) merely tried to prevent Christians from *paying* usury.[37] The supposed dichotomy has never been all that compelling, and I would now prefer to think of the Norman order—a judgement of the Exchequer of Normandy—as perpetuating the spirit of the earlier reforms and in small ways improving upon them rather than representing a new direction in or culmination of royal policy. The reason for this change of interpretation is that it now appears that the critical clause in the judgement is corrupt. What is undoubtedly the case, however, is that the king wished for Jews to "live from their own labors or from commerce without usury," even if he did not directly order them to do so in 1235.[38]

What he did order by the judgement was that Jews not frequent brothels or prostitutes and that they not be welcomed into taverns unless they were in transit and had to use taverns as inns.[39] He commanded Jews also to dismiss any Christian servants whom they employed and who were excommunicated.[40] The last two clauses of the order deal with rents owed by the king to ecclesiastical establishments and grain owed to him from unspecified (seigneurial?) tenements. The precise relation of the Jews to these matters is not spelled out, but presumably in some way a few Jews were involved in the transactions and they were being commanded to carry out their commercial roles with integrity.[41]

As fate would have it, the king's wish and expectation that the Jews abandon usury, as he understood it, did not come true.[42] But the point to be emphasized now is that in 1235 a reasonable person could think it might come true. Certainly, there was very little more that the crown could do in the matter, given the existing state of the administration. Maybe the king believed that there was no more it had to do in order for Jewish usury to wither away.

Making money from or through Jews was a useful expedient. Protecting Christians from exploitation earned the government moral capital. These were firm pillars of policy. Jews who entered under royal authority from regions that had not been part of the domain therefore came face to face with a coherent and antagonistic political program. The situation of southern Jews, those living in the two large *sénéchaussées* of the south, where the penetration of some aspects of the crown's program was slow, will be addressed in subsequent chapters. The only other Jews who came directly under the control of Louis IX but had escaped Capetian domination before his reign were those living in the county of Mâcon, which the king bought in 1238. Difficulties of governance with regard to the establishment of the royal administrative machinery and appointment of personnel may have delayed somewhat the full application of Jewish policy in the county. But this delay was only temporary, and, more important, nothing in the assimilation of the Mâconnais required any rethinking of the crown's fundamental administrative or fiscal policies, including those relevant to the Jews.[43]

So far as I can tell, then, the government had no other decisive points of interest in the life of the Jewish community down to the end of the 1230s except its value to the possible revenues of the crown and its interface with Christian debtors. Louis and his mother certainly do not seem to have taken seriously the notion, for example, that the Jews perpetrated outrages on Christian children in mockery of the crucifixion. Indeed, the sorts of rumors that had excited the apprehension of Louis's grandfather, Philip Augustus, were strangely absent in these years in France. There were no reports of ritual murder within the kingdom. The one "crime" of celebrity was elsewhere, in Fulda. Five boys were said to have been murdered by Jews; the boys "were entombed *venerabiliter*" in 1236. But the government of Emperor Frederick II moved with decisive swiftness to suppress the cult. And the papacy remained hostile to such charges.[44]

By 1240, however, the French crown did develop a new interest in the Jews. It became concerned with Jewish devotion to the Talmud. The trigger for this concern was the influence of Pope Gregory IX. The pope, with information supplied by converted Jews, came to believe that the Talmud had largely replaced the Bible as *the* book of the Jews and should therefore be banned. He was no longer content with the policy of his predecessors that the Talmud could be tolerated.[45]

It was not just that the Talmud had replaced the Bible; the charge was that it was replete with blasphemies and slurs. It was a book that, according to the pope in a circular letter of 1239 to Christian princes, "made Jews remain obstinate in their perfidy."[46] The French crown, confident in its religious duty under the pious Louis and Blanche, took the charges seriously and decided to investigate their merits. The investigation has sometimes been called a "disputation" or a "debate" because both Christians and Jews took part. Others have referred to it as a "trial," which is probably more appropriate. Some have gone so far as to see the inquisitional procedure of the church applied at the trial, which seems a little farfetched since in the late 1230s the Inquisition was still a young institution without fully developed procedures.[47]

The real problem with using the terms "debate" and "disputation" is that they raise questions about the reliability of the documentation, since there was a literary tradition of treatises written in the form of contrapuntal dialogs.[48] The reports that have survived of the Paris Talmud trial (on both the Jewish and the Christian sides) may enliven the proceedings by borrowing *topoi* from this literary tradition. Nonetheless, much of the reportage is straightforward, and since it comes from two different viewpoints, rather sophisticated judgements can be made about the course of events.

The converted Jew who had played the major role in the pope's rethinking of the Catholic position on the Talmud was Nicholas Donin.[49] It was at his instigation that the pope wrote to the princes and urged them to seize the copies of the Talmud in their domains. In France the books were seized on 3 March 1240. The trial that ensued was an impressive one. Queen Blanche was present and her interventions are recorded in the Jewish report. It does not record the presumably more hostile interventions of her profoundly anti-Jewish son. The crown was counselled by several churchmen who, during the proceedings, showed various levels of hostility to the Jews. Nicholas Donin directly interrogated the Jews, al-though this has been denied by those scholars who believe that the pro-cedures used were borrowed from the Inquisition, in which case the accused would have been denied the privilege of confronting their accusers.[50]

A number of Jews, chief among them Rabbi Yehiel of Paris, were questioned successively and in isolation by Donin, who had his own axe to grind.[51] Born in La Rochelle, he was a renegade from what he regarded as overly legalistic Judaism. He had been excommunicated by Jewish author-ities about 1225.[52] Subsequently, he converted—a guess would be under the influence of a Bishop Nicholas (hence, the convert's Christian name).[53] Donin devoted the early years of his apostasy from Judaism to inveighing against his former religion. There is naturally a denigration of him, which must be approached circumspectly, in medieval Jewish sources.[54] There is also a kind of denigration of his sincerity among modern historians of Judaism who assert that he was more a rationalistic rejecter of Judaism than a sympathetic adherent of Christianity.[55] To be sure, Christians themselves occasionally questioned the sincerity of converts.[56] But in the case of Nicholas Donin the only "evidence" adduced by scholars is the fact that some of Nicholas's ideas were condemned in 1277. By this criterion Saint Thomas Aquinas, a great many of whose arguments were censured at the same time, lacked sincerity.

In fact, it is a waste of time, given the state of the evidence, to impugn Nicholas's motives. Like more than a few Jews in young manhood in the Middle Ages, he was unable to sustain the demands of his elders for conformity.[57] The pressures that the French state brought to bear on Jewish life in the 1220s and 1230s made that conformity no easier. However he justified his conversion in his own mind, Donin's apostasy was part of a social phenomenon whose motivations and results varied considerably. Undoubtedly some converts or secret apostates had genuine misgivings about Judaism; others crossed the line for crass reasons of material benefit. Although conversion meant the loss of all chattels to the possessing lord, the lord who sponsored conversion usually sheltered or pensioned the Jew and offered him protection, including the symbolic protection of sharing his lord's baptismal name.[58]

Having converted or decided merely to abandon active loyalty to the old faith, men like Donin acted in a variety of ways. Some lived ordinary lives; some, like Donin's contemporary, Guillaume de Bourges, named after his ecclesiastical sponsor, wrote treatises *contra judaeos*.[59] Others remained or tried to remain veiled, informing secretly against those who thought them their brothers in faith.[60] The *social* aspects of conversion and apostasy generated a variety of responses: Jewish cursing of apostates in liturgical contexts, shunning of them in social contexts, licit killing of the unveiled informer.[61]

Donin's way was open and brutal: he denounced his former coreligionists as liars and blasphemers. The response, the utter contempt in which Jewish sources recall him, is hardly startling. Donin alleged that the Talmud reviled the persons of Jesus and of Mary, that it permitted Jews to treat Christians inhumanely, and that it perverted the clear meaning of scripture.[62] Rabbi Yehiel responded that the Jesus of the Talmud was not the founder of Christianity even in those passages in which a Nazarene is mentioned. In a beautiful irony—heretofore, I believe, unnoticed—the rabbi pointed out that not every Louis in the kingdom was the king.[63] The irony, of course, is that except for members of the royal family, the name Louis, like Philip, was relatively rare among Frenchmen other than converted Jews.

To the argument that Jews were permitted by the Talmud to treat Christians with contempt, Yehiel replied that the word *Christian* never appears in the texts cited by Donin, only words for pagans. And yet, as he particularly insisted, certain of the proscriptions against business dealings with pagans did not apply to Christians, as everyday life in Paris, including the teaching of Hebrew to Christian clerics, testified.[64] Finally, to the charge that the Talmud perverted the clear meaning of scripture, Yehiel explained, by analogy with Christian theologians' disputes, that the Bible was a difficult book, full of apparent contradictions and anthropomorphisms about God (God repenting, for example) that had to be explained and made consonant with the supervening truth of the spiritual nature of the divinity and its ineffability.[65]

The outcome of the trial was delayed but devastating. The Jews' arguments having been rejected, the seizure of their books was confirmed. Winds of change would soon blow in Rome.[66] Nevertheless, the Talmud was ordered burnt, and in 1242 twenty-four cartloads of the books were consumed in Paris.[67] Partly as a result of this and later burnings, only one full copy of the Talmud has survived from the Middle Ages.[68] The public burning "demeaned" Judaism to Christians in the same way as the burning of the books of heretics "demeaned" heterodox Christian beliefs.[69] Rabbi Yehiel himself, like many Jewish savants of the thirteenth century, managed to flee France for the Holy Land.[70] Scholars talk of a crisis of Jewish confidence in France, the decline of Jewish scholars in the north as the result of the absence of books, and an increasing number of laments in literary sources on the decline of learning.[71] An elegy on the suppression of the Talmud, written by Rabbi Meir ben Baruch of Rothenburg, who witnessed the events, is still included in the Kinot (penitential readings) of the Ninth of Av in the Ashkenazi rite.

> How were you given over to a consuming fire?
> How were you devoured by man-made flames
>   and the oppressors not scathed by your coals?
> How long, O lovely one, will you lie quietly,
> While my young ones bear your shame?[72]

This new incarnation of "the oppressors" was firmly anchored to the support of a wider Christian community. It is hard to know how much if anything ordinary Christians knew about the Talmud, but that is not the point. When they learned or heard that in such-and-such a book there were slurs, they could accept this judgement precisely because the sources for the little information they did have on Judaism were replete with stories that confirmed the accusation. Spurred by the revelations of converts, there were rumors about cursing of Christians in the course of Jewish worship, about solemn ritual "unbaptisms" of converts who came back to Judaism. It has been a scholarly tradition to deny many of these and similar allegations, as if the truth of them would somehow justify the Christian excesses of the Middle Ages. Yerushalmi and others have now shown that there was some truth in them: "The loathing that could not be expressed in the streets was sometimes released in the liturgy of the synagogue."[73] The books that attacked Christianity in a learned and philosophical manner are well-known.[74] There were also prayers of thanksgiving in which Jews thanked God that they were not born Christians (although strictly speaking it is not possible to be born a Christian anyway). There were Jewish prayers thanking God that they (Jews) did not worship "vanity and emptiness" as the Christians did and that they did not hail as God the "illegitimate son of a prostitute, . . . Mary a woman of voluptuousness and luxury." These prayers and imprecations achieved currency from the dawn of the crusades and were flourishing in the thirteenth century.[75]

The ritual "unbaptism" of contrite apostates has been strongly denied by confessional scholars because if this allegation were true it would imply that Jews regarded the Christian ceremony of baptism as efficacious. Without getting into high theology, however, such folk inversions of rites are common. We now know that whatever elitist rabbinic views might have been, an "unbaptizing" ritual was being practiced.[76]

All of this information, exaggerated and perverted perhaps by converts, poisoned Christian attitudes toward the Judaism of their own day. But nothing was more corrupting of relations than the belief in the reputed slurs of the Virgin. Earlier we saw how the miracle stories of the Virgin characteristically objectified the evil Jew. The gentle Virgin, more and more a divine-like cult object, contrasted sharply with the image of the hardhearted Jews in these popular tales.[77] The attribution to Jews of a litany of filthy slurs against the Virgin was (or must have been) profoundly upsetting to Christians. There is obviously a psychological component here on both sides. The Hebrew chroniclers vented their helplessness by denigrating Mary as the harlot mother, the menstruating mother, and denigrated her son's worshippers as the worshippers of a "putrid corpse."[78] Christians' resentment stiffened through their awareness of Jews' use (or purported use) of these unsavory phrases. The "exposé" of the Talmud in 1240 for containing blasphemies that were of a piece with these slurs helped perpetuate and intensify this resentment. Soon the condemnation of the book settled into the folk memory as an extraordinary fulfillment of the will of God. Those who stood in the way, like an unnamed bishop in one tale who, seduced by bribery, spoke out against the suppression, were cut down by the divine wrath.[79]

Together, then, with the economic policies of Louis IX and his mother, the attack on the Talmud signalled an intense rift in Jewish and Christian relations. It was not, however, the last act in the drama. Scarcely had the burning of the Talmud been accomplished when the general political situation in France began to usher in a new and more terrible phase in the history of royal policy toward the Jews.

9. The Evolution of Capetian Policy, 1242–1285

My intention in this chapter is to sketch the development of royal policy toward the Jews and some of its consequences from the middle of the reign of Saint Louis until the death of his son and successor, Philip III. This is a period and a subject that have engendered an enormous amount of excellent scholarship. On the other hand, the social impact of Jewish policy has either been ignored or the results of research into the issue have been buried in obscure places. The chapter that follows this one will therefore undertake to explore the social impact of royal policy toward the Jews by means of case studies of three regions of France. Out of this will emerge, it is hoped, a vivid sense of the pressures on Jewish life in France in the great age of mission of the Capetian monarchs. And it is possible that some of the conclusions will have wider implications for our understanding of the potential achievements and the limits of state power in principalities throughout medieval Europe.

The achievements of Blanche and Louis in the first two decades of the young king's reign were impressive in all respects.[1] A regency that might have been overthrown in its birth hours by any number of baronial factions had not only survived but had inflicted decisive defeats on the rebels. The count of Champagne, who sometimes acted the friend, sometimes the enemy of the crown, was also successfully thwarted in his overweening ambitions. After 1234, he spent increasingly more time away from Champagne in the distant kingdom of Navarre which he had inherited. The fact that armed forces in the deep south had managed to withstand the several flare-ups against Capetian rule was an added accomplishment of the regency government. Whether any of these accomplishments would be lasting, however, was another matter.

The English continued to watch the French situation develop and to await the opportunity to intervene in order to win back their continental possessions. Barons of the southwest, in Poitou, Limousin, Périgord, Quercy, Angoulême, who had always chafed under the external control of the Plantagenets, were no happier with the authoritarianism of the Capetians. Occasional disturbances in Languedoc reiterated the instability of the conquest of that region. These centrifugal tendencies manifested themselves most decisively around 1240. Trencavel, the former viscount of Béziers, emerged from his refuge beyond the Pyrenees to lead a rebellion that was crushed by local royal forces. Hardly had this drama unfolded when a much more serious rebellion took place in the southwest, which was joined by the count of Toulouse and supported by invading forces under the king of England.[2] The posturing that took place in late 1241 and the skirmishes and battles that were fought in 1242 have something like a last-ditch-effort sensibility around them. The barons of the southwest were ostensibly reacting to the granting of the county of Poitou in 1241 to the king's brother, Alfonse, as an appanage, that is, as a domain given over to his direct governance and responsibility.[3] They saw this as a direct challenge to their autonomy—as indeed it was or would prove to be. A decisive stand against this transfer of the county and against the oaths of allegiance to Alfonse that it required of local notables was the only way to forestall Capetian domination of political relations and arrangements in the southwest. The crystallization of this issue in 1241 signalled to other interested parties like the count of Toulouse and the English king that the time might be ripe for overturning the array of Capetian successes of the last forty years.

The war that ensued *was* decisive, but for the Capetians. In a very brief series of combats in 1242, the still-young king inflicted crushing defeats on the coalition mounted against him. His victories took a modest place beside Bouvines as another symbol of the invincibility of the French crown.[4] And yet, the defeat of the rebels was not followed by the kind of retribution one might have expected.[5] After negotiating the truces that effectively ended the war, the king does not seem to have thought it wise to undertake a policy of vengeance or terror. Despite the confiscation of some property, many lords who had taken part in the war were allowed to remain in possession of their estates. The count of Toulouse was one of these. No serious plans seem to have been made to invade the continental possessions of the English in Gascony, let alone England itself. It is something of an anachronism, but one can think of the king of France representing his kingdom to Christendom as a satisfied state, one whose "borders" or limits of influence were more or less fixed. There may well have been rather wilder hopes in the air, but the perception after 1242 was of a kingdom that had ceased expanding.

What confirmed this sensibility was the king's illness in late 1244 during which he swore the vow of the crusader. From late 1244 until his departure on crusade in August 1248, he was determined to marshal the resources of his kingdom for a successful war in the East. This involved many things. It meant convincing the English that the French had sufficient power to fight such a war and at the same time to resist any attempt at invasion in the absence of the king. It meant persuading the pope to caution the English about interfering in efforts of the French to fight the Holy War. It meant purifying the realm on the eve of the holy pilgrimage and settling outstanding disputes that might disrupt the crusade. And it meant, finally, whipping up enthusiasm in all quarters in France and abroad for the great undertaking.[6]

Most of these plans and preparations for crusade had grave consequences for the Jews. The papal legate sent to France to preach the crusade was instrumental, for example, in renewing the condemnation of the Talmud. When the new pope, Innocent IV, wrote the legate expressing some sympathy for the plight of Jews trying to carry on their worship and religious studies without the Talmud, the legate responded by rehearsing the history of the condemnation of 1240 and expressing in vehement words his support of the decision.[7] He was especially hostile to the idea of returning any books not yet burned. Later, he warned the Jews that he knew that some had sequestered other books, but that he would seek them out as well.[8]

On the financial side, preparations for crusade were devastating to the Jews. But it would not have had to be this way. Canon 17 of the First Council of Lyon, 1245, could be read to give some sort of license to the king to attach the profits of Jewish usury from crusaders.[9] But if royal policy since the ordinances of the 1230s had been strictly enforced, this should have been a rather minor issue, at least in the north. In the south it was potentially more significant, because the crown, having been restrained in its level of intervention into southern life and preoccupied in the same years with northern rebellions, had not pursued its Jewish policy vigorously. Eventually, of course, the crown would have imposed its policy with force in the south. But it was the First Council of Lyon in 1245 and a local council, that of the province of Narbonne held at Béziers in April 1246 (which reported tendentiously on Jewish commercial prosperity in the south), that were the trigger for the full application of Jewish policy in the Midi.[10] We possess two orders—one from July, the other from August 1246—that reveal the government pursuing vigorous measures including arrest and despoliation against the Jews in one of its two main administrative districts in Languedoc, the *sénéchaussée* of Carcassonne-Béziers.[11]

The king was also concerned with settling outstanding disputes in the realm between his government and his subjects. In the very first months of 1247 waves of Dominican and Franciscan investigators, commissioned by the king, traversed the realm in order to hear petitions from disgruntled subjects.[12] The investigators discovered that there were many kinds of complaints and an especially deep well of resentment against the crown for having failed to prevent its own officials from permitting Jewish usury in line with its published policy even in the north. Special panels of investigators were delegated to explore this matter fully. They were cautioned to hear only recent instances of the lack of action against usury, nothing that went back further than thirteen years, to 1234, the date of the last major legislation on the subject (the "amendments" to the Ordinance of Melun). They were apprised, too, that it might be difficult to figure out what the principal of debts as opposed to the usury actually was.[13] An extraordinary litany of complaints in the wake of these commissions convinced the government to take drastic action.[14]

The authorization of the First Council of Lyon probably envisaged nothing more than the suppression of interest on crusaders' debts per se. The crown, as I suggested earlier, even if it decided to seize this interest, could not have expected more than a modest return because of the restrictive legislation it had passed in the 1230s. Finding, however, that the legislation had not been enforced systematically at the local level, the king authorized a more general taking (*captio generalis*) of Jewish debts, both those outstanding and those paid since 1234. The usury was remitted to the Christian debtor; the rest went to the crown.[15] Alternatively, in Normandy in 1248, the crown authorized that one-third of the face value of every debt be forgiven the debtor; the other two-thirds was to be remitted to the crown, but it forbad distraint of Christians' real property or of their persons to force payment of outstanding debts. The crown also expressed concern in 1248 about whether the system in Normandy whereby the inheritance tax on Christian usurers was exacted to its benefit was being enforced properly.[16]

Additional evidence from Normandy tells us one thing more, namely, that the revelations about the situation in that province (and possibly elsewhere) had led the king to authorize distraint of Jewish goods until such time as the appropriate transfer of debts could be accomplished. A fragmentary account from Normandy in 1252 refers to these chattels being in the king's hands.[17] An ordinance from after the crusade (dated about 1257) explains that the king had originally had no intention of retaining these chattels, unless presumably this was the only way to get remuneration for the debts paid the Jews between 1234 and 1248.[18] The fiscal record from Normandy in 1252 shows that occasionally the sale of the chattels was necessary to accomplish this.[19]

There were masses of information that the friars accumulated for the king, besides that concerning the continuity of Jewish usury and the collusion of his officials in it. Louis learned of an enormous number of abuses of the population in the wars and rebellions that had characterized the first decades of the century. He learned of rapes and murders, extortion, and reprisals on people seeking justice against corrupt local officials. He learned that the kingdom he ruled was very poorly governed and that the intensity of dismay might put everything that he and his predecessors had accomplished at risk.[20] The evidence mounted quickly, and his reaction was swift. Men who had served the government for decades but who were shown to be on the take, abusive, or incompetent were fired or retired. Troubleshooters went into particularly difficult regions where the tradition of exploitation and extortion seemed to demand it. Several *baillis* were shifted from one district to another to break any developing ties with local elites or the underworld and to protect the residents from retribution for informing on them. So began the realization among Louis's Christian subjects that a new kind of monarch was on the throne, more activist and determined to root out crime and sin as far as he could, and to bring justice into the provinces.[21]

The atmosphere of retribution against the Jews affected popular expressions of distrust before and during the crusade. A few illustrations follow. The borders of France in 1247, at the peak of preparations for crusade, saw an accusation of ritual murder.[22] A "very tiny little girl" (*quedam puella parvula*), it was said, was lured to her death by the Jews of Valréas in the Jura. The inquiry that we have on this occasion conveys the haunting image of the little girl, named Meilla, last seen at twilight in the Jewish quarter of the vill. This may be a topos, like that of two seven-year-old boys in another report of such allegations, who "were wandering with childish abandon" (*in solaciis puerilibus ambularent*) in the strange neighborhood where the crime against them allegedly occurred.[23] The description was meant to evoke visceral hatred.

The father and mother of Meilla, upon interrogation, recalled the mother's search at twilight for her two-year-old daughter. The search wearied her; she was too exhausted (*nimis fessa*) even to seek official help. She laid that burden on her husband. Next day she prayed to the Virgin at the local church of the Virgin. Soon the girl's body was discovered and taken to the shambles. From the tiny corpse exuded a fragrant odor. Wounds on her forehead, on a palm (or both hands) and on her fingers, and a little hole in each foot confirmed the case for crucifixion by the Jews. She was interred with great honor under the floor of the church. Her mother added, "The pain and sadness of my own heart were much restrained because of the miracles that God did for my little girl."

One after another the confessions came. A Jew Bendig (Benedictus or Baruch), confessed that he had stabbed her. He then named his accomplices in perpetrating the further indignities on her body. Burcellas, a Jewish farmer (*rusticus judeus*), admitted that he was there, but said that Bendig was the person who had killed the girl by suffocation; and he admitted that this was a heinous deed for which he and all the others deserved to be burned. He also named accomplices—but the list was different from Bendig's. Then Durantus was summoned and confessed. His list of accomplices differed both from Burcellas's and from Bendig's. And so it went: Jew after Jew, under excruciating tortures, confessing; and when asked to repeat the confessions willingly (*sponte*) they either affirmed what they had said, out of fear of more torments, or denied everything.

A second illustration of the atmosphere created by the crusade relates to rumors of the difficulties the king was having against the Muslims in battle. These rumors gave rise to a popular rescue movement. Its impact on the military history of the crusade was minimal, but for a brief time in 1251 this "Crusade of the Shepherds" wreaked havoc against certain groups in France: nobles who were believed to be indifferent to the crusade; churchmen whose wealth offended the crowds; and Jews. In Bourges the synagogue was ransacked; the books of the law were consigned to the flames.[24]

The general attitude of the king toward the Jews was widely known at this time. His "hate" for them was remarked upon across the channel,[25] so it cannot be that the incidents in Valréas in 1247 or in Bourges in 1251 took place in an environment in which people failed to appreciate or to draw upon what seemed to be the official position of the crown. This is not to say that the king countenanced violence, merely that the atmosphere he helped create and the attitude of hate that intelligent people attributed to him were quite likely to stimulate violence against Jews or give it a hint of respectability unless he came out firmly against the excesses.

In 1253 the men who were ruling in the king's name in France (his mother, who had been acting as regent in his absence had died in December of the year before) received a missive explaining that they should send the Jews out of his lands into damnable exile, at least those who were unwilling to live by the labor of their hands or by commerce. Rumor had it that the king had been taunted by Muslims during the crusade, taunted that he suffered Christ's killers to live in his realm.[26] This may be an effort to explain anecdotally what was rather the result of the general frustration and vindictiveness following the defeat of the crusade. It suggests also that the king in the East had been reached by a swirl of innuendos and misinformation that made him think that in his absence the Jews were somehow corrupting his land and had undermined his ability to win the crusade. Hence his order. Yet if this interpretation is true, it must also be said that the return to France in 1254 that otherwise sobered the king did not make him renege on the order. In December of that year he repeated it (and reissued along with it the great ordinance of Melun): Jews were to live by the honorable labor of their own hands or by commerce. Those who did not wish to do so were to leave the kingdom of the Franks.[27]

Within a few years of this major statement, other relevant matters were clarified. In the first place, the king made clear that distraint of Jewish chattels before the crusade had not been ordered with the intention of seizing them. Nonetheless, information had come to him that besides the legitimate selling of such chattels for the *captio generalis* of debts otherwise irrecoverable, his men had used the expulsion order sent from the Holy Land in 1253 as justification to sell to the crown's profit all the Jewish chattels in their possession and had also seized any number of other goods from Jewish communities.[28] Many of these efforts could not have gone very far before the king returned to France, because there was much inefficiency in government after Blanche's death in December 1252.[29] Nonetheless, the king ordered that any goods whatsoever wrongly taken under the crown's control from the Jews ought to be returned to them forthwith.

"By the honest labor of their own hands or by commerce": these words made explicit the crown's commitment to accepting the Jews into the fabric of economic life. But on the other side there were great problems with Jews themselves fulfilling the command if they wanted to. The intention was for Jews to service their communities as Christian artisans and storekeepers serviced theirs. There was no expectation or hope that the Jews would be providing goods or services to Christians. What Louis's policy meant, therefore, was that Jews in general would have to remove themselves from the business of moneylending and, by taking up crafts that had a very restricted market (limited to other Jews), condemn themselves to grinding poverty. Realizing the dilemma, but determined that the choice of the alternative, clandestine moneylending, not be at all worth the risk, Louis renewed commissions to seize the property (excepting that protected as necessary for worship) of those who would not conform. Fragmentary as some of the evidence is, it still shows that investigations were relentlessly pursued.[30] The morally tainted profits that arose from these successful investigations were purified by acts of charity for which, with the advice and consent of his bishops, Louis used the money.[31] Right down to the time of the king's last crusade (1270) commissions of investigation were renewed and profits taken—not just from Jewish usurers who were more and more rare, but from Christians as well. Those Christians who preferred to live by usury were ordered to live elsewhere.[32]

A southern Jew, Meir ben Simeon, reacted with a stinging denunciation of the king that circulated in Hebrew. He attacked the king for exiling Jews who practiced moneylending. This stimulated, he said, many Christians to waylay and physically abuse the exiles. He lamented the seizure of property that accompanied the crown's repressive policies. The king's was a self-defeating policy; everyone, including members of the king's own entourage, knew that credit was necessary, but, Meir pointed out, Louis preferred to be oblivious to the facts of everyday life. Desirous of the wealth of the Jews, he condemned them, the rabbi averred, to a life of misery and hunger, banishment and death.[33]

The king, of course, would not have agreed with Meir's analysis of motive and he would have denied that he was intent on or a party to killing Jews. Nonetheless, if being a Jew was so difficult and so degrading, did it not follow that it made more sense to become a Christian?[34] Would it not be better to associate safely and freely with a large community of neighbors and friends? Would Jews not be happier to walk the streets without the defaming sign that Jews had to wear? (Louis was the first French king to enforce this requirement, which dates from the early part of the century.)[35] All of the ancient rhetoric was given new life that was to some degree sustained for years after Louis's reign came to an end. Pensions were offered adult male converts. These pensions were not necessarily extinguished at death. If the convert left a widow, she received half. The royal archives show mounting numbers of recipients.[36] The king actively pursued his role as sponsor at christenings, appearing himself and rejoicing in the *Ludovici baptisati* (children) and *Ludovici conversi* (adults) he brought to the font. Jewish orphans were cared for, having been baptized into the faith.[37] By 1260 a crescendo of conversions already necessitated special orders to facilitate the new Christians' integration into local society.[38]

None of this proceeded entirely smoothly. Some orphaned children fled rather than abandon their parents' religion. Some adults in crises of conscience repented of their conversion, were declared *relapsi* by ecclesiastical courts, and were handed over to the secular arm to be burned. A number of Jews simply became refugees rather than endure the pressures.[39] Others, finally, stood firm even though the king never tired of experimenting with ways, like forcing them to listen to sermons, to influence them to embrace the New Covenant.[40]

Philip III, the dutiful son who succeeded his father while both were on crusade in 1270, actively pursued the saint-king's policies. Most of the pressures he brought to bear on the Jews had been enunciated by his father or were even older in their application: segregation, no moneylending, heavy taxation.[41] Philip almost immediately confirmed his father's order that the Jews wear the sign of infamy on their outward apparel.[42] It was probably under him that the principle was universalized barring Jews from being witnesses in certain kinds of cases.[43] And of course he repeated the traditional legislation of the thirteenth century against new cemeteries, new synagogues, repairs to old ones, and loud chanting.[44] These reenactments of legislation were as much prohibitions to the Jews as they were predictions for the future. It simply was not conceivable that there could ever be a need for new cemeteries or new synagogues. When, in obvious contradiction to this expectation, the bishop of Béziers built or authorized the building of a new synagogue there in 1278, the king intervened decisively and had the building razed at the bishop's expense.[45]

Despite this evidence of Philip III's commitment to the policies of his father, modern scholars have accused him of laxity. The opinion goes back to Langlois's judgement that Philip III was a mediocre man in general and to Caro's perception that some moneylending was going on in royal France during Philip's reign.[46] Philip may have been mediocre in Langlois's sense or slack in Caro's. Compared to Saint Louis, few people make the grade for vigilance, determination, asceticism, or patience. Nonetheless, Philip's inability to eradicate usury is no measure of his commitment to the policy.[47] So much of the business of moneylending was clandestine—hidden behind the facade of non-usurious contracts or in pawning—that absolute eradication was scarcely possible. Even Louis IX could be fooled: he never saw the "usury" of the life-rent, for example.[48]

A more serious charge against Philip is that he *deliberately* ignored certain forms of usurious moneylending. This, too, is a modern judgement, an unjustified extrapolation, in my opinion, from Caro's more measured considerations. It is said that in 1282 Philip issued an order "which reveals the resumption of Jewish moneylending and, by dealing with some of the technicalities of such lending, implicitly condones this resumption." It is said further that "pawnbroking transactions . . . were the last financial operations to be outlawed [by Saint Louis], and they were the first to be legally resumed."[49] Unfortunately, all of this is false.

Louis IX never banned pawnbroking, although he regulated it.[50] The author of the passages quoted above provides no evidence so far as I have been able to determine that such a ban existed and therefore that Philip III could have overturned it. With this fact in mind, the order of 1282 which supposedly "condones (the) resumption" of usurious pawnbroking is seen to do nothing of the sort. What it does do is specify how long Jews must keep pledges before selling them.[51] In the legitimate business of pawnbroking, this was where the profit was: unredeemed articles could be sold. The old source of profit, manifest usury (a weekly charge until the loan was repaid), had long been banned and remained banned under Philip III.

The fair picture of Philip III reveals a man quite prepared to walk in his father's footsteps with regard to policy toward the Jews and other groups. He was not as able or as singleminded a man as Louis, but he was not whittling away at the great edifice of statutory pressure on the Jews. To be sure, he was well aware of the tendency of any administrative system to settle into routines, to hinder and impair the execution of policies from above. This is why he had to remind his officials in letter after letter that his legislation and his father's was there to be enforced.[52] On the other hand, also like his father, he was very careful to be a "just" king, as traditional notions required. During a succession crisis in Navarre (from 1276 onward), when Philip became deeply involved in Pyrenean affairs, we may discern this concern for justice. To protect his interests in the kingdom of Navarre, interests granted him by the regent, he appointed a French governor. In the bloody civil war that ensued, Jews, besides being subjected to Capetian anti-usury legislation, suffered physically at the hands of French forces. When tensions abated and the indignities were brought to his attention, Philip commanded his people to receive the petitions of any Jews who had not taken part in the resistance to his authority yet had lost their property in the war. The anti-usury legislation was retained.[53]

One can conclude, then, that the weight and thrust of Capetian legislation from the 1240s through the 1280s were unrelieved. Besides having the desired effect in the increasing number of conversions, the legislation was a major stimulus to emigration. The ancient Capetian policy that had striven to keep the Jews within the domain by means of baronial conventions or by command in order to allow for successful "taking" of them was modified to the extent that permission to emigrate was given to those Jews who did not want to conform to the political, economic, or social guidelines set out in the legislation. It goes without saying that the sources for exploring the demography of the situation are inadequate. In gross terms, the most that can be said is that the number of practicing Jews in the kingdom probably went down considerably from the 1240s onward. But we shall have to look at the local level to achieve any less vague impression of how much decline there was and what impact it might have had.[54]

Even the gross impression may be misleading. It was argued earlier that from the late 1240s onward the crown took the attitude that the congeries of provinces that constituted the kingdom was more-or-less fixed. Neither Louis IX nor Philip III systematically looked beyond the borders that were well-established in 1240. There were minor adjustments, acquisitions, and cessions of territory. A small band of territory in Périgord, Limousin, and Quercy was ceded to the English in 1259 in return for their recognition of the loss of Normandy, Anjou, Maine, Touraine, and Poitou, as well as for recognizing the feudal dependency of Gascony on the French crown. The loss of this territory was of virtually no importance to Franco-Jewish history because, given existing patterns of settlement, few Jews resided there.[55]

About the same time a more or less definitive boundary was marked out with the king of Aragon and Louis IX that recognized the Pyrenees as the line between their two kingdoms. This agreement ratified already existing political facts, although it left some anomalies behind. The town of Montpellier, for example, continued to be held partly by the Crown of Aragon.[56]

A real increase in territory (and the number of Jews under the crown) came from the annexation of Toulouse in 1271. The still large but truncated county of Toulouse, the result of the Treaty of Paris of 1229, had been attached to the appanage of Alfonse of Poitiers in 1249 on the death of Count Raymond VII. When both Alfonse and his wife Jeanne (the daughter of Raymond) died childless in 1271, the fief and Alfonse's other lands escheated to the crown. This may not have signalled a decisive shift in policy toward the Jews in these lands, but it offset some population loss from emigration.[57]

Finally some English Jews immigrated to France. The circumstances were these. English Jewry had been virtually ruined in the reign of king John. Whenever and however it might make a partial recovery, the English crown would move against it in takings or tallagings as the French were doing.[58] It is hard to say which monarchy was less hospitable. But the acceptance of a charge of ritual murder by the English crown against the Jews of Lincoln in 1255 might have been the decisive factor in Jewish perceptions. Nineteen Jews were executed for the "crime"; and the king of England himself led the way in harrying the Jews.[59] Or the decisive factor might have been the wave of massacres during the baronial revolt in 1264.[60] No matter. The point is that even though fiscal terrorism was equally practiced in both realms and though the pressure for conversion was probably heavier in France, English Jews in the mid-century were already beginning to petition their king for permission to emigrate.[61]

The continued attraction of England over France for some Jews was that moneylending remained licit in England until 1275, more than twenty years after Louis IX's prohibition. When, in 1275, English Jews were commanded by their king to desist from usury and live by crafts, agriculture, and legitimate business, the one last financial reason for preferring England evaporated.[62] For those who made the transition to "legitimate" commerce the rewards were not so happy. By 1278 Jews were being accused of coin clipping and otherwise undermining the English currency. For these crimes, in Powicke's words, they "suffered atrociously, and very many were hanged."[63] Shortly afterwards, in 1279, there was another accusation of ritual murder and capital justice at Northampton.[64]

Since the ancestral home of English Jews was Normandy, it is not surprising that those Jews who did manage to leave England—with or without permission—sought refuge with relatives and coreligionists there. A few years after Saint Louis's death we have evidence of a child smuggled out of England with his nurse and residing in the province.[65] When incidents like this became known to the authorities, further restrictive ecclesiastical and royal legislation was issued forbidding Jews to take up residence in small Norman vills. The intention was to prevent them from peddling or opening small shops, difficult to police and therefore difficult to prevent from operating as pawn shops and serving the Christian public illicitly. Examples of this legislation come from 1276 and 1283.[66] Presumably, however, some of the immigrants did successfully take up residence in the larger towns and added modestly to the number of Jews in the kingdom at large.

Already in the last several pages there have been allusions to the social impact of the policies that we have been describing: flight, conversion, and relapses; mob action; forced movement of population out of small towns; impoverishment. Yet social impact varied regionally and over time in the patchwork kingdom of France. To get a sense of the range and also of the depth of the commitment of the thirteenth-century monarchs to implementing, against all odds, the program of coercion that they hoped would bring about the conversion of the Jews, we must turn our attention to a set of regional case studies.

10. Communities in Flux: Picardy, the Narbonnais, the Toulousain

In this chapter we shall be looking closely at three regions in order to explore the implications for the Jews of the royal policies described in Chapter 9. These regions have been chosen not only because the sources exist but also because each in its own way illuminates very different facets of the historical experience. Picardy had been part of the royal domain since the time of Philip Augustus. The towns were commercial but small, and the mediation of local lords between the crown and the native population was weak. The Narbonnais, on the other hand, was an uncertain prize of the Albigensian crusade. Local authorities, particularly baronial, who were confirmed in their traditional lordship, remained strong and feisty. Commerce in this maritime province was extremely sophisticated; and the substantial Jewish population of the region had long played a role in it. Finally, we shall look at the county of Toulouse, an inland region, largely rural, dominated by a single great city. Until 1249 the county was semi-autonomous under its native baronial dynasty. Beginning in 1249 it became an appanage of a cadet of the royal house. In 1271 it was permanently attached to the royal domain. The transformations of lordship will be a factor that we can test against the evolution of policy and its application to Jews.

Picardy[1]

The region of Picardy, north of Paris, had been part of the royal domain since the late twelfth century. Lordly rights, other than those of the king, were extremely fragmented.[2] The greatest of all the towns (and most were quite small) was Amiens, which had no resident Jews.[3] The region was well-integrated economically. The towns exported and traded along the riverine network, the main artery of which was the Somme. Woad, for dyestuffs, and cloth were the principal native products, but there was a healthy trade in wines from eastern France to England and Flanders as well.[4]

The Jewish population was scattered through these small towns, with the notable exception of Amiens, whose religious establishment may in the twelfth century have managed to bar immigration. Elsewhere, at Saint-Quentin, Berlancourt, Sermaize, Amigny, and so on, there were families or small settlements that down to the 1230s were actively engaged in moneylending. Moreover, the legislation of the 1230s against moneylending does not seem to have brought an end to much of this business.

It was during the great investigations of the 1240s that the difficult situation in Picardy was revealed in all its vividness. What emerges, in detail, from the records of the investigation is a social and financial network of contacts among Christians and Jews that was shattered by the king's determination to purify the kingdom on the eve of the crusade of 1248. The evidence established the existence of an active market in consumer credit and the collusion of royal agents in all sorts of illegal activity connected to it. More especially, local officials accepted bribes from Jews to protect their moneylending businesses and enforce the collection of debts. In the 1230s the occasional intrusion of the state into these arrangements had been met not with overt defiance but with a kind of lying low until each crisis passed. Victims of local corruption revealed in the late 1240s that officials openly asserted that the intermittent investigations launched from Paris could be weathered and that they would retaliate against any who had the temerity to complain against them.[5]

Consequently, what the great investigations of the late 1240s permit us to observe is an elaborate and hitherto relatively open network of lending and borrowing. Christians, especially males and more especially noblemen, even Christian monastic houses, borrowed heavily from Jews; and when they did so, a group of Jews ad hoc or in an already existing small business (*société*) usually raised the loan. There was no expectation that the borrowers would default on interest payments. Informal, illegal pressures could be—and sometimes were—brought to bear. The word "sometimes" is significant in this context. Local officials who were willing participants in the enforcing of Jewish debts did not have to flex their muscles often to make their point.

It was the same for the myriad of small Christian borrowers, many of them women and many of these widows, who took advantage of the availability of loans from Jews. It is hard to believe that they seriously

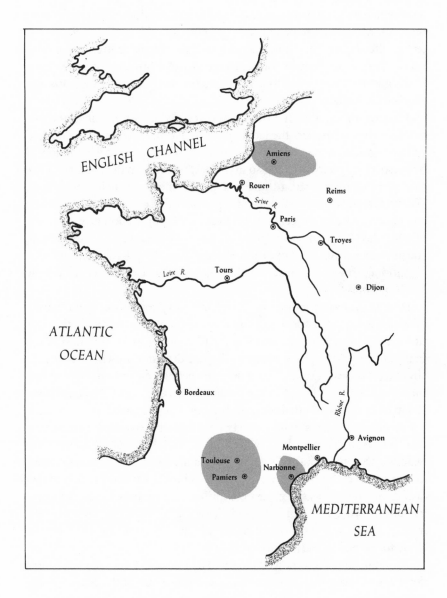

Picardy, the Narbonnais, the Toulousain

entertained the possibility of protesting formally about the paying of interest when local sergeants came (illegally) to their door to bring pressure on them. Most of these people did not know that this sort of pressure was technically illegal or that it justified a formal protest, no matter how galling it was. They were alert, of course, to the fact that brutality of any kind by local officials was wrong; but pressure, however intimidating, was not necessarily brutality.

The investigations of the late 1240s succeeded at last in bringing home to these small borrowers the fact that (1) local officials for a long time had had no right to coerce them to pay "usury" and (2) local officials who had been especially guilty of doing so in the past would be removed from office to prevent reprisals against those who gave evidence of their malfeasance. What surfaced was an accumulated repertory of resentments. Many of the complaints must have been exaggerated, or, to put it another way, much of what the Christians complained about had been accepted with relative equanimity before. The opportunity to get something back from the Jews conditioned their responses, so that the petitioners emerged as people much put upon.

Despite the exaggeration, the complaints carry conviction. A wide array of witnesses stepped forth to support the complaints. Some of this was tit-for-tat ("I will testify for you if you will do so for me"). But most of the testimony seems to me to consist of honest depositions. The message, in any case, was clear. For the first time many people came to understand that they were being exploited by (or in their words, "extorted" by) an illegal group of creditors and their corrupt helpers. The exchange, in and of itself if it involved usury, was wrong. To be sure, churchmen differed even in the mid-thirteenth century about what was usury.[6] And not all would have willingly accepted Louis IX's definition, namely, that usury was any interest whatsoever. But if there was a group of churchmen likely to accept this definition, then it was a group comprised of members of the still new mendicant orders, Dominicans and Franciscans, whom Louis had commissioned to carry out the investigations. Their denunciation of usury in all its forms was already commonplace.[7]

The complaints become a drumbeat. The Jew(s) extorted or stole usury; the shape of the complaints bespeaks the expectations of the friars not just the resentment of the borrowers. Christian after Christian laments that he or she "could never get any part of it back." All the accumulated frustration breaks out—not as violence, but as a series of publicly spoken recollections of past humiliations. Our records—clipped, formalistic, and laconic as they are—evoke numerous remembered indignities: for example, children recall their parents' involvement with the Jews, particularly how little the parents received when they pawned an heirloom worth so much.

Although the evidence demonstrates that the market in loans flourished right down to 1248 in some parts of Picardy, it also reveals that there were significant shifts in the nature of the loans and in the population served by the creditors. First of all, pawning became more and more the dominant form of credit exchange from about 1245 on, that is, as the atmosphere of the crusade and the obvious need for money that this entailed penetrated Jewish sensibilities. Jews themselves preferred under such circumstances to deal with the pledge of chattels rather than call upon sympathetic local officials to enforce the repayment of straight loans by threats or distraint of property. Moreover, prominent Christians tended to avoid, if they could, seeking loans from Jews at a time when this was likely to redound to their discredit in the eyes of those, also prominent, who were enthusiastic about the crusade and had the backing of the government in trying to stimulate further enthusiasm. Finally, corrupt local officials themselves were reluctant to be seen as the tools of Jewish usurers when the state was bent on rooting out corruption in its midst. The intrusiveness of the medieval state might be brief (though in this case it turned out not to be so), but even if brief, it was dangerous to those careless enough to ignore it.

The erosion of prominent people in the market for loans, the increased concern of Jews to secure pledges, and the generally tense situation had a curious effect on the percentage of the value of pledges returned as loans to borrowers. It went decisively up. That is to say, the Jews in confronting a constricted market were willing to give a borrower a higher percentage of the value of a pledge than had been given before. This was the only way to attract business under the threatening circumstances created by the preparations for crusade and more especially after 1246 with the commission and activities of the special Franciscan and Dominican investigators.

The little Picard towns, therefore, saw the credit system transformed. More and more it was only poor people—poor people who had absolutely no alternative—who turned to Jewish lenders and who pawned objects they could ill afford to part with, though in the circumstances they obtained relatively good deals from the Jews. I say that the pool of borrowers was more and more comprised of people who had absolutely no alternative because it is not to be supposed that poor people were oblivious to the atmosphere created by preparations for the crusade, any more than were

corrupt local officials or more high-born potential borrowers. They probably wanted to turn to other sources of credit, at least temporarily, but
found those sources (family, friends, taverners) closed to them because
they were undependable credit risks. So, in despair, they turned to the
Jews; and although the Jews in better times would not have looked upon
them as preferred borrowers, the difficulties of the late 1240s made many
of these poor people acceptable ones.

Not all local officials, of course, were corrupt. The investigations very
occasionally reveal that Jewish lenders had been under pressure before the
period of the most intense preparations for the crusade. One or two Jews
were cited in earlier times as having absconded with goods in their
possession.[8] Their flight clearly responded to official or popular antagonism. But what had been a trickle became a stream in the late 1240s.
Anticipating the coming of the investigators—and the reports of their early
successes in rooting out usury—many Jews fled with the pledges in their
possession in 1247 and 1248. Where they went is no mystery. Some undoubtedly were hidden by coreligionists or escaped to other small towns
of Picardy where the investigators had already completed their work or had
not yet arrived. Most sought refuge in Paris, where it was easier to efface
themselves in the relatively large Jewish population, a population surely
sympathetic from the religious point of view but just as surely tense because of the enormous body of evidence waiting to be discovered of
non-enforcement of royal decrees against usury in the capital city itself.[9]

Yet it is hard to believe, however heavily the royal presence in Paris
weighed on the Jews, that the city would not have been viewed as one of
the few possible refuges for people on the run. When they got there, of
course, and if they succeeded in blending into local life without being
caught out by the authorities, they would have faced an onslaught of ever-
increasing and humiliating pressures. Paris was a city of religious and
quasi-religious festivals. The most impressive recent one had been the
reception of the relics of the Passion in 1239. This had been the occasion for
the composition of expressive poetic outpourings—"lais, virelais, rondes,
complaintes et ballades." One of the greatest of the relics, the crown of
thorns, in a crown-reliquary of the apostles, was carried in a procession in
which representatives of various occupations took part. The Jews, however, were confined to their neighborhoods.[10]

This atmosphere of intense ceremonial piety re-emerged in Paris in the
1240s, making it all the more problematic for Jewish refugees to attain to
normal lives in the city. The same relics were celebrated at the dedication

of the Sainte-Chapelle in 1248. The king himself made a ritual progression through Paris on the eve of his crusade.[11] Jews who had lived on the outskirts of the city in the first few decades after Philip Augustus's readmission had, over time, and without any strong intervention against it by municipal authorities, managed to move into other areas of the city.[12] The result was that the processional displays and the pious enthusiasm in general encroached on more and more Jews as a daily fact of life. The very presence in Paris of this diffuse congeries of Jewish neighborhoods, a vivid reminder of the unfulfilled nature of his mission, helps explain Louis's penchant for issuing his orders and decrees about the Jews in a special form, or so it would seem, for Paris.[13] The late 1260s, on the eve of his last crusade, saw this emotionally supercharged atmosphere still again. In the space of a few months in 1268–1269 Paris witnessed the burning of a relapsed Jew, the royal commission of Paul Chrétien, a convert and Dominican, to preach to the Paris Jews, and the royal order to the Jews of Paris to wear the badge of Jewish infamy on the front and rear of their garments.[14]

All of these considerations make me believe that Jewish moneylending and pawnbroking and, in many ways, the general vigor of Jewish communal life in the north were broken by the saint-king. Jews of Picardy—or of Normandy or of the Ile de France—were unable to escape from the intense scrutiny of the crown even when they tried. The only place where escape might seem possible, the great city of Paris, was more a prison than a haven. That so many (or so I suppose) fled there anyway is a testimony to the power of fear in the countryside.

Now, if we again take Picardy as our test, we will find that the vigilance of the crown and therefore the fear of the local Jewish population never let up in Louis IX's reign. The province (in administrative language, the *bailliage* of Vermandois) in the 1250s and 1260s, the great epoch of the Holy Monarchy, came under the control of two of the most efficient and enthusiastic enforcers of royal policy known in the thirteenth century. One, Mathieu de Beaune, had a reputation for being the best *bailli* ever appointed by the king, and he had a penchant for progressing through his *bailliage* at every opportunity to check up on officials lower than he in the administrative hierarchy. He also maintained a reputation as being absolutely above bribery.[15] Geoffroi de Roncherolles, the other of these *baillis*, is somewhat more obscure. He had spent time in the south administering the *sénéchaussée* of Beaucaire-Nîmes before being transferred to Vermandois. That the king depended on him for both a troublesome southern province and the hinterland of Paris establishes that he was a first-rate man who took his job very seriously.[16] More concretely, the complaints against him which followed his retirement from the office of *bailli* (all *baillis* were subject after the crusade to inquiries that led to complaints) show a man liable to overzealousness in duty, not to lack of zeal. And in one especially revealing complaint, a widowed Christian moneylender denounced the *bailli* for protecting a debtor of hers from distraint, contrary to local custom (but consonant with royal law).[17]

In other words, in Picardy the battle against Jewish usury was decisively won. And it would not be surprising if the pattern of events in Picardy was representative of the entire north of the kingdom of the Franks. Paris, as we have seen, had the mature king to make the administrative system work. Normandy meanwhile had the great *bailli*, Julien de Peronne, who seems to have known more about even the most mundane matters in the *bailliage* of Rouen than one thinks possible.[18] And there were many other *baillis*, carefully selected, who were determined among themselves, either from genuine respect for the king's policy or from the egotistical desire to get ahead in the administrative hierarchy, to please the king.

Other princes conformed as well. In 1265 the monks of Saint-Florentin conceded to the count of Chartres, for example, rights of exploitation of the Jews at Bonneval and, in line with Saint Louis's decrees, the right to expel them if he wished to do so.[19] Everywhere in the north, it would seem, the machinery of government was supremely vigilant with regard to the Jews—everywhere, that is, that the king's authority and influence could make themselves felt. Four hundred miles to the south in the Narbonnais, life was different.

The Narbonnais

Jews had resided in Narbonne and its hinterland from at least the fifth century on.[20] The city became the political center of Judaism in southern Gaul in the early Middle Ages, although the role of the Jews in the wider society has been exaggerated at times.[21] By the end of the twelfth century the Jews were an integral part of municipal life.[22] They could own property outright, even property outside the jewry—a privilege extended (or affirmed *de jure*) in 1217 by the lay authority in the town, the viscount, for the *bourg*, that part of the town that fell directly under his control.[23]

The Jewish community was well-organized.[24] Its leading citizen was the *nasi*, usually translated as prince or king. Day-to-day authority rested on the Jewish consuls or municipal assembly, subject, of course, to the viscount or the municipal consuls whenever their interests were affected.[25] But the cooperation of the various authorities, so far as the evidence permits us to say, was not unusual; and it was grounded in a myth that told of the Jews' strong support of Charlemagne at the time of the establishment of the Spanish March.[26]

Part of Narbonne, the so-called *cité*, fell under the jurisdiction of the archbishop of Narbonne. In this section of the town, too, scholars feel that the position of the archiepiscopal Jews was strong from the Carolingian period until the late twelfth century. If in the thirteenth century synods and popes found the natural affirmers of their decrees in the resident archbishops, and if the religious enthusiasms of the Albigensian crusade and its aftermath spilled over occasionally onto the Jews, actual treatment of them does not seem to have degenerated.[27] Capetian pressures mounted as well, for despite the preservation of local lordship, Narbonne was from time to time after 1226 incorporated into the administrative framework of the kingdom. These Capetian interventions occurred whenever local factions, uneasy with the Capetian presence, demonstrated their opposition violently. In 1237 there was a short uprising that included the killing of a supporter of Capetian rule. Royal forces swiftly put it down. And the participants redeemed themselves by taking the crusader's vow. Some Narbonnais notables also joined the baronial rebellions against the king in 1242, but the city itself was forced to capitulate and new crusaders' vows were imposed on notorious offenders.[28] In all of this the Inquisition had a persistently disturbing effect on local society.[29]

The negative impact on the Jews was minimal. There exist charters of both viscomital origin and archiepiscopal origin that are rooted in local experience and establish this point. Gaillard, for example, has discerned resistance to Capetian policies in the viscomital charter of 1269, which permitted enregistering and enforcement of debts owed Jews and provided that no special sign of infamy had to be worn.[30] This charter reacts not only to Capetian directives but to the brief archiepiscopate of Guy Foucois, later Pope Clement IV, a southerner but a great friend of Louis IX and one of his former special investigators. As archbishop of Narbonne (1259–1265) he authorized the wearing of the sign, a policy that Louis confirmed late in the reign.[31] Guy also brought pressure on the Jews to hear sermons. The imposition of the sign and the forced sermon gave rise to a brief exchange between a Christian poet and a Jewish troubador, in which, with slashing sarcasm, the Jew replied to the Christian's denunciation of him as a Christ killer: if the poet wanted to preach, he should wear his own sign, the white robes of a friar.[32]

The viscount of Narbonne was determined that the royal policies adumbrated above not be interpreted by his Jews to mean that they were under a special ban of infamy. By also opposing the much more important legislation on usury, he was protecting his political and financial prerogatives over his Jews. That he could make this challenge in 1259 reflects the still uncertain character of some of the rights of the crown in the south. The situation would not have been tolerated in the north.

It was not just at Narbonne that questions of the limits of royal power were raised. Everywhere that local notables had supported the French in the Albigensian crusade or had made deals early, the crown, seeking to cement support, had been lavish in its confirmation of the historic privileges of the notables. By the 1240s problems were already intruding into the governance of the south as a result of these concessions. Moreover, the relative lack of good information on the customs of the south made the crown vulnerable to accepting some of the exaggerated claims of "loyal" southerners. Churchmen in the south, urged by the archbishop of Narbonne in the 1240s, claimed not to have to pay the crusading taxes. The count of Melgueil, who was bishop of Maguelonne, insisted continuously in the 1250s and 1260s on his autonomy in an array of matters, including the minting of money. The bishop of Albi argued forcefully for his autonomy in temporal affairs but was willing to compromise for a price.[33] The bishop of Mende claimed practically to be emperor in his diocese: Louis IX would be dead for thirty years before the bishop could be made to alter his position significantly.[34] Municipalities throughout Languedoc at times refused to contribute gracious aids to the king's Holy War.[35]

Given this background it ought not to be surprising that the crown, despite the fundamental concern with the Jewish question, could not move decisively to root out resistance to the enforcement or application of its decrees. It was willing to compromise to a degree that would have been unthinkable in the north; it was willing to tolerate enclaves of special treatment of the Jews that were inconceivable elsewhere in the kingdom. It did not do so with delight, but it did so. Thus, an archiepiscopal charter of 1284 from Narbonne regularized relations between Christians and Jews in the *cité* in what Regné regarded as the traditional positive spirit (the brief archiepiscopate of Guy Foucois notwithstanding). For instance, the archbishop regulated but did not undertake to destroy the Jewish pawnbrokers. He provided guarantees, too, against arbitrary exploitation.[36]

Nowhere was the crown's treatment of Jews in the regions neighboring the Narbonnais comparable. Consequently, Narbonne emerged as a haven for migrants. The famous denunciation of Louis IX that Meir ben Simeon of Narbonne circulated in Hebrew sometime around 1270 eloquently set life in his city against the oppression in the domains of the Frankish monarch, who thought he was more religious than the clerics.[37]

It was Jews of the crown seeking refuge in Narbonne in numbers that provoked a series of sharp royal reactions in the thirteenth century. Permission to emigrate from royal lands had been predicated on the notion that there could be no safe sanctuary in the kingdom itself for those unwilling to "live by the honest labor of their hands or by commerce" in the limited sense of servicing other Jews. The lords of Narbonne seemed to gainsay this high declaration of policy; and however much the crown was sensitive to intruding on the legitimate rights of its southern barons, it could not countenance this affront.

The lords of Narbonne were of two minds. They wished to retain Jews who were legitimately theirs—and it was not always easy to say who were and who were not theirs—but they also desired to remain on good terms with their suzerain, the king of the Franks. There is no doubt that a well-known census of the Jews (the *Haec est informatio*) is the culmination of this struggle both to determine which Jews belonged to whom and to monitor migration.[38]

This census, dated 1284 by Saige, has generated considerable scholarly interest. Even though I will be quoting from the manuscript, Saige's transcription is usually accurate and can serve in most cases for any discussion.[39] The refrain in this long and marvellous record is that royal Jews from royal towns—Béziers, Carcassonne, and a number of smaller settlements—had taken up residence in places like Narbonne (and Pamiers, to which we shall return). Once there, they claimed, in order not to be reclaimed for the crown, to be under the personal (and more benevolent) lordship of the local baron. They did so deceitfully, *tacita veritate* in the words of the census.[40] Elsewhere they sought residence at places to which political concessions had been granted creating franchises where the royal writ did not run. Limoux was a case in point: "which town," it was asserted, "does not belong to the lord king since the said town in a definitive act was transferred to Lord Pierre de Voisins." The claim, made by a Jew named Astruch, was met by a royal *nec obstat*: this concession, at least, did not extinguish the crown's rights.[41]

The royal conclusion to this evidence of deceit and to the inadmissibility of a few claims of special franchises was that the Jews who migrated remained under its authority to this extent: they were subject to its taxing power. The investigation depended on the *sénéchal* of Carcassonne-Béziers to ferret out information, and he searched the *acta* of old court cases and other *acta publica* and *documenta publica* to establish a list of those who had perpetrated this "most manifest injury."[42] Dozens of cases were produced and on one occasion the Jews of a "franchise," Mazères, not far from Pamiers, decided to make a common declaration of their dependence voluntarily. Even had they not done so the *sénéchal* claimed that he "could establish [the dependency] by means of *acta publica* and other law-worthy documents."[43]

Only twenty-eight of the migrants are listed by name. There were undoubtedly more, since the phrase "and his brothers" is appended to the name of one migrant (this would add at least two to the named total).[44] Moreover, as we have just seen, at one point in the document an entire community of a small franchise, Mazères, confessed its dependence. We are talking, therefore, about slightly in excess of thirty Jews. The women who migrated, if any did, are hidden behind the men, since the men constituted the tallageable population.

The men, in any case, may or may not have been married before migrating. In several instances the investigation makes plain that some of the migrants had been tallaged before they moved from the king's domains; others, it is explicitly indicated, had not been.[45] Those who had not been tallaged were thus in their teens when they migrated, young men striking out on their own. Certainly, they made good for themselves. Otherwise the royal government would not have been so determined to tap their wealth to its advantage. Indeed this concern to get at rich emigrants may explain the relatively low number of people targeted: these were the more glaring examples of the attraction of Narbonne and a few other places to the king's Jews.

It is reasonably clear, too, why the men, whether young or mature, left the king's lands. The primary reason was the oppression of the king's policies. As noticed, the *sénéchal*, in assembling the information to establish that so-and-so was a Jew of the king, might cite a record that showed that the Jew had already contributed to a tallage, "normal" taxation.[46] But he might also establish the fact from the record of a special or particularly difficult taking, such as the time "when the entire community of the Jews of Carcassonne was seized for the lord king's *taille*."[47] It made sense to try to escape these exactions, for the king routinely claimed not just the seisin of regular tallaging (*seysina* or *possessio talliandi*) but also of even more arbitrary exactions (*seysina exhigendi*; *possessio exhigendi*).[48] This distinction is similar to that in the law of serfdom between the servile *taille*, which was a customary annual and fixed render, and the *tolt*, which incurred none of the constraints of customary law.[49]

Little is recoverable about the skills of the men who migrated. Iusse Cohen, who left home as a mature adult (he had already contributed to tallages by the time he abandoned Béziers), was one of several sons in a family that had lived since time out of mind in Béziers. The census makes plain that his brothers did not join him in Narbonne, where he took up residence and went into business supplying rope for shipping.[50] Over and over again the census refers to families that stayed behind while one or two members migrated out of the king's lands.[51] It was hard to leave one's home. On this point, the census can almost wax poetic. It records the case of Mosse, a physician who migrated to Limoux, but it is much more revealing about those Mosse left behind—his father, who had spent his whole life in Béziers; his people and family had always resided there, and he himself "closed out the days of his life there."[52]

Although the number of named Jews is low, it is surprising how much information the royal administration was able to amass on these individuals, especially the details of their migrations. The government must have kept very close watch on movements. The information from Pamiers, where some of the migrants ended up, is, however, rather special. Pamiers had enjoyed a special status in the county of Toulouse. The lord of the town, the abbot of Saint-Antonin, had *dominium* over the Jews, and, although or because he was a churchman, had a reputation for fair treatment of them. Jews willingly sought out and bought his protection.[53] As late as 1279, years after the county of Toulouse came under direct royal governance, the abbot permitted his Jews to wear a modified and less obtrusive badge than that worn by other seigneurs' Jews, a privilege perhaps grudgingly confirmed by the crown in 1280.[54] But the immigration of royal Jews to Pamiers, as to Narbonne and certain franchises, disturbed relationships between the king and the abbot. Generously the abbot allowed the *sénéchal* of Carcassonne-Béziers access to the more recent Jewish residents of Pamiers to inquire of their past.[55]

At least ten refugees were uncovered. One man and his father had lived in the domains of the house of Aragon at Perpignan before moving to Port [-Sainte-Marie], a French royal town in the Agenais. They stayed there nine years before moving to Pamiers.[56] Another family, originally from Carcassonne, had also briefly inhabited Port [-Sainte-Marie] before moving to Pamiers.[57] Two brothers whose families came from roughly the same region were residing there as well.[58] All of this suggests that there was a form of chain migration operating, in which one family established itself, sent news back, and attracted other families to the same haven. From there someone else might strike out for even greener pastures, attracting other families in his wake. A pattern of migration emerged as a series of distinctly linked points.

While there was this distinct pattern of chain migration as well as many more examples of single definitive moves, one trek seems quite "individualistic." Bendig, a Jew of Pamiers, explained that his father, Astruch, had been born in Caylus but at different times in his life (*alternativis temporibus*) had lived in other royal vills, such as Gaillac and Cordes, before going to Pamiers.[59] Astruch seems more the restless traveller than the sober migrant making one definitive move or following the well-trod paths of preceding migrants to carve out a new life. Breaking with the past for them was not a lark but a considered decision, one that troubled them. There is something poignant in Jachob de Arelate of Pamiers mentioning (for it would not have been written down if he had not mentioned it) that his "father and grandfather and greatgrandfather and all [his] family were of old of the country of the lord king of France."[60]

The administrative machinery of the lord king of France followed the Jews into their franchises and stripped them of the tax immunity they thought was or might be associated with those franchises. It sought them out in baronies, like the viscounty of Narbonne, that could make a strong case that the crown's rights were circumscribed by ancient political arrangements. Nevertheless, even though the crown could and did bring pressure on these Jews and was successful in taxing them, much of their way of life in their new homes was preserved by determined native authorities who struggled to hold out against the growing prestige and intrusiveness of the Capetian state. The Jews of Pamiers, for example, continued to prosper under the administration of the abbot of Saint-Antonin (afterward bishop of Pamiers): the last confirmation of their privileges dates from 1302.[61] The Jews of the Narbonnais prospered until at least the same date under their charters as well.[62]

The Toulousain

The shape of policy toward the Jews in Toulouse and its environs is familiar. Works by Saige (1881), Nahon (1966), and Dossat (1977) provide us with a picture of a community established in the early Middle Ages which achieved, like many communities in the south, a modest level of integration with Christians.[63] The difficulty with Toulouse is that the evidence is thin in the critical years of the eleventh and twelfth centuries before the Albigensian crusade and north French domination of the region.[64] This has led historians to be rather more hesitant about the Toulousain than the Mediterranean littoral. As an inland province, the county of Toulouse had a level of trade that was probably inferior to that of a maritime city like Narbonne or Montpellier. Meaningful contacts with people representing different traditions were necessarily less frequent than in ports or cities near the coast.[65] And the few documentable incidents about early Jewish-Christian relations in Toulouse hardly encourage strong statements about the level of integration of the two communities.[66]

Only with the period of the Albigensian crusade do the documents become more abundant. Even so, the sources on the Jews remain thin. It is possible, however, to discern in Toulouse and the Jewish settlements nearby a relatively prosperous set of communities.[67] Intellectual life flourished to the degree that commentary produced by a Toulousain sage was cited by northerners.[68] Some Jews even served Count Raymond VI as administrators of his domains.[69] The majority of Toulousain Jews made their living from moneylending and commerce, or, at least, this has been suggested from later thirteenth-century documentation.[70]

Because of the Albigensian crusade, a body of ecclesiastical legislation was produced that tried to limit the boundaries of Jewish life, as if this would be one step in preventing further heresy.[71] The prevailing scholarly opinion is that even though Count Raymond VII, unlike his father, was always concerned to present himself as a loyal son of the church, this legislation was of little effect in the county except in the most egregious abuses. The application of ecclesiastical legislation to secular life, after all, was a matter that lay in the power of the prince; and existing "contractual" arrangements between Jews and princes usually continued to govern local life. To be sure, confirmation of these contractual arrangements might require on the Jews' part, some contribution or, less euphemistically, a bribe; but however they were achieved, the confirmations typically foresee the perpetuation of the traditional equilibrium.[72]

The change in Toulouse occurred after 1249, that is, after the death of Count Raymond VII and the entrusting of the county to Louis IX's brother, Alfonse of Poitiers. Almost from the earliest moment we find in him the hardliner.[73] Like his brother he forbad usury and defined it as anything beyond the principal of the debt; he forbad distraint of Christians' property to pay off debts to Jews. And also like his brother he began to apply some of these strictures to Christian moneylenders as well.[74] How effectively this legislation was enforced in the county is an important issue. The *sénéchal* of Toulouse and the *enquêteurs* of the count, modelled on his brother's friar-investigators, made an efficient and determined group of officials, but to a degree it was in the hands of the *viguier* of Toulouse to carry out the count's policy in the city of Toulouse proper.[75] There that official ran up against entrenched municipal interests and the interests of the clergy.

The Jewish quarter of the city was located in the very shadow of the count's seat of government, the *viguier's* castle. Dossat suggests that even though Christian residences were to be found in the quarter, the choice of site was deliberate. It assured a modicum of protection and also assured that adjudication of Jews in their disputes with Christians would rest with the *viguier* rather than with the consular authorities who, to some degree, constituted economic competitors with Jewish merchants.[76] As to how many Jews we are talking about in the mid-thirteenth century, the best evidence suggests that there were less than five hundred in this city of about 25,000, probably fewer in the rest of the county. This should be compared to the best figures we have for the city of Narbonne of the Mediterranean littoral. The Jewish population of that city was in excess of eight hundred in a total population of 20,000; the number of Jews in Narbonne, in other words, was roughly equal to the total population of all the Jews of the county of Toulouse.[77]

The first real attempt to penetrate the secrets of Jewish life came with the decision of Alfonse to accompany his brother on his last and fatal crusade. Alfonse and his wife died on that crusade, thus assuring that the county would pass to the crown in the person of Philip III. The evidence that scholars have assembled on Alfonse's exploitation of the revenues of the county of Toulouse and of his other lands in order to finance his contribution to the Holy War reveals a machinery of exploitation and collection that disturbed every level of provincial society. In this context, the exploitation of the Jews, first by tallaging, then by a more comprehensive *captio*, loses some of its uniqueness, but as we shall see, none of its fascination.[78]

The overall policies of Philip III in the properties that escheated from his uncle to the crown in 1271 were designed to perpetuate the burden of being a Jew. The burden was stressed time and again by the continued taxation or tallaging by the crown. This tallaging was heavy, but orderly. The king took care to respect the rights of other seigneurs to exploit their Jews, even as he was careful to guard his own from their exploitation. This pattern may be said to have continued even into the reign of Philip's son and successor, Philip the Fair, for a few years.[79]

It is not the intention here to flesh out with full details the sketch of policy that I have just completed, but rather to move beyond that sketch to probe certain aspects of social behavior that were affected by Jewish policy—and, insofar as possible, to do so with careful attention to concrete cases and individual acts. Those aspects of social life on which we shall be concentrating include questions of ritual humiliation and the different effects of the financially exploitative behavior of the government in the mid-thirteenth century, namely, dissension within the Jewish community, fatalism, and defiance through migration.

As we have seen, the Jewish community in Toulouse, dating from at least the year 1000 and probably long before, achieved a relatively sophisticated level of organization in the High Middle Ages. By the early thirteenth century the community possessed, among other properties, a synagogue, a hospital, and a cemetery.[80] It is with the cemetery that we will first be concerned. Like sanctuaries everywhere, cemeteries were under the special peace of the seigneur.[81] As we saw earlier, a Jewish cemetery was a consecrated space of particular significance. At the cemetery resplendent language honored the relationship of the dead to the martyrs of the past.[82] Unfortunately, only a handful of inscriptions from the Jewish cemetery of Toulouse have been recovered by antiquaries, but their existence confirms that large funerary steles marked the graves as in other Jewish cemeteries.[83]

To Christians, the Jewish cemetery was a forbidding social space partly because of the steles with their strange, incomprehensible Hebrew letters and partly because of the general aura of death that enshrouded it. The earliest potentially revealing incident that may be associated with the Jewish cemetery of Toulouse is its possible desecration by Christians during the highly charged period of the Albigensian crusade. Unfortunately, the evidentiary basis for documenting, let alone exploring, this incident is weak.[84] More lavish is the mid-century evidence to the effect that Christian authorities after Capetian domination paid increasingly little heed to the Jewish cemetery as an inviolable space; and this change in attitude is characteristic of Capetian policy as a whole in Toulouse. That is to say, the government neither encouraged nor tolerated popular action against the

Jews or their sanctuaries, but it enforced as narrow a policy as possible with regard to the maintenance of the outward signs of the spiritual health of the community.

In 1270 the count permitted the building of a bridge that required access through the cemetery of the Jews. The legal basis for this act was a congeries of doctrines that permitted public authorities to seize property for the general welfare. There was therefore nothing illegal in granting permission. Yet the tone of the act makes plain the attitude of the authorities, and from this we can deduce the reactions of the Jews. The count had received a request from the friars of the order of Saint Mary the Mother of Christ (the so-called Pied Friars) that a bridge be constructed over the fosse that separated the convent from surrounding neighborhoods. The *viguier* of Toulouse, who was familiar with the problem that the friars wanted to address, was ordered by the count to look into the situation further, but only to this extent. If he could be assured that a bridge might be constructed without prejudice to the rights of any Christians and without injury to the welfare of the town, he should permit the undertaking— "notwithstanding the cemetery of the Jews, from which he should take two measures of land, if necessary, for laying out the approach."[85] Dossat has discovered an order from 1278 which appears to show that the *viguier* did find this seizure the appropriate way to meet the two other conditions of the count's grant, namely, that no Christians be harmed and no municipal rights be compromised.[86]

Two years later what remained of the Jewish cemetery was at the heart of another controversy. Here the issue was the expansion of the castle— the seat, by then, of the *royal* government in Toulouse. As another act for the public good, the entire Jewish cemetery was confiscated. Presumably the steles and recent burials were removed before excavation of the site for the extension of the castle. The Jews were permitted to purchase from the chapter of Saint-Etienne of Toulouse rights to a field at a distance from the jewry that they were to hold for an annual rent of one pound of ginger, and that was to be used for a new cemetery.[87]

The violation of the Jewish cemetery in Toulouse for the "common good" in the thirteenth century was part of a broader insensitivity to and denigration of the Jews of the city and region. Just like Jews elsewhere, Jewish residents of Toulouse were to wear the *signa* of their religious confession on the front and back of their garments.[88] Order after order also enabled local authorities in Toulouse and its environs to take action to segregate the Jews. Given the present state of the evidence, it is impossible to say whether the segregative policies were exceptionally effective, but they were undoubtedly more effective than under the Raymonds. Kriegel notes that in general in Languedoc there was emerging in these years the sense that the Jews constituted not merely a group of people of a distinctly lower legal status, but a caste or "out-caste" properly called.[89]

In this context the extremely heavy tallaging that Alfonse of Poitiers inflicted on the eve of the crusade of 1270 plays a special role.[90] Perhaps it is a quirk of the survival of the texts, but the evidence reveals an intensity of encounter that is disturbing. The tallage assessments, 3,500 pounds for the city, 2,300 pounds for the rest of the county, were as nothing to the ruthless nature of the *captio* that succeeded the tallage. The Jewish apparatus of defense through bribery was not easy to invoke with a lord who ruled from Paris. The desire on the part of local authorities to please that lord with a large take in a province that had no index of what a large take should be created enormous difficulties and opportunities. The arrest of the Jews who were to be "taken" appears to have been particularly brutal. We know this only through the modifications of the arrest policy later. The count's men were to go through the Jews' houses for their financial books, for all their movable property, for all the pledges in their possession and, not least, for any hidden treasure (a point to which we shall return).[91] Later the count permitted his officials to "let out of prison poor Jews and especially the feeble and sick, women and children fourteen years old and younger, all of whose goods you are sure that you have taken into possession."[92] What this means is that the original arrest was indiscriminate—aged and young, healthy and infirm, men and women. All were lodged in the available holding places of Alfonse's lands.

The count, after releasing the *miserabiles personae*, kept in prison any "rich Jews and their wives concerning whom it will be presumed that they would hide or disguise their goods or pledges." More thorough searches or investigations were to be made into their affairs. Only after the count's men had "more fully" satisfied themselves about the comprehensiveness of the "taking" were these families to be released.[93]

Impoverishment accompanied the seizure, despite the fact that the real property remained in the Jews' hands. Arrears mounted on Jews' debts to Christians, for they had to borrow from the latter to begin life anew.[94] The impoverishment also led to internal dissent. One supposes that a community under such stress pulled together on the whole, but there is rarely evidence of this kind of reaction unless it took a particularly dramatic form. So we must imagine that many people simply gave support to one another, the kind of emotional and spiritual support that the great Hebrew poems of the north so often mention in similar context. Fortunately, the prison poems of a southerner, Todros Abulafia, exactly contemporary with the events being narrated here though relating to incidents on the Castilian side of the Pyrenees, give us a hint of the psychological sustenance among the Jewish prisoners of Count Alfonse.

> My rings have fallen off,
>   but I still have my fingers;
>   my glory is not in my wealth of rings.
> I still have my faith, my dignity, and my precious soul,
>   the legacy of my parents,
>   the patrimony of my ancestors.
> My heart harbours exploits and good deeds,
>   but having lost all my money,
>   I am at a loss to act.
> Yet I hope in the Lord.
>   Who is, was, and shall be.
>   that Time and its days will once again be in my service.
> Uphold me, Lord, for your will is mine.
>   How much longer shall the fool prevail?
> How much longer?[95]

The "legacy of my parents, the patrimony of my ancestors" uncovers to us a milieu that found sustenance in the reaffirmation of traditional values associated with the patho-centric images of northern Jewry earlier in the century. It is not my contention that this poem, contemporary though it is and southern in origin, precisely replicates the perception among the Jews taken into custody by Alfonse's men. But it seems reasonable to suppose that the gathering of children and parents, weak and strong, rich and poor, in the same context of confinement, degradation, and powerlessness evoked sentiments of a generally similar kind.

> Tell them, I pray you,
>   that they hunger and thirst,
>   though they feed on the bread of tears
>   and drink their heart's blood.
> They sit in a dark, vile dungeon,
>   [hidden away] like an untimely birth.

They lie among fleas, and man-eating lice.
....
The overseers assail them and harass them;
    the guards are under order not to give them food,
    and the ravens are too.[96]

It remains true, nevertheless, that the dissenters are what struck Christians. Certain Jews were instructed by the count's authorities in Toulouse to tallage the members of the community according to their worth. One Jew appealed against his coreligionists for their too heavy assessment, therefore taking his complaint outside his own congregation, contrary to Jewish law.[97] Yet, this breach was mild compared to the incident that led the count to suspect that hoards of treasure were being sequestered by Jews. A genuine turncoat was responsible here. This nameless and unsavory fellow, unsavory to both Christians and Jews, was kept apart from the other Jews in prison. He is said, in the Christian text that records this information, to have indulged his "hate for the other Jews." He was motivated, too, by a desire for the authorities to let him continue with his own business if he informed to their liking. He told them about money and precious goblets and jewels that had been buried by certain Jews. The Christians were dubious: no one trusts a traitor. But his story turned out to be true, and it provoked the count to issue an order that effectively turned the systematic search of Jewish homes into the ransacking of them.[98]

The records from the Toulousain increasingly reveal the Jews as being at a loss to carry on their way of life in the wake of the great *captio* of Alfonse's last years. The suspicion expressed in some of Alfonse's own orders that they would abscond—leave his *dominium* (as opposed to licit internal migration)[99]—and thus deprive him of his just due quickly became a fact of life. After 1271, when the county of Toulouse became crown land, it was new tallages that stimulated new dissimulation and migration. In 1282 we have an interesting example of a *sénéchal* of Toulouse being ordered to look into duplicity involving the *tailles*. The list of Jews identified as culprits in avoiding the heavy taxes in this instance is not long, but it provides a fitting climax to this section. The list includes one Abram d'En Boniso and his brother Isaac (along with six other Jews).[100] What is interesting is that their struggle, already long in 1282, to avoid the authority of the Capetians did not come to an end with their identification as dissimulators in that year. There was always hope of escape. They tried again.

We will find them two years later living in Pamiers or, rather, in the *franchise* of Pamiers, claiming immunity and trying to eke out a livelihood, when the Capetian state catches up with them once more.[101] The determination of these Jews in the face of the encroachments of the crown of France bespeaks an attitude quite at variance with that in another of the contemporary prison poems of Todros Abulafia; and it warns us against hasty generalizations. Todros would write, "This is the way of Time: he lifts up the dissolute, and as the base are raised the noble are debased."[102] His fatalism is a kind of retreat from action. Others, as we have seen, capitulated and informed. Yet, most—and if it had not been most, the Christian records would glory in the tale—most Jews endured and actively sought to improve their lot at considerable danger to themselves. When the pressures at last became too great, they neither retreated into quietism nor turned their back on the wisdom of the elders. They chose the very difficult path of exile.[103] The tragedy of the years to come was that the French crown, and western European principalities in general, gave a bitter imprimatur to this new diaspora.

III

Journeys to Dark Lands:
The Era of the
Last Capetians, 1285–1328

11. Prelude to the Great Expulsion

In 1285 Philip III died while undertaking a short but costly expedition against the king of Aragon. Called a crusade because the French were defending the political interests of the papacy by the expedition, the war ended in ignominious failure for the French.[1] It was an unexpected disaster. The history of French arms in Europe had been uniformly glorious since the great conquests of Normandy in 1202–1204. To be sure, Louis IX's crusades to the East had not succeeded. However, partly because the papacy could be blamed, partly because of the insufficient contribution of other princes, and partly because the "sins" of the army could be adduced for the failure of a "Holy" war, no undermining of French self-confidence per se occurred.[2] It seems certain that the new king, Philip IV the Fair, blamed the papacy to some degree for the fiasco in Aragon as well, but there is little indication in the sources that this was an effective excuse.[3]

The new king thus came to power in defeat, trying to make the best of a very difficult situation in the Pyrenees and to effect a sober retreat to Paris. He did not expect to have any other formidable problems immediately before him, despite the defeat. The latter part of the reign of his grandfather, Louis IX, and the reign of his father had brought more than thirty years of continuous peace to the kingdom. The economy was generally prosperous, although there was sluggishness in a few areas.[4] Local resistance to Capetian domination took subtle forms, such as we have seen in the legal defense of privilege in the Narbonnais.[5] Increasingly even this resentment was directed less against the Capetians per se than against northern functionaries who had "excessive" power in local affairs. Acceptance of the dynasty, in other words, was secure; patriotism, let alone respect for the people who ran the machinery of the government, was somewhat less so.[6] All the same, there was no sense of crisis, no serious fear that southerners might see the French defeat in the Pyrenees as an opportunity to turn back the clock on the conquest of the south as might have occurred forty years before.

In line with this sense of continuity in the face of defeat, there was no immediate reevaluation of major policies in the kingdom. The first order of business in 1285 was the securing of the Aragonese frontier, a matter that turned out to be relatively easy even before the Aragonese king died several months later (8 November 1286).[7] As the situation stabilized, the new king, who was in his late teens, was able to turn his attention to other matters, that is, to put his own personal stamp on governance. Whether he would go the way of his father and be content to follow in the footsteps of the revered Louis IX or would set off in a definitively new direction may seem a choice that only a modern could propose. Yet, while there was deep respect for tradition and custom at all levels of medieval society and political culture, there were ways and opportunities to give a distinctive style and edge to governance. Philip II Augustus had done so almost as soon as he became king in 1179 by shattering his father's policy toward the Jews. Louis VIII had accomplished something of the same thing when he, almost as his first act of state in 1223, overturned the considered policy of Philip Augustus toward the same group of people.[8]

Philip the Fair, unlike these ancestors, avoided the dramatic opening gambit that would distance himself from the past reign. Nonetheless, the group that had been targeted by Philip's ancestors was particularly situated for such a gesture in the 1280s. In location after location on the borderlands of France, princes and their counsellors were abandoning the policy, dear to Saint Louis, of attempting to coerce Jews to convert by means of economic and social disabilities and were offering them instead a starker choice: convert or depart. It is no secret that Philip eventually did adopt this policy, but only in 1306, a generation or so after the movement began in earnest in his neighbors' lands. Why he hesitated is an interesting and important question to which we shall have to return. For now we need to look at how the wave of expulsions outside of France from the 1280s on affected the political and demographic history of the kingdom.

Mass expulsion was not a new phenomenon. Philip II Augustus had expelled the Jews in 1182 and seized their real property, but had also provided that converts who remained could retain theirs. We have seen that his expulsion, given the size of the royal domain, affected only a few thousand Jews. There had also been an expulsion of the Jews from Brittany in 1240. Once again, the number of Jews affected was very small (at most a few hundred), and the sources on the incident are correspondingly thin.[9] From the time of the expulsion of Breton Jewry, however, expulsion or threats to expel tended to be directed against a particular group of Jews, namely "usurers." It is typically said that the old Augustinian argument had force here. The Jews had to remain as a remnant to testify to the truth of Christianity at the end of time.[10] Pressures to get them to convert were licit, expulsion of "criminals" like usurers was licit, but the mass expulsion of all Jews just for being Jews was not a policy affirmed or supported by the official church, one or two exceptional preachers notwithstanding.

Recently doubt has been thrown on the power of the Augustinian judgement to influence political life. It was all well and good to talk about the necessity for the presence of Jews to serve as witnesses at Judgement. It was quite another thing to say that this or that principality had to be the locus for the remnant and should not expel the Jews.[11] Increasingly, too, scholars are revaluing interpretations of the Last Days and especially the eschatological fervor in the time of Philip the Fair. It had long been thought that the Jews would follow Anti-Christ, though their conversion by the saints or prophets was a foregone conclusion.[12] This tradition became harsher in Philip's time, an indication of the intensity of the suspicion in which the Jews were held. Anti-Christ would be the Messiah of the Jews, born of the perfidy of the Jews, a Jew himself. Perhaps, some said, the Jews would not convert.[13]

Meanwhile, scholars' valuation of the preachers who urged banishment of the Jews has undergone a change. They no longer seem oddities but rather articulators of a wide range of social attitudes, such as those discernible in the enormously popular passion plays. In those plays audiences responded enthusiastically to the Jews as Christ killers and especially to one character, sometimes called Stephaton, who gave Jesus vinegar to drink immediately before his death on the cross. This man, depicted in manuscripts, stained glass, sculpture, and wall painting as a misshapen, bloated, perverse Jew, was widely regarded as the last tormentor of the living Jesus. Part sinister presence in the plays, with a voice that was more beastly than human, with a red wig or filthy clothes and perverse poses, he was also partly a clown. Consequently, good and sober churchmen frowned upon the excesses of the passion plays, but the plays retained their popularity.[14] When preachers evoked the image of the unnatural and beastly Jew they drew upon this popular lore and effectively opposed the milder Augustinian theme in Christians' understanding of the place of the Jews in salvational history. Theirs was a picture that deeply affected many princes as well.

Charles II of Anjou is a case in point. Charles was the nephew of Louis IX. His father, Louis's brother, had been granted the appanage of Anjou and Maine in 1246 and with it rights of governance in the provinces.[15] After his father died in 1286 and after his own liberation as a hostage in the negotiations to settle the issues that precipitated the crusade against Aragon, Charles II pursued his own policies. His first major act was the expulsion of Jews from his appanage. The order is dated 8 December 1289; the campaign in its wake must have taken at least several weeks, perhaps months.[16]

The action was comprehensively defended. The presence of the Jews, not just Jewish usurers, was reprehensible to the Christian religion: Jews sought to seduce both sexes from the true creed. Jews were indeed perfidious usurers. (So, too, Christian usurers were expelled.) But Jewish men dared to engage in sexual relations with the women of the true faith.[17] The Christian population granted a capitation tax of six pennies and a three-shilling hearth tax as a boon to their count for the expulsion.[18]

The Jews thus expelled, probably about one thousand, took the road as refugees northward to Normandy and east to the Ile de France. Most, because of the concentration of the Jewish population of the appanage in southern Anjou, would have moved into the neighboring Loire valley provinces of Touraine and Poitou. Few if any went across the channel to England, where the distressing plight of English Jews was already well-known.[19] And it must be presumed that none could have sensibly opted for Brittany, whose Jews had been expelled en masse in 1240.

Whether directly in concert with Charles II or not, King Edward I of England expelled the Jews of Gascony and England at about the same time—explicitly, in the English case (1290), for a grant.[20] This fact, which has made the expulsion appear to be an act of economic policy, obscures the long series of ritual murder accusations that characterized English life in the thirteenth century.[21] The force of the merchants' voices among others was that much stronger because they spoke to a shared notion of the Jews as nefarious. In the event, the attrition of Jewish population in England in the thirteenth century, the economic constraints put on them in the 1270s, and the charges of coin clipping made against them soon after created an opportune moment for Christian merchants to eliminate this source of competition. On less vulnerable competitors, like the alien Italian merchants, their cries for government action had less effect. They managed to have the Jews expelled not simply because they were competitors but because they were Jewish competitors.

The influx into royal France of Gascon Jews, expelled in 1288 (we shall return to the question of English Jews later), caused an immediate problem. They set out from their homeland very poor, having been subjected over the past two decades to extremely heavy taxation based, quite possibly, on an extensive investigation or census of them.[22] Some of these Gascon Jews went south into Navarre.[23] The vast majority either set out for cities in France, like Toulouse and Carcassonne to the east, or to thriving regions like Poitou to the north. It was the immigration to Poitou that precipitated a crisis. This immigration, combined with the forced migration of Jews from Anjou-Maine into the same region the year or so before, caused the authorities in Poitou to feel compelled to make their complaints known to the king. Philip IV responded by issuing orders on 1 May 1291 for the arrest of the refugees and the receivers of refugees in the county.[24] Jewish communities rallied to their coreligionists' defense and offered sufficient inducement to the king's ministers to bring about a change in policy. The king rescinded his authorization for a forced withdrawal of the refugees and their supporters from the county (not before a few had already departed)[25] in return for the Jews' submission to a residence tax of six pennies per hearth.[26] The king, nonetheless, supported the efforts of certain localities that, in the first flush of the arrest order, had expelled their Jews. Niort, for example, was confirmed in the removal of its Jews. The Jewish cemetery there was sold by 1296 and later reconsecrated as a Christian burial place.[27]

English Jews meanwhile crossed the channel to Normandy and, thence proceeded, many of them, to Paris. Philip the Fair resented the incursion, although the numbers (about one thousand, perhaps a few hundred more) were small. The slight numbers reflect the voluntary and clandestine emigration from England in the decades before Edward's expulsion. Some of these earlier emigrants, as we have seen, took up residence in Normandy. Their settlement there, in turn, ushered in a spate of restrictive legislation under Philip III in the 1270s and 1280s.[28] The new forced migration of 1290 confirmed the pattern of resettlement at least temporarily.[29] Because of restrictions on residence in Normandy, however, there was a decided bias among the migrants to abandon their temporary refuge in Normandy for the broader economic possibilities of Paris.

By the end of the thirteenth century a minimum of 7%, but possibly as many as 20% of the Jews of Paris (the total being variously estimated at one thousand to fifteen hundred in a city of over one hundred thousand) were English immigrants.[30] Moreover, if we compare the yearly tax lists of the city, it would appear that 76% of the Jews living in Paris in 1297 had not been taxable heads of households six years before.[31] Some of this, of course, was the result of natural attrition/replacement or, possibly, forced consolidated resettlement of the native city population.[32] Much of it was the result of English immigration and the setting up of new households. Still more had another source: forced migration out of small towns.[33]

In fact, Philip IV had originally forbad residence to the English expellees of 1290.[34] Many of their coreligionists were ready to fine for the privilege; so, the king relented.[35] Some smaller towns picked up this population. The Jewish population of Coutances, for example, seems to have increased around 1291 and 1292, prompting the naming of a street "rue aux Juifs" in the latter year or thereabouts.[36] The new Jews in towns like Coutances probably peddled second-hand wares and hawked folk medicine to eke out their livelihood. Despite distrust of Jews, no product was more seductive than curatives among people who were sick or in pain. Also, no commercial activity was more likely to provoke a swift reaction on the part of the crown. The king issued orders to crack down on the hawkers of these medicines and to make an example in punishing them (*punias quod pena eorum sit aliis in exemplum*).[37] At the same time he moved to prohibit new settlement in small towns and even broke up older settlements in some towns.[38] The demographic situation in Paris that we have already detailed owed much of its volatility to these acts of the king.

Even in the large towns, "new" or superfluous jewries or concentrations of Jewish housing were suppressed.[39] The indirect pressures to consolidate settlement may have been so severe in Paris that despite the influx of English immigrants, the net number of Jewish residences in the city declined in the 1290s from 125 taillable households to 86.[40] To be sure, the number of taillable hearths is not a perfect indicator of the number of residences. Some hearths may have left the tax rolls because of impoverishment. The wealth that the Lombards were accumulating by "commerce" in the 1290s may provide something of a yardstick here. The tax rolls show the Lombards growing in wealth. The richest Lombards by the end of the century were twice as rich as the richest Jews and there were far more of them. The Jews, in other words, were losing the economic war in Paris as well.[41]

It is possible but less likely that some of the Jews living in Paris at the end of the thirteenth century were immigrants from the southeast, the county of Nevers. However that may be, it was in 1294 that the count of Nevers, Louis I, also completed his expulsion of Jews in the tradition that his counterparts in the west had recently established. The situation in the county of Nevers was somewhat more complicated, however. The Jews of the Nivernais had long lived in a precarious but relatively prosperous existence in that county.[42] Jewish life has left documentary and archeological traces here and there throughout the region: at Cosne, Verriers, and the capital, Nevers, where a *rue aux Juifs* was located in the extra-mural parish of Saint-Arigle, commercially the "most important" parish in the city.[43] As late as 1909 traces of the synagogue were still to be seen.[44]

The count had earlier moved against the Jews of the county, but many had found temporary safety in the *bourg* of the capital city, a district under the jurisdiction of the priory of Saint-Etienne of Nevers, a religious house claiming royal protection.[45] The count recognized his problem but was not deterred. He sought with great effort and obtained the license of the king and the permission of the procurator of the priory to have the Jews expelled even from the *bourg* on 20 March 1294.[46] From that time forward Nivernais Jews would have had to seek refuge with their numerous co-religionists in the royal domain or in eastern regions with Jewish populations.

In sum, what all this means—the expulsions from Anjou and Maine, England and Gascony, and the county of Nevers—is that Paris and a few other great towns in royal France became centers of immigrant Jewish populations. The immigrants from great distances were joined by other persons displaced from smaller towns or from isolated clusters of residence in the larger towns themselves. Several of the Jews' occupations, like the hawking of medicine, fell under careful scrutiny and were proscribed. There was growing impoverishment because of new residence taxes on the immigrants or fines on the native Jews who petitioned in favor of the immigrants. The fact that many of the immigrants came to royal France with virtually nothing and had to depend on the generosity of already poor communities compounded the difficulties of the situation.

As to what the princes and their Christian subjects obtained materially from these scattered expulsions, much can be conjectured. Gascon and English Jews had very little left to them after years of exploitation. Edward I was kinder than most princes in letting the Jews depart with their chattels, and he was careful to see that they were not abused as they left his domains.[47] What he gained from the confiscation of the property that the Jews could not take with them he divided among the four mendicant orders.[48] In return for the expulsion, of course, he received a heavy subsidy in the form of taxation that is said to have more than offset the loss of the Jews to the royal fisc.[49]

In Anjou and Maine, scattered evidence shows that synagogues, cemeteries, schools, and market stalls were transferred from the Jews as lease-holders to Christian leaseholders.[50] We have already seen that at Niort the cemetery went into Christian hands as a result of the move against those Jews who welcomed immigrants in 1291.[51] The synagogue similarly changed hands in Niort.[52] The relative lack of documentation reflects both the small numbers of Jews affected by the expulsions from Anjou-Maine and Niort, and the fact that the real property in the Jews' possession in the Loire Valley was leased. Transfer of leases as opposed to transfer of ownership generates more ephemeral records.[53]

Nevers was rather different. The Jews in Nevers probably owned land and buildings outright. At least, tenure by "free allod" was common in the region.[54] Even so, little survives to document the transfer of property from Jews to Christians in the aftermath of the expulsion that was completed in 1294.[55] The municipal organization in the capital city that might have monitored or licensed such transfers was too primitive to preserve records.[56] The municipality itself had no purchasing authority, so far as I can tell; so it did not benefit from the expulsion.[57] The one possible relic of the transfer of property that I have found touches not upon Nevers itself but upon the count's expulsion of the Jews from the countryside preliminary to the expulsion from the city. It is a fragmentary *taille* roll of 1322 listing the payments of hundreds of dependents of the cathedral chapter of Saint-Cyr of Nevers, including those living at the village of Fontaines.[58] The residents of three small houses clustered together paid three shillings, one shilling, and two shillings for the *taille*. The houses are remarkable for having once belonged to Jews (or to people with Jewish names): Malochot, Sagetus, Michaelis Arrondoth.[59] If my conjecture is correct, this is evidence of a village with a small jewry that died almost without a trace—a fact that must be replicated in scores of other instances not only in the Nivernais but in Anjou and Maine as well. It suggests too that in the smaller expulsions that we have been discussing, property was transferred from Jews to many individual Christian lessees or owners, though in all cases the intermediary must have been the expelling prince who profited from the transactions.

This brief sketch of the series of expulsions in the borderlands of royal France and the pressure they exerted on the French crown needs to be contextualized by developments in Jewish policy more generally. As indicated earlier Philip the Fair did not use the Jews as an object to make a major statement of his authority at the time of his accession. Rather, he affirmed the traditional attitude of the crown as it had been expressed over the half-century before his reign. On the positive side, he renewed tradi-tional protection of property like synagogues and cemeteries necessary to the Jewish cult.[60] On the negative side he reaffirmed with perhaps added force the restrictions imposed by Louis IX and Philip III.[61]

The year 1285 saw the confirmation of the order for Jews to wear the *rouelle* or badge of their Jewishness on their clothing. A supplementary measure authorized the government itself to sell the badge, an innovation that assured uniformity.[62] Sales never brought in much revenue (this was hardly a major moneymaking activity); yet the move does betoken one of the most highly developed instincts of French government in Philip the Fair's time: the desire to have every administrative impulse or program pay for itself.

More important than the Jewish badge was the continuation in general of the policy against usury. Philip countenanced no relaxation of Louis IX's prohibition. He made this clear several times in the course of his reign.[63] Saige, examining the information for the south, sees hypocrisy at work here. Philip emerges in his portrait as a king who was determined to impugn the legitimate wealth of southern Jews and who, to do so, charged them with usury and presumed that even apparently legitimate debts (pur-chases on credit) had usury built into them.[64] This may be true, but the attitude was traditional. Louis IX too had become convinced that approx-imately one-third the face value of bonds for so-called legitimate debts was usury.[65] In 1292, when the *sénéchaussée* of Carcassonne was visited with an investigation that was designed to get at the hidden profits of usury, Philip was walking in the footsteps of his grandfather.[66]

Philip the Fair was also concerned, as his predecessors had been, with preserving his jurisdiction over the Jews. The problem here was no longer, as it had been under Louis VIII, primarily the pretensions of northern barons. Even the position of the count palatine of Champagne was irrel-evant, for Philip had married the heiress to Champagne and assumed the countship himself in 1284.[67] The problems were with the church and with southern barons. The ecclesiastical issue was grounded in the Inquisition's efforts to pry into the lives of heretics, suspected heretics, and friends and supporters of heretics in Occitania. It was bad enough, as Louis IX and Philip III had discovered, that southern barons claimed privileges with regard to Jews that seemed excessive.[68] That the Inquisition in its system-atic snooping should from time to time transgress the boundary of royal jurisdiction was intolerable. Philip the Fair was conventionally religious. He did not hate the church or its institutional apparatus, but his government zealously defended his prerogatives whenever these were threatened. Indeed, the orders that warn his officials to be very wary of moving against Jews, who were so-called *relapsi*, at the instigation of the inquisitors declare quite explicitly the king's full support for the appropriate work of the Inquisition.[69]

The successful defense of Philip's jurisdictional interests against the Inquisition, and, to a lesser extent, the maintenance against a few southern barons with special prerogatives of the tallageability of the Jews to the crown's profit, assured that there would be a good return in the south on the periodic exactions on the Jews.[70] This needs to be stressed, because the real concentration of Jews was in the south of the kingdom. It was recognized that any erosion of the king's prerogative over the Jews in this region would have a considerable impact on the financial value of taxing or taking the Jews.[71] Under Philip the Fair as under his father, taxing continued regularly, it seems. Abundant evidence survives for almost every year from the beginning of the reign down through 1301.[72]

Records from 1286, 1288, and 1293 establish that the government assigned Jews to collect the tallages.[73] The crown also issued safe-conducts for the execution of these assignments.[74] To the extent that his interest was in getting the tallages fully collected, Philip the Fair is known to have ordered government officials to compel the Jews' debtors to pay legitimate debts so that the king could be paid.[75] That is to say, if, for example, a Christian subject of the king living near Narbonne had bought an article on credit from a Jewish merchant of the city who was liable to the royal taille, the crown would enforce the payment of the debt in order to secure the alloted contribution of the Jew to the overall tallage. The care with which the crown directed its efforts to tax the Jews shows up in the returns. Partial figures demonstrate that sums as high as fifteen thousand pounds per year might be collected.[76]

This burden was significant. Arrears were commonplace.[77] Partly this was because Christians could not always pay their debts to the Jews swiftly. Partly, however, the arrears resulted from efforts on the part of Jews to provide evidence of some special exemption from taxation. In one notorious case in 1290, Philip annulled letters on exemption that he said had been fraudulently obtained.[78] A month later he ordered that southern Jews who were in arrears ought to be brought up to Paris to answer for their offense.[79] The concern with the taille grew and grew until the kind of census that we saw in the *Haec est informatio* of 1284 became almost a commonplace in the south; and searching after defaultors who claimed exemption or who fled to franchises and other lordships became a daily fact of royal officials' lives.[80]

Collection of the taille did not endear the Jewish assessors and receivers to their coreligionists in Philip's time any more than it had in the time of Alfonse of Poitiers.[81] We must keep in mind that the *taillatores'* task was a very difficult one. They walked a tightrope between maintaining the safety of the Jewish community as a whole against the royal wrath and the deep offense felt by tax-paying Jews at the participation of their brethren in the exploitation.[82] The charge made by some Jews was that these *taillatores* exacted far more from them than the king required and did so in order to line their own pockets.[83] Charges like this excited the crown's interest and precipitated careful investigations that in some ways undermined the solidarity of the Jewish community, but also, if they became too harsh and intrusive, must have reinforced it.

A final area in which Philip maintained the policies of his predecessors—with some brief interruptions—concerns the justiciability of Jews. Jews were under the ordinary jurisdiction of the seneschals in the south. As more and more disputes arose in the course of the heavy tallaging, the judicial authorities in Toulouse conceded a special judicature to the Jews, this probably in 1288.[84] Whether all the Jews were happy with this development or not, it was supported by influential members of the Jewish community.[85] Philip was of two minds. Not long after the establishment of the separate judicature he suppressed it.[86] On the other hand, not long after the suppression he renewed it in a much more limited way by commissioning one special judge.[87] The judge's name was Laurentius Paschalis (Lawrence Easter), a name which suggests that the judge was a converted Jew. Philip was certainly not opposed to using converts in high administrative posts; and this would have been an appropriate post for a man who read Hebrew. Philip's own godson, Philip the Convert, became one of the great administrators of the royal forests.[88] Nevertheless, by 1304, this special commission appears to have expired, and Jews, in the tradition of Philip's predecessors, returned to the ordinary justiciability of the seneschals.[89]

Philip's early policies toward the Jews evince a deep resentment and suspicion of them. This was vividly manifested not too long into his reign by an incident in Champagne. Champagne Jewry, as we have seen, had had its own rather distinctive history in the late twelfth and early thirteenth century. From time to time the counts palatine imitated the Capetians; more often they did not. Or such was the situation down to the mid thirteenth century.[90] Louis IX had exercised considerably more influence in Champagne for a longer period of time than any of his predecessors. Champenois contributions to his crusades, for instance, were extraordinarily high in military personnel.[91] When Louis "took" his Jews to help pay for his wars, the count palatine "took" his as well.[92]

Nonetheless, there is a pervasive sense in the literature that the insistently harsh policies of the Capetians were mitigated in Champagne as long as there was a native count who took an active interest in the governance of the county; and this was the situation from 1253 until 1284.[93] Jewish institutions thrived.[94] Jewish population thrived.[95] Moreover, Jews are seen in occupations other than moneylending, occupations that might have been catering to the needs and wants of the Christian community.[96] Wilder claims have also been made. Early historians saw profound intercultural relationships, and generalized far beyond Champagne to France as we know it—north, south, east, and west. Most of these claims are now rejected.[97] Yet in 1968 Kraus argued for a "cordiality of relationship" and "friendly [intellectual] intercourse" in Champagne in the thirteenth century on the basis of a single lancet of Troyes Cathedral that plausibly depicts a disputation.[98] Why a depiction of a disputation should suggest cordiality is not made clear. As recently as 1976, Weinraub argued at book length, that the Champenois poet, Chrétien de Troyes's *Conte du Graal*, above all the scene with the Fisher king, was a masterly reworking of the Passover seder.[99] People need to have close relationships to utilize each other's ceremonies in this way, it might be said. Here again, however, wishful thinking is at play; and a wiser argument rejects the Jewish origin of Chrétien's *Conte*.[100]

Although it remains true that the full panoply of Champenois evidence demands a reappraisal,[101] no one can deny that however good things might have been before the Capetian domination, they were very bad within a few years after. Taxation is not the issue: royal exactions only continued the heavy levies of the native counts.[102] The notorious incident was the scapegoating or framing of several Jews of Troyes, the capital, around Easter 1288 for the murder of a Christian. The frame-up succeeded to the extent that Dominicans (?) investigated the allegations and imprisoned and then turned over thirteen Jews to the local authorities to be executed.[103] How did the Dominicans have such authority? As with the Inquisition in the south, they did not. Consequently, we possess a royal order of 16 May 1288 prohibiting ecclesiastical punishment or incarceration of Jews.[104] Nevertheless, the sentences appear to have been confirmed and the property of the executed Jews went to the crown.[105]

Several elegies magnificently evoke the martyrological images of these events.[106] The overwhelming fear expressed in these elegies particularly rivets the reader (or, since these were probably synagogue poems, the listener).[107] The sense of fear and helplessness is the first emotion revealed, but it is neatly set off against the firm determination to act out an heroic martyrdom. Time and again the poet describes a situation in which the martyrs-to-be quaver; and time and again a determination, grown fierce, inspires a stoic, even defiant or swaggering, sense of the heroic. In succession each victim burns to death. The final judge is and can only be God Almighty.[108]

I do not know whether it really happened this way. I am particularly dubious of the alleged judicial execution of the children of the accused even with the loose judicial constraints that seem to have characterized all the proceedings. On the other hand, lynch law knows few rules. What *is* memorable and significant remains the riveting set of images: "Fear suffuses me," the poet says, and uses for *fear* the Hebrew word *rogez*, a word beloved of the author of the book of Job. "Fear," the translators say, or "sorrow" or "trouble," an emotion like the trembling of an angry sea.[109]

By 1294 the situation in Troyes had returned to a sufficient state of normalcy that a few of the Jews resident in the city attempted to repurchase the martyrs' homes. The crown, after the forfeiture, had conveyed the property to the count-king's valet. He, in turn, had sold it under royal license. By the close of 1294 five of the houses were back in the possession of Jews.[110]

Philip's attitude in all of this seems fairly straightforward. By confirming the sentence he accepted as fact that the Jews had conspired to carry out evil deeds like this murder and presumably other heinous crimes. But it is good to remember that this was no accusation of *ritual* murder. Indeed, no French king since Philip II Augustus had indicated any belief in the ritual murder accusation or the wilder fantasies of the blood libel (the alleged need in Jewish rituals for innocent Christian blood).[111] This may help explain why accusations of this sort or records of government prosecutions are so rare in the heartland of the kingdom in the thirteenth century.[112] Philip the Fair did, however, come to accept a new calumny against the Jews, namely, that when possible they tried to desecrate the host, the eucharistic wafer.

The mystery of the host—the central mystery of traditional Christian ceremony—was its transformation into the body of Christ. A consecrated host was such a holy object that when it was carried in procession, Jews were not to be in the vicinity.[113] It was a desired object for magic; its potency might be harnassed to good or bad ends. It was reputed that Jews and Christians sought possession of it for that purpose.[114] The host might also, through a miraculous effect on other material objects when in the possession of an unbeliever, be the means for the conversion of the unbeliever to the Catholic faith.[115] At times, it accomplished an even more arresting miracle. Many Christians reported that the consecrated host allowed its bodily attributes to be perceived. Joinville himself repeats a story of how the early thirteenth-century crusader, Simon de Montfort, was tempted to go see such a visible manifestation of the real presence, but declined to do so.[116] Indeed, the earlier thirteenth century seems still to have been dubious about purported miracles of this sort.

Changes in the administration of the eucharist in the 1260s, especially the introduction of the elevation of the host before the congregation, coupled with the later proliferation of the Feast of Corpus Christi, responded to and further stimulated a new and profound devotion to the re-enacted sacrifice of Jesus at the altar.[117] These developments undermined scepticism about the visible miracle of transformation, scholastic theory notwithstanding. What was more unsettling was that the sacrifice of the host was so often conceived as the sacrifice of the infant Jesus.[118] The justification for thinking in these terms is not entirely clear. Nonetheless, the most important model on which medieval Christian writers could draw to gloss this perception was the sacrifice of the Holy Innocents, the male children two years old and under whose slaughter Herod had ordered in hopes of killing the baby Jesus according to the Gospel of Matthew.[119] Since these children had not had an opportunity to reach the age of reason, they were superficially without the possibility of relevant *acta* or even relevant desires with regard to the substance of the Christian message.[120] Commemoration of them was based, instead, on their "substitutive" deaths for the infant Jesus. *Their* slaughter received theological closure by *his* own death in adulthood. So, somewhat like antetypes from the Old Testament, the Holy Innocents foreshadowed the full and perfect sacrifice of Jesus at Calvary.[121]

These themes came together with devasting effect in the Paris of Philip the Fair. The idea of the real presence in the host easily led some people to imagine bodily actions in it. It was a short step to the notion that "the worthy person" (*la digne personne*) in the host could be tormented just as Jesus on the cross was tormented—that it could weep or bleed all over again at the hands of the perfidious Jews.[122] The year 1290 saw the charge made in Paris.[123]

Various chronicles mention the incident, and there is also an extended report on it that reads like a sermon.[124] Although the sources differ on details, the overall picture is sharp and clear. A really quite poor Christian woman had pawned some of her clothing or linen. Despite the ban on usury, inhibiting the payment of interest on loans made through pledging was difficult. There is no doubt that in this case the rumor was that the Jewish pawnbroker had charged usury. When the Christian woman needed to get her pledges back, the Jew, it was said, offered to return them gratis in return for a consecrated host (*son* [her] *Dieu*). Thereupon, it being Easter, the woman went to mass and *sans dévotion* pretended to partake of communion but secretly sequestered the host in her mouth and later gave it into the Jew's hands. The sources make clear that she was grasping (*avara*) and shared with the Jew the principal characteristic associated with usurers, namely, cupidity (*convoitise*).

The Jew, either in the presence of his wife and two children (son and daughter) or not, is supposed to have subjected the host to various acts by which he wanted to destroy it. He tried to boil it away, but it would not disintegrate. He stabbed it; and it turned the water red (*rubefacta*; *vermeille*). He threw it into cold water and that turned red. In various versions he is said to have inflicted further and further torments. It was only when seen by another Christian woman, evidently in need of a hot ember to light a fire, that he desisted from his perfidy. Naturally, he attempted to bribe this women to get her help in destroying the host (*aider son Dieu destruire*). Less full of avarice than the woman who had given him the host, she was not led astray. She reported him; and the matter came before the bishop. Although the Jew tried to dissemble, the host made itself known by the childlike gesture of leaping into the Christian woman's container. Still, the Jew gave no sign of remorse. He was convinced that he could not be executed so long as he had a special book (of magic?, the Talmud?) in his hands. In fact, turned over to the lay authority, both he and his book were consumed. His wife and children converted, and so did many other Jews.

What is true and what is false about this story? A Jewish pawnbroker among whose customers were very poor people had become an object of intense hatred. It seems reasonable to assume that the first Christian woman, who did not want to spend the money necessary to redeem her clothing, spread the story to get him into trouble. To an extent her act came back to haunt her. Instead of showing sympathy for her poverty, popular opinion held that anyone who would steal the wafer was moved by filthy impulses.[125] The second woman's role seems equally patent. She was undoubtedly asked to help get the Jew in trouble by supporting the first woman's story.

The wafer and the instruments of the alleged torture were preserved. A cult grew up around the host. An extremely rich Parisian, Renier Le Flamenc, who paid taxes in Paris of forty pounds per year, one of the highest rates in the entire city, founded a church in its honor with the pope's license on the site of the Jew's house.[126] Renier was at the same time active in the administration of Philip the Fair.[127] The king himself conveyed a neighboring house in 1299 to the *capella Miraculorum* that Renier founded.[128] Under the inordinate pressure caused by the seizure and sentence of death on her husband, it would not be surprising that the usurer's wife and children nominally accepted Christianity. The proposition that conversion was more general seems farfetched.

The immediate effect of the acceptance of the host desecration accusation was limited. Philip the Fair still does not seem to have felt that the appropriate response was expulsion even though by 1290 the Angevin and Gascon expulsions were complete and the English in train.[129] His disgust with Jews as he perceived them was intensified; he essentially warned them that he was on the lookout for further examples of host desecration.[130] It was in the immediate aftermath of the accusation of 1290 that he tried to bar Jewish immigration to the royal domain and re-issued anti-usury legislation. In time, the king became increasingly *sensitive* about the Jewish "problem," but other matters delayed the full evolution of his policy toward the Jews.

Most important, Philip became more and more concerned with the south. We have seen this already in the care with which, even on the Jewish question, he kept authorizing careful scrutiny of the Inquisition, of purported exemptions from the Jewish taille in the *sénéchaussées*, and so forth. In reality his concern for the governance of the south, if particularly exigent on the question of the Jews, was much broader. The southern lands had been the locus of the opening event of his reign; and it had not been an encouraging event. It was noted earlier that the French failure in the Pyrenees in the crusade against Aragon did not precipitate any significant eruption of anti-French demonstrations in Languedoc, but the evident stability of the region notwithstanding, the king was determined to strengthen his position there.

Something of a tour de force was his success in securing a serious presence in the one great city between the Rhône and the Pyrenees that was not under French control, Montpellier. Montpellier in the thirteenth century was a city (technically a town) of multiple lordships.[131] The bishop of Maguelonne and the king of Aragon (later of Majorca) were the most important seigneurial authorities.[132] Yet, to a remarkable degree, the municipal or consular government was the real boss.[133] The two seigneurial authorities did not always treat their parts of the town alike. Jews, for instance, had better rights in leaseholds in the "Aragonese" lordship than in the episcopal; and the jealousy among the various authorities in general was extremely intense.[134]

In the mid-thirteenth century Louis IX had managed to secure some French influence in the town by offering protection to the bishop against the Crown of Aragon at a time when relations between France and Aragon were poor. He was solicitous of municipal authorities as well in their contests with the Aragonese prince.[135] This political influence had only marginal social consequences. Again, if we focus on the Jews, Capetian policies were not slavishly adopted by either the bishop or the municipal authorities. Jews engaged in pawnbroking, moneylending, various aspects of commerce with Christians, such as silk merchandising, and so on.[136] Even Jewish and Christian scholars enjoyed a community of interest, strictly limited, to be sure, by the problems posed by confessional hostility, but no less remarkable for all that.[137]

The special relationship that had developed between the bishop of Maguelonne and the French king in the mid-thirteenth century— formalized by the bishop's acknowledgement of his vassalage to the king— was the principal conduit for the expansion of French influence in the town.[138] As long as relations with Aragon were cool, French officials would play on the bishop's problems with other lords of the town to the benefit of the French government. On the other hand, Louis IX was scrupulous about not transgressing the rights of competing authorities and restrained his agents.[139] Moreover, after 1258 his own relations with the king of Aragon improved dramatically. In that year, the two kings worked out boundary problems in the Pyrenees, in the Treaty of Corbeil.[140]

Despite the king of Aragon's claim a little afterwards that Montpellier was not *of* the kingdom of France, he eventually conceded the point by accepting the judgement of a French court in 1267 that he held the town of Louis IX.[141] The French under Louis and his son behaved correctly and did not try unduly to encroach on the established authorities—seigneurial or municipal—in the town. In 1276, on the death of the king of Aragon, the *dominium* of Montpellier held by him was ceded to his younger son along with the kingdom of Majorca. The king of Majorca preferred and maintained an alliance with the French instead of with his kinsmen, the Aragonese. The relationship of Montpellier to the French crown was therefore strengthened by this development. If problems persisted, as they had to, given the complex layers of lordship in the town, they were solved amicably.[142]

It was only preparations for the crusade against Aragon that corrupted this modus vivendi. The Montpellierans themselves craved autonomy, an autonomy that might be achieved through playing off the Aragonese against the French. The king of France made his postion clear in 1284, when he permitted grain to be shipped into Montpellier from his domains, with the provision that the grain not be re-exported, presumably to Aragon or to lands allied with the Crown of Aragon.[143] The importance of the order is not in its substance per se, but in the clear implication that import of grain into the town might be stopped at any time if the Montpellierans, in defiance of their lord, the king of Majorca, gave active support to the Aragonese. After the fiasco of the crusade and despite the French defeat, the opportunity presented itself for the French to exercise enhanced influence in the town. When the bishop offered to sell his rights in Montpelliéret, the commercial appendage of the town in 1293, Philip the Fair jumped at the chance—or at least the sale went through very "quickly and smoothly."[144] It was not that the French crown, by the purchase, achieved hegemony in Montpellier; the tactics by which the other lords, including the king of Majorca, managed to thwart the French have become classic.[145] But the year 1293 does see a kind of dramatic reassertion in the south of the French presence over against the Aragonese that was really quite remarkable. In the event it also brought a cosmopolitan and wealthy group of Jews under royal control.

These Jews, whose varied commercial life and scholarly interaction with Christians has already been noticed, were truly integral citizens of the town.[146] They had enjoyed stability and prosperity under native lordship. They aided in the defense of the town: from 1208, during the unsettled period of the Albigensian wars when it was not clear whether or to what extent Montpellier would be involved, we possess an agreement whereby the Jews promised to furnish crossbow bolts in times of siege.[147] The Jews also had extensive proprietary rights in lands and buildings.[148] To be sure, when the Jews lent money, they lent at relatively lower interest and with longer repayment schedules than their Christian mercantile counterparts, presumably because exigency in these matters would have increased their vulnerability to reprisals, a good indication that all was not perfect in Jewish and Christian relations.[149] Moreover, it is generally agreed that over the course of the thirteenth century there was some worsening of the overall situation as the indirect influence of French policy in neighboring lands encouraged critics to denounce the relative degree of toleration characteristic of life in Montpellier.[150] Nonetheless, it was Philip the Fair's annexation of Montpelliéret that really signalled the decline of the Montpellieran Jewish community; heavy taxation followed the fleur-de-lys.[151]

The new initiatives in the south were not limited to the purchase of Montpelliéret. Much more dramatic was Philip's decision to do something about the English king's possession of Gascony. Edward I had been a great admirer of Philip's saintly grandfather. He believed that the agreements between Louis and his own father, Henry III, published in 1259 as the Treaty of Paris, had laid the foundation for a lasting peace between the two kingdoms.[152] Problems in the settlement had erupted almost immediately, but because both sides were determined that there be peace, these problems had never been permitted to constitute a *casus belli*.[153] It was not so under Philip the Fair. A good, but highly conjectural argument sees Philip's inability to sustain his grandfather and father's forbearance as an outgrowth of a young man's bravado and, perhaps, a need to redeem further the old disgrace in Aragon by some act of courage. Perhaps.[154] Whatever the truth, a series of incidents in Gascony was used as a provocation by Philip in 1294.

The war that began in 1294—and continued until 1297—changed virtually nothing of the territorial map of the kingdom. It was, after initial successes by Philip, essentially a standoff.[155] But it did whip up a sort of enthusiasm for the glory of French arms; and, since it had led to no defeat, it could be employed to shake off the memory of the Aragonese disaster. More to the point, it provoked a crisis in taxation as both sides burdened their people with inordinate levies. The church was taxed without the prior permission of the pope, an action first denounced but then accepted, in an embarrassing volte-face, by the papacy.[156] In France, the crown borrowed 200,000 pounds from the "bankers" of the Fairs of Champagne, 630,000 pounds from French bourgeois; it imposed new sales taxes which were expected to bring in as much as 150,000 pounds and "squeezed" 65,000 pounds out of the Lombards.[157]

It was inevitable that the Jews would be tallaged heavily in France (they had already been expelled from England and Gascony). This was still limited taxation, but it was an attempt to get a great deal from all the Jews—northern, southern, Champenois, French, inhabitants of the western provinces. The take, if it had all been collected, was supposed to have come to 215,000 pounds.[158] (Recall that an annual tallage of the Jews brought in fifteen thousand.) We must imagine that French Jewry was close to financial ruin as a result of this event. The year 1295, at the height of the frenzy to pay for the war, saw the Jews of the *sénéchaussée* of Beaucaire-Nîmes, accused of dissimulation, arrested en masse, sent to Paris, and despoiled of their money and outstanding debts by way of redemption.[159]

A further problem was that the financial exploitation was succeeded at the close of the war by a growing hostility toward the Jews. The crisis over ecclesiastical taxation had particular repercussions. It is from the mid-1290s that we begin to date those propaganda tracts that make of the French crown the guardian of public religion, that take a harsh and unfriendly view of the way ecclesiastics exercised and exceeded their authority or hesitated to help pay for the king's just wars.[160] This sense of the religious mission of the crown made its concern with the Jews all the more special. For the Jews represented an infection in the Holy Land of France, a raw spot among the New Chosen People, who, according to the propagandists, were the French themselves.[161] There were two ways to deal with an infection: heal it (conversion) or cut it out (expulsion). What we read in the wake of the Anglo-French War of 1294–1297 is a heightened language of pressure on the Jews, the sort of pressure that might bring them to convert.

Traditional prohibitions were once more reaffirmed. The year 1299 saw a repetition of the usury prohibition and of the prohibition against new synagogues and loud chanting at service, and the proscription of the Talmud "with its innumerable blasphemies of the glorious Virgin Mary."[162] It also saw the crown warning the Jews against circumcising simple-minded Christians, as if the infection in the kingdom were growing.[163] It warned them, too, not to succor fugitive heretics, a further indication of the perception at the summit of the state of the Jews as a cradle of religious infection.[164] On the other hand, the pressures had sometimes the opposite effect from what was wished. There is very little doubt that a clandestine market in usurious lending emerged here and there in the provinces, as Jews who were cut off from more open activities took desperate chances in the underworld.[165] In 1303 the anti-usury legislation of Saint Louis had to be issued with orders of enforcement once again.[166] Such tension had to be resolved. It had to be resolved—one way or another.

12. The Confiscations of 1306

Philip the Fair, sometime before 1306, re-examined his commitment to the policy of Saint Louis, which had been limited to the imposition of legal disabilities on Jews in order to encourage their conversion. The royal archives show that the traditional pressures had had some impact but that the vast majority of Jews remained steadfast in their allegiance to their religion.[1] Perhaps this steadfastness alone irritated the king who was becoming more and more persuaded of his own mission in the world. France, the satisfied state of the mid-thirteenth century, became more aggressive toward the end of the century—with the war in Gascony and also a nasty series of wars in Flanders.[2] The king, despite vicissitudes in his military fortunes, became convinced, or allowed his ministers to behave as if he were convinced, that France was a special land, beloved of God, whose special duty was to achieve a purity of faith and devotion that mirrored that of the kingdom of God.[3] Finally, the successful confrontation with the morally suspect papacy of Boniface VIII, who claimed an intolerable *dominium* over the French king, and Philip's own consciousness that he was the scion of a holy dynasty (the canonization of Louis IX occurred in 1297) gave a sharp point to his determination to purify the land.[4]

Moral or religious purity was closely tied to political loyalty. When, in the opening years of the fourteenth century, the usual complaints against the Inquisition became more strident, Philip visited Languedoc to see what he might do about the excesses of the institution. He was offended, however, by the strong emotions of the denouncers of the Inquisition and regarded their behavior as showing a lack of respect. When it was discovered that there was also a plot in the heartland of the old Cathar heresy to withdraw obedience from Philip and seek the protection of the king of Majorca, the enraged northerner moved swiftly to execute the plotters and redoubled his commitment to the Inquisition.[5] It has been plausibly suggested—although more evidence would have to come to light to prove the case—that one of the most important factors in the great internal struggle among Mediterranean Jews about the licitness of the study of philosophy (the so-called Maimonidean controversy) is related to these events.[6]

Many Jews of Languedoc were concerned about the matter of studying philosophy or gentile subjects. Some rejected the notion entirely; others wanted to defer study until a man was well into his maturity, since such study was potentially corrupting. Others, in various degrees, were much more open to this kind of learning. When, about 1300, the crisis came, Jews who opposed or wanted to put strict limits on such study sought support wherever they could find it; and one source of support was the influential rabbi of Barcelona, Solomon ben Adret (Rashba). Conservative Jews could not have been entirely happy, however, with the method Rashba chose to express his support for them, namely, issuing the ban (*herem*) on the study. The problem was that the ban required the prior approval of the Christian seigneur, in this case the king of Aragon (cousin of the king of Majorca). Saperstein has argued that the appeal outside the borders of France to a rabbi of a land with a recent history of conflict with France and, more especially, the ratification of that appeal by his king might have been seen as a provocation, even a kind of treachery, by the crown of France. The language of criticism Jews themselves used to deplore the ban is suggestive: "What kind of man will go and shriek about the inhabitants of one nation before the king of another?"[7]

Whether or not Philip knew of and in some sense responded to this behavior with his order to expel the Jews in 1306 remains moot. Other factors are undoubtedly relevant to the timing of Philip's order. The cost of war is one of these. Expenditures for war were so great, so draining of resources, that all sorts of expedients were being used in the 1290s and after to provide the government with income to sustain itself.[8] The king seems to have bought a number of Jews from other seigneurs, principally his brother, Charles of Valois, in the 1290s. This may reflect the intention on the king's part to despoil these Jews.[9] Equally likely, it may have responded to the not infrequent poverty of the king's brother, who was always committing himself to expensive, desperate projects hoping to win a crown.[10] On the other hand, much more obviously an expedient on Philip's part to finance the wars was a debasement of the coinage that overnight gave the crown triple its buying power. In the long term the debasement crippled the economy and led to charges of malfeasance, a kind of moral breaking of faith, that deeply affected Philip the Fair until the end of his life.[11]

No one of the factors that I have sketched explains entirely why Philip chose to repudiate the traditional policy of Saint Louis, which burdened but tolerated the Jews. Of course, it may be said that expulsion or the threat of expulsion was a burden in itself that might encourage conversion.[12] Yet no one could have deluded himself after observing the expulsions of the 1280s and 1290s on the borders of royal France that that approach would lead to mass conversion. Expulsion, then, was not complementary to Saint Louis's policies; in essence, it acknowledged them as failures. That the present king by expelling the Jews would make France Christian and receive an enormous amount of money in doing so would, however, mitigate self-reproach for diverging from the footsteps of the saint-king.

The king's intention was the *captio* of the real estate in the Jews' possession and of the money and chattels belonging to them, especially the books in which they recorded the amounts of their loans to Christian debtors. His aim was to have his subordinates carry out this policy not only in his own domains, but *throughout the realm*, including those baronies in which local, powerful Christian lords actually had *dominium* over the Jews and permitted moneylending at interest.[13] The total number of Jews thus affected is variously estimated by scholars.[14] There is no point in reworking these estimates here, since at every stage in the discussion to this point I have tried to sketch the shifting demographic profile of the regions studied. The most conservative estimate would count 45,000 royal Jews. The largest plausible estimate might be 140,000. If we choose a rather low figure, say, 70,000, and supplement it with a 30,000 figure for Jews under the *dominium* of other lords—in Narbonne, Pamiers, Montpellier, Burgundy, and so forth—we will get an approximate total of 100,000. I believe this is on the low side and that a combined figure closer to 150,000 might be more accurate. Nevertheless, 100,000 will serve us throughout the discussion as our best estimate of Jews in the realm of France on the eve of expulsion.[15]

As confident as they may have been about local lords submitting to their policies, Philip the Fair and his advisers still kept the planned expulsion secret until the last moment and entrusted it to special deputies. There were several good reasons for this approach. (1) A public statement would have led to remonstrances, quibbles, and delays from lords who, even if they acknowledged the crown's authority in the matter, were opposed to expulsion and the consequent loss of a taxable portion of their population. What they did once they were informed proves this contention.[16] (2) Experience taught that the Jews themselves, if given advanced warning, would try to flee the royal wrath with as many of their own valuables and books and the pledges in their keeping as they could—to the injury of the king's profit.[17] (3) The crown desired to forestall uncontrolled popular enthusiasm on the part of its Christian subjects, many of whom relished the thought of sacking the Jews' houses for loot and for the books that recorded debts that they owed the Jews. Without the books, the king's men, again relying on historical precedent, would have had to employ other, far less reliable or far more lengthy methods to generate information (the empaneling of local inquests, torture).[18] To be sure, the account books to which I am referring were often in Hebrew and might require the crown to allow a few expellees to remain in the New Holy Land (or return to it) until the financial details of the confiscations were completed.[19] Though galling, the presence of a handful of Jews was a minor inconvenience. When their work was over, they too could be forced to leave their homes and *patria*.[20] (4) Secrecy and the use of special agents also inhibited the crown's less dependable local officials (suborned by bribery) from softening the blow of the seizure and from further diminishing royal profits. Such behavior was well-documented on similar occasions.[21]

As we now watch the campaign unfold we shall see that the situation was more complicated, more problematic than had been predicted. The intention was clear: a swift, massive arrest. Philip II had accomplished this with a few thousand Jews in 1180; both Philip Augustus and John of England had probably done something similar to a few thousand Jews in 1210.[22] In 1278 the English had successfully arrested for false coining six hundred Jewish heads of households in a lightning thrust (an episode that historians once regarded with doubt but that is now substantiated in the documentary record).[23] The French in 1306 intended to effect the same swiftness of arrest for 100,000 Jews or more in a kingdom that stretched from the North Sea to the Mediterranean, from the Atlantic coast to the Rhône and the forests of the Franche-Comté.

Documentary evidence on the Christian side sets out the plan. Let us take the case of the *sénéchaussée* of Toulouse, a large region but with a small Jewish population. Oral orders were given in Paris on 21 June 1306 to the commissioners who were to direct the confiscations in Toulouse. They arrived in the great southern city in July. An order of 17 August already looks forward to the sale of the seized properties. By 20 November the commissioners were well along in the process.[24] These commissioners were extremely high-ranking men of the likes of the intimate royal counsellor, Guillaume de Nogaret, and the royal clerk of accounts, Jean de

Saint-Just.[25] They seem to have entered into their tasks with enthusiasm, mobilizing local officialdom in a well-choreographed effort to confront and constrain the Jews. After locating the Jews (easily arranged from the informative censuses that had been built up over the decades) and performing the mass arrests, they entered upon a long and difficult task of identifying property and inventorying goods, and when they were recalled to Paris, they felt confident in assigning the finishing touches to local authorities.[26]

The evidence for the date of the expulsion from narrative sources seems less confident—22 July; around 22 July; sometime in August; 10 August; in August and September.[27] Partly this variation reflects dating from various phases of the *captio*. Partly, however, it reflects the fact that from the very beginning there was, among local Christians, incompetence, foot dragging, and indignation at the unannounced royal program. It was not that many Christians played the role of righteous gentiles, but they did have their grievances against the crown. Lords protected their jurisdictional interests.

In Pamiers, where the Jewish community was under the protection of the Abbot of Saint-Antonin and paid an annual tax to the lay lord, the count of Foix, the situation was particularly grim for royal officials.[28] The great thirteenth-century census of renegade Jews, the *Haec est informatio* referred to earlier in this study, had identified Jew after Jew who had deceitfully emigrated from royal domain lands and claimed to live under the personal lordship of the seigneurs of Pamiers, a state of affairs that had resulted in condemnations and recriminations.[29] Yet Pamiers remained something of a haven even after the dust of the inquiry had settled. As recently as 1302 the count of Foix had granted the Jewish community a lenient charter of liberties.[30] Into this situation a special royal deputy had to be sent, Gérard de Courtonne, a canon of Paris, who ultimately worked throughout Languedoc.[31] The Pamiers business seems still to have been churning as late as 1311, possibly because latent popular resentment of the Jews came to the surface even in this supposed haven. In that year the town agreed to pay a fine for multiple infractions of the peace, including "the forced baptism of a Jew detained in the castle."[32]

The situation in Pamiers, requiring the despatch of a special deputy, is merely one example of a wider set of problems caused by local lords, many of whom the crown could not easily bully. Whatever their other objections, they insisted on their fair share of the loot.[33] Careful delineations followed—and more delays. The final agreement in Montpellier with the

co-seigneur, the king of Majorca, came in February 1309; that for Mende
with the very lordly bishop who imagined himself king in his see, in April
1309.[34] Other arrangements followed: the viscount, archbishop, and municipal authorities of Narbonne reached accord with the crown in June
1309; the abbot of Alet in 1311; the abbot of Saint-Gilles in March 1313; the
abbot and religious of Notre-Dame de la Grasse, in July 1313.[35] A special
deputy, Jean de Crépy, "the superintendant of Jewish affairs at Toulouse,"
had to be expressly instructed to deal with the stubborn lord of L'Isle-
Jourdain near Toulouse.[36]

Besides the lack of smoothness in the *captio* that can be attributed to
lords who zealously protected their rights, there was collusion with Jews
among the people picked to carry out the expulsion. Geoffroy de Paris, a
chronicler, alludes to diversion of expected revenues by greedy officials.[37]
There is a revealing instance of this in records from 1314.[38] A sub-delegate
of the commissioners who had been appointed to effect the *captio* in the
north was punished in that year. This official, a sergeant of the Châtelet
(that is, of the royal administration in Paris), with the aid of two Jews, had
illegally sequestered goods. The *récits* of this case note that the properties
of the sergeant—one Jean Vendomeau, a burgher of Chartres—were sold
as punishment (the pain was actually inflicted on his heirs, however, since
he was dead by the time of the judgement). The *récits* go on to refer to an
ordinance by whose authority the punishment was inflicted, the so-called
Ordonnance de Creil, otherwise unknown, but whose very existence indicates the perceived scale of the problem.

Saige assembled evidence of numerous accusations of embezzlement
(some of the accused, to be sure, were later exonerated). These accusations
were most frequently directed at men of middling status: *bayles* or second-
level functionaries.[39] One particularly interesting case was that of Jean
Beucet, a *bayle* of Narbonne, who confessed that he, his wife Berengère, a
female domestic servant Marthe, and another associate (one Benoît of
Narbonne) had embezzled considerable funds entrusted to him by the
commissioners. It would appear that he ultimately cooperated with the
special investigators whom the crown sent to inquire into this sort of
peculation (which was widespread). Beucet himself got off with a remarkably light punishment. He paid a fine, ceded his office, and gave up any
right to resume it, but no physical punishments were inflicted.[40]

As intimated, this was a widespread problem. Soon a number of special
investigators were deputed to investigate charges of malfeasance. Master
Raoul de Joie worked in the *prévôté* and viscounty of Paris. He and Master

Etienne d'Antogny, who was sent into the *sénéchaussée* of Beaucaire-Nîmes, were instructed to look into the question "of embezzled goods" and these "financial matters" more systematically.[41]

The confrontational tactics of lords and incidents of collusion and embezzlement delayed the completion of the *captio* and gave popular anger an opportunity to manifest itself. If the king was being hindered in taking the property of the Jews, then ordinary people might feel justified in acting against them in his stead (paradoxically devouring some of his expected profits). Within a year and a half of the initiation of the *captio*, a king's clerk would describe these popular executions of the royal will as an "offense to the royal majesty."[42]

In the confusion, as it were, some Jews escaped with their chattels and the precious records of their financial relations. This occurred, for instance, in Montpellier, where, as we have noticed, negotiations with local lords interrupted the operation of the *captio* for a considerable length of time.[43] Nevertheless, escapes seem to have been the exception, the very rare exception.

As remarked earlier, it was the special commissioners who authorized and supervised the first phase of the *captio* (1306–1307). To the names of Guillaume de Nogaret and Jean de Saint-Just in the *sénéchaussée* of Toulouse and Albi we can add a handful of others.[44] The dirty work was carried out by the *baillis* or seneschals and their subordinates. They made the arrests, declared the seizure of the buildings, books, and other goods, including, scandalously, holy objects pawned by clerics and thieves.[45] They poked their noses here and there and arranged for the disposition of the real property. The procedure was the following, to illustrate from what took place in the *bailliage* of Orléans:[46] once a piece or pieces of property were deemed by the commissioners ready to be sold, the local crier made his rounds. We may watch Jean Chicho, the crier of Orléans, performing this task on four late summer and autumn Saturdays (17 September, 24 September, 8 October, 29 October 1306). He spread the news: the former small synagogue (really a big house) and two other houses taken from the Jews in Orléans were available for purchase. As a package these made a quite substantial holding. The bidding was brisk: 120 pounds *parisis* (l. p.); 130 l. p.; finally, 140 l. p. The delivery of seisin of the properties to the winner, however, was anything but smooth.

It emerged that the successful bidder, Guillaume Garbot, had bid not for himself alone but also for one Jean Dreux, who had agreed to go in for half the sum. At the same time, probably under judicial threat, Guillaume admitted to the king's officials that he was selling his interest in the property to Alain du Val, a cleric and lawyer. The situation was more complex still. Alain had already ceded his interest, because of a prior obligation, to Guillaume's original partner, Jean Dreux. There is a story behind these machinations which is difficult for us to get at and was difficult for royal officials to reconstruct. They were dissatisfied, so they demanded and obtained the full 140 l. p. from Jean Dreux in November, but held up the transfer of seisin until they had re-opened the bidding, as an added precaution against sharp practices. The crier, Jean Chicho, was commanded to beat the bounds again, this time in winter. He made new rounds on four Saturdays, 28 January, 4 and 18 February, and 4 March 1307. Only when no larger bid was received was Jean Dreux's title affirmed.

Not every disposition of confiscated property was as complicated as this one, but the process was not easy. Most serious, perhaps, was that local officials had to keep a wary eye on the church and on knights, two estates that were forbidden to acquire the property or to have it transferred to them, except with special royal dispensations.[47] Consequently, it was absolutely essential to investigate—to go behind the scenes—to see whether these excepted groups were making arrangements through front men. It is true that some churches *did* manage to acquire property. Their bishops, priests, and abbots were clever; they played on the king's piety and sometimes his good sense. All the same, despite a few startling successes, churches on the whole failed to obtain much material benefit from the *captio*.[48] Local functionaries must have been largely responsible for this successful enforcement of royal policy.

The hard work of the local officials and special deputies was compounded by the royal obsession with hidden treasure. Jews had been arrested, their houses ransacked and inventoried (*super inventario bonorum*).[49] Many of these Jews seemed poor. On the other hand, they could not be poor. The popular belief in their wealth was too strong to accept superficial evidence of poverty. Treasure there was, for treasure there had to be—hidden treasure.

It was not simply a question of law. Yes, the right to a treasure trove was regalian. So it seemed legitimate that any treasure found in the confiscated property, even after it was auctioned, should revert to the king.[50] But we must try to imagine the local officials going about, checking here, checking there, digging, opening, prying, tapping for hollow places, while always at the same time trying not to diminish the value of the property before it could be auctioned. They are known to have forced one successful bidder to swear on the gospels to reveal the hoard that they expected him to find. In this case they had clearly overdone the prying in a house in Nîmes, to such a degree that they could not obtain the price that it should have commanded.[51]

Dreams of treasure were not pure fancy. Occasionally the king's men poked and did find more than the modest pledges of hard-up Christians. Some fiscal accounts of the precious "jewels of the Jews" seized in 1306 (*rotulus jocalium dictorum Judeorum*; *rotulus . . . de jocalibus auri et argenti Judeorum*) are mentioned in the surviving records.[52] The existence of a few caches of precious objects stimulated the imagination to believe that there were more and more and more. It was a feeling that would not go away. Fifty years after the expulsion, a small hoard was discovered in the niche of a rock near the Burgundian village of Arnay-sous-Vitteaux. The popular imagination immediately concluded that it had been hidden by a fleeing Jew in 1306 who was never able to retrieve it.[53]

An even more oppressive (but considerably more lucrative) assignment than ransacking for treasure while simultaneously preserving properties in a state suitable for profitable sale was tracking down the debts owed the Jews. The number of explicit references to the collections made under this rubric (*de debitis*) is enormous.[54] And, of course, many other general references to the *captio Judeorum*, *finance Judeorum*, *negotium Judeorum*, or some such phrase refer to this activity as well.[55]

Even with the account books in their possession and Jewish informers in their train, the royal agents encountered in the Christian debtors a resistance that was frustrating. As time went by the resistance became infuriating.[56] The authorities became so abusive in Bourges that by 1310 the local population protested threateningly. The central government intervened to caution its people to obey the proper rules of procedure.[57] Proper rules only meant producing "reasonable" evidence of debt.[58] Failure on the debtor's part to repay might mean imprisonment, forfeiture of property, and its resale at auction to pay the outstanding sum.[59] Such procedures, even properly applied, led to any number of complaints.[60] Thus, by August 1311 the government decided to abandon the pursuit of debtors, except for notorious cases.[61] It had conceded the year before that really ancient debts, those over twenty years old, also would not be collected and that Christian debtors would not be imprisoned.[62]

Despite all the problems that have been noticed, it remains the case that the *captio* was an enormously dramatic and dreadful statement of the administrative capability of the Capetian monarchy. There would be arrears for decades.[63] There would be investigations and lingering problems with some of the administrators' performances.[64] In the hope of streamlining procedures there was a movement toward collecting money and auditing accounts by more traditional methods than the use of special commissioners.[65] This did not solve all the problems.[66] Yet Philip the Fair had not failed. His narrow-minded conventional piety was satisfied with an expulsion that made France as pure as the golden lily that was its emblem, and he could only be delighted by the extremely large amount of money that entered the royal coffers.[67]

The men who brought that money in had worked hard. Days, weeks, months had gone into the awesome task of inventorying, appraising, arranging auctions, conveyancing, collecting payments, auditing, chasing down debtors, negotiating disputes, hunting for treasure. Hugues de la Celle worked 151 days "on taking the Jews" in the bailliage of Bourges in late 1307 and early 1308.[68] In the bailliage of Tours, Pierre de Bourges put in 85 days on the business in early 1308.[69] On and on it went as functionary after functionary collected his wages *in captione Judeorum*.[70] They could not have found everything or stopped every Jew from salvaging something. They did not in all cases get the prices they thought auctioned property should get. But if they were not perfect, they were substantially effective.

Given the state of French financial records it will never be possible to know precisely how effective the king's confiscators were. That is to say, the overall profit of the *captio* to the crown is irrecoverable from the sources. Excellent historians (Schwarzfuchs, Saige, Strayer), with a notion of the structural weaknesses of medieval states, have suggested too quickly that the crown was disappointed financially or found the *captio* only "fairly profitable."[71] Despite my respect for the work of the people who have concluded this, the conclusion itself is wrong. Even the fragmentary figures that can be collected point to an enormous windfall, followed, because of the auction of the real property, by a transfer of fixed capital to the most productive and aggressive members of the Third Estate.

In the seizures of the single *sénéchaussée* of Toulouse (1306 and forward), where the data are reasonably good, we know that over 87,000 pounds *tournois* (l. t.) were received. This is accounted weak money, that is, according to the debased currency. The strong or good money equivalent was about 30,000 l. t.[72] (All figures will be expressed henceforth in terms of good money.) Since there were about 1,000 Jews in the county of Toulouse,[73] the crudest estimate for the return from 100,000 Jews throughout the realm would be 100 times the amount collected in the county, or 3,000,000 pounds. Before accepting this figure, however, it might be wise to explore the other available hard evidence.

The county of Champagne, which certainly had more Jews than the county of Toulouse but far fewer than the great maritime *sénéchaussées* of Carcassonne-Béziers and Beaucaire-Nîmes, produced revenue of 35,000 l. t. from the *captio* of the Jews down to 1310.[74] Burgundy saw receipts as high as 18,000 l. t., of which 11,000 came from the capital Dijon. More important, about two-thirds of this sum originated in the collection of debts. The other one-third came from the value of pledges discovered in the Jews' possession, from chattels, and possibly from the sale of steles from the Jewish cemetery which were used in building. The value of the real property was a distinctly modest proportion of the overall total. Twenty-two houses in Dijon were sold for an average slightly in excess of 100 l. t. per dwelling.[75]

Figures such as the ones presented give us the opportunity to make reasonable estimates of regional returns from areas heavily populated with Jews. Take Narbonne. There were almost as many Jews in the city of Narbonne as there were in the whole county of Toulouse. There were 165 hearths in Jewish hands in 1300, giving a population of roughly 800 to 1000.[76] Eighty-four pieces of property were sold in the *captio*: "53 large residences, 26 houses, five fields, gardens and other pieces of real property." The average price for one of these units was 35 l. t.; the total value close to 3,000 l. t.[77] If the ratio of profits from real property to profits from other sources in Narbonne is roughly similar to the ratio in Dijon, then Narbonne would have generated about 10,000 l. t. in the overall confiscation. Narbonne, of course, was a much more lively commercial center than Dijon; profits from debts payable were undoubtedly higher.[78] This discrepancy was accentuated by the fact that in contrast to Narbonne the local lord of Dijon, the duke of Burgundy, had followed the Capetian lead over the course of the century in periodically taking the Jews and enforcing a policy of no usurious moneylending.[79] It is easy to see, then, that Narbonne, which suffered none of these disabilities, would have produced profits in the confiscation far in excess of 10,000 l. t., perhaps twice as much or even more.

Beaucaire, Nîmes, Béziers, Saint-Gilles, Carcassonne, Montpellier were all cities in the maritime *sénéchaussées* with sizable Jewish populations that would have returned excellent sums, not the 20,000 l. t. of Narbonne or the 30,000 l. t. of the county of Toulouse, perhaps, but substantial sums.

The lowest estimate of the population of Jews in Montpellier, for example, makes the Jewish presence there about 30% the size of Narbonne's.[80] That would mean that something like 6,000 l. t. or 7,000 l. t. came from the Jews of Montpellier in the *captio*.

The older parts of the royal domain were less well-settled by Jews, but the data allow us to note collections from the *captio* in Normandy, Vermandois, the Sénonais, the Orléanais, Touraine, the *bailliage* of Bourges, and, of course, Paris.[81] When figures are available they show good, sometimes substantial profits: 5,500 l. t. from Normandy; thousands from Paris.[82] Moreover, we should recall that all of these figures are fragmentary. It has sometimes been said that merely 800 l. t. were collected from Bourges, but this figure constitutes the value of only part of the collection accounted for by only one collector, Jean Barmont, from 1306 to 1310.[83] We know that other commissioners were active as well. Although they did not work as extensively as Jean, they accounted for sums, exact amounts unknown, in 1306 and 1307.[84] The evidence from the Touraine, too, has not been given its due. Certainly only a little money came in during 1306 and 1307. Yet the amounts got larger and larger as the campaign continued in 1308, 1309, even as late as 1313.[85] Unfortunately, only one of these data has been used to estimate the return from Touraine, that which refers to one portion of the collection of 1309. Even that is not bad: about 1,500 l. t.[86]

It should be added that there were regions in which collection was going on where Jewish settlement was very, very sparse. One can mention Auvergne, the Rouergue, Cahors-Périgord.[87] All the same, a region like Auvergne could produce more than 1,500 l. t. for the royal coffers.[88] A return like this makes the partial figure from Touraine, where there were close to a thousand Jews, look very partial indeed.[89]

Increasingly, then, the idea of extrapolating from the Toulousain figure, 30,000 l. t. from 1,000 Jews, seems reasonable. But there are problems. First, Jews owned real property outright in the south; except for a few houses they usually leased properties—fields, cemeteries—in the north. Consequently, there was not much to be made from this source in the north.[90] Second, in large parts of the royal domain, especially the north, the ordinances against Jewish moneylending had been well-enforced since the days of Saint Louis.[91] Thus, the recovery of debts was less lucrative than in places like Narbonne, where moneylending was permitted. Finally, lords with *dominium* over Jews, as we know, managed to obtain a large part of the profits of confiscation. Whatever the value of Jewish property that was confiscated in 1306—and it can willingly be conceded that it probably was far less than 3,000,000 pounds—probably only about 60% or 70% of the total ever reached royal coffers. Again, it is hard to put a firm figure down on paper, but 1,000,000 pounds for the crown is probably not far off the mark. It is, in any case, a fairer estimate than the 200,000 l. t. figure that is sometimes given, which is less than the war tallage of about 1295 (215,000 l. t.), which did not involve the confiscation of real property, the seizure of all chattels, the confiscation of all pledges and which did not apply to all franchises.[92]

So much for what the king got. The money and treasure remained with him to be spent according to the needs of the crown. The real estate, in one way or another, was conveyed to the king's subjects at auction. We have already seen that knights and the church (if not individual clerics)[93] were prohibited from bidding for the confiscated lands and buildings. My own scrutiny of published and of about forty unpublished ecclesiastical rent rolls, cartularies, obituaries with endowments from rents, and *terriers* with information on fourteenth-century holdings confirm that the prohibition was successfully applied.[94] Who, then, got the property? In a number of cases municipalities purchased or leased it. The mayor and *jurés* of Rouen secured a lease in their city for 300 l. t. per year to the holdings of the Jews.[95] The consuls of Narbonne purchased at least twenty-four large buildings for 862 l. t. In 1313, the former residence of the head of the Jews of Narbonne became the quarters of the consulate. Still later it became the seat of the royal *viguier*.[96]

Most frequently those who benefitted were middling types: squires; lawyers, and judges; notaries; royal administrators such as sergeants; physicians; merchants; artisans like carters and pelters.[97] Most of the purchasers who remain unidentified in the sources by status or occupation were probably merchants or artisans of the same sort and condition as have been listed. Take Jacques Gervaise of La Ferté-sous-Jouarre, a vill less than fifty miles up the Marne from Paris. He bought houses and a synagogue (a big house) at Lizy-sur-Ourcq, a village that was just across the river and a little upstream. The cost was 80 l. t.[98] Skilled workmen were earning about 25 l. t. per year. Well-paid but not the highest-ranking royal officials were making from 60 l. t. to 100 l. t. per year; judges were earning toward the upper end of that scale.[99] A purchase like the one made by Jacques Gervaise, a man who probably earned more than a workman, less than a judge, must have been the chance of a lifetime, the answer even to his dreams of becoming a *rentier*.

Guilhem Gozi of Toulouse, with a bid of 135 l. t., purchased a workshop

that two Jews, husband and wife, had operated in 1306.[100] Other work-
shops came into the hands of Pierre Bergognon and Jacques Mercier,
whose last name possibly tags him as a small shopkeeper wanting to
expand or relocate his business.[101] Lesser properties—some in bad repair,
like the house with the leaky roof in Blois, whose lease Jean Guérin
obtained—also came on the market.[102] Sums were expended to pay bids
and purchase leases of this variety by any number of men who were
determined on improving their lot: in Toulouse, Narbonne, Melun, An-
delot, Sézanne, Dun-le-Roi, Monjuyf, Pavie-en-Gers, Janville, and so
forth—in short, all over the kingdom.[103]

It might be said that the stratum of French society represented by these
people was confirmed in its loyalty to the crown by the acquisition of
Jewish property through its good offices. Possibly, in a small way, this is
true. It is at least as likely that the king (or his government) also lost
something just as intangible, namely, the good will of many other people.
Where there are victors, there are losers. Failure in the bidding necessarily
nourished a certain bitterness, especially when there were so many charges
of peculation on the part of the officials who carried out the confiscation
and disposition of the property. Much more significant, I think, but not
documentable, is the likelihood that among the discontents the image of
the Jews suffered. Recriminations by losers about the disposition of the
property in the Jewish matter would become a bitter memory of the time
the Jews were expelled; and there would be, irrationally perhaps, deeper
resentment if they were ever to return.

13. "Every Jew Must Leave *My* Land"

"Every Jew must leave *my* land, taking none of his possessions with him; or, let him choose a new God for himself, and we will become *One People*." The statement quoted is attributed to Philip the Fair by the sixteenth-century author, Yosef ha-Cohen, and aptly declares the ostensible purpose of the expulsion of the Jews as they perceived it.[1] To be sure, most scholars have preferred to see the expulsion as an expression of the avarice of the king. This is fair enough, but it goes too far to say that the expulsion "added nothing to the religious aura of the most Christian king."[2] The event must be seen in context. The struggle with Boniface VIII, in which Philip challenged the right of the pope to interfere in affairs of the kingdom even when these affairs put the life of a bishop at risk, is a key point here. When Bernard Saisset, the bishop in question, was accused of treason and arrested in 1301 and the pope came to his defense in the name of clerical immunity, Philip and his ministers, in the struggle that followed, formulated a more-or-less comprehensive interpretation of the king as sovereign and principal protector of the church. This formulation was rooted in those other ideas of the majesty of monarchy, the holiness of the dynasty, and the sanctity of the people and kingdom to which we have referred before. As a result of the successful contest with Boniface VIII, the repertory of metaphors employed to glorify the realm took on new and enhanced shades of meaning.[3]

The active persecution of heretics which Philip encouraged, even if he also suspected that the Inquisition encroached on his jurisdiction, further supported the militantly holy image of the monarchy.[4] The persecution and expulsion of the Jews was of a piece with this. To be sure, the manipulation of the coinage and the enormous problems it caused up to 1306 tarnished the luster of Philip the Fair, so that the attempt to polish his reputation by expelling the Jews might have generated less enthusiasm than he wished.[5] Nonetheless, the chroniclers show that there was genuine approval.[6] They delighted in recalling how he ordered the Jews out on pain of death, how he expelled them "never again to return" (though, in laments and with echos of the same words, they recall their readmission years later).[7] Several annalists found the expulsion of the Jews the only thing worth mentioning in 1306.[8] Many others bracket the expulsion with the destruction of the Templars on charges of peculation, sodomy, and heresy in the next year.[9] Indeed, the destruction of the Order of the Temple was the crowning achievement of the militant Christianity the French king had come to represent. Not even Saint Louis in all his glory, one writer declares, had succeeded so well.[10]

The expulsion was a stimulus to conversion for a few (*pauci*) Jews.[11] The chroniclers would make more of the point if they could. It has even been shown that among those few who did convert there was some apostasizing.[12] It may be that Philip, if he was really interested in conversion, misplayed his hand. The relatively short duration of the imprisonment of the Jews before they were commanded to depart the kingdom put insufficient pressure on them to convert.

The only Christians, aside from barons worried about their rights, who seem to have protested the expulsion in a vigorous way were some of the poor in Paris.[13] Much has been made of this, but it is not likely that their sentiment reveals a relative lack of religious hatred in the "working class" or anything similar. It was merely an economic fact of life that in the underworld of pawnbroking and moneylending Jews charged less interest than Christians in order to attract any business at all.[14] The absence of the Jews was likely to be detrimental, therefore, to the position of some of the poor.

The arrest and detention of the Jews is extremely difficult to explore in depth. At Auxerre and Issoudun Hebrew graffiti have been found scratched into the tower or dungeon walls that lament the imprisonment of the Jews—but whether in 1306 or sometime earlier is unclear.[15] Any population of 100,000 would have had its share of the aged, the sick, small children, and pregnant women, some of whom would have found the detention and the travel afterwards very difficult. Yet, it must be said that this consideration does not seem to have had much force in French thinking.[16] The leprosarium of Provins and the hospital or alms house of Narbonne, to mention two Jewish institutions for the sick, gave up their inmates to the exile.[17] We are informed that the crown permitted the Jews some travelling money and the clothes on their backs but was insistent on a speedy departure "on pain of death."[18] The journey itself was a miserable one. For some families who lived in the heartland of the kingdom, the nearest frontier was two hundred miles away. The toll in human lives is not recoverable though one chronicler tells us that "many died along the way through exhaustion and suffering."[19]

The exile left a deep impression on French and European Jewry.[20] There are large numbers of exile poems and prose allusions to the catastrophe in Hebrew sources.[21] The following is illuminating for its staccato-like evocation of the dispersal of the tribes of Israel in the prophecy of Genesis 49:7.[22]

> My enemy said to me yesterday:
> I will destroy the country of your dwelling,
> I will take away all that your ancestors have amassed.
> I will pursue
> I will overtake
> I will divide
> I will scatter the promise of God . . . [23]

Those responsible are cursed over and over again.[24] The age is repeatedly described as one of calamity and oppression.[25] More than anything else, it is the loss of books (and with books, sacred learning and the possibility of pursuing sacred learning at a high level) that is lamented.[26]

What this chapter will concentrate on is the movement of the exiles into new lands—the achievement of license to settle, the initial adjustments to a new way of life, and the reaction of native Jews and native Christians to the exiles' presence. Much information on the immigrants in their new lands is scattered in local journals, but except for a brief, helpful article by Blumenkranz a quarter of a century ago, this information has never been systematically brought together. The aim of this chapter is to do so. The presentation has been divided into three sections: those exiles who took up residence in principalities along the northeastern frontier of the kingdom, roughly from Flanders to the Franche-Comté, are considered first; those who crossed the Rhône to Dauphiné, Savoy, the Comtat-Venaissin and Provence, second; and those who settled in the Iberian kingdoms, third.[27]

The Northeastern Frontier: Flanders to the Franche-Comté

The principalities on the northeastern frontier of the medieval kingdom of France were uneven in Jewish settlement before the French expulsion of

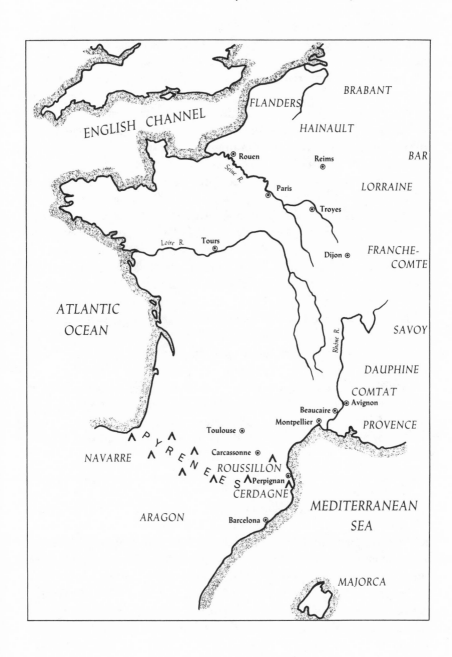

Lands of exile

1306. There has long been debate on patterns of residence and density of population. As a general description, it may be said that density became heavier as one followed the arc of principalities southward from the North Sea provinces of Imperial Flanders and Brabant through Hainault, Bar, Lorraine, and the Rhenish lands, with a marked falling off in the heavily wooded Franche-Comté and what we now call Switzerland. In Imperial Flanders there were possibly resident Jews in Bruges and Ghent in the thirteenth century.[28] Residence in Brabant is undoubted in the thirteenth century, but localization is difficult owing to the lateness and lack of specificity of the texts. The best reconstruction suggests that Jews were present in at least seven or eight towns in 1306.[29] The sources are problematic for Hainault, but there may have been Jews at Mons and Ath before 1306.[30] Undisputed evidence of Jews in Bar dates from the 1220s and 1230s.[31] Lorraine and Rhenish principalities boast several old and well-known Jewish communities: Metz, Colmar, Mainz, Speyer, and so on.[32] But Jews of the Franche-Comté (the *County* of Burgundy) are documentable only from the very late thirteenth century, not before.[33]

The history of the Rhenish communities is the best known. There the flourishing Jewish settlements of the eleventh century were traumatized by the so-called popular crusaders in 1096. This event led, as we earlier saw, to a decisive shift in the self-perception of the Jewish communities, an intensification of the martyrocentric attitude of writers, especially poets, and it contributed to a continuing "debate" in the twelfth century between those Jews who wanted to reduce contact with gentiles to an absolute minimum and concentrate on holy living (the *hasidim*) and those who were optimistic about the possibility of reconstructing a more intimate modus vivendi.[34]

The twelfth and thirteenth centuries, despite the crusades and internal dissent, did witness the evolution of a new set of social relations between Christians and Jews, less limited than that advocated by the *hasidim* but founded on deep suspicion of each other nonetheless. This did not prevent Jewish community life and sacred scholarship from flourishing. Much of the great collections of twelfth- and thirteenth-century rabbinic material by Finkelstein and by Agus comes from German or Rhenish Jewry.[35] Yet, the level of suspicion was such that a whole series of confrontations developed in the course of the thirteenth century. A few illustrations will help make the point.

We may begin with Metz. The history of the Jews of Metz was checkered. Jews' role in trade and merchandising was eclipsed by the early thirteenth century, and it has even been argued that the community itself ceased to exist for part of the century.[36] When this community was re-established or when it revived, it came under great stress. Several Jews and lepers seem to have been burned alive in 1269.[37] The martyrdom of another Jew by judicial murder in 1276 is memorialized in a famous poem that speaks of the martyr (*kadosh*) as having been imprisoned for ten years before his execution by burning.[38] This is a strange and problematic as-sertion by the poet. Why should a Jew (or any prisoner) be held for ten years awaiting execution in the Middle Ages? The only argument that seems reasonable to me is that Jewish communities or individuals ex-pended a great deal of effort to influence a variety of authorities to delay the execution of a man who, in the poet's description, was a rabbi su-premely just. If we take the ten-year period as approximate, then the martyr's fate had probably been sealed about the time of the execution of the Jews and lepers in 1269; but the strong intervention of other Jews delayed the enforcement of the sentence of death against him for several years. The point is that the situation in Metz continued to be difficult; the tension never abated. Nor did the poet see the sacrifice of his hero as the end of the story, for each stanza of the poem closes with the invocation of Job 17:18: "Cover not my blood, O earth." Blood uncovered pleads to heaven for vengeance.

The outrages in Metz were not isolated incidents, as massacres at Col-mar and Weissenburg in the 1260s demonstrate.[39] An incident at Wesel in 1287 also adds to our picture of the rumors about pressures on Jewish life in the French borderlands. Wesel, in the *pays de Trèves*, saw itself become the locus of an accusation of ritual murder in 1287.[40] A child or adolescent whom the sources call that "good and devoted Werner," that "blessed youth" had been found dead. It was commonly said that he was killed by Jews. He became the object of devotion "by certain simple people" (*a quibusdam christianis simplicibus*). Forty Jews were slaughtered for the al-leged crime; their rabbi was clapped in irons. Note the similarity to the events in Metz where, again, the rabbi did not immediately share the fate of his flock. Ultimately, the emperor, Rudolph I, successfully intervened at other Jews' behest, and, it was said, at their financial offering, to destroy the cult. He went so far as to "order the archbishop of Mainz to solemnly preach that the Christians had caused the greatest injury to the Jews and that 'Good Werner' . . . ought to be incinerated and the ashes of his body scattered to the wind and reduced to nothing."

What the cluster of data from Metz, Colmar, Weissenburg, and Wesel suggests is that there was a deep well of resentment against the Jews throughout the Rhineland that nothing but the extreme dedication of higher officials to the enforcement of the law could restrain. Partly, this was a legacy of the crusade massacres. Partly, it was tied to the charge that the Jews were usurious moneylenders squeezing the life's blood out of poor Christians. The duchess of the Brabant was so concerned about this problem that she sought out the aid of Thomas Aquinas to help her formulate a general anti-usury policy in the 1260s.[41] One of the few hard facts about the livelihood of the Jews of Bar is that they engaged in moneylending.[42] One of the equally few hard facts about the Jews of the Franche-Comté is that they did so as well.[43]

Whereas it may be possible to argue that the presence of Jews in moneylending in principalities like Bar and the Brabant, where commercial networks were strong,[44] would not have been considered blameworthy among thirteenth-century Christians at large (a position I dissent from), the same cannot be said about Jewish moneylending in the Franche-Comté. This forested and underdeveloped region began to attract Jews only when local nobles came under desperate pressure toward the close of the century.[45] The county as a whole, like its counterpart Brittany in the west, where the Jewish presence was equally precarious early in the century, remained essentially rural and parochial in outlook.[46] The tradition reported by Morey that the abbot of Luxeuil organized fairs and local markets in his domains on Saturdays to protect against participation of Jews represents the general attitude, a provincial xenophobia which held the usury of the Lombards in the same contempt and put comparable restrictions on them.[47]

The Jews had come to the province in the wake of a series of disputes in the later thirteenth century in which local lords opposed the French and anti-Imperial policy of their count and found it increasingly difficult to do so without ready cash.[48] The situation was aggravated by a series of agreements with France, the Treaty of Ervennes (1291) and the Treaty of Vincennes (1295), by which the count of Burgundy agreed to have his daughter marry one of the younger sons of Philip the Fair. He also agreed to entrust administrative control of the county to Philip in his son's name as part of the settlement. (The concession brought the count 100,000 l. t.) The barons of the Franche-Comté, xenophobic and independent-minded, rose unsuccessfully against this arrangement (1296–1301). After their failure Capetian influence remained firm for a long time, but the net result of the barons' commitment of so many resources to the rebellion was extremely heavy indebtedness to the Jews and to Lombards as well.[49] Later developments would see the tensions resulting from this indebtedness escalate into fury.[50]

The incidents that I have been relating are obviously not the whole story of Jewish and Christian relations in the principalities on the northeastern frontier. Nonetheless, in the circumstances of the French expulsion of 1306, these traumatic events loomed large. Jews exiled from Normandy, Picardy, the Ile-de-France, Champagne, and the Duchy of Burgundy had to make serious decisions about where to take up residence. To decide to go elsewhere than the principalities on the northeastern frontier would have meant enormously long journeys to lands beyond the Rhône or to Spain. We know that many of the refugees did just that.[51] Sometimes, of course, the choice was logical. It made more sense for a Norman Jew to take ship, if he could, to Navarre than to seek refuge in Imperial Flanders where, even though it was closer, there were virtually no Jews.

The popular sensibility about what life would be like even in those lands of the northeast where Jewish settlement was dense was also negative but for different reasons at the turn of the century. Sometime in the 1290s, for example, a young Jewess, unhappy with her marriage and overcome by her responsibilities as a mother, converted to Christianity and came to Colmar in the heartland of Jewish settlement on the Rhenish frontier. There she denounced the Jews in the most extravagant terms. Certain Jews, she said, who were descended from those who had shouted to the crucified Jesus, "His blood be on us and our children," were in fact stricken with fluxes— the whites and diarrhea. They could save themselves only by the blood of professing Christians.[52] Around 1295, another rumor arose that accused the Jews of profaning the host.[53] The accusation may reflect a recently heightened sense of the miraculous host in this region, since only a few years before, according to the Annals of Colmar, a youngster had seen "a most beautiful little boy" (*puerum pulcherrimum*) during the elevation of the host at mass.[54]

Many other anti-Jewish incidents of a spectacular nature are recorded in the Annals of Colmar for the 1290s.[55] Any number of these and other accusations circulated widely. In 1298, for example, a Christian woman, believed to be possessed, publicly denounced the authorities for tolerating Jews whom she knew by supernatural insight had murdered a poor itinerant skinner nearby.[56] The year 1303 saw an accusation of kidnapping and murder against the Jews of the Rhenish town of Soultz. The alleged victim was a child. The effective dissemination of the accusation is evident from the fact that miracles came to be attributed to this child and his passion.[57]

For most northern French Jews—at least those living at any distance from the Atlantic Coast—the possibility of alternative emigration to the Provençal south or to Spain was just not possible. This would have been especially the case with the old, the sick, and women in the last term of pregnancy. Is it any wonder, then, or any better proof of desperation, that Soultz, the site of a ritual murder accusation in 1303, turns out to be one of the towns in which French Jews took up residence in 1306?[58] Is it likely to have been easy for immigrants to take up residence in Speyer, where the weight of an oppressive regime had been causing native Jews to emigrate since the 1280s?[59]

The new French residents were not necessarily welcomed by the princes. They were poor and, therefore, only potentially valuable sources of heavy taxation. Presumably, native Jews smoothed the transition by offering money to the princes or by paying the special fees that some authorities demanded. At Metz, for instance, each immigré was charged a thirty-pence entrance fee.[60] In Hainault a seigneurial residence tax was imposed, documentable from 1308.[61] Other lords might have been less amenable to immigration: no one can say for sure whether the count of Bar decided to imitate Philip the Fair and expel his Jews, but it is suggestive that there is no positive evidence of any Jews resident in his county between 1306 and 1315.[62] Why the count, if he did so, should have gone out of his way to imitate the French king is uncertain. Because of earlier grievances he had little or no love for Philip the Fair.[63]

What there is no uncertainty about is that a number of principalities on the northeastern frontier accepted refugees. Brabant appears to have done so, and Hainault certainly did.[64] Besides Metz, we can include Worms and Strassbourg among Rhenish towns that accepted Jews in numbers.[65] Blumenkranz believed at least twenty-five towns in Lorraine received refugees.[66] In the Franche-Comté and the Swiss borderlands, the vills of La Loye and Auxonne and the town of Basel became homes for Jews.[67]

These Jews came, as has already been intimated, from the north of France. Many were English refugees who had spent sixteen years in northern France; others were native French from places like Troyes and Verdun-sur-Doubs in Champagne. Still others are only identified as northerners from the tombstones inscribed at their deaths: *ha tsarfat* (*le français*) or *mi-tsarfat* (*de France*). The retention of the geographical surname was in no way unusual; yet it does raise the question of whether the Jews were or became well-integrated with the native Jewish communities. There is very little evidence on this point for the principalities of the northeast. We do know, however, that the transition was not altogether smooth. In Worms the newcomers were "excluded from candidature to the council of the [Jewish] community."[68]

The effect on the Christian population of this wave of immigration is impossible to measure with precision, but nevertheless seems quite clear. There is evidence of a flurry of popular demonstrations against the Jews in the immediate aftermath of their resettlement. The little town of Gennape in the Brabant suffered a massacre of its Jews in 1308.[69] The incident was touched off by what seems to have been an ill-organized gathering of people, mostly artisans, for a crusade. It turned into an attack on the Jews in defiance of the duke of the Brabant, who ultimately had to open the castle of Gennape to the Jews for protection and descend on the town himself to disperse the so-called crusaders.[70] Strassbourg also saw a brief eruption of persecution of the Jews around 1309.[71]

More generally, certain tombstones that have been recovered in the Rhenish provinces and appear to date from slightly after the period under discussion here are inscribed with martyrdom formulae that praise the parents of the deceased.[72] These may reflect incidents in the generation of the parents' death of the kind of random violence that the immigration of even a small number of "undesirables" would provoke in the vills and towns of the northeastern frontier. This violence and that described in the preceding paragraph stimulated further migration. Like the English Jews who found only a temporary home in France from 1290 to 1306, French refugees frequently abandoned their homes for the hope of safety and prosperity further east. A century after the French expulsion there were Jews in Budapest, descendants of the exiles of 1306, still speaking French.[73]

Beyond the Rhône

Jewish population in France in 1306 was concentrated in the south. Hence the migration to French principalities beyond the Rhône and to Spain dwarf the movements discussed thus far. The larger migration has generated larger quantities of material, and the picture that emerges from these materials is fuller and contrasts sharply with that of the fate of the northern refugees.

The major principalities beyond the Rhône were four in number: Savoy, Dauphiné, Comtat-Venaissin, and Provence. The northern two, Savoy and Dauphiné, were lightly settled by Jews before 1306.[74] The Comtat, however, possessed approximately twenty towns and vills with Jewish settlements, including Carpentras, Avignon, Cavaillon, Vaison, and Orange.[75] Provence possessed about fifty such settlements, most of which were concentrated along the eastern banks of the Rhône or along the other major artery of internal communication, the Durance. A few important Jewish settlements were located apart from these concentrations: Aix, for example, was midway between the Durance and the Mediterranean coast, and Marseilles was directly on the coast.[76]

Almost nothing is known about the situation in Savoy or Dauphiné with respect to the Jews before 1306, so we can profitably turn our attention in the first place to the Comtat-Venaissin.[77] For nearly a century before the French expulsion, French political influence had been important in the Comtat. The decisive event was the conquest of the chief city, Avignon, under Louis VIII in 1226. Juridically, the county as a whole passed to the papacy in 1229. In reality the concession to the papacy was not enforced until 1274. Indeed, it had been agreed in 1229 that the king of France should exercise guard over the county at least to 1235. After 1235 Capetian influence might have been expected to wane, but Alfonse of Poitiers, Louis IX's brother, inherited the count of Toulouse's claims to property in the region and became an active promoter and patron of the local ecclesiastical establishment. As a result, he built up a considerable bundle of rights in the region. Louis's other brother, Charles of Anjou, after his marriage to Beatrice of Provence in 1246 and his acquisition of titular sovereignty of her homeland by that union, also had claims in the Comtat-Venaissin, with especially strong ones in Avignon, and took an active interest in affairs there. The two brothers ultimately became the de facto rulers of the Comtat. It was not until the early 1270s that the crown reimposed the original settlement and confirmed the Comtat to the papacy in 1274.[78]

In Avignon a municipal *viguier* acted as the Capetians' representative after Charles took control of the city in 1251. The Jewish population was circumscribed in its economic activities, but the full panoply of Capetian restrictions do not appear to have been applied here, possibly because of the technical limitations on French authority, but also, one supposes, because of the tendency noticed earlier in the French crown's treatment of Languedoc to defer to local customs in an effort to consolidate the conquest.[79] (The situation with Narbonne makes a nice parallel.)[80] Whatever the reason, the Jews in Avignon seem to have flourished even under the Capetians in those aspects of economic life that were permitted to them.[81] In intellectual life the latter part of the thirteenth century saw the careers of a number of important Jewish savants in the city.[82]

Elsewhere in the Comtat, as we might expect from the unsystematic nature of the Capetian political presence, other authorities exercised more power than Alfonse of Poitiers or Charles of Anjou. At Carpentras and Cavaillon, the Jews were under the jurisdiction of ecclesiastics. The immediate nature of the authority over them sometimes put the Jews at risk. A "good" bishop might be lenient and encouraging; a "bad" one could be ruinous. The uncertainty made life more precarious in these towns and, consequently, less prosperous.[83] The materials whereby this issue might be fleshed out are fragmentary, controversial, and demand further study than can be given here. There is a hint of a local expulsion of the Jews from Carpentras in the early thirteenth century but with Jews drifting back (or being allowed back) by 1263. What happened a few years later is also controversial. Either there was a new expulsion in 1269 or there was a general restriction of settlement in that year. This hiatus in the Jewish history of Carpentras was brief, however. It was upset in 1274 when the papacy took more active governance of the Comtat. Residence in Carpentras was soon confirmed to seventy-five Jewish families.[84]

About one-third of the seventy-five families bore Languedocian place surnames.[85] Many of this group were probably people of more or less remote Carpentras origin who had settled on the western bank of the Rhône (only thirty miles away) when the hostility against them from the bishop of Carpentras waxed strong and had migrated elsewhere in the region as circumstances permitted. In other words, whether there were formal expulsions of Jews from Carpentras before 1274 or not, voluntary emigration during periods of great pressure on the Jews amounted to much the same thing and would have given observers much the same impression. What intellectual activity has come to be associated with the Jews of Carpentras dates from the period after the firming up of papal control in 1274, control which, at least during the period before 1306, seems to have been typically restrained or moderate.[86]

If we look further south, into Provence, uncertainty yields to a richness and stability of Jewish community structures and Jewish-Christian relations that was a consistent feature of life. Numerous authors have stressed the social harmony that existed in Provence.[87] Some see an almost idyllic set of relationships and conjure the evidence of intellectual vitality in the Jewish community as support of this view. A world of enmity or active hostility would not have permitted the efflorescence of the large number of writers—theologians, philosophers, and doctors—that was seen in Marseilles or Arles, for example.[88] Yet, everybody is agreed that the penetration of Capetian influence in the guise of Charles of Anjou and his Angevin successors upset this stable environment.[89] Charles himself was not the culprit entirely. Gross, over and over again in his great book, reminds us that the brother of Saint Louis was somewhat more lenient than the king.[90] Nonetheless, Charles and his administration constituted the conduit for certain Capetian ideas on Jewish policy to penetrate the fabric of life in Provence, although there was no systematic attack on moneylending in this commercial environment.[91]

Dissident voices have sometimes been raised against the rosier versions of the above picture, and one community stands out for the variety of information that it has produced and the vigor with which that information has been investigated: Manosque. Legend has it that long before the coming of the Capetians Manosque was settled by northern Jews with different ways from the Provençal Jews with whom they came in contact. It is said, too, that the Jews of Manosque kept to their ways and attitudes despite the life that was being lived all about them.[92] On top of this, the town of Manosque had a very active Inquisition that aggressively sought out certain Jewish targets, namely, the families and friends of converted Jews who, it was alleged, tried to bring the converts back to Judaism.[93] While the Order of Knights Hospitaller of Manosque, which was the seigneur of the town, was as zealous as any lord in trying to preserve its jurisdiction, there was an evident willingness to yield to the Inquisition on the matter of apostasy and support for apostasy.[94] So Manosque looks like a place ripe for northern fears and northern hates, like the accusation of ritual murder (or so it is categorized by Joseph Shatzmiller). A relative of two Jews charged in Manosque in 1284 with trying to secure the apostasy of their daughter from Christianity was the victim of such an accusation a decade later. Other rumors flew through the town: about profanaion of the host and desecration of the cross.[95] The real question is whether the Manosque case is generalizable to Provence as a whole and whether it owes any of its more startling details to the influence of Capetian ideology. That question cannot be answered definitively at the present time, given the state of the research. But a few remarks may be of value.

The Angevin presence in Provence need not have been disruptive. By the very nature of this presence (acquisition through marriage) there was the possibility of a relatively peaceful transition to Angevin rule. Natives who resented the marriage were provoked from resentment to action more by Charles of Anjou's style of governance than by any one act of his. A major locus of resistance was the independent commune of Marseilles. There was a long tradition among the citizens of Marseilles of playing off various forces in Provence to assure the independence of the city. In the early part of the century, this tradition had entailed balancing the pretensions of the bishop, the count of Toulouse, the emperor (Provence was an imperial fief), and the native count of Provence.[96] As the empire drifted into turmoil in the mid-century, it became a less important factor in Provençal history. After Charles of Anjou became count of Provence in 1246 and Alfonse of Poitiers, count of Toulouse in 1249, the traditional approach of the citizens of Marseilles to preserving their autonomy made little or no sense; but they were not averse to seeking new allies against their Capetian antagonist.[97]

In spite of this—and primarily because of his involvement in so many other enterprises and his consequent absences from the scene in Provence—the count made no determined effort to suppress the independence of Marseilles. Similarly, the town's mercantile elite, the ecclesiastics who controlled part of the town and those citizens who favored the Angevins, worked together to achieve a modus vivendi with the count. Many of these people wanted to benefit from the boom in economic activity that came from the first crusade of Louis IX and recognized that a favorable relationship with the king's brother could only help them achieve their ends.[98] Underneath (or alongside) the spirit of compromise went a strong suspicion of the northerner and his intentions and an equally strong nativist impulse for independence, both in the city and in the province at large.

Charles of Anjou's capture and brief imprisonment on crusade with his brother in 1250 was one of many opportunities for nativist elements to give vent to their hostility. When Charles returned from crusade after his ransom, he no longer put off the process of bringing the province and Marseilles to their knees. At intervals Angevin troops were prepared to lay seige and take the city, but the city fathers and other interested parties usually succeeded in working out compromises, which were followed, after a time, by new anti-French alliances and demonstrations that further provoked Charles.[99] The deteriorating situation was enshrined in the compromise or capitulation of 1257, the so-called Chapters of Peace, that

effectively suppressed the commune. There were insurrections and demonstrations after this date; and even though Charles was restrained in his
reactions, he ultimately moved with decision against those who plotted to
overthrow his rule. By 1264, after a large number of executions, Marseilles
was definitively integrated into his domains.[100]

War brought what there was of latent tension between Christians and
Jews to the surface. Of course, thanks to the Albigensian crusade, there was
a long tradition, even in this part of the south that had suffered little from
the crusade, of ecclesiastical councils harping on the theme of segregation
of the adherents of the two religions, as if permitting social commerce
between Jews and Christians would lead to tolerance of Christian
heretics.[101] Despite this tradition, Jews in Marseilles and elsewhere continued to enjoy profitable relations with Catholics. They served as doctors
for them. They were employed in municipal offices. They played a modest
role in maritime commerce. They were brokers, landholders, rentiers, and
artisans of many sorts who serviced the Christian population as well as
their own.[102]

Nonetheless, the ecclesiastical pronouncements were hardly voices cry-
ing in the wilderness. To be sure, the picture is not one of Manosque writ
large. Social relations between Jews and Christians remained profitable and
varied through the first several decades of the thirteenth century. Yet there
is evidence both from individual incidents and from general secular pronouncements that the roots of social harmony were, if not superficial, not
very deep. The municipal authorities of Marseilles coupled Jews with
prostitutes and slaves in closing the baths to them; they limited the number
of Jews who could take ship at any one time and what they could do once
on board; and they were quite concerned with the sort of activity, like the
practice of medicine, that might endanger Christians' lives.[103] Concerns of
this sort seem particularly sharp in the period of great contention with
Charles.[104] But that may only suggest that the ground was already fertile
for such antagonism.

The reformulation of policy toward the Jews in Marseilles with the
suppression of the town's independence in the 1260s addressed the problem of their immunity from taxation by the count. The immunity had been
conceded in the Chapters of Peace of 1257. It was revoked in 1262.[105] From
the 1270s the income generated by the count's taxation of the Jews has left
good records, showing that the return, from the city and in Provence
generally, was substantial: it ranged annually from about 1,200 l. t. to 1,500

l. t.[106] Together with the annual taxation went the count's support for the ecclesiastical proscriptions enforced in Capetian lands. Jealous of his jurisdiction vis-à-vis the church he may have been, but he supported Jews' wearing of the distinctive sign on their clothing as mandated by the church, the inadmissibility of testimony against Christians, and the prohibition of work on Sundays.[107] Although, as Crémieux argued, these proscriptions were mitigated in practice, especially in the fourteenth century, I do not find evidence that the distinction between Jew and Christian came to be of no juridical importance in life in Marseilles, as he believed.[108]

Focussing on Marseilles with its strong Jewish community while acknowledging the problems associated with Jewish-Christian relations there permits us to put the picture of Manosque in proper perspective. The evidence from Manosque must not blind us to the generally successful level of commercial integration between Christians and Jews in Provence. Incidents and legislation which betoken certain tensions in local society are not the same as state prosecution and executions on the charge of ritual murder, elaborate cults of child-saints, or the massacres that came to signal Jewish-Christian conflict in England or the Rhenish provinces.[109] Even the taxation can be used as evidence of the successful continuity of Jewish prosperity and community. The early taxes were, as one might expect, collected by the Jews themselves. For this purpose, the various local communities were organized into sub-regional units; this may very well represent or reflect an internal sense of organization on the Jews' own part. Moreover, later taxation (early in the fourteenth century) will show us syndics of the Jews paying the lump sums required in taxation even before the individual assessments were collected, a fact that suggests both a high degree of community responsibility and the existence of some Jews with very large fortunes.[110]

It was, then, communities like the one at Marseilles,—not idyllic, but large, fiscally healthy, full of intellectual vigor—that would have been most attractive to the refugees from France in 1306. Constraints of distance, however, necessitated that some refugees take shelter or become residents of less flourishing towns with much smaller Jewish presences. In Savoy and the Dauphiné we find migrants settling in tiny vills. These seem to have served less as permanent residences than as way-stations on the road to Piedmont and northern Italy.[111] Occasionally more permanent settlements sprang up, as, for example, in the small Dauphinois vill of Serres and at Grenoble.[112] In and near the Comtat-Venaissin such settlements were less rare. Orange counted a number of families toward the end of the four-teenth century whose ancestors had emigrated from France in 1306.[113] And widespread immigration is documented in the province as a whole. [114]

All the same, Provence was the region that really attracted permanent refugees from eastern France. Tarascon, where an established if not ancient community of approximately one hundred Jews resided in the late thir-teenth century, received a number of immigrants, a few of whom may have come to the town before 1306 in any of one or more of the waves of voluntary migration that characterized Jewish demography in later thirteenth-century France.[115] The Jews of Aix (about 250 families or 10% of the town) accepted a large number of immigrants in the early fourteenth century as well.[116] Arles, whose Jewish population exceeded one hundred, took in immigrants, including famous learned rabbis like Abba Mari of Lunel, whom Gross called "the famous champion of obscurantism" for his opposition to gentile studies.[117] Marseilles also offered much to refugees— the full repertory of amenities of Jewish life: an historic neighborhood or neighborhoods, a *scola major* and a *scola minor*, a hospital, an almshouse, a *mikva*.[118] Many took up residence there and in much smaller towns, like Trets, where a good living waited to be made.[119]

Influenced by the upbeat interpretation of life among Provençal Jews before 1306, most scholars talk about the "welcoming" of Jews in the time of the French exile.[120] "Welcoming" (the word has even been used of Grenoble in the Dauphiné) seems inappropriate. Grenoble charged an entrance fee of forty pounds and a residence fee of ten pounds per year.[121] The "welcoming" count of Provence in 1306 was Charles II of Anjou, the same man who had expelled the Jews from Anjou and Maine in 1289. Perhaps because of the large numbers of Jews already in Provence or because of the existing charters to the Jews, he had not expelled them from Provence at that time and he did not follow the lead of Philip the Fair in 1306. It may be, however, that Charles II was no longer actively governing his domains in 1306, for that year saw Charles's son and heir, Robert, issue instructions on a wide variety of matters pertaining to the administration of Provence, including the limits of licit Jewish activity.[122] They were traditional in scope: Christians ought not call upon Jewish doctors; Chris-tians and Jews ought to establish separate markets; Jews ought to wear a distinctive badge. But they in no way mimic the oppressive program of the recent years of Philip the Fair's reign. Even so, what some scholars have called "welcoming" must have been greeted with far more suspicion by the immigré Jews themselves.[123]

The integration of the Jews who crossed the Rhône had both spectacular successes and some spectacular failures. We have already noticed how in the Dauphiné and Savoy temporary residence was frequently followed by new displacement to lands with larger Jewish populations far to the east and south. There must have been greater success in the Comtat-Venaissin, especially in a town like Carpentras, where so many of the resident Jews had themselves recently spent time in eastern Languedoc. The people who went to Carpentras, I would suggest, were friends and relatives of the residents there.

In some cases—and here the Provençal sources are helpful— immigration to small towns put great pressure on the Jewish communities.[124] It has been suggested that Saint-Remy-de-Provence was an entirely new community.[125] This would make sense if we postulate that immigrants made a brief sojourn in one town to renew their prosperity before buying permission to set up on their own elsewhere, thus taking pressure off the community that first received them. But this kind of process was in no way the model. More often a small town was transformed by immigration. Trets is a case in point.[126]

On the eve of the French expulsion there were only four or five Jewish families in Trets although the community was an old one going back perhaps before 1143. It had not been an entirely isolated community. Marriages were sometimes made with outsiders who took up residence in the town. In general, however, the community, like its Christian counterpart, was parochial; and the status of the Jewish community was demographically precarious. Any imbalance in migration or slight rise in infant mortality would have wiped it out.

Within a few years of the French expulsion the Jewish population had doubled from four or five families to ten, in numbers from twenty or twenty-five to fifty. In the absence of any strong mendicant presence representing the Inquisition, life in Trets was dramatically opened up. Contacts with other immigrants created more elaborate social and business networks than had existed before. The immigrants, needing to establish themselves and prosper, worked actively in the rural hinterland of Trets (if Trets can be said to have had a hinterland) providing credit. They effectively displaced their coreligionists who had serviced the credit needs of the local population from more distant centers at Aix and Saint-Maximin, probably by undercutting their interest rates.

On the one hand, the enhanced presence of Jews in Trets saw the rise of anti-Judaism. The Christians were wary of permitting competition in

the agricultural or artisanal sphere that was at the heart of the rural economy. Moneylending and also medicine were more tolerable (there were no
Christian doctors in Trets). The Christians, or rather their seigneur, required the Jews to do a form of homage, the *osculum pedum* (kissing of his
feet), that was more humiliating than that performed by non-Jews; and he
imposed restrictions on the alienation of real property to Jews. Nonetheless, the situation in Trets became extremely favorable to the Jewish community. What was unthinkable culturally before 1306 became possible with
the advent of the new immigrants and a little time: a synagogue, more
comprehensive community "political" organization— essential for the continued well-being of the community vis-à-vis Christian, especially the ecclesiastical elite—and a sense of the social dignity of the Trets community
over against the claims of larger jewries. There is no call for romanticizing.
Resentment there was among the Jews themselves: natives of newcomers,
newcomers of natives. Still, the social history of Trets was transformed
fundamentally in the ripple effect of the French expulsion of 1306.

The Iberian Kingdoms

Along the Pyrenean border of France in 1306 three kingdoms presented
themselves as possible new homes for refugee Jews: Navarre, Aragon, and
Majorca (whose continental possessions included Cerdagne and Roussillon). The westernmost of these kingdoms was Navarre, ruled by Louis of
France, the son and heir of Philip the Fair. Louis had been invested with
Navarre and the county of Champagne on the occasion of his mother's
death and the transmission of her rights to him in 1305. As his father's vassal
for the county of Champagne, Louis dutifully carried out the orders of
expulsion.[127] He did not expel the Jews from Navarre, however. He even
permitted the exiles from his father's kingdom to seek refuge in
Navarre.[128]

Strayer argued in his study of the reign of Philip the Fair that the young
Louis (he was seventeen at the time of the expulsion) was not allowed to
act with much independence in general, either in Champagne or Navarre,
a fact that makes his behavior with respect to the exiles all the more
peculiar. Nonetheless, the evidence brought together by Strayer also shows
that Louis did make changes in Navarre within a year of his accession to
the throne there that suggest a break with royal policy. He spent three
months in Navarre in 1307 after having dismissed (or had transferred) the

governor of Navarre who had served as Philip's representative for the ten years before Louis's coming to the throne.[129] Much more telling is the fact that it would be Louis as Louis X of France who would reverse Philip's expulsion and allow the Jews to return to the kingdom of France in 1315, a year after his father's death.[130]

The role of Louis is critical to understanding one of the real differences between the exile experiences on the northeastern frontier and beyond the Rhône, on the one hand, and those in Spain, on the other. In the northeast the Jews met great hostility and many continued their journeys, leaving France and its culture far behind. Some "French" characteristics persisted, but eventually these Jews became Central and Eastern Europeans. Beyond the Rhône, especially in Provence, integration into Provençal life went relatively smoothly. One gets the impression of a world that accommodated the Jews and received them willingly. There were some difficulties, but the Jews who immigrated to Provence became Provençal Jews; they established flourishing businesses and made permanent settlements. On the other side of the Pyrenees from France, however, there persisted a kind of homesickness that was almost suffocating. It is as if the Jews who left France were merely waiting to return. That Louis of France had shown himself willing to accept the exiles from his father's land into his own must have given them hope that when he came into the kingdom of France he would undo the evil that his father had wrought.

At the same time there were worries among Jews of the other two kingdoms about whether the refugees would be admitted. In Majorca there were even worries that they themselves might be expelled. Certainly the recent history of legislation toward the Jews of Majorca was not encouraging. The king was intent on segregation, and he had shown considerable animosity to freedom of residence and "excessive" usury.[131] Furthermore, as vassal of the king of France for the lordship of Montpellier, he had followed Philip the Fair's policy in the town.[132] Consequently, the Jews of Majorca petitioned their lord with the prayer that he would not expand his actions in Montpellier to all his domains. He reacted favorably to their entreaty and also permitted Jews from France to enter his lands.[133]

Aragon, too, did not turn the exiles away. The Aragonese saw the Jews as a useful part of the tax base. Already in Aragon "Jewish communities contributed 22% of all direct taxes. . . . In Catalonia the proportion contributed by Jews was probably higher. . . ."[134] The Jewish communities in Aragon, in other words, were rich and were capable of influencing their king with money to permit the immigration of the refugees from France.

Navarre was overwhelmed with Jews from France. Earlier there had been immigrants from the expulsion from Gascony of 1288, as evidenced by residents in Navarre with surnames like *de Tonneins* and *de Bergerac*.[135] The refugees of 1306 came from many scattered and distant places: Saint-Maixent in Poitou, Saint-Pourçain in Auvergne, Chartres in the Beauce, Pont-Audemer and Passy in Normandy. The integration of these people of vastly different backgrounds was difficult. Each remained "el françes."[136] The Christian population eventually reacted with considerable ferocity at the increase in numbers—or so it seems from the later destruction of the jewry of Estella in 1328. That jewry had grown enormously after 1306 and although there was some out-migration about a decade later, it was still much larger in population than it had been in the thirteenth century.[137] The real proof, however, of the failure of integration is what Béatrice Leroy calls the massive return of the immigrant population to France in 1315.[138] If she is correct (there may be some danger of exaggeration),[139] the importance of Louis X in Navarre must be stressed in all of this.

Majorcan and Aragonese Jews provide us with the literary echo of the great return that Leroy alludes to. One senses the overwhelming pall of homelessness—"the poverty of exile"—and the radical uncertainty of the future. Even though Aragon and Majorca were physically comfortable lands, and even though the history of contacts between the Jews of Languedoc and Spanish Jews was long and intimate, the situation of the exiles was different from that encountered through occasional business and social contacts and far different also from the situation that had faced the steady stream of voluntary exiles who had crossed the Pyrenees since the time of the Albigensian Crusade.[140] For the Jews of 1306 came in droves from the great cities of Languedoc—Narbonne, Montpellier, Béziers, Carcassonne, Toulouse, Pamiers—and with virtually no resources. They were utterly dependent on the good will of their coreligionists. We will later explore some of the ramifications of this fact. For now it is sufficient to try to recreate the sentiment of uncertainty among the refugees themselves.

This uncertainty gave rise to many metaphors.[141] Poems and recollections speak of journeys to "dark lands," to "desolate lands," to lands of "shadows." The exiles express the fear of their deliverance from the rapacious "lions" who were the French into the clutches of the equally dangerous "lions" who awaited their arrival in Spain. They were stripped naked in the lands of exile. They feared, if the poems can be trusted, being unable to master the tasks of ordinary daily life: the language of the

Auvergne was not that of Barcelona; speech itself would always stigmatize the refugees as outsiders. The refrains, ultimately, are monotonous, but no less moving on that account: there is no rest, no repose, no respite from the poverty of exile. The time of exile is composed of "days, nights and months . . . passed in sadness."[142]

In fact, throughout the Majorcan lands and Aragon, Jewish communities went out of their way to welcome the refugees and by doing so assuaged the initial feeling of anomie. It was asserted as recently as 1962 that the Jewish subjects of the king of Majorca were perhaps less successful in this than were their coreligionists in Aragon. Indeed, Blumenkranz has suggested that the counties of Cerdagne and Roussillon on the mainland refused entry to Jews. These counties had already absorbed so many Jews in the course of the thirteenth century that the outlook for new Jews was dismal. Perpignan, the chief city, was, in Blumenkranz's words, "no longer able to offer any economic opportunity to new immigrants."[143] In the nineteenth century both Saige and Renan published a little evidence that Jews did take up residence in Perpignan in the wake of the French expulsion, but this evidence could have been and apparently was regarded as documenting exceptional or isolated examples.[144] More recently, Assis has shown that the examples are not exceptional at all. Significant numbers of Jews took up residence in Perpignan (it was the principal haven) and throughout Cerdagne and Roussillon and on the island of Majorca. Assis concluded that "access to all these territories was accorded to Jews expelled from France."[145] He noted that there was occasionally some resentment at allowing in people who, by taking sides in the Maimonidean controversy, had offended the Jews of Perpignan;[146] but even in these cases, initial hostility was rather quickly overcome when faced with the obvious need of the immigrants.

For native Jews of Aragon and Catalonia, the welcome or access given the refugees was very costly.[147] The resident Jews of the towns paid enormous sums to obtain permission for the refugees to enter: one thousand shillings in Gerona, for example, for the settlement of ten new families.[148] Separate communities took in greater or lesser numbers as they could: sixty families in Barcelona, ten in Lerida, four in Montclus, forty-five, thirty, and so on elsewhere.[149] In Catalonia we find Jewish communities experiencing growth in the decade after 1306 of approximately 40%.[150] No estimate of absolute numbers is possible with regard to the level of immigration to the crown of Aragon and Majorca. Since their location was immediately adjacent to the largest concentration of Jews in the kingdom of France, a total of many thousands of refugees does not seem an unreasonable guess.[151]

The large numbers created internal tensions—which in turn help to explain the persistent sense of alienation in recollections of the exile and in exile poems. Sixty new families in Barcelona—anywhere from one-sixth to one-third of the total Jewish population of the town[152]—put enormous pressure on the charitable and productive resources of the jewry and raised the psychological tension between natives and immigrés once the first wave of sympathy for the latter had abated. One can imagine the same problem in other communities. Taken aback by the logical consequences of such an influx as took place in Barcelona, Assis, in opposition to the explicit statements of the texts, suggested that the sixty families may have been distributed through Barcelona and its hinterland.[153] Whether or not this is so, the Jewish immigrés would still have constituted an extraordinary burden on the natives.

An additional burden was the influx in 1307 and 1308 of a few Jews who had converted during the great confiscation in France and later apostasized. In the abstract, their return to their confession brought joy to their coreligionists. And we should not underestimate the psychological pressure to which they were subjected to become Christians or which they endured from the disgust that their brief abandonment of Judaism also provoked among some Jews who had held fast against the "persuasion" of the Capetian state. But the real issue was the potential harm they brought to their new haven. Ecclesiastical authorities, seeking the *lapsi* out as heretics, would undermine the equilibrium of the Jewish communities that received them. Assis has traced the actions of the Inquisition in ferreting out suspected re-converts so thoroughly as to put entire jewries in jeopardy.[154]

There is, too, another dark side to the immigration. It does not appear that the wide variety of ugly incidents, rumors, and charges of devilry that met the migrants in the provinces of the northeastern frontier were encountered by Jews who crossed the Pyrenees. All the same, not long before they arrived in Spain, there had been an accusation of ritual murder in Barcelona, which had not been successfully prosecuted.[155] Less than three years later there were similar rumors in Majorca and Catalonia.[156] Again, though little came of these charges, they do betray a heightened sensitivity to the enhanced Jewish presence south of the Pyrenees. The residence fees paid to the king of Aragon are sometimes tied to his protection of the new Jews from hostility.[157]

Internal tensions arose in more mundane ways. Take work. A little town in Provence like Trets could stand having a Jewish immigrant doctor. It had probably had no doctor before. A town like Barcelona accepting sixty refugee families probably got one or more new doctors who, if allowed to practice, would have competed with native physicians. Presumably, in a glut of supply, the newcomers would have worked for natives of the same occupation until they could make enough to strike out on their own away from active competition with those who had succored them. What we know for sure is that hostility to the immigrants, no matter how careful they were, was repeatedly expressed and led some to seek new places of residence.[158]

The problem of marriage was another vexing one that made the situation of the exiles among the natives uneasy. The parchment contracts that accompanied Jewish marriage were seized in the *captio* in France. When couples reached the land of their exile, it became a question of Jewish law whether they could enjoy conjugal rights in the absence of the records. The resolution, as we might expect, was positive, but a number of "husbands," when apprised of the problematic character of their marriages, used the opportunity to renounce their ties and obligations and even made second marriages.[159] Inevitably these machinations, though by no means widespread, soured the environment, gave rise to a distancing between natives and "those refugees with their sordid problems." At least, things of this sort would help explain some of the clannishness. The "French" Jews of Barcelona set up their own "sinagoga dels francescos."[160] The sense of separation implied by this foundation lasted, just as it lasted with the immigrants to Navarre, so that a "significant" number of the exiles returned to France, what was termed, "our mother," in 1315.[161]

Conclusion

This survey of exile environments cannot be comprehensive. Much work remains to be done in local archives and in recovering data already published in obscure or neglected journals and books. Nor should it be assumed that there were no other exile environments. If Majorcan Jews could travel to Tunisia, refugees from France could also do so; and a few

Jews may have gone to Palestine.[162] To be sure, the latter would have been disappointed. Graboïs has gathered together some of the impressions of Jewish life in the late thirteenth and early fourteenth century in Palestine (after the Muslim reconquest of Acre and the slaughter of Jews whom they regarded as allies of the crusaders). These include a lament at "the murder of all the scholars of Acre together with all the members of their households when the Ishmaelites conquered the town" and a description of Palestine by a Jewish observer "who makes frequent mention of the graves and tombstones of scholars and rabbis, as if to emphasize the fact that Palestine was no longer the land of the living."[163]

Nonetheless, despite gaps in the record, a few clear conclusions emerge. First is the inhospitable nature of the sojourns of the Jews in the short term and long term in the lands of the northeastern frontier and the consequent movement of population further east. Second, we learn from the Provençal experience that modest numbers of Jews could be successfully integrated into a land where relations between Christians and native Jews were reasonably good and where lords did not tolerate popular excesses. All the same, the critical point here is the modest numbers of immigrés. Far more Jews crossed the Rhône into Provence than moved into the Rhenish provinces, but nothing like the number of Jews who crossed the Pyrenees or took ship to Majorca or the east coast of Spain from the coastal cities of Languedoc (Montpellier, Béziers, Narbonne) or took passage in the north, in Normandy and Picardy, on vessels bound for the Biscay ports of Castile that allowed access to Navarre. Whereas the Jews who immigrated to Provence from eastern Languedoc spoke essentially the same language and easily adapted to and were well integrated into Provençal culture, the Jews who immigrated to Spain, having come from an enormously wide geographical area, had only one thing in common: they were refugees from the kingdom of France. There were so many of them and they put such pressure on the resources of native Jews that they never successfully integrated in the short time they were given. Many of them were particularly hopeful of a return to France precisely because one of the kings of the Spanish kingdoms, Louis of Navarre, was the son of the king of France yet had generously opened his Navarrese lands to them, an act that was full of promise for the future. I do not think that with the presently available data it is possible to say that most or even half of the immigrés to Spain returned to France in 1315, but the sense of anomie revealed in their writings speaks volumes on why scholars are willing to entertain the possibility at all.

14. Disillusionment

When Louis X became king in 1314, France was already caught up in a flurry of rebellion. The accumulated disgust with the heavy taxation of Philip the Fair and the suspicion that his ministers were grasping and determined to squeeze the people dry and to usurp all liberties had led to a series of leagues and demonstrations in opposition to the crown.[1] The uprisings made the last days of Philip the Fair all the more tragic, for the year 1314 had opened with the scandal of his three daughters-in-law who were charged with adultery (ultimately one was exonerated).[2] The holy monarchy was, as it were, tainted from within. The rebellions proved that lack of trust was widespread. Much of 1314 and 1315 was spent by Philip and after his death by Louis X in trying to reduce tension, to prevent a flurry of rebellion from becoming a fury.[3]

Louis X struck the note immediately on his accession. He would confirm the liberties of provinces and groups and he would ceaselessly invoke the memory of his great-grandfather, Saint Louis. He did not intend to go to his deathbed as his own father had done, implicitly lamenting his failure to rule the kingdom as had the great saint.[4] On 19 March 1315, he confirmed the liberties of the Normans.[5] On 1 April he issued a more general confirmation of liberties, one section of which addressed the particularly sensitive problem of Languedoc (*lingue occitane*), where the hunt since 1306 for debtors who owed the Jews had caused tempers to flare. By calling off further collections, except for notorious cases, he was following his father's lead, but in this instance there was an implicit promise that "notorious" would be more narrowly defined.[6]

On 12 April the north received relief from the new notarial system that had recently been imposed in administration.[7] The Burgundians received confirmation of their liberties in the same month.[8] In May, ordinances of reform following precedents laid down in earlier reigns were issued on matters of administration, to specific administrative districts and to historic provinces like Champagne.[9] At the same time, additions were made to confirmations only recently given. The speed with which Louis had acted meant that some questions that had been glossed over needed to be clarified.[10] One of the most important statements of his ideal of governance was the promise to end the subvention for the army in Flanders. The settling of the tax issue was of paramount significance.[11]

All the same, the retreat from the authoritarian style of governance that had come to be associated with Philip the Fair had its risks. The crown needed money; and to get money Louis began immediately to employ expedients—expedients that were less objectionable than general taxation to the political nation at large. Royal serfs were freed on 3 July 1315 in return for subsidies to the royal treasury.[12] Italians and their businesses were regulated to the economic benefit of the crown in precisely the same week.[13] And later in the month, on 28 July 1315, the Jews were readmitted to the realm.[14]

As early as 17 May the king had expressed some willingness to entertain such a return.[15] But it was not an easy decision.[16] Still, if rejecting his father's policy was hard, this was mitigated, in a sense, by going back to the policy of Saint Louis. Perhaps more significant, final permission to return was purchased by the Jews for 22,500 pounds plus a yearly subvention of 10,000 pounds.[17]

The nature of the agreement was spelled out in great detail. By convention the ordinance that contains the agreement is divided into twenty sections.[18] On the whole, these sections repeat bits and pieces of the legislation of Saint Louis. The Jews were to live by the labor of their own hands or by commerce.[19] At the same time, they were permitted to engage in pawnbroking, though not quite as the saint had envisaged it. Rather, license was given them to charge interest at two pennies per pound per week.[20] Even so, pawnbroking was discouraged by the ordinance and could not involve church ornaments, bloody or wet garments.[21] Old-fashioned moneylending under bond was forbidden.[22]

Outside of financial matters, Louis X followed his saintly predecessor. He imposed the wearing of the badge and forbad slander or disputing of the Christian religion.[23] He offered himself as the protector of the Jews in all the privileges that they had enjoyed before the expulsion (unless modified by the ordinance of readmission), and he appointed two commissioners to oversee Jewish affairs in the future.[24] The king allowed Jews to collect on old debts that they could prove and that the crown had not already seized, an obvious admission on the crown's part that some of the Jews' financial books had escaped the *captio* of 1306. Of those debts which they eventually collected, they were to retain only one-third, with the other two-thirds going into the royal treasury.[25] Otherwise the government would not bother them about objects allegedly smuggled out in 1306 or about any other residual matters.[26] The government did not intend to look behind that year to prosecute Jews, nor would it raise any questions about what the Jews had been doing between 1306 and the readmission.[27]

In a gesture of generosity, perhaps, or at the insistence of the Jews, Louis gave them license to repurchase or lease their synagogues and cemeteries at cost from the new owners or lessees.[28] If by chance (*par aventure*) this was impossible (if, for example, building had occurred on the emplacement of the cemetery or the old synagogue had been torn down), the king offered to provide suitable locations and buildings at reasonable cost.[29] To facilitate worship, all the books of the law still in the government's possession (that is, which had not been sold) were to be returned, the Talmud only excepted (*excepté les Talameus condamnés*).[30]

The agreement was to last for twelve years. The king promised to give a year's notice if he intended to expel the Jews at the expiration date.[31] In the end the agreement foundered after seven years, and the whole period of "re-integration" turned out to be one of great disillusionment.[32] In this chapter our task is to try to determine how and why this was so.

From the beginning there were bad signs. The principal locus from which the Jews returned was the Spanish kingdoms. Immediately there were incidents as some of the returnees were waylaid on the roads back.[33] Nonetheless they settled in many communities from which they had been expelled in 1306—north, east, west, and especially south. As far as possible the returnees took up residence in the former jewries. This was the case in Orléans, Dijon, Poitiers, and Troyes, for example.[34] Consonant with the ordinance on their readmission, they retook possession of their old cemeteries in Montpellier and Toulouse, but such significant changes had been made in the topography of other towns (Orléans and Dijon are instances) that this was not possible.[35] Almost from the beginning they set up shop as pawnbrokers but, since many of them were poor, they did so on a very small scale, as at Narbonne.[36]

Within a couple of years it was clear that despite the detailed resettlement ordinance, an enormous number of problems were overwhelming the returnees.[37] They were being forced in some instances to answer criminal charges against them by trial by battle in defiance of their longstanding exemption from having to engage in the bilateral ordeal. Royal administrators were being particularly harsh on them, by such acts as imposing fines far above the level imposed on Christians for similar offenses. Officials were jailing them for torts for which Christians, accused of similar wrongs, could provide sureties, thereby retaining their freedom until adjudication. There was mounting harassment about the pledges they accepted in pawn, even pledges not in the category of prohibited articles, in a kind of constructive expansion of the definition of "interdicted chattels." The most minor officials were vexing them, jailing them, seizing their property without recourse to the license of higher authorities. Occasionally these officers followed them to the fields where they labored at tending their grapes: seeing them at work without the garments on which they had sewn their badges, the officials arrested and fined them for contempt of the law.

We know about these developments because they were addressed in an ordinance of 1317 which prohibited further injustices of the sort described.[38] The ordinance is important also because it confirms that the new king, Philip V the Tall, was going to maintain the policy of his prematurely deceased brother (Louis X died in 1316). We may wonder whether, if Louis X had lived, the sojourn of the Jews in France would have been different. In 1317 it was enough to know that it would continue at all, let alone that the crown would address some of the returnees' grievances sympathetically.

Philip V's concessive response to the Jews' grievances was not limited to the problems described above. It is quite certain that other problems disturbed him because they intruded into the efficient collection of revenue for the crown. For example, local officials had been hard on the exaction of the taille, a fact that gave rise to disgruntlement. The problem seems to have been the officials' unwillingness to spend the time to work out a fair assessment based on careful inventory of each head of household's possessions. On the other hand, they were also loath to compel debtors to pay debts to Jews; these officials still lived in the shadow of the resentment engendered in the campaign from 1306 to 1315 to force Christian debtors to pay up, and they faced the added resentment against the Jews' that they had returned at all. Unless the debts were paid, however, the tailles could not be paid. Consequently, while Philip V instructed his officials to make more rational individual assessments of the taille, he also ordered them to enforce those debts necessary for the Jews to pay the assessments.[39]

Alongside the Jewish grievances there were Christian ones. Some of the harshness with which local officials were treating the Jews seemed justified in their consciences by the accusations of sharp practice that Christians levied against the returnees. There were apparently charges of rackrenting, and there were certainly charges that the returnees were peddling inferior merchandise. To answer these problems the crown prohibited Jews from leasing to Christians and directed that profits on sales of defective merchandise would be forfeit to the crown.[40]

To the charge that the Jews were disposing of pledges at sale before they could equitably do so, the crown answered with more concrete instructions about redemption. Pledges liable to deterioration did not have to be offered for redemption after more than a year of being held. Objects made of gold or silver were to be held two years.[41] An additional problem with the redemption of pledges was the disposition of the pledges on the death of the pawnbroker. Some of the king's own men were treating the Jews as if they were mainmortable, that is, as if they had no rights of inheritance, so that all their goods escheated to the king at the Jews' demise. Obviously, the king could benefit from the redemption or sale of the pledges or the collection of the unpaid debts. Nonetheless, this interpretation of the special relationship between the king and the Jews was quashed in 1317.[42]

We might have expected that the transition to normal life would have been a difficult one for the returned Jews under the best of circumstances. Yet, as we have seen, the range of problems was extraordinarily wide during the first two years. The situation got much worse, however, for in 1319 Philip V announced his willingness to mount a crusade to the East. Some scholars have doubted, others have affirmed his sincerity, although in the end he did not fulfil this goal.[43] On the other hand, the announcement excited mass enthusiasm, especially because the recent past had seen a succession of famine years (1315–1317).[44] A crusade would purge the land and reconcile an angry God to His people. Early in 1320, small groups of rustics called Shepherds began coalescing in an attempt to form crusading armies. Defrocked priests played an active role in leading these contingents, which began their destruction by attacking Christians in France whose luxury or authority targeted them for resentment. Masses of them carried out acts of terrorism and outrages even in Paris.[45]

Support—or tolerance—of the Shepherds' actions against the rich was extensive in some localities. Certainly there was also fear of antagonizing them when it seemed as if the government was too paralyzed to act. Since, however, the object of their wrath increasingly became Jews, as the motley bands moved south into the regions most heavily repopulated by Jews, some of this fear abated. The Shepherds became avenging heroes of a sort to many Christians.[46] To be sure, when royal forces did begin to act with vigor, they found this support puzzling and distressing. To them (and it should have been the same for the local elite in their opinion) the Shepherds were merely disturbers of social order and carriers of the seeds of social revolution. By attacking the Jews, they were attacking not only a valuable royal commodity, they were defying the authority of the king himself.[47]

The Jews, then, became particular objects of protection as the royal forces began to confront the Shepherds and to a degree local authorities followed the lead of the crown as the repression gained in vigor. In the end the royal forces won the day and either massacred the Shepherds or chased them across the Pyrenees, where the Aragonese finished the job.[48] Yet in many ways the victory came too late. The attacks on the Jews before the effective suppression of the Shepherds were brutal: killings (at least 115 deaths in Toulouse alone), forced baptism or threats of such (an issue to be minutely investigated later by ecclesiastical inquisitors), and the burning of the registers of Christians' debts.[49] There is an element of frenzy in the reports of the brutality. Partly, this may be related to the fact that the "crusade" had begun in the Lenten fast, creating a fanaticism that imprinted itself on the whole history of the movement. This fanaticism provoked acts of terror on the other side: remnants of the Shepherds were literally starved to death. Resistance, too, became a dedication to martyrdom. The reports of Jewish mass suicide may be exaggerated, but they testify to the intensity of emotion observed by eyewitnesses to the carnage.[50]

Curiously, the French royal government got a financial windfall as a result of the violence. Fines and confiscations were imposed on the Shepherds who were captured—and not all were quite so poor as one might have supposed. More fines were imposed on those local authorities who were lax in moving against the Shepherds. And some of the property of the Jews who had been killed came into royal hands, despite the recent ordinance against their mainmortability. Perhaps these were Jews who had no close relatives to inherit. Or perhaps the crown's men at the local level took a narrow view of the circle of people who could legitimately do so. One chronicler recognized the duplicity being practiced here. Maybe Jews were not mainmortable, but they were certainly being treated like serfs, those of mainmortable status par excellence.[51] The value of the escheated goods of the murdered Jews in the Toulousain and its environs came to at least 1,485 l. t.[52]

What the uprising of the Shepherds revealed was the depth of the resentment of the return of the Jews to France. The kingdom had not seen this kind of massacre in a century or more. Under Saint Louis a similar uprising of Shepherds had been terrifying, but the cost in human life was not comparable.[53] One would have to go back to the wilder brutalities inflicted by Philip Augustus in Brie-Comte-Robert in 1192 or in Blois by the count of Blois in the 1170s to find a similar manifestation of terror.[54] For these twelfth century examples, however, one could argue that the seigneurial and royal actions might not necessarily reflect popular animosity. This was certainly no longer the case, if it ever had been. What was particularly disillusioning in 1320 was the failure of the crown in the one business that all recent kings from Saint Louis through Louis X had taken seriously, their duty to protect their Jews from violence. I do not mean that the failure was deliberate, but even if not deliberate it bespoke a frightening incapacity of the crown to restrain vigilantism against the Jews.

The next year saw the supposed Lepers' Plot. The story was that the Muslims in Granada, wanting to avenge the Christian reconquest of Spain, enlisted the help of the Jews and the Jews of the lepers to poison the wells of Christendom.[55] The rumors spread, gained official sanction here and there, and a kind of mass hysteria engulfed Christendom. Lepers in number were tortured, burned alive, immured, and Jews received their punishment from angry mobs.[56] In Chinon in the west Jews were condemned to the flames.[57] The case is a useful one to explore, for the picture we have of the jewry of Chinon long before the expulsion by Philip the Fair is of a thriving community, its residences concentrated near the marketplace, making the *rue de la Juiverie* "the most commercial street" in the town.[58] Over the course of the thirteenth century complaints about the Jews had mounted: they were thieves and usurers; and these perceptions provoked, it would seem, countercharges by Jews that local Christians perpetrated outrages against them.[59] The taking of Jewish debts for the king in any number of the *captiones* of the thirteenth century stirred up the resentment of the Christians who were forced to pay and who, despite occasional proscriptions to the contrary, were distrained in body and chattels to do so.[60] Bitterness over owing money to Jews (and, by transference, toward Jews themselves) became the common denominator of Christian society in Chinon. Then, in 1306, all the Jews were gone. Their return in 1315 deepened the Christians' resentment, and in the leper scare of 1321 this resentment achieved a ritual dimension in the slaughter of the Jewish community and the desecration of its holy objects. Even the stones of the Jewish cemetery with their Hebrew markings were tainted with these memories, or so it appears, and, though valuable, these stones lay discarded and unused until the seventeenth century.[61]

The government did not effectively contain the violence, but again it benefitted financially from the events. In 1321 it inflicted a huge fine of 150,000 l. t. on the Jews because of the "plot."[62] Such a figure, impressive to be sure, was not remotely similar to the great fines that had successfully been imposed before 1306.[63] There were just too few Jews in France and they were poorer than their forebears. By the end of March 1322 the crown realized that even 150,000 l. t. was too great for the communities and reduced the fine to 125,000 l. t. In fact, as Viard showed there is a great probability that the crown collected only about 75,000 l. t. in the entire campaign.[64]

Later in the year, another new king, Charles IV the Fair, the last of the Capetians, succeeded his brother and, realizing the failure of the resettlement of the Jews, decided once more to expel them.[65] One verse historiographer writing in the year 1322 found it a particularly hard year, with high prices and poverty.[66] This helps contextualize Charles's decision; it was a way of assuaging popular discontent at the governance of the state, its failure to bring the blessings of heaven to earth. But Charles had two administrative objectives. First, he wanted to carry through on recovering as much as possible on the fine that had been imposed in 1321. Commissioners worked thoroughly in all the *bailliages* and *sénéchaussées*, including lands held by courtesy by the queen dowager.[67] Some of these people had worked years before, in 1306, on the great confiscation of Philip the Fair, or had helped him destroy the Order of the Temple in 1308. They were professionals who knew their job.[68] Yet it was a limited job, for Charles did not intend to strip the Jews of all their belongings as his father had done. Hebrew sources affirm that he allowed the Jews to depart with their goods intact.[69] How far this perception should inform our evaluation is problematic. Probably what is meant is that the Jews were allowed to take chattels that were their own but neither their pledges nor outstanding debts that could help defray the fine of 1321. I say this because the treasury books of Charles IV report the confiscation of treasure or the discovery to the crown's profit of treasure consisting of jewels that must have been pledged: "a round stone similar to a crystal worth three silver gros [tournois]"; "small rings and necklaces of gold and silver with stones which were among the goods of the Jews."[70]

As to the collection of debts, that this was done is clear from the necessity of employing Jewish collectors, that is, men who could read the Hebrew registers.[71] Occasionally the treasury books and other fiscal records are explicit about the collection of debts.[72] And obviously only a *captio* of some sort, modest though the Hebrew sources imply, could explain the residual problems of collecting the fine. There was embezzling throughout Languedoc. An official in Roquemaure in the present Gard was charged with keeping a horse seized from the Jews. There were cases of fraud in the bailliage of Tours.[73]

The best illustration of the moderate nature of the *captio* is the series of accords with Haginus, a Jew of Corbeil (but his case is only the best documented of several similar ones).[74] Two-thirds of the debts owed to Haginus were to go to the king; Haginus was permitted to retain one-third. He was instructed, however, to transfer the part owed the king to a knight whom the king himself owed. Haginus kept careful records or receipts of these matters (*de quo habet cedulam*), which betray the difficulties and delays in debt collection from Christians; it was a common problem.[75] As always, therefore, arrears mounted. As late as 1334 (or even 1344) there were still outstanding debts from the fine of 1321.[76]

Because of the restricted nature of the *captio*, because fewer Jews were taken and because the transfer of leases has left much less evidence than the transfer of freeholds (particularly in the south) in 1306, we know less about the disposition of the properties of the Jews in 1322. Raymond Ysalguier, a *changeur* who had been active in carrying out the great confiscation of 1306, purchased the cemetery of the Jews of Toulouse in 1325.[77] The disposition of part of the cemetery of Dijon is known as well. One-half of it, worth 600 pounds, was sold to the abbey of Bussière by the duke in 1331.[78]

As with the transfer of property, so, too, with the impact on the Jews there is less evidence of the meaning of 1322. The great expulsion always remained 1306. Nonetheless, for those who had taken up residence south of the Pyrenees but had never reconciled themselves to exile and had come north again in 1315, the disillusionment was cruel.[79] The impact on them was as bad as it had been for the exiles of 1306, but there were some differences. The new exiles may have arrived in Spain shamefaced at their naive belief that a return to France was possible, but they came back to communities full of relatives and friends who had not returned to France, people who in the sixteen years since the expulsion of 1306 had put down roots and whose children were growing up as natives to Navarrese or Aragonese culture, with little or no longing for the land their parents had left.[80] There was also more resentment at the French than in 1306, for the act of expulsion of 1306 was an act of state, preceded by no great massacres, no great popular demonstrations against the Jews. This was not the case in 1322. The uprising of the Shepherds and the Lepers' Plot were nasty revelations of the depth and extent of popular hatred. Many Jews had already fled because of these disturbances; many who had been forced to convert, even if by the church's narrow definition of "forced" they were voluntary converts, also fled to homes in Spain. (As *lapsi* they were sought out by the Inquisition, of course.)[81] The point is not that Spain offered them all the hopes that had been exploded in France. Far from it; the Spanish situation was itself becoming more and more unfavorable. The point is that the history of the Jews in France was at an end. After 1322, there was really no turning back.

Epilogue: The Capetian Legacy, 1322–1394

After 1322 there were virtually no Jews in France.[82] The history of medieval French Jewry was played out instead in the borderlands.[83] It is well-known that that history was not a happy one. Besides heavy taxation, the fourteenth century saw massive persecution of the Jews before and especially around the time of the Black Death, as if they were responsible for the epidemic that brought profound demographic catastrophe to their own communities.[84] Still, the desire to strike out at some group—Jews or lepers, eventually witches—was so compelling in the fourteenth and fifteenth centuries that governments found it impossible to contain the violence. Some, in fact, actively supported or endorsed it. In the wake of the cataclysm messianic dreams became more vivid among Jews and dreams of the Second Coming more vivid among Christians.[85]

It is true that in 1359, purely as a business enterprise, a small group of Jews led by a family from Vesoul near the Swiss border made an agreement with the crown to open business and maintain residences in France.[86] We know, thanks to the work of Schwarzfuchs and the even more exhaustive industry of Roger Kohn, that the government permitted this resettlement because of the terrible need for money during the Hundred Years War.[87] Settlements were kept extremely small and were given extraordinary protection.[88] No attempts were made to convert these Jews or, within reason, to interfere in the internal life of their tiny communities so long as they remained strictly segregated from the Christians.[89] The authorities probably turned a deaf ear to rumors that the Jews had copies of the Talmud with them.[90]

Every possible privilege was given the Jews to make money, for by their making money the crown benefitted in the higher task of provisioning an army to save the kingdom. High interest was allowed: four pennies per pound per week. Jews were not to be prosecuted for possessing stolen articles or merchandise as pledges. They were exempt from all exactions except those specifically levied by the crown. They were in Kohn's analysis pure outsiders, like foreign merchants, who had temporary charters that needed to be periodically renewed.[91] They constituted no cancerous part of the body of the holy kingdom; they were conveniences like useful beasts of burden. To the crown they were not seen as threatening to the social or religious health of the larger community. But, of course, theory and legalisms yield to social realities. And the fundamental social reality was war, a war that was rapidly sapping the life's blood of the French crown and the many elite institutions that were its partners in governance.[92] Great nobles like the duc de Berri went thousands of pounds in debt to the Jews.[93]

The effort, therefore, to insulate the tiny business communities of Jews was always tentative. There is reasonably good evidence that the crown toyed with reversing its policy a number of times, perhaps believing that the image of a holy monarchy (one that excluded Jews) was to be preferred to the money collected from taxes on Jewish business.[94] In the end, however, internal squabbles among the Jews themselves brought the crown to lose confidence in the ability of the community to control its members. There is no reason to go into detail on these squabbles here since they have been treated in great depth by Schwarzfuchs. They make a depressing story of struggle for power between two rival Jewish families.[95] The struggle occurred at precisely the time that the government's own authority was being challenged in France. Extremely violent anti-government riots in the 1380s carried with them a strong anti-Jewish component because of the debt burden of the Christians. The cry, "Aux juifs!" could be heard in the streets of Paris in 1382.[96] Challenges to the Jews contained the charge of deicide: "False Jewess," one rioter is reported to have said to one woman, "who forged the nails with which God was nailed, if you do not become a Christian, we will put you to death." When she refused, she was murdered.[97] Records of debts were sought out; places of refuge provided by royal officials were besieged; the Jews were humiliated, or converted by force, or, following their defiance, murdered. A few Christians would later return some of the baptized children to their mothers.[98]

Through all of this—riots in Paris, in Orléans, Montereau[99]—the crown sustained the Jews because of the revenue they provided, but even the revenue began to decline as the community suffered. Increasingly, there-fore, the crown supplemented annual taxation with special levies that essentially ruined the Jews.[100] By the 1390s the situation was critical. It was exacerbated by the explosive news from Spain in 1391 of a wave of massacres unparalleled in the history of the West.[101] A terrible sense of despair came over western Jewry. A few Spanish Jews escaped to France.[102] Some made their way to Paris, but by 1391 there was virtually no livelihood to be earned there licitly. We see some of these Jews as vagabonds and thieves, playing roles in the seamy underworld in the often unsuccessful fencing of stolen goods.[103]

On 24 September 1394, there came a new and final order of expulsion. It was executed successfully by the end of January 1395.[104] There was not much property to distrain. But the difficulties of the past several years had put some Jews at psychological risk. They converted rather than make new journeys to "dark lands."[105] The majority who did leave—and we should recall that the total number was very small (perhaps only hundreds or a few thousands)—found it hard along the way to avoid being waylaid or hu-miliated by angry Christians.[106] Many of the refugees fled to the region near modern Switzerland where the families that had negotiated the read-mission in 1359 still maintained second residences. To some degree the history of Jews in Switzerland begins from their influx following the expulsion.[107] Doubtless their presence can help explain what will emerge as persistent judaizing charges in the witchcraft accusations in the decades to come in that region.[108]

When an adolescent Philip II Augustus expelled the Jews from the tiny royal domain in 1182, his biographer greeted the event with great praise. For him, the act was closely connected to the king's right to bear the title *rex christianissimus*.[109] Eustache Mercadé, the author of the mystery play "La Vengeance Jhesucrist," was probably only a teenager himself when the expulsion of his day (1394) occurred. Yet years later, when he wrote his play, he remembered that expulsion as the deed of a new Vespasian, the figure of the avenging hero of Christ's execution whom he crafted for his mystery. His dedicatory to the architect of the expulsion, King Charles VI, who had also been a youth of eighteen at the time of the order, praises Charles for hating the Jews and for hating their nation: "Celuy bon roy, second Vaspasien, a tant hay les juifs . . . . Il hait leur natïon."[110] It was a wonderful hate, an admirable hate, a hate that, in Mercadé's universe of virtue, equally merited the title "Most Christian."

Plus ça change, plus c'est la même chose.

15. Conclusion

Nowhere were relations between Jews and Christians stable in the 150 years from 1179 to 1328; and it would have been legitimate and appropriate in this study to concentrate our attention on certain key economic or religious events to mark the evolution of relations over the course of these years. I have tried not to ignore these events, but the fact that I have chosen in this book to make the *political* aspects of French history the organizing theme of the presentation should not be surprising given the clear and explicit determination of the crown to transform social relations between Jews and Christians. A preliminary theoretical defense of this approach seemed unnecessary and, in any case, would have been vapid. The certainty that the *political* theme is a crucial one, perhaps *the* crucial one, necessarily had to be justified in a concrete consideration of the material that has survived.

When commentators say that medieval states were weak, they mean that relative to early modern states they lacked the extensive bureaucratic infrastructure of the "New Monarchies" of the late fifteenth century and the sixteenth century, they lacked standing armies of any size or dependability, and they lacked mechanisms of taxation that would be commonplace in the Renaissance. To be sure, not all "states" developed at the same rate, and certain of the "New Monarchies" were weakly developed in key areas. Nonetheless, the gross comparison seems a fair one: judged by the early modern western state, its medieval predecessor had access to fewer resources, mobilized those resources it did have less efficiently, and controlled the process by which programs emerged from serious political decisions with far less consistency than was typical two or three hundred years later.

Personality affected deeply the variations among medieval states. Louis IX (Saint Louis), ever vigil, managed to do more and do it with more success than his counterpart Henry III in England or his successor Philip III in France. But even a determined, intelligent, and hardworking saint on a throne was no final answer to the systemic weaknesses of medieval government in the thirteenth century, although every "improvement" a man like Louis IX made—if it were incorporated into the permanent apparatus of government—contributed step by step to the power and authority of government. The "New Monarchies," after all, were not made out of whole cloth.[1]

Besides personality, it must be said that a determining factor in the relative efficiency or success of any single princely policy was the group at which it was directed. Secular states might mobilize their resources to take on this or that aspect of the ecclesiastical establishment; but the danger was always real that the official church would mobilize its own considerable resources in opposition to these thrusts. When it did so, the application of princely policies was jeopardized though not necessarily rendered null. The same was true when princes tried to interfere in or control traditionally free towns or enclaves of feudal privileges. They were not necessarily stymied by the opposition these moves engendered, but their success was always problematized. So it is right that historians tend to emphasize the limits of state power, even when ostensibly successful, in undermining many of the characteristic features of the institutions or societies with which princes struggled.

The Jews constituted a group that, almost uniquely, could call on no deep resonances in Christian (majoritarian) society for support against medieval governments. The official church was always careful not to endorse the more exploitative aspects of princely policy. It especially stood opposed to expulsion. Yet it did not mobilize its resources to bring a halt to the program. Merchants and townsmen in general might have had at least ambivalent feelings about the Jewish presence in the great cities, but they were never willing to jeopardize their status via-à-vis the princes in an attempt to protect the Jews. Feudatories were extremely jealous of their rights over against the king's; and insofar as possession of Jews was a lucrative right of exploitation, they put obstacles in the way of royal policies that sought, however delicately and inconspicuously, to enhance royal control of the Jews. Yet, again, they could be bought off—and they recognized that in the give-and-take of conflicting jurisdictional claims, some rights, like rights over Jews, were better to cede or at least compromise on than to die for.

For the Jews what this meant—and we have seen it over and over again in the preceding pages—was that there never emerged any persuasive *strategic* response to the pressures on them from Christian states. Tactical measures were developed aplenty. The oppressing lord might be bought off. If he could not be bought off, appeal to the papacy or to sympathetic churchmen might avail. If that failed, escape to territories that were already in a hostile or unfriendly relationship with the oppressor regime might be attempted. Time and again, of course, these various tactics failed. Some lords simply could not be bought off; others could be bought off only at a price that rendered the Jews destitute. Sympathetic churchmen might well have been more common than we know, but sympathy and movement are two quite different things. Our sources reveal few enough Saint Bernards ready to back up sentiments with actions. And escape was always fraught with danger: it delivered the Jews into the hands of different lords and made them bargaining chips in the larger political struggles of France and of Europe.

The one great force that might have buffered the political and financial demands of the crown was popular sentiment—the kind of popular feeling, for example, that helped insulate the Cathar heretics from the aggression of the French crown and the Catholic Church for generations. On this point, with regard to the Jews, opinions differ considerably. Undoubtedly before the age of the crusades there was genuine personal sympathy between Christian families and Jewish families in regions throughout France. These personal felicities might have constituted in their generality a social phenomenon of importance. But always in this fideistic culture there loomed the fact that Jews were not Christians, that they did not share in the central religious and social ceremonies of the faithful in Christ, and, more ominously, that they practiced forms of worship and devotion and had habits of leisure, diet, and burial, for example, that by their very existence challenged Christian practices. It matters not one jot that Christians did not always live up to or practice the specific rituals laid out by ecclesiastical officials. They knew what these rituals were and knew that they were supposed to follow them. They knew, too, that their Jewish neighbors did not subscribe to this repertory of habits.

The crusades, in their parallel manifestation of hatred toward the Jews at home, reveal how deep the suspicions actually were. All the same, the view has to be qualified. In some places the increasing concentration of the Jews in moneylending to Christians was progressively corrupting relations, marking a transformation from traditional religious suspicions to profound social tensions. Meanwhile, the increasing segregation in some regions and the heightened frequency of calls for segregation everywhere emphasized the spiritual distance between the adherents of the two confessions. Where these conditions, for whatever reasons, were not so strong, the degeneration in Jewish and Christian relations or, rather, the violent manifestation of the social distance between the two confessions was less pronounced. To make a gross generalization, it was the north that first and most profoundly endured the violence in the twelfth and thirteenth centuries, while the south remained significantly more "civil."

The Capetian government brought northern policies and perceptions of Jews south. Here is where the discussion of the power and authority of the medieval state seems most critical. We have seen that the south in the thirteenth century was a congeries of conquered provinces. The natives of these provinces had no deep affection for northerners or for their king and his agents. To the extent that the northerners recognized this and wanted to forestall rebellion they were very careful, after the military conquest, to be circumspect about the application of Capetian policies in the south, and they were very solicitous of confirming the southerners' legitimate rights (which were rather generously defined). Even with regard to the Jews this policy may be noticed in the immediate aftermath of conquest. But with the Jews it did not endure. One way that the crown made itself respected was by concentrating on a group that did not have strong support among those natives of the region it wanted to cultivate. Individual attempts on the part of southern lords to resist the encroachments of the Capetians do exist. We may remember the viscount of Narbonne, the bishop of Pamiers, even the king of Majorca as lord of Montpellier. But the essence of their situation in no way turned on their defense of the Jews. They would grudgingly cede their authority over Jews for money or would willingly adhere to Capetian exploitation for a part of the take so long as their legitimate position in the hierarchy of vassalic relations was recognized and affirmed by the crown.

If all this sounds too pat, too manipulative, we should perhaps remind ourselves of an important point. It is that even where there is manipulation there may be strong feeling. Philip Augustus surely wanted to make a dramatic statement of his rulership by opening his reign with a brutal attack on the Jews. Louis VIII surely wanted to achieve something of the same sort by making the first important act of his rule a statute diminishing the privileges of the Jews. But if nothing else, the powerful propagandistic potential of these moves was overshadowed in the first case by the emotional state of Philip Augustus and, in the second, by the real sense of sin that Louis VIII associated with his government's traditional policy of letting usurious deals be struck in its offices and sealed with its seals.

No medieval king could afford to ignore the Jews by the thirteenth century. Their practice of moneylending made them a valuable taxable minority. The fact that the moneylending was frequently "usurious" in Christian terms made them an object of concern for the king as a moral prince. Their obstinacy—their resistance to conversion—made them a challenge to any king, most assuredly to kings who came routinely to call themselves Most Christian.

Thus in the end there was something inexorable about the development of royal policy. In the Jews the crown discovered a group that it could confront, humiliate, and exploit for moral, political, and financial purposes. It discovered that the extent and intensity of sympathy for the group were extremely small and that what there was of it could be defused with relative ease. It found that when it concentrated its resources on this single group it could be almost always positive of success, a fact that often led to dramatic gestures that in a certain sense helped resacralize the monarchy when things were otherwise going ill—when a crusade failed, for example, or when a debasement of the coinage undermined respect for the crown. At the same time, there was a genuine emotional commitment to the enterprise of disciplining the Jews. In the middle of the thirteenth century the purpose of this discipline was conversion. By the end of the century, this seemed an unrealizable goal. For even if the network of support for Jews in the Christian community at large was weak, the long tradition of Jewish solidarity, founded on the culture of martyrdom and of suffering for the integrity of their worship of God, permitted and encouraged the Jews to maintain their identity in the face of the Capetian challenge. In the end, Capetian policies did transform social relations between Jews and Christians; but finding the result unsatisfying and the goal of conversion unfulfilled, the crown chose finally to expel the Jews and to refashion—a few brief experiments aside—a new and enduring ideal of the purified Christian state, an ideal that persisted until the close of the Middle Ages and left its considerable imprint on the powerful state of the early modern period as well.[2]

Yet if this study has explicitly adopted a political narrative, the testing ground for the success of policy has been the social milieu within which Jews and Christians acted daily, whether in France (a term with varying regional connotations) or beyond its borders. What appears to be the case, to pursue a theme sketched above, is that longstanding suspicions between the adherents of the two confessions received a stimulus and direction from the constant articulation and repetition of harsh royal policies. The spokesmen here were functionaries ordered to carry out the policies, and they were seconded, though not always slavishly, by the widespread popular preaching and storytelling about the nefarious Jews. Ordinary people did not necessarily agree with every aspect of policy or every critical note sounded against the Jews by popular preachers; but usually they had no vested interest in gainsaying it.

To be sure, there were exceptions to these generalizations. When princes demanded the rapid repayment of debts owed the Jews in order that the princes themselves might benefit, there were protests. These were not protests on behalf of the Jews but self-interested attempts to cushion the debtors from the intrusiveness of state power. All the same, the benefit did sometimes redound to the Jews, shortening the campaigns against them, for example.

On the other hand—and this is considerably more significant—the political program at any one time was always less important than the conclusion in the minds of people at large that their lives were being disrupted because the crown chose (with powerful moral arguments) to attack the Jews. Hence, the Jews became the devalued object in every crisis. Debtors, when asked to pay up to the king the principal of loans owed the Jews, pleaded "extortion" by the Jews, sometimes claiming thereby that the interest or usury was higher than it actually was. The language of extortion became the language used to describe what had became the most fundamental social relationship of Christian and Jew in the thirteenth century. It was part of a transformation or debasement in the vocabulary of sensibility toward the Jew that was much more widespread: lend money at interest/judaize; felon/Jew; and so on.[3]

We have seen, too, that princes were not consistent. Philip Augustus was capricious in the extreme, but his behavior—his shifts and reversals, his changes in emphasis and tone—may be found in lesser degrees in many other princes. For the Jews the erraticism was profoundly disturbing, but the erraticism also affected the crown's officials, who were themselves unsure about how to proceed, and with what vigor, against the Jews. If one day the king told them to act decisively to enforce debts owed to Jews and the next showed himself angry at Jewish "extortion" of his poor Christian subjects, officials were confused and moved very circumspectly, uncertain just what they were supposed to do. And no love was lost between the king's subjects and his officials as a result. The former obviously focused their dismay on the officials as the agents of caprice. Even Philip Augustus had to threaten his men to do his will in the face of popular hatred of their doing it and of the way they did it.

The inconsistency was therefore a contributory factor to the exacerbation of social tensions between Christians and Jews at large. For a few years Jews might be gone, as from 1182 to 1198. All the force of the moral arguments, whatever misgivings there were about these arguments, could be marshalled or twisted to justify the exile. Even those who were opposed to Philip Augustus's expulsion must have seen it as the natural culmination of his other policies. For him to reverse himself, to bring back the Jews, confounded his supporters and opponents alike. At the same time, however, for him to permit and occasionally after 1198 to encourage the moral condemnation of Jews' business dealings with Christians — dealings which he otherwise tolerated — could only further bewilder and frustrate the mass of his subjects. For the mass, Jews might not have been personal objects of active hate, but a group that was supremely disagreeable because, in the perversion of logic, they were perceived as the cause of the inconsistencies that marked royal policy and its application.

One might think that any number of ordinary Christians rose above these sentiments. Some no doubt did. But they had no profound interest, beyond their own moral fiber, in standing opposed to the policies of the Capetian kings. They had no jurisdictional claims to protect as the nobility and clergy had. They had no strictly defined role as the functionaries of the official church in setting out in limited terms opposition, say, to expulsion. And in any case it would have been dangerous to denounce any of the exploitation. Thus, I am persuaded that to the vast majority of their Christian subjects, the sometimes erratic and frequently grinding policies of kings toward the Jews, which indirectly disturbed Christian lives, only reinforced the perception that the Jews were the real problem and therefore encouraged a kind of indifference to their plight or, rather, a profound desire that they would just go away for good.

Such sentiments did not perhaps come to the surface very often in ordinary times. But we know that they were expressed in the heat of the moment — a quarrel in the market, an altercation along the road, the stress following the disappearance of a child. The Jews were quite aware of the animosity and sometimes emphasized the need for social distance, but again — and especially in the south — they underestimated the danger. The anomie of southern Jews living in exile in the Iberian peninsula after 1306, their profound desire to return, and their utter disillusionment at popular violence during the brief return, fundamentally establish this point.

A gloomy tale all in all—a difficult one to write—but I believe that it is the truth.

Notes

1. The discussion of the domain is based on Newman 1937, ix-xv, 1–85; Fawtier 1960, 96–109; Bautier 1980b, 11–12; Baldwin 1986, 12–13.

2. The general remarks on demography depend on Russell 1972, 25–68, and Cipolla 1980, 3–5.

3. Cf. Fourquin 1964, 63–64.

4. I have made this list by correlating the information in Chazan 1973b, 10, 31, on Jewish settlement before 1182 in northern France with the material assembled by Newman 1937, 59, 95, and Baldwin 1986, 465–66, on the royal domain.

5. On the Jews of Saint-Denis before 1182, see Graboïs 1969, 1187–95; on the royal concession, Newman 1937, 59.

6. Newman 1937, 58–59, 95.

7. So Chazan 1973b, 11; the text is printed in Hebrew in Finkelstein 1924, 149.

8. *Intermédiaire des chercheurs et curieux*, vols. 34–39 (1896–1899). This material has been collected and combined with other similar material in Blumenkranz 1980, 307–87.

9. Gueneau n.d., 152–53; Villand 1982, 57–58.

10. Chédeville 1973, 476; Dahan 1980b, 16–20; Villand 1982, 55–59. For two illustrations of the problems but from non-domain towns, consider Châteauroux (Indre) and Toulouse. The *Intermédiaire des chercheurs* duly noted a *rue juive* in Châteauroux in 1897 (vol. 35, 173). Further study reveals that early modern land registers identify a *rue juive* there; *Inventaire des AD: Cher, série G*, G 32, 356. But there is also a reference to a *rue des juifs* in 1630 which may or may not be the same, and a further reference to a *Cimetière aux Juifs* as early as 1452; *Inventaire-sommaire des AD: Indre, série A*, A 105, 107. With all these references — and the variety of them — I am convinced that there was a significant Jewish presence in Châteauroux at sometime in the Middle Ages, but there is not a single reference in Jewish sources to such a settlement and no medieval Christian evidence that would make it possible to describe this community; cf. Gross 1969/1897. As for Toulouse, much ink has been spilled in the past hundred years about the extent and precise location of the well-attested jewry there. The argument has revolved around the toponym Joutx-Aigues (variants: Juzaigas, Jusaiga, Jusaic) and whether it is a derivative of Latin *judica[e]* or a corruption of a Latin phrase for an underground aqueduct in which the second part of the toponym, *aigues*, is said to reproduce the plural of Latin *aqua* (cf. the port of Aigues-Mortes). For the debate, see among

others Thomas 1885, 439–42; Douais 1888, 118–19; Blanc 1896, 195–99; Bréal 1896, 88–91; Chalande 1906–1909, 367–72; Dahan 1980b, 20.

11. In general see Dahan 1980b, 20, 24–25; for examples of several foci of residence within individual towns, see Chédeville 1973, 475 n. 276 (Chartres had two); and Shatzmiller 1980d, 218–19 (Marseilles had three). "Jewry" when capitalized will refer to Jewish regional culture or civilization (German Jewry; north French Jewry, etc.); in lower case letters, it will refer to an area of a town or village with a cluster of residences inhabited by Jews.

12. *Intermédiaire des chercheurs et curieux*, 34 (1896), 334, 649; 35 (1897), 301; 38 (1898), 490–91.

13. *Intermédiaire des chercheurs et curieux*, 34 (1896), 649.

14. In general on settlement in the north, see Rabinowitz 1938, 29–34.

15. See Cipolla 1980, 176, to read an enthusiastic encomium of the growing towns.

16. Schwarzfuchs 1957, 22–23; Assis 1983, 286. Cf. Finkelstein 1924, 13– 15.

17. Anchel 1938, 6; Anchel 1940, 45; Cochard 1895, 113; cf., for England, Lipman 1984, 1–19.

18. Cf. Dahan 1980b, 23–24, for caveats to earlier ideas.

19. Roblin 1952b, 20.

20. Sivéry 1984, 14.

21. For the methodological problems of determining the early population of Paris, see Cazelles 1972, 131–40. My corrective is based on the fact that Paris seems to have grown rapidly in the late twelfth and early thirteenth century (cf. the evidence of its walls; Baldwin 1986, 343). If this is the case and if the population was really about one hundred thousand in 1250 as Sivéry asserts, a major "corrective" of the sort I suggest is necessary. On the fiscal contribution of the city to Philip Augustus, see Baldwin 1986, 158.

22. Roblin 1952b, 12–13, 18–20; Anchel 1940, 46–47.

23. Delaborde 1882, 12; Rigord says that the "liberality" of the French and the peace established in their lands inspired the migration, especially to Paris. For an evocative portrait of the Jewish community at this period in Paris, see Temko 1955, 228–39.

24. Schwarzfuchs 1975, 55.

25. In general see the study of Liebeschütz 1983 (in reality, an up-dated annotation of a work from 1938).

26. Cf. Parkes 1938a, 31–38.

27. Liebeschütz 1959, 97–112; Grayzel 1967; 427–37; Touitou 1984, 3–12. For the earlier period, cf. Katz 1937; Blumenkranz 1960; Bachrach 1977.

28. But cf. Golb 1966, 1–63. If there were considerably more violence in France than is presently acknowledged, as Golb argues, it would merely strengthen my point about the psychological effect of the crusading massacres, but to be candid I do believe that Golb goes too far.

29. Hyams 1974, 271–72; Agus 1969; Finkelstein 1924. Cf. Graboïs 1984, 246.

30. Smalley 1952, 149–72. See also Cohen 1986, 593–604, and Touitou 1986, 51–53.

31. Touitou 1985, 35–39; Shereshevsky 1968–1969, 268–89. A more moderate view is in Graboïs 1984, 252–53.

32. It is clear to me that Berger 1986, 587–91, would take issue with the emphasis

of my analysis. The matter might be worth pursuing. But I come down on the side of Gavin Langmuir: " . . . it seems impossible to imagine that Jews and Christians could ever have agreed on their interpretations of Hebrew Scripture and the Old Testament or even on crucial passages in them. The fact that a few, *remarkably few*, Christian scholars, such as Andrew of Saint Victor, occasionally expressed pride in their knowledge of Jewish interpretations in a way that contradicted their fundamental convictions hardly modifies the picture." See Langmuir 1986, 622 (with my emphasis) and more generally, pp. 622–23. One minor point: although Langmuir directs the quoted excerpt to the work of Cohen 1986, it seems to me much more relevant to that of Berger 1986 (all three essays appear in a special forum published in the *American Historical Review*, volume XCI).

33. Graboïs 1984, 252–53; d'Alverny 1982, 427–28; Berger 1986, 587–91.

34. Rosenthal 1960, 115–35; Lasker 1977, 3; Smalley 1983, 364; Graboïs 1984, 251. Cf. Talmage 1967, 215–21.

35. Châtillon 1984, 184; Alverny 1982, 428; Häring 1982, 193–94; Smalley 1983, 110, 365. It is difficult to take issue with a book, like Smalley's, which was pathbreaking, but although she was fully aware of the tensions aroused by Christian interest in the so-called *veritas hebraica*, she consistently ignored its wider implications. She also conflated the impact of Andrew of Saint Victor as a source to be pillaged by later commentators and the influence of his attitude toward Jewish exegesis, which was never popular. Still, her exploration of Andrew's own work per se (Chapter 4 of *The Study of the Bible*) is a masterpiece.

36. Genesis 34 and 49:5–7; the story is also recalled in the book of Judith 9:2–5. English quotations are from the *Jerusalem Bible* 1968.

37. Modern "scientific" exegesis, while rejecting traditional rabbinics and Catholic scholasticism, is virtually incoherent on the story. There is no agreement on its "real" meaning. Cf. Driver 1954, 307–08; Lewy 1955, 120, 135, 195; Von Rad 1961, 324–30; Noth 1972, 86, 151; Cohen 1983b, 341; Wifall 1983, 197–209. More enriching approaches—both more literary and anthropological—to the Dinah story and similar tales are provided in Pitt-Rivers 1977; Oden 1983; Alter 1981; Kee 1983.

38. *Encyclopaedia judaica*, VI, 55–56. The quotation is from the Me-am Loez (Culi 1977–, III, 173), an anthology of antique and medieval Jewish interpretations that first appeared in 1730.

39. Rashi 1905, 70–71, 94.

40. Culi 1977–,III, 172, 179; cf. Ramban 1971, 414, 419; *Sefer Ha-Yashar* 1887/1965, 97. These interpretations were anchored on the early Jewish apocryphal literature (Jubilees 30:25 and Testament of Levi 6:9 in the edition of Charles 1913) and Talmudic sources, e.g., *Babylonian Talmud* 1948–1952: Seder Nezikin, Sanhedrin II, xi, 102a.

41. Jewish criticism of this attitude, the "overabundance" of allegorizing even New Testament texts, is noticed in Baldwin 1970, I, 94.

42. Cyril of Alexandria: *PG*, LXIX, 281; Gregory the Great:*PL*, LXXVII, 108; Isidore of Seville: *PL*, LXXXIII, 267; Hrabanus Maurus: *PL*, CVII, 614–15;

Glossa Ordinaria: *PL*, CXIII, 160–61; Marbod of Rennes: *PL*, CLXXI, 1682–84; Petrus Riga 1965, I, 66–67; *Bible moralisée* 1911–1927, I pl. 21, IV pl. 724.

43. The church father who led the way in this interpretation was Ambrose ("Jacob and the Happy Life"; Ambrose of Milan 1972, 165), Ambrose's writings on the Old Testament being "particularly prized" in the Middle Ages—Leclercq 1982, 97. The opinion entered the *Glossa ordinaria* in the twelfth century: *PL*, CXIII, 736; and was repeated over and over again. It took on special force in the artistic depictions that shared the two Christian traditions of interpreting Dinah's tale, namely, heavy allegorizing (Virtue against Vice) and the typology of the church. The sources for exploring the iconography of the Dinah story in Christian art include the following manuscripts that I have consulted from photographs catalogued at the Index of Christian Art, Princeton University, and from those kindly provided me by the institutions possessing the originals: Klagenfurt, Landes Mus., MS VI 19, fol. 47; Rovigo, Bibl. Accad. dei Concordi, fol. 25; Berlin, Mus., Stl. Kupferstichkab, MS 78 A6, Psalter, fol. 5 v.; London, Brit. Lib., MS Egerton 1894, Genesis, fol. 17 v.; Lausanne, Bib. Cant. et Univ., MS U 964, Bible, fol. 12 v.; Zurich, Zentralbibl., MS Rheinau 15, Rudolf von Ems, Weltchronik, fol. 45 v.

44. Richard of Saint Victor, *Benjamin minor*: *PL*, CXCVI, 40.

45. I have not seen a manuscript of Richard's *Benjamin minor*, but the editor of the Dinah commentary in *PL*, CXCVI, 36–43, peppers the parts of the text that seem to be reacting to Jewish interpretations with exclamation points, suggesting that the impression I am taking from the text is not eccentric.

46. Besides the research of Smalley already cited, cf. Shereshevsky 1968/1969, 268–89, on the work of Peter Comestor and contacts in Troyes, but although Peter's contacts with Jewish exegesis in Troyes or Paris (Häring 1982, 194) are real, much of the argument seems labored. See also Cochard 1895, 134.

47. For example the *Lapidarium* of the great polymath, Marbod of Rennes, of the turn of the eleventh/twelfth century was translated into Hebrew; cf. Rosenthal 1957, 127–37, on the possible identification of the translator, a polemicist if he is right. Again, evidence from Troyes on the Latin knowledge of Rashbam, Rashi's grandson, is marshalled by Graboïs 1984, 253. Cf. Berger 1986, 589–90 n. 68.

48. Haskins 1955, 278–302; Alverny 1982, 421–57.

49. Alverny 1982, 457; Knowles 1962, 223–34.

50. *Glossa ordinaria*: *PL*, CXIII, 114–15; Davidson 1967, xix; Trachtenberg 1939, 89, 262; Culi 1977–, I, 419–20; Smalley 1983, 362.

51. Joubert 1854, 129–32. The inscriptions, now highly restored, on Angers Cathedral (which is being referred to here) are difficult to date in their present state; Joubert, of course, observed them at a more opportune time.

52. Cf. Leclercq 1982, 241–44, on the roots of this development.

53. Cf. Abrahams 1932, 387; and for the Hebrew reference to crusaders as a "people of strange speech," Marcus 1986, 10.

54. Trachtenberg 1939, 28, 75, 82, 102–03. (See also late examples collected in

Schrire 1966, 54–58.) Cf. on Jewish mystical lore on the Latin alphabetic signs, Trachtenberg 1939, 264; and Gaster 1925–1928, I, 600–13.

55. Davidson 1967, 192; Stroumsa 1983, 287; Schrire 1966, 36–37.

56. On the *hasidim*, see Marcus 1980, 227–54; and, at greater length, Marcus 1981.

57. See, especially, Davidson 1967, 192–93. Somewhat more probing but less clear is Stroumsa 1983, 269–88.

58. Grayzel 1933, 74 n. 145.

59. For a collection, see Davis 1888. As legal instruments these deeds may have influenced and been influenced by Christian contractual practice; cf. Pollock and Maitland 1968, I, 475; Palmer 1982, 187, 215.

60. For Dobson's criticism of Roth, Dobson 1974, 28 n. 88.

61. Cf. Davis 1888, x.

62. Stein 1959, 39.

63. This fact, which has sometimes been disputed for Jews, the contrary argument being that they spoke a distinct judeo-vernacular in Europe or even Hebrew in daily life, is sustained by the evidence of the contemporary Hebrew-Old French glossaries and the vernacular glosses of many Hebrew texts in northern Jewry. More than one generation of scholars made their reputations studying these fascinating texts: Neubauer 1871–1875, 163–96; Darmesteter 1872, 146–76; Blondheim 1909, 1–18; Blondheim 1926, 379–93; Bannitt 1961, 259–96; Kukenheim Ezn 1963, 89–107; Levy 1964; Bannitt 1968, 188–210. See also Gaster 1925–1928, II, 715; *HL*, XXVII, 440, 498–99; *HL*, XXXI, 354–55.

64. Cf. Baron 1952–,IX, 35–36.

65. But cf. Cohen 1983a, 1–27.

66. Langmuir 1984, 820–46; cf. Langmuir 1985, 109–27.

67. Langmuir 1984, 844.

68. James and Jessopp 1896, 15; *AASS*, III March 590.

69. For a brief conspectus of the ritual murder accusations, see *Encyclopaedia judaica* 1972, s.v. "Blood Accusation."

70. Chazan 1973b, 48; Chazan 1968, 16 n. 6.

71. James and Jessopp 1896, lxxxv; *AASS* III March 494, 502, 588, 591, etc.

72. *AASS*, III March 591. These more or less contemporary allegations were later embellished in Richard's life by Robert Gaugin; *AASS*, III March 593–94.

73. *AASS*, III March 592. This and other details were later popularized by Alphonsus de Spina ca. 1471, cruelty 2.

74. *AASS*, III March 591–92. For later embellishments of this theme in Richard's *vita*, see Alphonsus de Spina ca. 1471, cruelty 2. Also James and Jessopp 1896, bks. III-IV; *Chronicle of Jocelin of Brakelond* 1951/1949, 16; *Chronica de Mailros* 1835, 91, for comparisons with other so-called child saints.

75. Delaborde 1882, 15. Chazan 1973b, 49.

76. The Blois incident has been studied in Chazan 1968, 13–31. Unless otherwise directed the reader should assume that the summary of the events here is adapted from this work. He places the incident in the context of ritual murders and cites Robert's assertion that a crucifixion had taken place (16 n. 4; cf. *AASS*, III March 591).

77. Baldwin 1986, 14.

78. Below Chapter 2, text to nn. 33–44.
79. Stow 1984, 4–5.
80. In Chazan 1973b, 14–15, 37, drawing on his own earlier work (Chazan 1970, 217–21; Chazan 1970–1971, 101–18), he puts considerably less emphasis on the Blois incident than on remoter and obscurer crises, but he continues to insist on a general significance for Blois (Chazan 1973b, 48–49). I say "remoter and obscurer" because one of these "earlier" incidents (1007) is believed by some scholars (cf. Stow 1984, 27–33) to have occurred in the mid-thirteenth century, the date in the original records being an error. On the other hand, Chazan has tried to raise serious problems about Stow's analysis; Chazan 1987, 728–31.
81. Excerpts of two laments on the martyrs of Blois are translated in Carmi 1981, 384–87. Significantly, they are Rhenish poems, pointing once again to the fact that northern Jewry was of a piece culturally.
82. The bulk of these missives exists in reduced form as part of the *responsa* literature, but for the use of the circular letter system for emergencies, discounting many of the older ideas (Finkelstein 1924), see Chazan 1968, 13–31.
83. This theme runs through Baron 1952–.
84. Marcus 1982, 40–52; Marcus 1986, 7–26.
85. Several of the poems with these motifs are readily available in English; Carmi 1981, 372–75, 379–84. I have treated this theme at greater length in Jordan 1987b, 531–43.
86. Usually Jews had separate cemeteries, the location of which is not always easy to determine now (cf. Weyl 1974, 123–25); there are only a very few examples of joint Jewish/Christian burial grounds, but see Lévy 1889, 246–47 (in the county of Bar), and Rabinowitz 1938, 193 (northern France). That the stones were upright is nicely shown from a print, published in Metz, of the Jewish cemetery in the 1500s; Bégin 1842–1843, facing p. 336.
87. Cf., though the example is southern, Kahn 1889, 264.
88. Vincent 1930, 290 n. 4; cf. Rabinowitz 1938, 196, and Champion 1933, 851, on apparent Christian superstition at Jewish burial practices.
89. On the size of the stones, some as large as 1 m. x 2 m. x .15 m., see Longpérier 1874, 659–60, 669–70; Schwab 1884, 137; Schwab 1887, 296–97; Macler 1906, 221; Ramette 1971, 464. Their removal and use in building are addressed in Lazard 1888, 213; Grandmaison 1889, 269; Marilier 1954–1958, 176–78; Weyl 1974, 125–26; cf. Nahon 1976, 38–43.
90. In general, see Schwab 1904. Dating of the artifacts is extremely tentative, and few go back before the early thirteenth century, but more than 50 markers have been recovered for Paris (Champion 1933, 850; Schwab 1909, 113–16; Roblin 1952a, 8–9). For the relics from the environs of Mantes, Saint-Germain-en-Laye, Bourges, Senneville, and Orléans, see Schwab 1884, 137–38; Schwab 1887, 296–97; Schwab 1897, 205–06; Macler 1906, 221–23. For Lozère, Mâcon and Dijon (nearly forty markers), see Loeb 1882, 105–06; Gerson 1882, 224–29; Ramette 1971, 464. Cf. southern examples, Schwab 1897, 189–90, 194.
91. Trachtenberg 1939; Abrahams 1932, 391; and Sirat 1966, 391–94 (for her data if not her conclusions). Rabinowitz 1938, 204–10, downplays French Jewry's "superstition."

92. See the twelfth-century (?) example in Macler 1906, 221–23, for Bourges.
93. For one example, below to n. 96.
94. Weyl 1974, 130.
95. Schwab 1904, 279; this is a nice and rather complete example (most of the stones are broken or effaced in places). Because it is Parisian and more or less intact, I quote it even though it dates from 1248. Fragmentary remains, sometimes undatable precisely but which seem to be older, appear to demonstrate that this stone reflects earlier practice (cf. the date below at nn. 96–97).
96. Longpérier 1874, 55; Weyl 1974, 130, 138 no. 17.
97. Longpérier 1874, 654.
98. Weyl 1974, 130; Weyl says the single word *harug* without the accompanying *al* . . . is not sufficient to establish that the reference is to a martyr.
99. Davis 1888, 6, 18, 122, 323.
100. Carmi 1981, 375. How much "activist" martyrdom actually occurred is uncertain; cf. Chazan 1984, 185–95.
101. Carmi 1981, 385.

Chapter 2

1. On the example of the goldsmiths of Paris particularly, see Lespinasse and Bonnardot 1879, ci, cix–cxx, cxxvi, etc.; Franklin 1883, 128. Other examples in Paris and elsewhere of the pattern: Omont 1905, 1–3; Hanawalt 1984, 21–37; Geremek 1976, 79–80.
2. Rabinowitz 1938, is full of essential but somewhat haphazardly organized information. Specific questions pertaining to these matters will be addressed in subsequent pages.
3. For general background see Richards 1977.
4. Delaborde 1882, 24–25.
5. Delaborde 1882, 28.
6. The declining presence of Jews in agricultural pursuits all over Europe is reflected in the fall-off in the number of papal bulls requiring Jews to pay tithes (in kind); Grayzel 1940, 3. See also below n. 16.
7. Rabinowitz 1938, 131–33; Agus 1965, 750–808; Agus 1969, 341–56. Much material on Jewish occupations is also scattered through Baron 1952–, XII.
8. Shatzmiller 1983a, 149–64.
9. On the Christian side, Grayzel 1933, 62, with full citations; on the Jewish side, cf. Abrahams 1932, 110–11.
10. An English translation of the Hebrew text that describes Polcelina is in Chazan 1980, 303.
11. Grayzel 1933, 74, with full references; Chazan 1973b, 17.
12. The translation and the editorial matter are all taken from Shatzmiller 1982a, 588 n. 13, 593.
13. This clause simplifies the range of possible reactions by the Jewish woman too much. What if her son had died? She might have reacted either with self-

recriminations at her failure to use the relic, or she could have redoubled her affirmation of faith, that is, with the thought that even though he died she had stood fast in his agony, trusting that God would reward her for doing so. The storyteller is making an exemplum, a one-dimensional moral lesson, out of a problematic encounter, though, to be sure, he would not have chosen to make this point with this story unless the woman had held firm. In any case, my aim is not to get at the personal psychology of this woman—I cannot do so—but to suggest that we have to think hard about the logic of, and the constraints on, situations like the one described in the exemplum.

14. Delaborde 1882, 24–25. On Brother Bernard, Baldwin 1986, 39, 49.
15. The failure of Rabinowitz (Rabinowitz 1938) to keep this in mind vitiates much of his book. I have tried to be careful by citing only those pages of his work where his conclusions seem to be drawn mainly from northern evidence of the appropriate period. For a good general treatment, see Caro 1920–1924, I, 356–60.
16. Finkelstein 1924, 10–11; Grayzel 1940, 3; Stein 1955, 28.
17. Stein 1955, 28; more generally, Abrahams 1932, 260–64.
18. Rabinowitz 1938, 29, alludes to the importance of the guild exclusions but never develops the point or offers specific evidence. Much material is summarized by Abrahams 1932, 243–44, on the effect of the exclusion in various regions.
19. Below Chapter 9, text to nn. 27, 62 (but cf. text following n.29).
20. Roblin 1952b, 20–21; Langmuir 1960, 207; Chazan 1973b, 15–17, 33; etc. Cf. Grayzel 1933, 43–44.
21. I use "quasi" advisedly. Many moneylenders engaged in the activity only temporarily, and many merchants made moneylending a very small or occasional part of their business. See Jordan, "Women and Credit," nn. 54, 57.
22. There is a brilliant exploration of the avoidance of commercial language as it pertains to real property by Maitland in Pollock and Maitland 1968, II, 10–28.
23. Jordan, "Women and Credit," 33–38. To the references cited in that article, add Langholm 1984.
24. Jordan, "Women and Credit," n. 30.
25. Delaborde 1882, 24–27.
26. Delaborde 1882, 28–29, for Rigord's reference to Philip's steadfastness against the Jews, a steadfastness uncorrupted by importunity and the promise of money—things that had moved his predecessors.
27. For the emergence of Jewish notions of the permitted parameters of lending at interest to Christians, see Stein 1955, 3–40. For the Christian background on moneylending, the literature is vast and exceptionally learned. General reference may be made to Gilchrist 1969, 62–76, 104–16 (with texts). References will be made to other more specialized works in subsequent chapters.
28. Below Chapter 10, text to n.7.
29. Langmuir 1980, 24–54.
30. Cf. Langmuir 1980, 24–54.
31. Quoted slightly differently both in Langmuir 1980, 37 (indirectly from Roth), and in the translation of Chazan 1980, 122–23. The Latin (*Rotuli litterarum*

- *patentium*, 33) is: "quia si cuidam cani pacem nostram dedissemus deberet inviolabiliter observari."
32. Delaborde 1882, 15–16. Bautier 1980a, 46.
33. Baldwin 1986, 51.
34. Delaborde 1882, 16 n. 1; Chazan 1973b, 64; Baldwin 1986, 51.
35. Stubbs 1876, II, 4.
36. Among the difficulties: Rigord makes a point of mentioning the coronation date; thus, it may be that he wants to emphasize regnal years. But Rigord shaped (distorted?) his text in such a way as to make the adolescent Philip rather more heroic and kingly in his mien than he might have been (cf. Baldwin 1986, 29). Ralph de Diceto, on the other hand, is sometimes just bad on dates; see Stubbs's introductory remarks (Stubbs 1876). Although the year for which he enrolls the raid would be 1181, new style (which agrees with my analysis), the day he gives is *XV* (not XIV or XVI) Kalends of *February* (not March). This can only mean, I think, that he misfigured by one when he counted backwards from the first (Kalends) of March and then wrote "Kalends of February" when he meant "February." Some support for my feeling that the raid should be dated 1181 also comes from a reference to a Christmas 1180 argument between the Archbishop of Sens and Philip over the issue of Christian servants (*mancipia*) of Jews, the ban on which was not enforced by his father. At that time, he followed his father's policy, but subsequently repented, that is, after Christmas 1180. The raid, in this chronology, would be one of the uglier manifestations of his repentance. On the dispute, *Gallia christiana*, XII, 54; discussed by Caro 1920–1924, I, 359–60.
37. Urbach 1955, 108. The Hebrew source provides no date, but Urbach of course followed the traditional chronology. Chazan 1973b, 64, translates *shomrim* as officials; but the word "guards" or "watch" (representing an underlying Old French *bidaus* or *guête*) seems more precise for the situation.
38. Delaborde 1882, 25, 27.
39. Stubbs 1876, II, 4.
40. Cf. Baldwin 1986, 54. Normal predictable revenue was not *all* revenue (indeed there was usually a lot more), but the magnitude of the Jewish ransom is startling nonetheless.
41. Delaborde 1882, 24–25, for Rigord's evidence of enforcement; Chazan 1973b, 35–36, cites evidence of enforcement from the royal domain town of Etampes in 1179.
42. Delaborde 1882, 25; *Recueil des actes de Philippe Auguste*, I, no. 62. The remarks of Guillaume Le Breton, the continuator of Rigord, add nothing to the story; Delaborde 1882, 181.
43. As far as I have been able to determine, the Orléans incident is based only on a very late tradition. Cochard shows that scholarly references to another Orléans incident of 1171 are themselves based ultimately on a misreading of this late tradition; Cochard 1895, 40.
44. Delaborde 1882, 27–28.
45. Delaborde 1882, 28.
46. Above Chapter 1, text to n. 22. See also Anchel 1940, 50.

47. Delaborde 1882, 28 (Rigord), 181 (Guillaume Le Breton). Also below n. 48.
48. Cf. Roblin 1952b, 13.
49. Delaborde 1882, 30–31 (Rigord), 181 (Guillaume Le Breton).
50. *Recueil des actes de Philippe Auguste*, I, no. 90. All scholars mention this dramatic transformation; see Champion 1933, 848; Roblin 1952b, 12; Chazan 1973b, 66.
51. Delaborde 1882, 31–32; *Recueil des actes de Philippe Auguste*, I, no. 99, and II, nos. 617, 658; Grayzel 1933, 357–58.
52. Roblin 1952b, 12–13; Baldwin 1986, 52.
53. *Recueil des actes de Philippe Auguste*, I, no. 95.
54. *Recueil des actes de Philippe Auguste*, I, no. 94.
55. *Recueil des actes de Philippe Auguste*, I, nos. 166, 263, and II, no. 627.
56. *Recueil des actes de Philippe Auguste*, I, nos. 134, 223.
57. *Recueil des actes de Philippe Auguste*, I, nos. 133, 402.
58. *Recueil des actes de Philippe Auguste*, II, no. 665.
59. But cf. Chazan 1973b, 68.
60. Cf. Legeay 1889–1890, 214; Morey 1883, 1–2, 4; Nordmann 1925, 5–6.
61. Delaborde 1882, 28. Chazan 1973b, 68.
62. Above Chapter 1, text to nn. 76–77.
63. Souchet 1867–1873, II, 508. On the jewry and its sharply defined topography, see the document published in Guérard 1840, II, 367.
64. Chédeville 1973, 475.
65. Grayzel 1933, 77–78, 293.
66. Cf. Legeay 1889–1890, 214.
67. Above Chapter 1, text to nn. 5–6. The abbey of Saint-Martin of Tours was under royal patronage and Tours in general was susceptible to French influence; Baldwin 1986, 68–69. The close relationship of the royal abbey of Saint-Denis with the Capetians need not be dwelt upon. Philip, however, had recently had his bride crowned queen there, a clear mark of the continuing importance he accorded the abbey; Baldwin 1986, 16.
68. Baldwin 1986, 396.
69. Graboïs 1969, 1187–95.
70. Baldwin 1986, 6–27.
71. Fawtier 1960, 111–12.
72. Jordan 1984, 155–56. A *rue des juifs* in Amiens must relate to a later settlement (cf. *Intermédiaire des chercheurs et curieux*, XXXV, 253).
73. Chazan 1973b, map pp. 210–11 (examples: Saint-Quentin, Ribemont, Roye, etc.)
74. For these matters I follow Baldwin 1986, 16, 24, 80–82, 200.
75. Baldwin 1986, 187, 278.
76. Baldwin 1986, 77–80.
77. Delaborde 1882, 118–19, 194; Chazan 1980, 305–06. I have used the neutral phrase "one of his dependents" to describe the Christian. Chazan 1980, 305, says "serf"; Chazan 1973b, 70, says "vassal." The Hebrew (from Habermann 1945, 128) is *eved*, which could mean servant, serf, or reeve.

78. Chazan 1969, 1–18; Chazan 1973b, 69–70 (the earlier with references to the wide variety of scholarly opinions).
79. Delaborde 1882, 119 n. 1. Bautier 1980a, 46, accepts the Brie identification.
80. The Hebrew text spells the name bet-resh-yod-yod-shin (unvocalized, but probably pronounced 'Bryis' or something like it). The s-ending is decisive. In Old French, Brie not Bray was spelled Bris (HF, XXIV, 284, 290 — Latin documents, but with location names frequently in the vernacular). In Latin both Brie and Bray could be spelled Braia (cf. HF, XXIV, 278*, nos. 29, 33); and until the sixteenth century one called Brie-Comte-Robert, Braye-Comte-Robert (Anselme 1674a, 361 and elsewhere).
81. Lewis 1985, 145–79.
82. Recueil des actes de Philippe Auguste, I, no. 423.
83. Lewis 1985, 147, n. 6. Chazan's argument that the existence of a good-sized Jewish community at Brie is not otherwise documented is not telling, given the paucity of documentary records before 1200 and the fact that, by the time the documentary record becomes richer, the community had been destroyed.
84. Delaborde 1882, 119: "subito, nescientibus suis familiaribus quo pergebat"; "gressu velocissimo"; "velociter venit."
85. Chazan 1980, 305–06.
86. For various explanations: Chazan 1973b, 75; Baldwin 1986, 160; Baron 1952–, XI, 213; Blumenkranz in Encyclopaedia judaica, XIII, 392; Schwarzfuchs 1975, 75.
87. Delaborde 1882, 141.

Chapter 3

1. Delaborde 1882, 141.
2. For the theories, cf. above Chapter 2, text to nn. 29–31. See also Langmuir 1960, 210; Thibault 1933, 720, and cf. Grayzel 1933, 355 no. xvii.
3. See the collection of opinions assembled by Chazan 1973b, 77.
4. It is Rigord who informs us that the readmission dates from July; Delaborde 1882, 141. I am assuming in all I write that the Jews were active in the royal domain from July, or whenever Philip first made known his willingness to readmit them, until September, and that this, as we shall see, raised thorny legal problems. I do not subscribe to the view of certain authors (Baldwin 1986, 160, following Chazan 1973b, 68) that an agreement of September 1198 confronting these problems (below nn. 5–7) can be used as evidence that from 1182 to 1198 Jews had managed somehow to provide credit clandestinely in the royal domain, at least to any substantial degree (there might have been some of this near the "borders").
5. I have had to extrapolate from the documents as best I can. Since both Philip and Theobald of Champagne dated their charters at Mantes, I presume that there was a face-to-face meeting. For the texts: Recueil des actes de Philippe Auguste, II, no. 582; Layettes, I, no. 479. Cf. Caro 1920–1924, I, 362–63.
6. Recueil des actes de Philippe Auguste, II, no. 583.

7. The agreement touches all debts contracted in the domain before the Nativity of the Virgin, 8 September 1198. The two-year repayment schedule runs from All Saints, 1 November 1198, to All Saints 1200. The three weeks or so between 8 September 1198 and All Saints would have been used to publicize the agreement with the king's officials and to make a determination of the debts that had been contracted.

8. Baldwin 1986, 505 n. 122. The reference is to Lot and Fawtier 1932, CLXXXIII, CCI: 466 pounds, 66 pounds, plus perhaps 50 pounds of the debts owed to an individual Jew; also (CL, CCII) large debts (?) of 40 pounds and 60 pounds collected from individual Jews at Sens and Montlhéry.

9. *Rotuli de oblatis et finibus*, 73. I am generalizing from an order which was directed against one particularly wealthy Jew.

10. Delaborde 1882, 141. Baldwin 1986, 92–93.

11. "Ex Chronologia Roberti Altissiodorensis": *HF*, XVIII, 262–63. (There is a misprint in Chazan 1973b, 75, of "returned" for "retained.") Gutsch 1928, 190.

12. *Recueil des actes de Philippe Auguste*, II, no. 678. For a discussion of this record, see Baldwin 1986, 278–79.

13. The word census, left untranslated, has a particular meaning here as "element of domain income" rather than mere "rent" or"quit-rent"; cf. Baldwin 1986, 45.

14. *Recueil des actes de Philippe Auguste*, II, no. 582; *Layettes*, I, no. 479: the general conventions have the saving clause, "nisi assensu (ipsius) comitis [or nostro, *for the king*] ex ore suo [nostro]." Of course, those Jews who had done so without the assent of the lord had their existing debts confiscated, even if they were then allowed to reside outside the lordship of their birth; cf. above n. 8 on the debts seized in the royal domain (for the count of Champagne) of Jews residing at Sens and Montlhéry.

15. *Recueil des actes de Philippe Auguste*, II, no. 776, dated 1203.

16. On moneychanging, cf. Baldwin 1986, 159.

17. Baldwin 1986, 61.

18. There is no positive evidence of this before 1204, but on oath taking, cf. Saige 1881, 54.

19. Below Chapter 4, text following n. 33.

20. Below n. 32.

21. On the *prévôts* of the Jews, a resurrection of an office that flourished under Louis VII, Baldwin 1986, 160–61; Chazan 1973b,40, 90; Lot and Fawtier 1932, 71. On regulations regarding pawning, below chapter 4, text following n. 36.

22. In general, below chapter 4, text following n. 36. On the Jews' attitude, cf. Kisch 1938, 22–25.

23. Below chapter 4, n. 36.

24. Baldwin 1986, 156, 160.

25. Lot and Fawtier 1932: revenue from the Jews generated by the use of the seal (*sigillum*) or the authentication of bonds (*littere*) at Senlis (CLIII), at Pontoise (CLXXVI, CLXXVIII), at Béthisy (CXCVII), at Poissy (CXCIX), and at Mantes (CCIII). For rents or, rather, general sums from the Jews, *de judeis*, which are probably rents: at Senlis (CLVII), at Orléans (CL), at Mantes? (CLIV), at Paris (CCII[= ?CLXXXII]). For the levy on wine at Sens, CLI; I

see no compelling reason to regard this as a charge against (?imported) wine from Champagne as the editors seem to think, p. 58. For levies on other unspecified produce (*esplees*) at Orléans, CL.

26. Above nn. 8, 25. Although not from the fiscal records, one can add Corbeil to this list. Chazan 1973b, 86, says that a "specific grant" was made to Saint-Spires of Corbeil "to exclude Jews." This overstates the case. What we find in the cartulary of the church, which was located on dower land of the queen, is that one Jew had rented part of the house of a burgher located in the precincts of the church property. The queen was reminded that, from of old, Jews were prohibited from this area, and she confirmed the prohibition in 1203; Coüard Luys 1882, 50.

27. Delaborde 1882, 141.

28. Cf. the reference in Dion 1903, 61, to the "Old Jewry" of Paris, 1218.

29. For all that follows I have depended on various scholarly reconstructions. Some are more cavalier than one might like about bringing evidence from diverse periods together, but the general outlines seem authentic: Roblin 1952b, 14–17; Anchel 1940, 52; Champion 1933, 849– 50. Cf. above n. 25 on rents for leased property at Paris and elsewhere.

30. Delaborde 1882, 141; *HF*, XVIII, 263.

31. Baldwin 1970, I, 296–311. See also Poliakov 1967, 69–71.

32. Brundage 1969, 179–83.

33. Innocent's views are neatly summarized in Langmuir 1960, 207; the texts are available in Grayzel 1933, 86–142.

34. Above nn. 11, 30; also Chazan 1973b, 86.

35. On the euphemisms, cf. De Roover 1948, 127.

36. *HF*, XVIII, 262; Baldwin 1970, I, 309. Also Le Goff 1986, 9–68, 83–99.

37. Cf. Le Goff 1986, 48.

38. Rigord mentions judaizing in the context of conversion of Christian domestic servants of Jews to Judaism: Delaborde 1882,24. For further discussion, see Mann 1930, 244–59; Rabinowitz 1938, 109; Blumenkranz 1952, 54; and, though wildly exaggerated, Wacholder 1960–1961, 288–315. On reconverts, see Shohet 1931, 30.

39. Cf. Kirschenbaum 1985, 286–87.

40. Blumenkranz 1960, 64; Baldwin 1970, I, 198; Stow 1981, 179; Stow 1984, 28; Le Goff 1986, 37–40.

41. Little 1971, 44.

42. I follow, in general, Dahan 1980a, 41–48, 56–68, on the interpretation of the work of Gautier.

43. For his career, Koenig 1955–, I, xviii–xxx.

44. Dahan 1980a, 41–48. See the critical edition of Koenig 1955–; the handsome older edition (Poquet 1857) is nicely illustrated and worth consulting.

45. Cf. Kunstmann 1981, 3–5, 11–12, 45–49, 69–71. Gautier has much in common with his contemporary, the Anglo Norman Adgar in the treatment of Virgin-and-Jew miracles; Adgar 1982, 14, 33, 42 43, 143–47, 257–64.

46. Dahan 1980a, 60–67. Over eighty manuscripts survive; Koenig 1955–, I, xxxiv–xxxviii.

47. Quoted in Dahan 1980a, 67.
48. For the interesting mystical names of the Virgin, such as the one quoted, see Assisi, MS 695, fols. III, 236 and 236 v. In general on the twelfth century cult of the Virgin, especially in its connection with the vulgar literary sources that include popular tales, see Ahsman 1930, 79– 103 (more particularly, pp.84, 93–94, 97, 100 on miracles with a Jewish leitmotiv).
49. Beaumanoir 1884–1885, II, 299–301.
50. Cf. Pflaum 1930, 125–27, for the evidence from dramatic literature, and Levine 1986, 291–96, for satiric *topoi* based on Jews.
51. *HL*, XXVII, 499.
52. Jordan 1982, 50–57.
53. Below Chapter 4, text to nn. 1–31.
54. Baldwin 1986, 191–96, 207–19.
55. Baldwin 1986, 220–58, 289–93, 304–28; Strayer 1932.
56. Baldwin 1986, 304–28; Fawtier 1960, 149–50; Delisle in *HF*, XXIV, *157–*60, *187.
57. Chazan 1973b, 73, 94; Baldwin 1986, 230–33; Richardson 1960, 201–12.
58. Above Chapter 2, text to nn. 71–75.
59. Baldwin 1986, 278–79.
60. Above nn. 24, 26–27.
61. Above Chapter 1, text to nn. 3–4.
62. Nortier and Baldwin 1980, 14.
63. For an inventory of relevant documentation, Nahon 1975a, 5(C 64/5, 24 and 25 February 1203), 6 (C 64/5, 31 January 1203), 7(E 370/1/3, 1199), 8 (E 373/7), 9 (E 505/4, after 1 May 1203; E373/18, 1195). Also Delisle 1852, 134–35; Richardson 1960, 203, 206.
64. Which is not the same as saying they were spectacularly rich: this is the force of Richardson's unfavorable comparison of Norman Jewry with English; Richardson 1960, 206.
65. Chazan 1973b, 69–73; Delisle 1852, 133–34. For a translation of the charter (1201) of John to the English and Norman Jews, see Chazan 1980, 77–79.
66. Cf., however, Nahon 1975a, 5 (C 62/3, 12 November 1203), 7(C 66/6, 11 November 1204), for evidence of some loyalty and financial interests.
67. In general, Roth 1941, 1–131 (notice especially, p. 34); Caro 1920–1924, I, 351, 499. On population, see Shatzmiller 1977–1978, 173; but cf. Baron 1952–, XII, 6–7, for a different estimate of population (criticizing the 5,000 figure that ultimately goes back to Caro's analysis, according to Baron).
68. Roth 1941, 32–37.
69. Above Chapter 2, n. 85.
70. Below Chapter 4, text to nn. 79–95.
71. Chazan 1973b, 213–20 (supplemented where Chazan does not give dates with Gross 1969/1897, 136–39, 476–83): *L'Aigle*, Alençon, *Arques-la-Bataille*, *Argentan*, Aumale, Bernay, *Bonneville-sur-Touques*, *Brionne*, Caen, Caudebec-en-Caux, Coutances, Domfront, *Elbeuf*, *Exmes*, Falaise, Fécamp, Gisors, *Gournay-en-Bray*, *Hodeng-au-Bosc*, Lillebonne, Lisieux, Longueville-sur-Scie, *Lyons-la-Forêt*, Montivilliers, *Orbec*, Pacy-sur-Eure, Pont Audemer, Rouen,

Saint Cénéri-la-Gerei, Sainte-Scholasse-sur-Sarthe, Sées, *Verneuil-sur-Avre, Vernon*. (Gisors was already under Philip's control before the major conquest of the province.)

72. Nahon 1975a, 4, 7–9: Auffay, Beaumont-le-Roger, Chambois, Trun, Veules-les-Roses.

73. Nahon's "Troarn" is omitted as doubtful (Nahon 1975a, 5), but his "Andelys" is open (p. 7). Although the Jew of Andelys he refers to was a transient, there was a *rue aux Juifs* at Andelys (reported in *Les Intermédiares des chercheurs*, XXXV, 68), but it might go back only to a post-1210 settlement. I think "Evreux" also had a pre-1210 community of Jews, but Gross 1969/1897, 38–43, can only show that a rather senior teacher taught there "before 1224."

74. The twenty villages and towns where there is evidence of one Jew are the five identified by Nahon (above n. 72) and those italicized in my abstract of Chazan's list (above n. 71), though I do not see why he says "one" for Gournay-en-Bray; cf. Gross 1969/1897, 136–39.

75. See, among others, the citations to Gross in n. 71. above. Cf. also the rabbinic material for routine references to the Jews of Normandy in Finkelstein 1924, 155, 166–67, and Rabinowitz 1938, 148. But far more comprehensive now is Golb 1985.

76. Cf. Shatzmiller 1980a, 141.

77. Caro 1920–1924, I, 482; Golb 1985, 85–99.

78. On these matters there rapidly appeared a large and disputative literature. See Golb 1977; Golb 1979a, 24–31; Golb 1979b, 8–23; Golb 1985. Also, Blumenkranz 1978, 37–42; Talmage 1987, 648 (review of Golb 1985).

79. Richardson 1960, 202–07. This is what he means by calling Norman Jewry "small, and relatively poor." I would prefer to say the Jews were modest in numbers and modest in wealth.

80. Nahon 1975a, 9 (E 505/4, year 1200–01).

81. Above Chapter 2, text to nn. 37–42.

82. First of all, a levy is one thing and receipt another. Second, the problem of inflation from 1180 to 1200 ought to be taken into account. We know English inflation was very high in this period (the pound may have eroded in value by 70% from 1180 to 1220). If this inflation, which was not characteristic of Europe in general, carried over into Normandy, we would have to conclude that far fewer residents were necessary to produce four thousand pounds than would have been necessary to produce the same sum in 1180, the date of our figures for the royal domain. If, as it has been urged, the English inflation depended on activity in the landmarket incident to the possessory actions in property law, then there is no reason to extrapolate the extreme inflation to Normandy, though there might have been some reaction. In any case, Normandy had shared some of the reforms of property law with England, but they never revolutionized the legal system. See on all these problems, Palmer 1985, 375–96. It is only fair to add that I do not feel persuaded by Palmer's argument from property law on English inflation.

83. It seems to me that Richardson's comparison's (Richardson 1960, 204–07) with England (given the population of English Jewry) point to the same

general conclusion: the existence of about 2,000 Norman Jews around the year 1200. Golb would undoubtedly raise the figure; he believes that Rouen at its height had at least 2,000 Jews; Golb 1985, 13 14. I find this assertion difficult to accept.

84. On the relative absence of towns: Richardson 1960, 202.
85. For the Norman situation, Richardson 1960, 201–02.
86. On the few Norman towns, see Strayer 1932, 81–90.
87. On the incident in Silli, Nahon 1975a, 3, 7, 9 (the word "massacre" is Nahon's).
88. Richardson 1960, 207. On pledging, *HF*, XXIV, 56 (no. 416).
89. Still another cluster was Lisieux, Bonneville, Orbec.
90. On the routes from Rouen were Elbeuf, Lyons-la-Forêt, Lillebonne, etc.
91. In the east an exception was Coutances; along the Atlantic coast, Fécamp and Montivilliers. Richardson also noticed the general unevenness of Jewish settlement in Normandy; Richardson 1960, 201.
92. Richardson 1960, 206.
93. Richardson 1960, 206; Powicke 1960, 157 n. 183, 216, 240–41.
94. Powicke 1960, 254 n. 8.
95. Powicke 1960 (page listings s. vv.).
96. *HF*, XXIV, 32–34, 54–58, 69–71.
97. *HF*, XXIV, 731.

Chapter 4

1. Golb misconstrues Philip's actions by predating records from 1210 to 1204; Golb 1985, 289–90. Cf. below, text to nn. 53–78.
2. *Recueil des actes de Philippe Auguste*, II, nos. 790, 806: "non capiemus . . . ad occassionem usure, nisi denarium pro denario vel equivalentiam alicui commodaverit." The *non capiemus* must apply to the estates of deceased usurers under traditional Norman law; cf. also, II, no. 879–80; III, no. 1000.
3. Baldwin 1986, 231. The definitive edition of the record of these oaths will appear in the fifth volume of the *Registres* of Philip Augustus (no. 1). Professor Baldwin kindly shared the edited copy of the record with me. See also Caro 1920–1924, I, 363.
4. On Beleassez as equivalent to Rachel, see Rabinowitz 1938, 240–41.
5. Cf. Baldwin 1986, 222–23.
6. Or three other sets if the bonds offered by two brothers (value sixty pounds) are considered together.
7. Boussard 1938, 76–96.
8. Cf. Chazan 1970, 217–21; Legeay 1889–1890, 213–14; Blumenkranz in *Encyclopaedia judaica*, XI, 892–93. Most unreliable is Saillant 1934, 62.
9. The charter to the Norman Jews of 1201 also applied to Angevin Jews. Hence my generalization; see Chazan 1973b, 72. Cf. Marchegay 1883, 285–86; and Musset 1902, 149.
10. Brunschvicg 1894, 231–32.

11. Finkelstein 1924, 155, 166–67.
12. Brunschvicg 1894, 229–31.
13. Vincent 1930, 269–70; Musset 1902, 149.
14. Dornic 1960, 47, 54–55. Dornic estimates the entire population of Le Mans at "4,000–5,000?".
15. *Encyclopaedia judaica*, XI, 892–93; Chazan 1973b, 207–20.
16. Above Chapter 3, text to n. 89.
17. Besides the references collected below, nn. 10–12, see on medieval Anjou, Dornic 1961, 26–47. The relative underpopulation and lack of towns has little to do with the "power" of feudal seigneuries; cf. Boussard 1938, 15–22.
18. *Encyclopaedia judaica*, III, 22–23; XIII, 704; XV, 1287–88; La Borderie 1896–1914, 338; Chazan 1973b, 207–20; Métais 1893–1904, II, no. dcxix. One might factor in "rue des Juifs" and similar topographical names which besides confirming some locations would raise a possibility for others, namely, in Anjou, Jarzé and Château-Gontier; *Intermédiaire des chercheurs et curieux*, XXXVI, 25.
19. Blumenkranz in *Encyclopaedia judaica*, III, 23.
20. On the problems of 1240, below n. 96.
21. Nahon 1966, 180, would probably prefer a slightly higher population.
22. On, for example, the Poitiers neighborhood, see Vincent 1930, 267–70.
23. Chédeville 1968, 156; Farcy 1895, 157.
24. Chédeville 1968, 348 (ownership), 276 (renting).
25. I follow Blumenkranz in *Encyclopaedia judaica*, XI, 892–93. Similarly in Poitiers, see Vincent 1930, 267–70.
26. Chédeville 1968, 340.
27. Merlet and Jarry 1896, no. IX; Métais 1893–1904, II, no. dcxix.
28. Chédeville 1968, 341.
29. Denis 1911, 109–10, 153–54: "judeos creditores."
30. Baldwin 1986, 194–95.
31. *Recueil des actes de Philippe Auguste*, II, nos. 829–30.
32. The charter is published in *Recueil des actes de Philippe Auguste*, II, no. 955. Much of this document has been misunderstood. The Latin extracts in some of the following notes are meant to provide the text against which my interpretation may be assessed. Chazan's translation must be approached with caution; Chazan 1980, 205–07. See also Caro 1920–1924, I, 364–65.
33. Champenois problems were notorious. In 1202 a monastery had to be taken into receivership it was so heavily indebted to Jews and other creditors; Lalore 1875, IV, 288–89.
34. " . . . neque judeus computare poterit cum debitore suo infra annum nisi debitor computare et reddere voluerit infra annum, et quandocumque debitor computare et reddere voluerit, judeus id ei denegare non poterit." Chazan's exegesis of this passage seems to be in error; Chazan 1973b, 84; Chazan 1980, 205. Baldwin 1986, 232, follows Chazan.
35. " . . . et si infra diem statutam non fuerint sigillata, ex tunc in antea non reddetur eis aliquid quod exigant per vetera sigilla."
36. "Si quis autem fugitivus fuerit aut in peregrinatione detentus, ejus debitum

arrestabitur, et ex tunc non curret lucrum nisi duo denarii pro libra per ebdomadam." *Fugitivus* was a technical word here for any person who abandoned his land to go into exile with John. The issue of what would happen to these lands was far from resolved. The *fugitivus* ought not to be penalized unjustly in case some sort of compromise would be reached later on; cf. Powicke 1960, 284–85 especially n. 28 for this usage of *fugitivus*. *Fugitivus* in the ordinary sense of an outlaw (cf. Tardif 1881–1903, I, 32–33) would not make sense.

37. Cf. Baldwin 1986, 524 n. 50; Chazan 1973b, 88.

38. *HF*, XXIV, 56. John the Warrior (Johannes le Guerrier, in the sources) was, so his name indicates, one of those mercenaries who vigorously pacified the countryside; cf. Powicke 1960, 231.

39. Cf. below Chapter 5, n. 69.

40. Powicke 1953, 80–104; Jordan 1979b, 15–16, 25–26.

41. Poole 1951, 425–86; Cheney 1976.

42. Richardson 1960, 165–75, for the details that follow. See also Poole 1951, 422–23.

43. This obsessive fear was still being manifested a half-century later during the baronial take-over of government from Henry III; see Treharne 1971, 110.

44. *Chronica de Mailros*, 109.

45. Cf. Chazan 1973b, 79: "Again the financial needs of the crown led Philip Augustus to exploit his Jews, just as John Lackland was despoiling his." Golb unfortunately misdates the material on the crisis of 1210; Golb 1985, 289–90.

46. Cf. Bedos 1980, 207–08, 218–19, and more recently Friedenberg 1987, 94–103, although the general remarks (pp. 101–03) in his catalog are not entirely clear.

47. Chazan 1973b, 88; Bedos 1980, 218–19 (a third Champenois bond of similar content is noticed by both authors).

48. On the "lull" in fighting, 1206–1212, Baldwin 1986, 196–207.

49. *Recueil des actes de Philippe Auguste*, III, no. 1106.

50. *Recueil des actes de Philippe Auguste*, III, nos. 1132, 1154. Baldwin 1986, 197, 279.

51. *Recueil des actes de Philippe Auguste*, III no. 1227. Baldwin 1986, 203–04.

52. Below, n.83, on Bray-sur-Somme; and for the Châlons example, *Recueil des actes de Philippe Auguste*, III, no. 1130.

53. Above n. 33.

54. See, e.g., Quantin 1873, 6 no. 13.

55. *Recueil des actes de Philippe Auguste*, I, no. 34; II, no. 741.

56. Baldwin 1986, 178.

57. Powicke 1960, 115.

58. *Recueil des actes de Philippe Auguste*, III, no. 1095.

59. Whether this debt was one of many or the sum of all debts owed *erga Judeos* (below n. 60) I cannot determine with certainty. Consolidation of Jewish debts in the way I have suggested did sometimes occur, however; see Lalore 1875, I, 250–52, 255, 266–67, 271–72, 304.

60. "Aliter enim non poterant liberare ecclesiam suam ab usuris quibus tenebatur erga Judeos."

61. This document, from the crown's Register E, will be published in the *Registres* of Philip Augustus in volume seven, no. 16. It is undated; so, the speculation

as to its place in the events that I am reconstructing is purely my own. But as we will see, the content of the list leaves little doubt of its relationship to the story as a whole. Professor Baldwin graciously permitted me to examine the copy-edited version of the document in advance of publication.

62. *Chronica de Mailros*, 109. The impression is truly contemporary for the chronicle was kept up to date by more or less current hands from 1140 to about 1275 (pp. xvi, 222).

63. " . . . subtili fretus astucia, per omnes Galliarum provincias simul ut omnes Judei carceribus manciparentur edixit."

64. A new edition will appear in the *Registres* of Philip Augustus, volume II (L). The tentative head notes there will suggest a date 1208–1212. But nine *baillis* are mentioned by name. Using Baldwin's lists, the only year that all these men were *baillis* was 1210; Baldwin 1986, 428–33. For earlier editions, see, for example, *HF*, XXIV, *277. For a brief analysis, Caro 1920–1924, I, 506.

65. Morel de Yainville, identified above, for example, is known to have been kept in prison even after some Jews were released; below n. 71. Supporting evidence that the arrest occurred no earlier than 1210 comes from the fact that one of the Jews, Dieudonné de Bray, whose debts were enrolled in 1210 (above n. 64) and who was kept in prison after some releases (below n. 71), had been carrying on business as usual as late as August 1209; *Recueil des actes de Philippe Auguste*, III, no. 1091.

66. *HF*, XXIV, 15, no. 97.

67. The *bailli* mentioned did not become a *bailli* in Normandy until about 1205; cf. Baldwin 1986, 432.

68. *HF*, XXIV, 9, no. 56, 10 no. 61, 32 no. 251. Dating is not perfect in these old-age recollections, but they mostly seem to go back to 1210 or the long aftermath of collections (cf. below n. 69).

69. For the document, Nortier and Baldwin 1980, 18; but Nortier is wrong in referring this "old debt" to the ransom of fifteen thousand marks (from 1198 he says, wrongly, for 1180 or 1181). It cannot be a twelfth-century debt, for the arrears mentioned in the fiscal account he edited come from Caux in Normandy which, of course, was not in Philip's control in the 1180s or 1190s.

70. For example: *Recueil des actes de Philippe Auguste*, III, no. 1236, dated 1212.

71. Not for the last time I want to thank Professor Baldwin for sharing with me the edited copy of this record which will appear in the *Registres*, volume seven, no. 17.

72. For the publishing details, the *Registres* will supply full information. One of the problems with early editions was the unfamiliarity of editors with the Old French or Latinesque versions of Hebrew names. For example, given the peculiarities of thirteenth-century calligraphy, it would be easy to read a certain word as either Bonevie or Bonemie. The choice should fall on Bonevie if we are dealing with a Jew's name; Bonevie is the equivalent of the not uncommon Hayim Tov.

73. Baldwin 1986, 232; Chazan 1973b, 80.

74. This record, hitherto unpublished, will appear in the *Registres* of Philip Augustus, volume seven, no. 18. (Baldwin provided a photocopy of the edited

copy.) The word surety is not used. It is my speculation; Baldwin 1986, 524 n. 53, earlier refers to the lists as "not yet" having "found an explicable context."

75. Chazan 1973b, 87.

76. Delaborde 1882, 233. See also Bautier 1980a, 46.

77. *Chronica de Mailros*, 110.

78. For the text, see Grayzel 1933, 306–07; and his speculations about date (1212 or 1213) and location (Paris or Reims) for this synod held by Robert, presuming it was different from the council held in Paris in 1210. Our Scots chronicler says that Robert de Curçon played a prominent role in the Paris council of 1210, which makes me think that the text in Grayzel might originate in that meeting; cf. *Chronica de Mailros*, 110.

79. For Jews in the area, below nn. 81, 91. Further on Brittany, below nn. 92–97.

80. On royal tutelage in Flanders, Baldwin 1986, 279. On the absence of Jews in Flanders, see Stengers 1950, 3, 11; cf. Dobson 1974, 7 n. 24.

81. *Layettes*, I, no. 922, dated at Mantes (not Meaux, which the editors suggest).

82. *Recueil des actes de Philippe Auguste*, III, no. 1127—also at Mantes. In October 1210 the Champenois and Burgundians made a similar agreement; Grayzel 1933, 352.

83. The town of Bray-sur-Somme was purchased and granted a communal charter, but whether Bray had any Jews at the time is doubtful. The communal charter reads as if there were none, and the *rue aux Juifs* attested in the modern period may relate to a much later settlement. *Recueil des actes de Philippe Auguste*, III, nos. 1121, 1128, 1117; Josse 1882, 200, 202–03.

84. Above Chapter 3, text to n. 11.

85. *Layettes*, I, no. 923.

86. Cf. Graboïs 1979, 67; Chazan 1973b, 86–87.

87. *Recueil des actes de Phililppe Auguste*, III, no. 1115.

88. "Quia vero ibidem capellam construere tenebantur, de voluntate nostra eis remisimus, et volumus ut ibidem cappelam construere de cetero non teneantur."

89. Baldwin 1986, 232.

90. On the matters summarized in this paragraph, Baldwin 1986, 94–95, 198–99, 239.

91. On the geography, culture and history of medieval Brittany in general, there is much up-to-date discussion in Delumeau 1969, but there is a faddish concentration on some subjects to the exclusion of others. On the general absence of Jews, La Borderie 1896–1914, III, 336. One minor point: Chazan 1973b, 60–61, retranslates a twelfth-century rabbinic text from Finkelstein 1924, 153, 155. Where Finkelstein reads "inhabitants of Normandy and the shore of the sea," Chazan substitutes "Brittany" for "the shore of the sea." I do not doubt (see Blumenkranz in *Encyclopaedia judaica*, IV, 1383), that there were a few Jews in Brittany before 1210 or even 1200, but perhaps "the shore of the sea" means "the Norman march with Brittany."

92. La Borderie 1896–1914, III, 336.

93. Durtelle de Saint-Sauveur 1957/1935, I, 230.

94. La Borderie 1896–1914, III, 337.

95. *Encyclopaedia judaica*, IV, 1383, for all except Fougères. For Fougères, I am arguing back from information in La Borderie 1896–1914, III, 338. *Rues des juifs* and similarly named locations raise the possibility of settlement in a few other towns and villages (Rennes, Saint-Malo, Le Croisic, Saulnières and certain lost hamlets and domaines); *Intermédiaire des chercheurs et curieux*, XXXVI, 24.

96. La Borderie 1896–1914, III, 337.

97. La Borderie 1896–1914, III, 337–38; Grayzel 1933, 344–45. (References to the details of the expulsion order are from Grayzel's printing, Latin, English facing.) See also Chazan 1973b, 134; Nahon 1970, 23; Brunschvicg 1894, 233–34; and for an easily available translation, Chazan 1980, 312–13.

98. La Borderie 1896–1914, III, 338.

99. Graboïs 1979, 67–79. See also Kanarfogel 1986, 191–215.

100. Translated in Graboïs 1979, 67 n. 3.

Chapter 5

1. See in this regard the hostile remarks of the poet, Guiot de Provins, against the count (of Champagne); Orr 1915, 26. The work where these remarks are found can be dated 1204–1209, probably 1206 (pp. xx–xxi). Also Chazan 1973b, 89.

2. Grayzel 1933, 138–41 (the pope's letter with allusion to Philip's; dated 1213 or 1214). Grayzel is right to point out that the pope refers to usury, not Jewish usury per se. The pope's letter, in other words, is a general indictment of the king's policies. See also Stow 1981, 176.

3. The directive can be consulted in an old edition *Ordonnances*, XI, 315, where the editors rightly refrain from dating it precisely. The newer edition (*Recueil des actes de Philippe Auguste*, IV, no. 1555) on the grounds of its place in Register C of Philip's archives dates it 1219–1220. Baldwin 1986, 231–32, who discusses the directive, implicitly rejects the modern editors' dating because they make the directive follow a comprehensive ordinance that is completely at variance with it. Again, however, except for regarding the directive as before 1219 or so (which it certainly is), he does not attempt to date it more precisely. The directive is also briefly addressed in Chazan 1973b, 85, 90. He translates it in Chazan 1980, 208, but his translation does not make good sense.

4. Above Chapter 4, text to nn. 32–36.

5. Below n. 7.

6. Cf. Baldwin 1970, I, 283.

7. Baldwin 1986, 231–32, has provided good, fresh data, but he has not fully liberated himself from Chazan 1973b, 85, whose discussion of these matters is not entirely coherent.

8. Baldwin 1970, I, 212, 273.

9. Cf. on the normal procedures of financial administration, Baldwin 1986, 144–52.

10. Baldwin 1986, 405–07.

11. There were several thousand Jews in the old royal domain by 1210 and four thousand or so in the newer lands of Capetian domination. Total population

was likely three million: more than one million for the Ile de France; more than one million for Normandy; and the population of the other western fiefs—Anjou, Maine, Touraine, northern Poitou—even with their vast empty spaces (northern Anjou, most of Maine) must have added significantly, many hundreds of thousands, to the total population as well.

12. *Layettes*, I, no. 977; *Recueil des actes de Philippe Auguste*, III, no. 1200.
13. On Norman custom, cf. Tardif 1881–1903, I, 40.
14. Above Chapter 4, n. 71.
15. Cf. Quantin 1873, no. 254, for a somewhat more explicit Jewish case. Also Jordan 1986b, 23, on customs about serfs.
16. *HF*, XXIV, 278*–79*, no. 33. On Barthélemy, see the index entries in Baldwin 1986, but especially pp. 109–11. On his *manerium* at Gonesse, cf. *Recueil des actes de Philippe Auguste*, IV, no. 1787.
17. I have put the names into French; so, for Dieudonné the original has Deodatus (it is, of course, the Hebrew Mattathias).
18. I have also rendered these in French. Gautier de Nemours (*Nemosis*), who served briefly as marshal, is also on the list.
19. Grayzel 1933, 306–07 no. IX.
20. Cf. Stow 1981, 162–67, for various suggestions.
21. Grayzel 1933, 306–07 no. IX: "[principes . . .] non sint Christianis infesti." The *Christiani* here must be *clerici* even though this is not specified, or else the decree would lack sense.
22. Grayzel 1933, 308–11.
23. See especially Grayzel 1933, 312–13 no. XIII.
24. For these directives, see Grayzel 1933, 140–43 nos. 31, 32; 144–45 no. 35.
25. Baldwin 1986, 207–12.
26. For the estimate I am extrapolating from Baldwin 1986, 239–48.
27. Baldwin 1986, 213–19.
28. Powicke 1953, 8–15.
29. Cheney 1976, 326–400.
30. Baldwin 1970, I, 19–23.
31. Delaborde 1882, 303–04.
32. Baldwin 1970, I, 23.
33. For the decree, Grayzel 1933, 313 no. XIV; on Philip's "congenial" relations with Pierre, see Baldwin 1986, 181–82.
34. Above Chapter 4, text to nn. 53–60.
35. *Layettes*, I, no. 1159; *Recueil des actes de Philippe Auguste*, IV, no. 1415.
36. *Recueil des actes de Philippe Auguste*, III, no. 1293, dated, late 1213.
37. Cf. Baldwin 1986, 104–05.
38. *nullus judeus poterit manere in terra Ligoliensi*. I do not know why, in opposition to the editors of the *Layettes* and the *Recueil des actes de Philippe Auguste*, Blumenkranz makes Ligueil into Longueil (*Encyclopaedia judaica*, XV, 1287–88) and Chazan makes it Liquiel (Chazan 1973b, 86).
39. Below nn. 41–42.
40. Grayzel 1933, 352–53 nos. V, VII (cf. also VIII). These lords were men set up by Philip Augustus as a result of the annexation of Auvergne by the crown

(Baldwin 1986, 200). Auvergne did have a few Jewish inhabitants to welcome immigrants, but not much is known about them before the middle of the thirteenth century; Blumenkranz in *Encyclopaedia judaica*, III, 934, and Jordan 1978, 49–50.

41. Since she co-sponsored the ordinance of 1206 (above Chapter 4, n. 33), she was permitting two pennies per pound per week plus interest penalties.

42. Grayzel 1933, 150–53, no. 39.

43. Cf. Baldwin 1986, 319, and below.

44. *Recueil des actes de Philippe Auguste*, IV, no. 1510.

45. *Layettes*, I, no. 1282.

46. Cf. Baldwin 1986, 386.

47. *Recueil des actes de Philippe Auguste*, IV, no. 1538.

48. The ordinance is published in *Recueil des actes de Philippe Auguste*, IV, no. 1554. The chronicler Robert of Auxerre quotes some of it; *HF*, XVIII, 286. It is discussed intelligently in Caro 1920–1924, I, 367–68.

49. So in the *Recueil*. Chazan breaks it down differently in his translation; Chazan 1980, 209–10.

50. Above text to n. 4.

51. *Agricola* could preserve its classical meaning "farmer" and *carpentarius* might mean "carriage maker" (Chazan's translations), but farmers and carriage makers tend to have a lot of property. Hence, my rendering. Even "carpenter" might be too elevated; cf. Delisle 1882, no. 200.The chronicler Robert of Auxerre adds to the list of exemplary occupations that of *pelliparius*, "skinner"; *HF*, XVIII, 286. Caro 1920–1924, I, 367, has a translation similar to mine: "Ackerbauer, Schuster, Zimmerleute."

52. Above text following n. 8.

53. Jordan, "Women and Credit," n. 9.

54. Chazan translates *ferrum carruce, aut animalia carruce* as "implement of a coach or the beasts of a coach" instead of "plowshare and plow team."

55. Above Chapter 4, text following n. 36.

56. Orr 1915, 40.

57. There is no doubt about the reading; the contemporary chronicler, Robert of Auxerre, who summarized part of the ordinance, used the same phrase (*HF*, XVIII, 286; on the date of Robert's work, see Baldwin 1986, 399).

58. Blum 1978, 80.

59. Chazan 1973b, 85.

60. For the Norman section, cf. Golb 1985, 293 (NB: the old style dating there).

61. "Draft animals" in preference to Chazan's "coach animals" (the Latin, *animalia carruce*).

62. Cf. Chazan 1973b, 85 n. 85.

63. Jordan, "Women and Credit," nn. 31–32. But even with the survival of information from criminal investigations, data on pawnbroking is quite limited.

64. Above Chapter 4, text following n. 46, and this chapter, text to nn. 9–10.

65. Below Chapter 6.

66. *Recueil des actes de Philippe Auguste*, IV, no. 1586.

67. *Recueil des actes de Philippe Auguste*, II, no. 610; IV, p. 230 n. 1.

68. *Recueil des actes de Philippe Auguste*, IV, no. 1710; and see also above, text to n. 62.

69. In general, cf. Chazan 1973b, 94–95. For relevant texts, Lalore 1875, I, 250–52, 255, 266–67, 271–72, 304.

70. Above Chapter 4, n. 34, on the original subscription. A case might be made from scanty available materials that the Champenois put pressure on the Jews in 1210 as Philip and John of England did; cf. Grayzel 1933, 351–52 nos. III, IV. The pressure, if genuine, would explain an agreement that the Champenois made with the Burgundians not to retain the others' Jews in October 1210 (no. IV), since such agreements usually indicate that Jews were fleeing one lordship for another they deemed more hospitable. A good, serious and comprehensive study of Champenois Jewry is much desired. Gerson 1899, 173–261, is outdated.

71. Cf. Chazan 1973b, 94–95. For relevant texts, Grayzel 1933, 353–54 no. IX (cf. also no. X).

72. *Recueil des actes de Philippe Auguste*, IV, no. 1791. For Pope Innocent III's use of the phrase, "usury upon usury" (*usuras usurarum*) in 1205, see Grayzel 1933, 106–07. The "ordinance" of 1222 in the French "copy" of the sixteenth century has *"ussures sur usures."*

73. This so-called ordinance is troubling in other ways. It asserts, in concert with many modern authorities, that from (in this case) 1222 distraint was forbidden for the collection of bad debts owed to Jews. If the editors of the *Recueil* are correct and the sixteenth-century copyist has merely given us in general a bad and misdated copy of the constitution of 1219, then he misread the temporary clemency clause on recent bad debts in the same way as some modern scholars have.

74. Lazard 1887, 234–35; Langmuir 1960, 214, 222; Chazan 1973b, 105–06.

75. See especially Chapter 9.

76. Berger 1986, 579–82, 585.

77. Jordan 1979b, 85 n. 138.

78. Cf. Bautier 1980a, 52–54, on the difficulty of trying to get into the head of this king; and see, too, Baldwin 1988, 195–207, for his interesting speculations.

79. The names were not chosen at random. These are Jews who enjoyed successful businesses before 1210, yet were arrested and despoiled in 1210, then allowed to reestablish themselves, only to find their livelihood seriously curtailed by the later ordinances.

Chapter 6

1. Petit-Dutaillis 1894, 222.

2. Confirmations of offices: Petit-Dutaillis 1894, 449–50 nos. 5, 6. Extensions of truces: Petit-Dutaillis 1894, 451–52 nos. 20, 21 (cf. nos. 22, 23). Much other predictable routine business is recorded in the first fifty or so of Louis's *acta* (that is, those of July through December 1223).

3. Petit-Dutaillis 1894, 438 (the itinerary of the king).

4. Petit-Dutaillis 1894, 222–23.
5. All references to the subscription version of the *stabilimentum* (8 November 1223) are to the edition in *Layettes*, II, no. 1610. The sequence of events given in this paragraph is my reconstruction based on the record itself and on data that will be furnished presently. It differs fundamentally from the reconstruction in Chazan 1973b, 104–06; and, to a lesser extent, in Petit-Dutaillis 1894, 414–17. There is a translation in Chazan 1980, 211–12; the head notes there repeat some of his earlier conclusions.
6. The earlier version is in Martène and Durand 1724–1733, I, 1182–83. It is not simply a "more complete" version as Petit-Dutaillis says; cf. Petit-Dutaillis 1894, 415 n.2. It is the *royal* ordinance. The version of 8 November is, if you will, the "treaty" with the barons, that is, that part of the original *stabilimentum* to which they would agree. For the distinction of tenses: the version of 1 November refers to those who *juraverint*; that of 8 November to those who *juraverunt*.
7. On the presence of the archbishop in Paris, see again, the catalog of Louis VIII's acts published as Appendix VI to Petit-Dutaillis 1894, no. 37. It is possible that one or more of the bishops of Angers, Le Mans, and Poitiers were also present; cf. nos. 32–36.
8. The preamble of the version of 8 November refers to the *stabilimentum* (of 1 November) having the original assent *archiepiscoporum, episcoporum, comitum, baronum et militum regni Francie. Comites, barones et alii prenominati* affixed their seals on the eighth. The order of names (and seals) is hierarchical and follows the order on numerous other formal documents, facts that merely indicate that a number of the close familiars of the king were induced to subscribe.
9. " . . . qui Judeos habent et qui Judeos non habent."
10. The references I will be giving do not always show that Jews were living in the domains of the subscribing lords precisely in 1223, but the references are typically to the thirteenth century or, rather, before 1306. In many cases I have already provided the citations in earlier discussions; and in these instances I have directed the reader to those remarks. In one or two cases I have not been able to establish with absolute certainty that Jews lived in the domains of the subscribing lord. Clearly, however, given the weight of the other evidence, the presumption must be that the surviving records are uneven; and the general argument should cause us to look more closely at the existing manuscript evidence for their domains for possible confirmation. Other (non-subscribing) lords regarded this list as a list of barons who had *dominium* over Jews; *Layettes*, II, no. 1620.

The bishop of Chalons as Count of Perche: Jews lived in Illiers and Dangeau in the region of Perche; Chazan 1973b, 214, 218. Cf. also Gross 1897/1969, 439.

The count of Boulougne was Louis VIII's brother Philippe Hurepel; he was also count of Clermont-sur-Oise; Petit-Dutaillis 1894, 334. There is evidence of Jewish residence at Clermont; Chazan 1973b, 218.

The duchess of Burgundy possessed large numbers of Jews; Marilier

1954–1958, 171, and above, chapter 4, no. 82.

The countess of Nevers: see Lespinasse 1909–1914, II, 31–32, 44, 99, 116–17; and above chapter 4, text to n. 85, on Jews in the county of Nevers.

The count of Blois: despite the massacre of Blois in 1171, Jews continued to reside in the county; cf. Chazan 1968, 13–31.

The count of Chartres;: for the Jews of the county of Chartres, see above chapter 2, n. 63.

Robert of Dreux was count of Brie. There were Jews at Dreux; Chazan 1973b, 214. There were Jews at Brie: for the massacre of the Jews of Brie, see above chapter 2, text to nn. 77–85; children were not killed.

The count of Brittany: above chapter 4, text to n. 92.

The count of Saint-Pol had Jewish communities scattered about his lands; above chapter 4, text to n. 81; also, possibly, Gross 1897/1969, 642.

The brother of the count of Saint-Pol, Hugues de Châtillon, subscribed; his lands, as seigneur of Châtillon, included Crécy-en-Brie and Pierrefonds with Jewish settlements; Rémy 1881, 77–81; Chazan 1973b, 218–19.

The count of Namur: Namur was an Imperial fief, but the count or marquis was a member of the Courtenay-Nevers family. I do not know what land he held in this line; cf. Anselme 1674a, 414.

The count of Grandpré had *dominium* over Jews at Sainte-Menehould and Saint-Jean-sur-Tourbe; *Layettes*, II, no. 2752; Longnon 1877, 304 no. 1333; Chazan 1973b, 216–17.

The count of Vendôme, Jean de Montoire: ?.

Robert de Courtenay, butler: Robert possessed, among other properties, Nonancourt which had a Jewish settlement; Baldwin 1986, 254; Chazan 1973b, 216.

Mathieu, the lord of Montmorency, the constable: the fief of Montmorency had a Jewish settlement; Chazan 1973b, 219.

Archembaud of Bourbon: on the Jews in his *dominium*, cf. Grayzel 1933, 352–53 nos. V, VII.

Guillaume de Dampierre: there is a great deal of evidence; see, e.g., *Layettes*, II, no. 1619; and, more especially below text to nn. 32–41.

Enguerran, lord of Coucy: on Jews in the town of Coucy, see Chazan 1973b, 214.

The hereditary *sénéchal* of Anjou held dispersed lands in Anjou, among which, for example, was Baugé, which had a Jewish settlement; Baldwin 1986, 236, and above chapter 4, n. 18.

Dreu de Mello, the lord of Loches: for Jews at Loches, see Chazan 1973b, 215, and further, above chapter 5, text to nn. 35–38.

Raoul, viscount of Beaumont and Sainte-Suzanne: Raoul would eventually succeed to Perche, but he already had Jews at Beaumont near Sainte-Suzanne; *HF*, XXIV, 114 no. 171; *Layettes*, II, no. 2131.

Henri de Sully: Despite Gross 1897/1969, 434, Graetz was probably right to read Sully in the Martyrology of Ephraim of Bonn. Through his wife, Henri had claims in the county of Dreux. Presumably part of her dowry included lands with Jews, since she was the daughter of Gui de Dampierre(Anselme

1674b, 486) who had *dominium* over many Jews. Cf., on later claims, *Layettes*, II, nos. 2761, 2870, 2871.

Guillaume de Chauvigny was lord of Châteauroux; *Layettes*, II, n. 2004. On the Jews of Châteauroux, see the data adduced above chapter 1, n. 10.

Gaucher de Joigny was enfeoffed in the county of Nevers where there were several Jewish settlements and indeed had significant holdings (evidently dependents and rights) in the city, which also had a Jewish population until 1231; see *Layettes*, II, nos. 1592, 2133, and the references collected in this note under the countess of Nevers (above).

Jean (lord) of Viévy: there was a Jewish settlement at Viévy-le-Rayé, the capital messuage of the fief; Chazan 1973b, 217.

Guillaume de Sillé was lord of the Loire Valley fief of Sillé. He played a role in the pacification of this region and was summoned to the coronation of Louis IX in 1226. I can only presume that he possessed high justice and *dominium* over Jews. He must be sought out in the records indifferently as *Guillelmus* or *Willelmus de S(a)iliaco*. See Baldwin 1986, 535 n. 39; *Layettes*, II, no. 1826.

11. *Contra* Chazan 1973b, 105.

12. Petit-Dutaillis 1894, 415 (but the explanations summarized and suggested by Petit-Dutaillis for this must be treated with caution).

13. " . . . et hoc intelligendum est tam de hiis qui stabilimentum juraverunt quam de illis qui non juraverunt." (I quote the version of 8 November with the perfect tense.)

14. Above on the early introduction of sealing, chapter 3, text to n. 17.

15. "Judei de cetero sigilla non habebunt ad sigillandum debita sua." Rabinowitz 1938, 49, seems to have misunderstood the implications of this text.

16. " . . . si quas [litteras] per quinque annos celaverunt Judaei in fraudem, nec ullam de eis mentionem fecerunt infra quinque annos proximo & ultimo praeteritos, eas dicimus non valere, & debita in illis contenta reddi non debere." This clause makes it seem as though some debts would be repaid to Jews not lords, a fair impression explained below n. 22.

17. Above chapter 4, text to n. 33.

18. Grayzel 1933, 353–54 no. IX (dated June 1222).

19. "Debent etiam Judei facere inrotulari, auctoritate dominorum quibus subsunt, universa debita . . . " These *debita* are later referred to as being recorded in *littere* or (below nn. 20, 23) in *carte*.

20. "litteras . . . de debitis suis continentes longius et remotius sue confectionis tempus quam a quinque annis proximo et ultimo preteritis, statuimus eas non valere."

21. On which, above chapter 5, n. 48.

22. "Si infra quinque annos de litteris illis mentionem fecerint Judaei, & debita illa quae in illis litteris continentur petierint interim, sicut debuerunt, & ubi litteras illas non dicimus non valere: immo debita in illis contenta praecipimus & volumus eis reddi."

23. Cf. Delisle 1864, no. 368 and n. 2. The bonds enforced are called *carte*.

24. *Layettes*, II, no. 1612.

25. *Layettes*, II, no. 1620.
26. *Layettes*, II, no. 1615.
27. Chazan 1973b, 106.
28. *Layettes*, II, no. 1615: " . . . et super hoc litteras [the letters imposing the *stabilimentum*] nostras patentes per clericum vestrum vobis transmittimus."
29. Petit-Dutaillis 1894, 394.
30. On her role as tutrix, Petit-Dutaillis 1894, 394. No distinct record of her confirmation, however, has come to light.
31. On the position of the Jews in Brittany, above chapter 4, text to n. 93.
32. The lord of Dampierre had wanted to marry Alice of Cyprus who had claims to the whole county of Champagne. On the dispute and its resolution there are a few useful pages in Arbois de Jubainville 1865, IV, pt. 1, 223–25.
33. For the earlier agreements, Grayzel 1933, 352–53 nos. V, VII.
34. Inferred from *Layettes*, II, no. 1619.
35. *Layettes*, II, no. 1619.
36. "Notandum etiam quod ego Judeas uxores videlicet et familias Judeorum, qui de terra mea venerant in terram comitis, recredidi domino comiti, ita quod per xv. dies ante terminum positum in septembri proximo, ad requestam meam vel meorum ex parte mea, eas mihi reddet; ita quod per recredenciam istam quam ei facio, nullum sit prejudicium nec ipsi comiti quin per omnia mihi salvum sit jus meum, et ipsi domino comiti, quod habebamus vel habere debebamus, alter contra alterum, tempore facte recredencie.—Ipse vero dedit mihi respectum de debitis, que a me vel militibus meis de terra mea, burgensibus vel hominibus meis de corpore, ratione predictorum Judeorum petebat, usque ad sepedictum terminum in septembri . . . "
37. Petit-Dutaillis 1894, 459 no. 79, has the reference. Grayzel 1933, 354 no. X, gives the transcription in full but unfortunately under the wrong date.
38. Inferred from *Layettes*, II, no. 1648.
39. On Cochin, cf. Grayzel 1933, 351–52 no. III.
40. "Duos filios Cochini judei de Sancto Desiderio, et uxores et familias eorum quos teneo, reddam comiti Campanie.—Comes Campanie Th. creantavit mihi, tanquam dominus meus ligius, quod redimet bona fide, sine auferre membrum et sine occidere, Cochinum et duos filios ejus supradictos et etiam Judeos quorum uxores recredidi eidem comiti; et de redemptione dictorum Judeorum habebit dictus comes medietatem, et ego aliam medietatem habebo.—Si comes Campanie debet aliquid alicui Judeorum sepe dictorum, inde penitus erit quitus. Et si ego debeo aliquid alicui Judeorum jam dictorum, vel si pater meus debuit aliquid alicui eorumdem, inde similiter penitus ero quitus.—Omnis etiam hereditas eorumdem Judeorum que est in terra mea, et omnes gagerie quas ipsi habent in feodo meo, quod tenetur de me in capite vel in domanio meo, remanent mihi sine parte comitis sepe dicti. Omnes supradicti Judei et uxores et familie eorum post redemptionem istam remanent comiti toti quiti sine parte mei."
41. "Si habeo aliquos plegios de Jacob de Dampetra et de Salemino de Dampetra judeis super aliquo debito de fine facto, et propter hoc voluero gagiare plegios

meos, si plegii vel ipsi Judei conquerantur inde comiti Campanie, ego inde stabo juri coram ipso comite."

42. Petit-Dutaillis 1894, 456 no. 55, 459 no. 73; *Layettes*, II, no. 1630; and above n. 37.

43. Petit-Dutaillis 1894, 486 no. 273, 521–22.

44. Petit-Dutaillis 1894, 524. For some reason the account in which this figure is found is variously dated. I follow Fawtier 1930, xlv, who depended on Borrelli de Serres 1895–1901, I, 58–73 (Borrelli confused the issue by dating the document Candlemas 1226 and yet seeing a reference to "the queen" in it as an allusion to Blanche's regency in 1227). Nortier (Nortier and Baldwin 1980, 7) gives 1227; and Baldwin 1986, 352–54 and elsewhere, follows Nortier.

45. This conclusion is again based on a number of extrapolations and is merely intended to show that a substantial proportion of royal income came from Jewish debts. See the comprehensive discussions of income in the early 1220s in Petit-Dutaillis 1894, 374–89; and also Baldwin 1986, 352–53.

46. Below chapter 8, text to nn. 5–9.

Chapter 7

1. The discussion in the next several paragraphs is drawn from Petit-Dutaillis 1894, 224–56.

2. Besides the discussion in Petit-Dutaillis 1894, see also Strayer 1971a, 123–28, but the discussion there as in most treatments offers us no certainty about why Louis broke off the southwestern war.

3. In addition, once again, to the discussion in Petit-Dutaillis 1894, see Powicke 1953, 24–27, 87–92.

4. Gross 1897/1969, 312, 462, 26* (the last reference is to additional material on La Rochelle and new material on La Réole). See especially Vincent 1930, 269–70, 277, 292–96, for the toponymic evidence. Also, *Bulletin de la Société des Archives de la Saintonge et de l'Aunis* 1897, 456–57.

5. Sometimes even the apparent exceptions dissolve. Early evidence for substantial Jewish settlement in Limoges, asserted by Gross 1897/1969, 308, is challenged in Chazan 1970, 217–21. For slightly further south, Rodez, the evidence of a large Jewish presence is exploded in Golb 1979a, 24–31.

6. Gross 1897/1969, 312; Musset 1902, 149.

7. Cf. Petit-Dutaillis 1894, 232, on this claim.

8. Cf. Petit-Dutaillis 1894, 255 (on Savari de Mauléon in Poitou, earlier an official of the Plantagenets); *HF*, XXIV, 188* and 198* (on Thibaud de Blaizon, a native appointment in Poitou and the Limousin) and 210* (on the Lusignan count of La Marche's appointment in Périgord and Quercy; this appointment was, of course, a political sop to the Lusignans rather than an expression of sympathy with the desires of the local population for the appointment of a native).

9. Petit-Dutaillis 1894, 468–71 nos. 138–46, 157, 160 (see also 162); cf. nos. 147–56, 158–59, 161.

10. Strayer 1971a, 11–14.

11. Le Roy Ladurie 1962, 30–34; Wolff 1967, 183–88; Strayer 1971a, 8–9; Cholvy 1982, 152–54.

12. See the summary in Lafont 1974, 38–40.

13. Cf. Baldwin 1986, 380–89.

14. Fawtier 1960, 118, 158.

15. Assis 1983, 286; Septimus 1979, 198–202; and most comprehensively Kriegel 1979.

16. Lewis 1976, 151–52; Le Roy Ladurie 1962, 27–29.

17. There is much useful material scattered about in Lejeune 1979. See also Le Roy Ladurie 1962, 30–34.

18. Cf. Le Roy Ladurie 1979, 69–135, though this section deals with the shepherds around 1300. I am not arguing that the population in general moved about freely (cf. Cholvy 1982, 162) merely that it is proper to think of both sides of the Pyrenees as parts of the same region.

19. Strayer 1971a, 4.

20. Gouron 1984, essay XX.

21. On language, see Lafont 1974, 17–20; Wolff 1967, 143–44; and Strayer 1971a, 3, 12–13, and more especially pp. 9–10: "The northerners thought that the southerners were undisciplined, spoiled by luxury, a little soft, too much interested in social graces, too much influenced by contemptible people such as businessmen, lawyers, and Jews. The southerners thought the northerners were crude, arrogant, discourteous, uncultured, and aggressive." A northerner would not even have found the aristocratic pastime par excellence in the south, the good old head-cracking tournament, which would have confirmed his prejudiced view of the southerners as soft; cf. Paterson 1986, 72–79.

22. Coulet 1985b, 371 (with references).

23. Weiss 1888/1889, 289–313. Weiss ties the tension closely to the various phases of the Maimonidean controversy.

24. Cf. Saige 1881, 51–58, 61–62.

25. Saige 1881, 7–8; Bachrach 1980, 11–19.

26. On the distinctiveness of the urban culture of the maritime cities, see Wolff 1967, 158–60.

27. Strayer 1971a, 14; Lewis 1974, 504–16.

28. Cholvy 1982, 155–56; Strayer 1971a, 5–6.

29. Baldwin 1986, 68, 305; Fawtier 1960, 71.

30. Below to n. 56.

31. On the political integration, below chapter 10, text to n. 79. The demographic discussion, in concentrating on "royal" lands, leaves aside Gascony and Provence for the time being except for comparative purposes. Within what would seem to be the natural geographical extent of the *sénéchaussées* discussed here, one territorially small but important area did not wholly and permanently come under Capetian rule until long after the original conquest of the south. This was Montpellier, on which see below chapter 11, text to nn. 131–51.

32. Le Roy Ladurie 1962, 50; Wolff 1967, 217.

33. Cholvy 1982, 137.

34. Le Roy Ladurie 1962, 44; Cholvy 1982, 176–77.

35. Cf. above chapter 1, text to nn. 2–3.

36. Kriegel 1979, 72.

37. Kriegel 1979, 72–73.

38. Drouard 1973–1974, 54, 56–59; Kriegel 1979, 73–74.

39. Cf. Kriegel 1979, 72.

40. Cf. Szapiro 1966, 395–97; and below chapter 10, text to nn. 66–67.

41. Blumenkranz 1962, 18; Nahon 1962, 68–73. These are estimates of royal Jews, and of course they include for the period around 1300 Champenois Jews, since Champagne had entered the royal domain by then (below chapter 11, n. 67). One would also have to add perhaps as many as 30,000 baronial Jews to the number of royal Jews in order to obtain the total number of Jews in 1300 in the geographical area that looks roughly like the map of modern France.

42. Cf. the case of Béziers, for example; Le Roy Ladurie 1962, 44, and below nn. 71, 95–101.

43. On allodial or fully owned holdings, Saige 1881, 9, 60–64, 78–86; on occupations, below nn. 46–50.

44. See especially the ecclesiastical denunciations directly addressed to the Midi printed in Grayzel 1933, 124–25, 296–99, 302–05, 310–11.

45. Cf. Saige 1881, 13–18.

46. Kriegel 1979, 88–93, summarizes the research, but the attentive reader will recognize that much of the data assembled there is late and already reflects an extraordinarily well-advanced constriction of the Jewish occupational profile.

47. Saige 1881, 65–66.

48. Cf. Kriegel 1979, 96.

49. I am extrapolating from the ordinances against such vending; cf. Jordan 1976, 32–33, 42; Kriegel 1979, 96; Coulet 1978b, 209–21.

50. Cf. the data assembled in Coulet 1978a, 80–84, and Kriegel 1979, 95.

51. On northern matters, above chapter 1, text to nn. 30–45.

52. Cf., for example, Himmelfarb 1984, 73–78.

53. On the political situation of Montpellier, Jordan 1979b, 71–74, 137–39, 200–02. On the role of Montpellier in these scholarly contacts, see Shatzmiller 1977a. Cf. also Romano 1977, 366–77.

54. Cf. Dossat 1972.

55. Cf. Jordan 1977, 213–19.

56. For background, see *Cathares en Occitanie*, 15–197; Borst 1984, 81–84; and *Cahiers de Fanjeaux* III (although some of the essays in this collection which appeared in 1968 have been superseded by the later research of the same authors). On Bernard, see Roquebert 1970, 58–61. On the mission of Dominic and of the later Dominicans, see in general *Cahiers de Fanjeaux* I. It is not at all certain that Dominic was dealing with the same kinds of heretics as Bernard; Moore 1974, 1–10. For comprehensive treatments of medieval heresy, see Moore 1985 and Lambert 1976.

57. There was one other group that was frequently singled out, namely the Wal-

densians or Vaudois. For a variety of discussions of their role in the events being narrated here, see the collection of essays in *Cahiers de Fanjeaux* II.

58. *Cathares en Occitanie*, 202–53; Borst 1984, 124–81. For available texts and criticisms of texts, see, among many others, Thouzellier 1973; Thouzellier 1977; Dröes 1982; Borst 1984, 214–32.

59. Borst 1984, 181–88.

60. The classic, Schmidt 1983 (originally published 1848–1849), 195–98, may exaggerate the political support for the Cathars, but it was substantial; cf. Strayer 1971a, 47–48.

61. O'Brien 1968, 215–20; Yerushalmi 1970, 342–44; Wakefield 1974, 61; Berger 1975, 287–303; Lasker 1977, 164; Shahar 1977, 344–62.

62. *HGL*, VI, 172; Madaule 1967, 60; Sumption 1978, 84; and cf. Manselli 1977, 251–66.

63. Sumption 1978, 68.

64. Roquebert 1970, 137–39; Strayer 1971a, 47–48, 50.

65. Roquebert 1970, 201–02.

66. Discussed in context, above chapter 5, text to n. 29.

67. Roquebert 1970, 211–19; Strayer 1971a, 51–52.

68. On the late emergence of Simon, Roquebert 1970, 279–85; on Simon as a personality, Dossat 1969, 281–88.

69. Strayer 1971a, 51.

70. On the evident confusion surrounding Raymond's behavior, cf. Roquebert 1970, 227–28, 235–43.

71. Roquebert 1970, 245–61; Sumption 1978, 92–93; and more generally, Belperron 1967, 183–210.

72. Roquebert 1970, 262–75.

73. On the role of Capetian vassals, see Roquebert 1970, 288–89; Strayer 1971a, 52.

74. On the campaigns of 1209, Roquebert 1970, 291–320, and more especially on the reversals of 1210, pp. 321–33.

75. Belperron 1967, 245–74; Roquebert 1970, 335–44, 367–82; Sumption 1978, 104–55.

76. Madaule 1967, 72–74; Griffe 1973, 74–101; Sumption 1978, 156–70. Also, Belperron 1967, 275–304.

77. Madaule 1967, 74–78; Belperron 1967, 305–36.

78. Cf. Strayer 1971a, 94–95.

79. Griffe 1973, 103–04.

80. Griffe 1973, 105–14.

81. Strayer 1971a, 106.

82. Cf. the nuanced (especially with regard to Narbonne), but generally unfavorable picture in Dossat 1969, 288–96. Also, Strayer 1971a, 106.

83. Cf. Timbal 1950, 24–25.

84. Cf. above chapter 4, text to n. 2.

85. Belperron 1967, 338–42; Strayer 1971a, 108.

86. Madaule 1967, 78–82; Griffe 1973, 115–18. Also, Belperron 1967, 337–51.

87. Madaule 1967, 82–84; Belperron 1967, 351–61; Dossat 1969, 298–300.

88. Belperron 1967, 366–68.

89. Madaule 1967, 86; Griffe 1973, 123–29; and most comprehensively, Belperron 1967, 363–78.
90. On the overtures of Raymond VII to the pope, cf. Sumption 1978, 208–09.
91. Belperron 1967, 372–74.
92. Strayer 1971a, 121–22.
93. Cf. Saige 1881, 4, 78–79. The ecclesiastical councils that expressed the northerners' normative view of what a transformed southern society in regard to the Jews should look like stressed the ideal of segregation and subordination (canons of the councils of Saint-Gilles and Avignon, 1209; discussed in *HGL*, VI, 278, 304).
94. Gross 1897/1969, 57.
95. On the *ribaldi*: Guébin and Lyon 1926–1930, I, 91–92.
96. On the Jews who left Béziers, Meyer 1875–1879, I, 18; II, 22; on the Cathars, Guébin and Lyon 1926–1930, I, 90.Also Belperron 1967, 187; Sumption 1978, 89–90. With regard to the possibililty of Jewish deaths at Béziers, cf. Gross 1897/1969, 98. For the migration: Assis 1983, 287.
97. Sumption 1978, 89.
98. They had some Jewish (and Christian) reeves at Carcassone and at least one at Béziers; *HGL*, VI, 208.
99. Cf. Sumption 1978, 93.
100. The quoted phrase is Strayer's; Strayer 1971a, 64.
101. *HGL*, VI, 39. Gross 1897/1969, 98. The incidents occurred in the late 1160s. Cf. the similar behavior of the Jews of Beaucaire vis-à-vis their lord in 1195; Gross 1897/1969, 120.
102. Moore 1987, 152–53, on the "formation of a persecuting society." On the legate, see Strayer 1971a, 62–64, 71.
103. The narrative provided from this point to the end of the chapter is based largely on Petit-Dutaillis 1894, 297–316; Belperron 1967, 381–417; Strayer 1971a, 123–38; and Sumption 1978, 212–25. The authors differ among themselves in emphasis, but there seems to be overall agreement.
104. The body of Raymond VI remained unburied until the sixteenth century, by which time there was almost nothing left to be buried; Sumption 1978, 208.
105. For these and similar quotations see Sumption 1978, 217, 220; Petit-Dutaillis 1894, 298. Cf. Madaule 1967, 88. "History abounds in seemingly inexplicable phenomena such as this, where the explanation can be found only in vast, irresistible, underlying forces," in this case, the prestige of monarchy. But more work needs to be done.

Chapter 8

1. For a masterful short introduction to the question of medieval state formation, see Strayer 1970.
2. Strayer 1971b, 44–59.
3. Sumption 1978, 230–35; Strayer 1971a, 143–58. The precise date of the formation

of the Inquisition has always been in dispute. One theory holds that it was instituted in 1230 (cf. Jordan 1979b, 157 n. 130); but even if this date is not accepted, it is certain that it was operating during the mid-1230s.

4. Below chapter 9, text following n. 10.

5. The evident failure in the early years of the reign of Louis IX to apply the strict Jewish policies of the north to the south has always been regarded as a bit perplexing; cf. Nahon 1977, 74–75. For a general survey of Louis IX's legislation, cf. Golb 1985, 325–39.

6. Above chapter 6, text to nn. 14–15.

7. Above chapter 6, text to n. 12.

8. This text is available in Martène and Durand 1724–1733, I, cc. 122–23. Both Chazan 1973b, 108–09, and Langmuir 1960, 222, discuss it with an assurance that belies the difficulties. See also Caro 1920–1924, I, 507. I have consulted with other Latinists on the matter; and all agree that parts of the text are obscure. In any case, what is certain is that the directive incorporates references to the order of 1227, probably of Saint John's day, 24 June. An undated order of clarification (Martène and Durand 1724–1733, I, c. 1294) is attributed to the same period by Caro 1920–1924, I, 507. From its tenor, it probably was issued after the directive of Saint John's day, 24 June 1227, since it refers to an earlier directive, and before the directive of 31 May 1228, which treats the same matters more comprehensively.

9. The use of *catallum*, usually meaning chattel, in this context is not a happy one, nor is the syntax "quod sint catallum". From Martène and Durand in the eighteenth century to the present, however, *catallum* has been taken to be a peculiar usage for "capital" or "principal"; and a very few other examples of the usage are attested in contemporary Latin.

10. Paris, AN: J 943, nos. 17, 18.

11. *Layettes*, V, nos. 372–73.

12. I am assuming that where the word *nichil* or the phrase *isti non soluerunt* or *pagaverunt* does not appear the debt was collected (sometimes this is explicit: *isti soluerunt*). One large debt, that of the *domina Longueville* is printed in *Layettes*, V, no. 372, as 117 pounds (l.). If I read the manuscript rightly, it was actually 1,117 l. She was paying installments of 113 l. which means nine installments at that sum and one more at 100 l.

13. One list of debtors goes nearly to one hundred, but the debts are not owed to a single Jew, rather to "Avo . . . and others" (*Layettes*, V, no. 373). Of the approximately sixty creditors in the texts, almost half had fewer than five clients.

14. It is not the assertion here that these surnames are all accurate occupational epithets, but in the early thirteenth century they can be used to get a general sense of social status; cf. Jordan 1986b, 105 n. 18.

15. For the loans in kind, see, e.g., *Layettes*, V, no. 372: "Rodulfus (*sic* Radulfus) Cointe . . . iiii qu[arteria] avene." For the comparison with Philip Augustus's Jews, above chapter 4, text following n. 69.

16. Martène and Durand 1724–1733, I, c. 1223: "Debita autem post dictum festum S. Johannis contracta consimilia usque ad hanc primam diem Junii reddentur

Judaeis per conventiones habitas inter ipsos & Christianos sine usuris curren-
tibus. Nullum debitum Judaeorum curret ad usuram, nec faciemus reddi Judaeis usuras, quae currant ab hac prima die Junii inantea."

17. *Layettes*, II, no. 2083. The translation of this ordinance in Chazan 1980, 213–15,
is inaccurate, particularly the clause in section 2, "whatever the custom which
the Jew may enjoy under the rule of another or in another kingdom." The
Latin is: "quantumcunque moram fecerit Judeus sub alterius dominio vel in
alio regno." It should be rendered: "whatever length of time the Jew was
under another's lordship or in another kingdom." Cf. below, text to n. 30, on
the importance of this clause.

18. "Usuras autem intelligimus quicquid est ultra sortem." Cf. Graetz 1897–1911,
VII, 108: "Er [Louis] war in diesem Punkte buchstäblich noch päpstlicher als
der Papst" (figuratively, not literally).

19. Paris, AN: J 1028 no. 2.

20. *Layettes*, V, no. 371.

21. Occupations: *carpentarius, sutor, tisserant, le macon, mercator, presbyter, le vilain*.
The argument is the same as the one advanced above, n. 14.

22. NB: the references in the manuscript, "pro blado," and, more puzzling, "pro
blado judeo."

23. Of the twenty or so creditors mentioned, fifteen had fewer than five clients
each.

24. Cf. Langmuir 1960, 224–25.

25. Above chapter 6, text to n. 13.

26. Above chapter 7, text following n. 105.

27. Richard 1983, 36–47.

28. Richard 1983, 45–47.

29. Cf. above chapter 6, text to nn. 18, 24–25, on the count's actions in 1223.

30. Langmuir 1980, 24–54.

31. *Ordonnances*, I, 54–55.

32. Grayzel 1933, 232–35. On Louis's relations with the Latin Empire, see Richard
1983, 150–51.

33. The text is obscure here, for after the warning that *catalum suum amittent*, the
scribe added, "et per jus tamquam Christiani deducentur." This might mean
that the Jews (and perhaps the Christians) would undergo further unspecified
punishment as well. The eighteenth-century editor of *Ordonnances*, Laurière,
recognizing the difficulty of getting any fully satisfactory meaning out of this
passage, suggested this paraphrase: " . . . les gages seront ostez, ou imputez
aux Juifs comme à les Chrétiens, qui auroient presté sur gages."

34. *HF*, XXII, 577–78.

35. *QTur*, no. 1421. The court costs amounted to 4 l. 10 s.; yet, the widow
requested reimbursement for 8 l. 10 s. Hence, my estimate of the debt allegedly
owed the Jews is the difference between the two sums. It is possible, however,
that the 4 l. 10 s. constituted the debt and that the residual of 4 l. was the court
costs that she incurred for both the original litigation and her appeal of the
decision.

36. Delisle 1864, no. 581.

37. Strayer 1932, 50; Parkes 1938b, 217; Chazan 1973b, III; Jordan 1979a, 47.

38. Delisle, who edited the judgements, normally depends on a manuscript he denominated, "Compilation 1." There were four other compilations of lesser dependability. Compilation 3 he described as *très-imparfait*. In judgement no. 581, however, which is now under discussion, he substituted a reading from Compilation 3 for that of Compilation 1. For the reference to Jews "qui vivant propriis laboribus sive mercatura sine usura," he substituted a jussive clause, "quod vivant de propriis laboribus sive mercatura sine usura." So, what the best manuscript expresses as a pious wish was transformed into an order. To be sure, the jussive clause does appear in legislation from two decades later (below chapter 9, nn. 26–27), but this was issued under quite different circumstances. Unfortunately, Delisle used the later syntax as a justification to alter the earlier.

39. The clause forbidding the frequenting of taverns obviously aims to prevent routine fraternizing, but perhaps as well to prevent pawnbroking to men at risk by being drunk. The tavern as locus for pawnbroking was a traditional concern in medieval Europe; Jordan, "Women and Credit," nn. 31, 64–68.

40. Christians in good standing were not supposed to have any social or business relations with excommunicates. This was a form of pressure that, it was hoped, would bring them to make peace with the church. If Jews offered excommunicates jobs, then the financial pressure on some excommunicates might be relieved sufficiently so that they delayed seeking reconciliation with the church.

41. Alternatively, these clauses may represent an independent judgement conflated with the order about the Jews: " . . . de redditibus qui debentur a domino rege ecclesiis vel locis religiosis, ut perfecte solvantur; de bladis domini regi debitis, ut in terminis assignatis recipiantur." Cf. also Golb 1985, 329 n. 18.

42. In general, see Jordan 1979b, 51–63. For a full discussion of the material on the Jews and for references to the large body of recent scholarship, see below chapter 9.

43. On the problems of the administration of the Mâconnais, see Fournier 1959, 473–78.

44. "Annales Marbacenses," in *MGH, SS*, XVII, 178; Grayzel 1933, 274–75. Grayzel also critizes the view that there had been a rumor of ritual murder at La Rochelle in 1235 and suggests that the texts actually allude to Fulda; Grayzel 1933, 340.

45. Papal policy, in general, permitted the Talmud. Occasionally, as with Gregory IX, it was not tolerated. Papal policy did not, as it is sometimes said, encourage expurgated editions; rather, this was a device employed by other authorities, either Jewish or Christian; cf. Rembaum 1982, 203–21; Maccoby 1982. On the general context of the suppression of the Talmud, see Baron 1952–, IX, 64–71.

46. There are many editions/translations of the letter and associated texts: Maccoby 1982, 21–22; Grayzel 1933, 238–43; Chazan 1980, 222–24. In general, I will refer to the work of Maccoby 1982.

47. Cf. the summations of various opinions in Maccoby 1982, 23–24; Rembaum 1982, 214. Also Baron 1952–, IX, 79–83.

48. In general on this issue and specifically on the place of dialogs between Jews and Christians or Synagogue and Church, see *HL*, XXIII, 216–34; XXVII, 556–71; Pflaum 1930, 127–32; Pflaum 1934, 250, 263–307; Blumenkranz and Châtillon 1956, 40–60; Blumenkranz 1963; Lazar 1967, 132–33, 138, 140–42. Whether many of the encounters that these "literary" dialogs record actually took place or, if cast in allegorical form, represent real incidents is much in dispute. Cf. Rosenthal 1957, 134; Stein 1959, 57; Werblowsky 1960, 69–77; Blumenkranz 1964, 125–40; Blumenkranz 1977, no. XXII; Abulafia 1981, 153–74; Abulafia 1984, 55–74.

49. Below text following n. 51.

50. Nahon 1970, 22; Rembaum 1982, 214; Maccoby 1982, 20–24.

51. Maccoby 1982, 21, 23.

52. Maccoby 1982, 153.

53. Only two bishops Nicholas seem likely candidates, Nicholas de Roye, bishop of Noyon, 1228–1240, and Nicholas de Brie, bishop of Troyes, 1233–69. Since the Jewish text of the trial (Maccoby 1982, 156) speaks of Donin's apostasy in general terms as having occurred fifteen years before the trial of 1240, and if the conversion occurred soon after, Nicholas de Roye seems the better choice; but cf. Grayzel 1933, 340, on the possibility of a later date for the conversion.

54. Cf. Mann 1926, 375.

55. Maccoby 1982, 20; Rosenthal 1956/1957, 70; Baron 1952–, IX, 64; Graetz 1897–1911, VII, 94.

56. Cf. Saige 1881, 20–22.

57. Jordan 1987b, 531–43.

58. Grayzel 1933, 285 n. 1; Rabinowitz 1938, 103; Blumenkranz 1960, 151. In an interesting instance from eastern France, Lord Raymbaud d'Esparron of the Dauphiné sponsored a young woman convert (once probably known as Regina; Hebrew, Sarah). She adopted the Christian name Raymbauda. She spent two years in the household of Lord Raymbaud and his wife as their *filiola*, being taken to hear mass and to receive the eucharist, learning to fast at the appropriate seasons and to say formulaic prayers. All availed little: she maintained an illicit conjugal liaison with an unconverted Jew which produced six children and got her into trouble with the Court Christian; Shatzmiller 1973b, 56–57.

59. Guillaume de Bourges was sponsored by Archbishop Guillaume de Dongeon of Bourges around 1210 and published his book not later than the 1230s; see the edition and introduction of Dahan to the *Liber bellorum domini*, Guillaume de Bourges 1981.

60. Jordan 1987b, 537–38.

61. Shohet 1931, 22; Rabinowitz 1938, 124; Yerushalmi 1970, 357–59.

62. The full translations of these charges, as extracted from the Christian and Jewish reports of the trial, are available in Maccoby 1982.

63. Maccoby 1982, 156–58, in the Jewish account; 165–67, in the Christian account. Maccoby emends the Jewish account in one place, probably rightly, where there is a lapse and the Jews admit the identification of the Jesus in one passage of the Talmud with Jesus Christ.

64. Maccoby 1982, 153, 158, 160–61, 165.
65. Maccoby 1982, 158–62, 164–67.
66. Innocent IV who first vigorousl supported the suppression had, by 1247, modified his position; Grayzel 1933, 251–53, 275–81.
67. Rosenthal 1956/1957, 72; some sources say fourteen cartloads.
68. For later orders to seize or burn the Talmud, see Grayzel 1933, 336–37, 341–43. Baron in a somewhat perplexing passage suggests that all those who think that the multiple suppressions of the Talmud were the cause of the overwhelming loss of examples are just victims of a "lachrymose" conception of Jewish history; Baron 1952–, IX, 71. So be it.
69. Rembaum 1982, 204. For an evocation of the scene in Paris, see Temko 1954, 446–55.
70. Graboïs 1979, 67.
71. Marcus 1938, 145–46; Rembaud 1982, 203; cf. *HL*, XXXI, 659, 663.
72. This excerpt is taken from the translation in Chazan 1980, 229–31. See also *HL*, XXVII, 453.
73. Yerushalmi 1970, 363.
74. Lasker 1977, 8–10, 66, 86, 116.
75. Yerushalmi 1970, 354–57, 359–63.
76. Yerushalmi 1970, 363–74.
77. Above chapter 3, text to nn. 48–49.
78. Cf. Marcus 1982, 49.
79. Marcus 1938, 149–50.

Chapter 9

1. The discussion in the next several pages is drawn from Jordan 1979b, 42–43; Richard 1983, 36–49, 87–120; and Sivéry 1983a, 374–97.
2. Jordan 1979b, 15–16.
3. On the appanage system, see Wood 1966.
4. Stories, with a legendary component, were told about the victories; cf. Smyser 1937, 26 n. 1.
5. The level of destruction seems to have been low; and this may explain the relative leniency. There are only the slightest hints in the surviving sources of the impact of the rebellion on the Jews; cf. *QTur*, no. 1637.
6. Jordan 1979b, 3–104.
7. Grayzel 1933, 275–79; Marcus 1938, 146–48.
8. Grayzel 1933, 279; Marcus 1938, 148–49.
9. The canons are printed in Purcell 1975, 192; Matthew Paris 1872–1883, IV, 459. Berger 1893, 136, has a brief discussion. The assertion in Jordan 1979b, 85, that the canon authorized the seizure of usury is wrong. For the interplay of the themes of the policy of the church toward the crusades and the Jews, cf. Synan 1965, 107–19.
10. *HGL*, VI, 779; Jordan 1976, 32–33.

11. *HGL*, VIII, 1191–92. *HGL*, VI, 779, 783 n. 2.

12. Jordan 1979b, 51–63.

13. BN, fonds Dupuy, vol. 532, fol. 88 v., "a tredecim annis citra usque ad ultimam generalem captionem," 89 v., "de solutione usurarum licet de quantitate confuse deponant, et perplexe." I would date this record to 1247 or 1248.

14. The evidence is explored in Jordan 1978, 39–56; Jordan 1979a, 47–55; Jordan 1983, 141–52.

15. Note the phrase "ultimam generalem captionem", above n. 13. See also Delisle 1864, no. 735, for a similar reference to Jews "quando ultimo capti fuerunt." The first record is from 1247 or 1248; the second definitely from 1248. I would therefore date the *captio* to 1246 or early 1247.

16. The Norman material, for Christians and Jews, is published in Delisle 1864, nos. 735–36.

17. *Layettes*, V, no. 581, p. 197.

18. *Ordonnances*, I, 85: "non tamen animo retinendi."

19. *Layettes*, V, no. 581, p. 197: "De catallis Judeorum receptis per burgenses Falesie, XXXXIIII l. XVI s. I d. — De catallis eorumdem per burgenses Cadomenses, LX l. V. s. — De catallis eorumdem per burgensis castri Vire, XII l. X s."

20. To the discussion and references in Jordan 1979b, 236–46, add Bartlett 1981, 83–96, and Sivéry 1983b, 3–24. Sivéry 1983a and Sivéry 1984, two major studies of Louis's reign and the French economy, incorporate much material from these investigations.

21. Jordan 1979b, 57–63.

22. The depositions on this allegation are published in Molinier 1883, 128–33. The case has been discussed more recently and set in a broader context in Langmuir 1977, 235–47.

23. Cf. Alphonsus de Spina ca. 1471, cruelty 12.

24. To the discussion and references in Jordan 1979b, 113–16, add Barber 1984.

25. Matthew Paris 1872–1883, V, 441. According to Guillaume de Chartres Louis could not bear to look upon Jews, those who were abominable to God and *odibiles* to men; *HF*, XX, 34.

26. Matthew Paris 1872–1883, V, 361–62. Golb 1985, 336.

27. *Ordonnances*, I, 73–74.

28. *Ordonnances*, I, 85. The ordinance says that the king had the chattels in his hands before he set out for crusade—and afterwards (*postmodum*) he expelled the Jews. This must refer to the expulsion of 1253. But it has traditionally and erroneously been referred to an otherwise unknown (chimerical) expulsion of 1248 or 1249: Loeb 1887a, 39; Michel 1910, 319; Roth 1932, 657; Strayer 1932, 50; Parkes 1938b, 328, 361, 380; Jordan 1979b, 85 n. 145.

29. Jordan 1979b, 116–25.

30. *HGL*, VIII, 1358; *HF*, XXIV, 5–6. Nahon 1970, 19, 20, 22. See also Stow 1981, 176, 183.

31. Nahon 1970, 21; Jordan 1979b, 184.

32. Nahon 1970, 19–20; Chazan 1973b, 148–50; Jordan 1979b, 215.

33. Chazan 1980, 218–20. Nahon 1970, 19–24; Chazan 1973b, 123.

34. On the dominance of the conversionary impulse in Saint Louis, see Mousset 1950, 83–84; Chazan, *Daggers of Faith*, appeared too late to be used.
35. Chazan 1973a, 591; Chazan 1973b, 150.
36. Nahon 1962, 76–78; Nahon 1970, 23.
37. Nahon 1962, 76–78; Nahon 1970, 23; Jordan 1979b, 156–57; Baron 1952–, X, 60.
38. Jordan 1979b, 156–57.
39. Nahon 1962, 76 n. 2.
40. On the forced sermons, see the chronicle published in Delisle 1877, 189; and the various reports in Chazan 1980, 261–63. See also Golb 1985, 373–78.
41. Mignon 1899, no. 2113 (see also no. 1389); Saige 1881, 221–23 no. 9. Golb 1985, 378–80.
42. Nahon 1970, 24; Chazan 1973b, 155.
43. Nahon 1970, 20. The information comes from the so-called *Etablissements de saint Louis*, now dated in the reign of Philip III; *Ordonnances*, I, 216 (chapter 129). Cf. the similar canonistic view (datable to 1272, with much earlier precedents): Marcus 1938, 153.
44. Summarized in Chazan 1973b, 156, with allusions (pp. 32–33, 43–44, 50) to earlier forms of these prohibitions that ultimately go back in part to the Theodosian Code.
45. Saige 1881, 34; Baron 1952–, IX, 11.
46. Langlois 1887, 5, 9–10; Caro 1920–1924, II, 68–75. See also Baron 1952–, X, 64.
47. Golb says interest seems to have been permitted in the 1270s; Golb 1985, 380. His evidence is a text he refers to 1273 (in fact it is undated, and the editor's suggestion is 1273–1275). The text, published by Langlois, is the miscellaneous notes of an unknown cleric taken at an unspecified session of the royal court. The passage in question reads, "Pro indecenti usura et superflua Judeorum Aurelianensium. —Concordatum est nihil" (Langlois 1888, 89). It suggests that the cleric was incensed at the "indecent and unnecessary usury" or "indecent and excessive usury." Golb argues that if some usury was indecent and excessive, then some was not, implying that Louis IX's legislation had somehow been modified, but I do not think the text can bear this interpretation and, in any case, it seems highly dubious considering that Louis's legislation had just been confirmed.
48. Jordan 1981, 303–05.
49. Chazan 1973b, 157 (also pp. 155, 158, 160–61, for similar statements).
50. Above chapter 8, text to n. 33.
51. Langlois 1887, 440 no. XXI.
52. Langlois 1887, 411 nos. 146, 151 (Saige 1881, 212–13 no. 2); 418 nos. 179–80.
53. In general on Navarrese affairs, Langlois 1887, 97–109; and Leroy 1985, 58–60; for the order restoring property to Jewish victims, Langlois 1887, 406 no. 124.
54. See below, chapter 10, text to nn. 38–60.
55. On the peace with England see Jordan 1979b, 197–99; on settlement in Périgord, Quercy, and Limousin, above chapter 7, text to n. 5.
56. Jordan 1979b, 199–200.
57. For additional information, below chapter 10, text to nn. 38–60, 99–101.
58. Powicke 1953, 36, 102.

59. Langmuir 1972. And, more generally, see Stacey 1988, 135–50, on the decades 1240–1260 as a "watershed in Anglo-Jewish 'history.'"
60. Powicke 1953, 184.
61. Matthew Paris 1872–1883, V, 441. On the conversion impulses of the English, see Hyams 1974, 276.
62. Powicke 1953, 322.
63. Powicke 1953, 633 (especially, n. 1).
64. Langmuir 1977, 242.
65. Nahon 1975a, 7.
66. Dahan 1980b, 21; Chazan 1973b, 156; Golb 1985, 378.

Chapter 10

1. The discussion of Picardy draws substantially from three articles of my own: Jordan 1978; Jordan 1979a; Jordan 1983. Normally, only where I am supplementing the conclusions of those articles with the work of other scholars have I provided footnotes.
2. In general on Picardy, Fossier 1968.
3. Jordan 1984, 155–56.
4. Doehaerd 1950, 145–65; Sivéry 1984, especially maps three and four.
5. Jordan 1979b, 55–56, n. 112.
6. Stow 1981, 161–84.
7. Le Goff 1986, 9–68, 83–99, draws on the considerable *exemplum* literature, much of Dominican origin, but he also notices the counter argument (less clearly recoverable from mendicant texts) that moderate interest was not necessarily equivalent to usury (Le Goff 1986, 75–77).
8. Jordan 1979a, nos. 173–75.
9. Cf. Graboïs 1970, 5–22.
10. Avenel 1878, 177–79.
11. Jordan 1979b, 109 (and more generally, pp. 105–10).
12. Roblin 1952b, 16.
13. Below n. 14.
14. Delisle 1877, 189. The chronicle printed here specifically denominates these as Parisian orders.
15. Jordan 1979b, 166–67.
16. *HF*, XXIV, 70*, 233*.
17. *HF*, XXIV, 699–700 no. 8, and for other complaints, pp. 698–704.
18. On Julien, see Jordan 1979b, 166.
19. Chédeville 1973, 475–76.
20. Regné 1908, 2.
21. See the criticisms by Bachrach 1980, 11–19, of Zuckerman 1972.
22. Gaillard 1920–1922, 103.
23. Saige 1881, 74–76; Regné 1909, 81–88.
24. For a full discussion, Graboïs 1977, 142–56.

25. Regné 1909, 104.
26. Bachrach 1980, 11–19.
27. Regné 1909, 207–09.
28. Jordan 1979b, 19.
29. Emery 1941.
30. Gaillard 1920–1922, 105–06.
31. On Guy, See Chazan 1973a; Dossat 1972; Kriegel 1979, 51, 185. For Louis's order, *Ordonnances*, I, 294.
32. Kriegel 1979, 51.
33. On all these matters, see Jordan 1979b, 81, 88, 138–40.
34. Strayer 1980, 192, 383.
35. Jordan 1979b, 97–98.
36. Regné 1909, 209–13.
37. Above chapter 9, text to n. 33, for a discussion of the denunciation. Scholars differ on the dating: Regné 1910, 61 n. 1, argued for 1246; Nahon 1970, 18, suggested 1245–1260; Chazan 1973b, 116, refers it to the mid-century; Stow 1981, 171, argues persuasively for 1270.
38. BN: Languedoc Doat, vol. 37, fols. 165 r.–170 v. For a discussion of the circumstances of its formulation, cf. Regné 1910, 62–67.
39. Saige 1881, 213–17. (Where Saige and I differ substantially in readings, it is indicated in the notes.) The date 1284 (perhaps late 1283) is certain; all references in the document make a point that the relevance of the matters being discussed goes back no further than fifty-four years, that is, to the fundamental guidelines on the royal annexation in the Treaty of Paris, 1229; see above chapter 7, text following n. 105.
40. Fols. 165 v.–166 r. Jews had received a false judgement exempting them from the royal *taille*, "quare sententia, quae dicitur lata fuisse pro eis domino Regi non praeiudicat in hac parte cum lata fuerit tacita veritate et in ejus manifestissimam lesionem."
41. Fol. 167 v., "nec obstat si dicatur quod longis temporibus idem Astruch Limosi steterit, quae *Villa domini Regis non est, cum dicta* villa sub certa forma in dominum Petrum de Vicinis translata fuerit." Unfortunately Saige 1881, 215, dropped the critical italicized clause in his edition.
42. Each case asserts, "sciat dominus senescallus." The preamble makes clear that, "Haec est informatio domini senescalli facta super Judaeis qui sunt de resortis senescalliae Carcassonae et Bitterris, super eo quod talliae domini Regis contribuere teneantur." References to "difinitiva sententia lata in dicta causa per iudicem Carcassonae," as well as the phrases quoted in the text are at fols. 167 r., 168 r., 169 r.–170 r. For the phrase, "most manifest injury," above n. 40.
43. Fols. 170 r.–171 v. "Super Judaeis vero universis de Maseriis sciat dictus dominus senescallus quod ipsi Judaei se domino Regi [Saige: *Rege*] sponte [Saige adds *se* after *sponte*] solempniter obligarunt [Saige: *obligaverunt*] ad contribuendum in talliis domini Regis, et dominus Rex est in saysina seu possessione talliandi et exhigendi easdem Judaei recognoverunt et confessi fuerunt in iudicio constituti se iudaeos fore domini Regis Franciae supradicti, prout de his constare potest per acta publica, et alia legitima documenta."

44. Fol. 165 v. "Quod Usdas [Saige: *Judas*] de sancto Tibario [Saige: *Tiberio*] et eius fratres . . ."

45. For those that had already been tallaged in royal lands, the clause used is, "contribuerunt in talliis Regiis secundum (*or* iuxta) proprias facultates," or words to that effect; fols. 166 v., 168 r., 169 r. For those who had not yet become tallageable or been tallaged at the time of migration, the clause used indicates that the son should follow the condition of his tallaged father, "quare filii patris conditionem in similibus sequi debent"; fols. 166 r., 166 v., 168 v., 169 r.

46. Above n. 45.

47. Fol. 167 r., "cum Universo collegio Judaeorum Carcassonae pro tallia domini Regis captus fuit."

48. Fols. 166 v., 170 r.

49. Jordan 1986, 26.

50. Fol. 166 v. Iusse's occupation is given as *canabasserius*, that is rope maker or dealer in hemp. While the record refers to him as one of many "sons," it targets him alone as the migrant. The family had lived at Béziers for more than a half century.

51. For example, so it appears with the family of the brothers Vitalis and Creschas who immigrated from Béziers to Narbonne (fol. 166 v.).

52. Fol. 168 r.: "longis temporibus fuit incola Bitterris domini Regis, et inde tam natione quam genere, et ibi dies suos clauserunt [Saige: *clausit*] extremos." I am adopting Saige's emendation in my translation of the text above, but if the plural form of the verb is admitted, the passage would be even more poignant.

53. Blanchet 1889, 140, with reference to a family willing to pay the abbot one gold *marabotin* annually at Christmas for residence privileges. The reference is dated 1256.

54. Blanchet 1889, 139–40. But cf. Pales-Gobilliard 1977, 97.

55. It is only in the Pamiers sequence of cases that the record refers to direct testimony. For example, fol. 168 v., "Quod Creschas de Appamiis contribuere teneatur sciat dominus senescallus quod Creschas in iudicio est confessus . . ."

56. This is the family of Creschas of Pamiers, preceding note. Cf. Pales-Gobilliard 1977, 112 n. 4 (this reference is relevant to nn. 57–58 below as well).

57. The family of Samuel de Port of Port [-Sainte-Marie] (Samuel de Portu), fol. 168 v.–169 r. Samuel explains that "from of old" (*ab antiquo*) his family was from Carcassoone.

58. The family of Abraham den (or D'En) Bonyo and Isach were originally from the region around Saintonge and Angoulême (*natione santonensis et Ingolosmenensis*), fol. 169 r. D'En was a title of respect.

59. Fol. 169 v.: "pater praedicti [Bendig] domicilium suum fovit alternativis temporibus in Villis domini Regis de Castlucio, de Galliacho, de Cordoa."

60. Fol. 170 r.: "pater, avus et proavus, et totum genus dicti Judaei ab antiquo fuerunt de Franciae domini Regis natione."

61. Pales-Gobilliard 1977, 97, and below chapter 12, text to nn. 28–31.

62. Below chapter 12, text to n. 77 on the extensive holdings of the Jews of Narbonne in the early fourteenth century.

63. Besides the studies listed, see also Szapiro 1966, 395.
64. Dossat 1977, 117–18.
65. In general on the comparative regional economic development of southern France in this period, see Lewis 1980, 57–83.
66. For an example of ritual humiliation at the paying of taxes to the church in the tenth (?) century, cf. Mann 1931–1935, I, 16–21, 27–30, and II, 1458 (emending the text transcribed at I, 27–30). For a homicide of the early eleventh century, with a Jew the victim of a Christian chaplain, cf. Szapiro 1966, 395.
67. Dossat 1977, 123–24 (but notice that most of Dossat's evidence comes from the mid to late thirteenth century).
68. Gross 1969/1897, 214–15 (additional bibliography at p. 19*).
69. See the ecclesiastical legislation attacking Raymond VI for employing Jews; HGL, VI, 278, 304, 623; Grayzel 1933, 302–03, 316–17. Also Saige 1881, 19. As late as 1274, an eighth of the returns on one of the tolls of Toulouse was going by a kind of hereditary right to a Jew. The Jew was obliged to part with it by sale; Dossat 1977, 134.
70. Dossat 1977, 132–35.
71. For the range of ecclesiastical decrees pertinent to Languedoc, see HGL, VI, 172, 278, 304, 623, 779, 795, 840, 862.
72. Cf. Saige 1881, 38–49.
73. Jewish policy in Alfonse's other lands may be studied in Layettes, III, nos. 3782–83, and in Boutaric 1870, 318. Cf. also Baron 1952–, X, 61–63.
74. Fournier and Guébin 1959, 62 nos. 34–36 (dated 1251).
75. With regard to the administration of the county, see Fournier and Guébin 1959, xxxiv-xlv, lxxvii-lxxxvii, and index s.v. "vicarius."
76. Cf. Dossat 1977, 126–27.
77. I follow Dossat 1977, 128, and Lewis 1980, 78, here rather than Nahon 1966, 180, whose estimates are slightly larger for the Jews of the Toulousain.
78. Below, nn. 90–98.
79. Saige 1881, 34–35.
80. Szapiro 1966, 395; Dossat 1977, 129–31.
81. Marcus 1938, 154.
82. Above chapter 1, text to nn. 95–98.
83. Schwab 1897, 189–90.
84. Szapiro 1966, 396.
85. Fournier and Guébin 1959, 319 no. 249: "si sine prejudicio christianorum hujusmodi pons possit fieri et sine gravamine ville, fiat, non obstante ceme-terio judeorum, de quo accipiat 2 braçatas, si necesse fuerit, ad viam facien-dam." The braçata was perhaps an arm's length. If so, the path was to have had a breadth of six or eight feet through the cemetery.
86. Dossat 1977, 130–31.
87. Szapiro 1966, 397–98; Dossat 1977, 131. One might compare the problem of the Jewish cemetery of Montpellier, part of whose land was granted to the Cis-terians by the lord of the town, the king of Aragon, in 1263. The Cistercians contributed ten pounds to the exhumation and carriage of the corpses to a new Jewish cemetery. As to the impact of this on the Jewish community, one can

refer to the Hebrew stele recovered from Montpellier, which, if reported accurately, declared (in the translated French of the antiquary who saw it): "Nous ne sommes même pas libres dans nos tombeaux et la mort qui deslie les autres nous tient toujours liés," Kahn 1889, 264–65.

88. Molinier 1894–1900, I, no. 1003.

89. Kriegel 1979, 37–69. The argument is long and subtle and touches on several centuries and lands. The significance of the Jewish badge in Languedoc is emphasized at p. 51. A measured rebuttal of Kriegel for Provence may be found in Coulet 1986, 203–19.

90. For what follows: *HGL*, VI, 906–07; Caro 1920–1924, I, 382–83; Bisson 1965, 79; Nahon 1966, 191; Dossat 1977, 128.

91. Molinier 1894–1900, I, nos. 646, 709, 890. Nahon 1966, 205–07, seems to think that the only books seized were religious books and that they were deliberately held hostage until the end of the *captio*. I think that all books were seized to get evidence of moneylending, while religious books, the Talmud excepted, were returned.

92. Molinier 1894–1900, I, no. 646: "Pauperes vero Judeos et maxime debiles et infirmos, mulieres et eciam pueros eorum etatis quatuordecim annorum et citra, quorum omnia bona mobilia credideritis vos cepisse et habuisse, a prisione deliberetis." See also no. 890.

93. Molinier 1894–1900, I, no. 646: "divites autem Judeos et eorum uxores, de quibus presumendum erit quod absconderunt vel subterfugerunt bona sua aut pignora que habebant, captos teneatis quousque vobis reddiderint bona et pignora antedicta, et cum hoc plenius feceritis, vos volumus similiter a prisione liberari."

94. Fournier and Guébin 1959, 345 no. 455.

95. Carmi 1981, 415 (and 415–16 for all the prison poems). The incidents date to 1281 (p. 117).

96. Carmi 1981, 416. The reference to the ravens, according to Carmi, is to 1 Kings 17.6: "The ravens brought [Elijah] bread in the morning and meat in the evening; and he quenched his thirst at the stream."

97. For the case, Fournier and Guébin 1959, 297 no. 70. The position of Jewish law is noticed in Rabinowitz 1938, 77.

98. Molinier 1894–1900, I, no. 709: "quod quendam Judeum separatum ab aliis sub fida tenebat custodia, qui in odium aliorum Judeorum et propter commodum suum quod sperabat exinde consequi, revelavit eidem modum et formam qualiter inveniret et habere posset thesaurum omnium Judeorum, et quia dubitabat . . . " The original betrayal occurred in Saintonge; the order to ransack by digging about (*fodiendo*) in the Jews' homes was applied throughout the count's domains, including the Toulousain.

99. Cf. on licit migration, Dossat 1977, 123.

100. Saige 1881, 211–12 no. XLIII (1).

101. Above n. 58.

102. Carmi 1981, 416.

103. Recall the lament (of about the year 1270) of Rabbi Meir ben Simeon of Narbonne on the pathos of the exiles. The text is discussed above chapter 9, text to n. 33.

Chapter 11

1. Strayer 1953, 102–13.
2. Jordan 1979b, 25–34; Siberry 1985, 87–88.
3. Cf. Strayer 1953, 112.
4. Sivéry 1984, 27.
5. Above chapter 10, text to nn. 30–32 (cf. also nn. 33–35)
6. Strayer 1980, 388.
7. Strayer 1953, 111.
8. Above chapter 2, text to n. 33; chapter 6, text following n. 4.
9. On these matters, above chapter 2, text to nn. 44–60; chapter 4, text to nn. 97–98.
10. Cf. Menache 1985, 352.
11. Menache 1985, 352–53.
12. Emmerson 1981, 27, 46, 90–91, 127, 129, 134–35; Rauh 1979, 133, 161–62, 405.
13. Emmerson 1981, 46, 79–81, 175–77; Rauh 1979, 227–28, 405.
14. Jordan, "The Last Tormentor of Christ," 21–47.
15. Jordan 1979b, 39–40. Information and sources on the Jews of Anjou and Maine have been brought together above chapter 4, text nn. 7–29. See also Bouton 1963, 711–23.
16. Chazan 1973b, 185–86; Bouton 1963, 721; Brunschvicg 1894, 238; Hucher 1869, 467. A translation of the text of the decree is available both in Chazan 1973b, 185–86 (partial) and Chazan 1980, 314–17 (complete).
17. Brunschvicg 1894, 238; Rabinowitz 1938, 109.
18. Chazan 1973b, 186.
19. Cf. above chapter 9, text to nn. 58–65.
20. Powicke 1953, 513.
21. Menache 1985, 354–58. Cf. Hyams 1974, 288–93.
22. Malvezin 1875, 41–42; see also Salzman 1968, 95.
23. Leroy 1984, 35–39.
24. Vincent 1930, 289.
25. Cf. Assis 1983, 290. In time numbers of Jews returned to Gascony illegally with the collusion of local officials and to the consternation of higher authorities; *Gascon Rolls . . . 1307–17*, 307, 314–15, 347, 488.
26. Vincent 1930, 289.
27. Vincent 1930, 290.
28. Above chapter 9, text to nn. 65–66.
29. Cf. Saige 1881, 223 no. 10.
30. Blumenkranz 1962, 18; Roblin 1952b, 20.

31. Roblin 1952b, 21: sixty-six of eighty-six taillable Jews listed in 1297 were not listed in 1292.
32. Cf. Dahan 1980b, 22.
33. Rabinowitz 1938, 33–34.
34. *Formulaires*, 18 n. 2.
35. *Formulaires*, 18 no. 11.
36. Cf. Villand 1982, 55–56.
37. *Formulaires*, 19 no. 12.
38. Saige 1881, 223 no. 10. Dahan 1980b, 21; Chazan 1973b, 183; Golb 1985, 381.
39. Cf. Dahan 1980b, 22.
40. Roblin 1952b, 18.
41. Roblin 1952b, 18–19; Baron 1952–, X, 64; Caro 1920–1924, II, 74.
42. Lespinasse 1909–1914, II, 31–32, 44, 99, 116–17.
43. Cormier 1944 [= AD: Nièvre, MS 166], 15; Lespinasse 1909–1914, II, 225–26.
44. Gueneau n.d., 152–53.
45. AD: Nièvre, H 58 (A), "Privilèges de St. Etienne de Nevers"—a compendium of notes assembled in 1674 (with subsequent, often nasty corrections in a later hand)—p. 117. See also, AD: Nièvre, 36 J 22, pp. 8–9 (these are the notes of Alfred Massé, a cabinet minister from Nièvre who after studying the records still in existence at the turn of the nineteenth/twentieth centuries wrote this unpublished sixty-chapter study of Nevers).
46. Lespinasse 1909–1914, II, 364, 373; Lespinasse 1908, 112.
47. Salzman 1968, 96.
48. Salzman 1968, 95.
49. Powicke 1953, 508, 513; Prestwich 1980, 25.
50. Brunschvicg 1894, 238; Legeay 1889/1890, 215–19; Hucher 1869, 466.
51. Above n. 27.
52. Vincent 1930, 290.
53. With regard to the numbers of Jews in Anjou-Maine, above chapter 4, text to nn. 14–21. The variety of property holding is noticed in Dahan 1980b, 26. Most records would be generated by the conveyancing of large community properties—synagogues and schools, cemeteries, vineyards, shambles, market stalls, and ovens (but cf. Shatzmiller 1984b, 67–70, to the effect that the ovens at least may not always have been "community" properties).
54. Cf. AD: Nièvre—AC: Nevers II. 4 (year 1270) and II. 1 (year 1290). Also AD: Nièvre 12 G 166[1] (years 1347, 1361). All of these references, of course, are to allods held by Christians.
55. *Dictionnaire topographique* . . . *de la Nièvre*, x: "Ces archives fort peu riches . . ."; Soultrait 1873, cc. 765–66, "La plus grande partie des archives de notre province a disparu."
56. Cormier 1944 [= AD: Nièvre, MS 166], 42.
57. Cormier 1944 [= AD: Nièvre, MS 166], 59–65.
58. AD: Nièvre 2 G 19, MS "Rotulus talliarum de Fontenanis [*or* Fonteranis] de anno xxij."
59. The three entries referred to are reasonably close together in the list (implying topographical closeness): "Osanna eius [i.e. Michaelis Bergers] uxor qui mor-

atur in domo malochot"; others were living "in domo puerorum Sageti" and "in domo Michaelis Arrondoth." I would conjecture further that the Jews referred to here and that others of the neighborhood were expelled by Philip in 1306, that these three returned in 1315 and managed to secure their old residences after some effort. They would then have been kicked out again in 1322, which explains why a record of 1322 would mention their names as recent residents. On the later events (1306, 1315, 1322), see below chapters 12 and 14.

60. Saige 1881, 219, no. 6, 224 no. 11.

61. Chazan 1973b, 163–79, seems to misunderstand a number of the developments in the reign of Philip the Fair. There is a brief conspectus in Baron 1952–, X, 65–67, and also in Golb 1985, 380–82, as developments affected Norman Jewry.

62. *Journaux . . . de Philippe IV*, xvi; Saige 1881, 219–20 no. 7.

63. Stow 1981, 175.

64. Saige 1881, 91.

65. Above chapter 8, text to n. 32.

66. Saige 1881, 227–28 no. 13.

67. Strayer 1980, 9.

68. Above chapter 10, text to nn. 30–35.

69. *Formulaires*, 19–20 no. 14; Saige 1881, 231–34 no. 18. The decree in Saige appears in translation in Chazan 1980, 182 (see also p. 183).

70. This is not to say that all barons in the south accepted the king's right to tallage their Jews or even Jewish immigrants to their lands; cf. Saige 1881, 218–19 no. 5, 241–42 no. LXVI.

71. Cf. Saige 1881, 234–35 no. 19.

72. Mignon 1899, nos. 1146, 1362, 1389, 2113–14; *Formulaires*, 17–18 no. 9; *Journaux . . . de Philippe IV*, xvii. Chazan 1973b, 166–71; Caro 1920–1924, II, 75–76. Cf. Nahon 1977, 55–57.

73. Saige 1881, 217–20, nos. 4, 7; *Formulaires*, 17–18 no. 9.Nahon 1977, 59.

74. *Formulaires*, 17–18 no. 9; Luce 1881, no. III.

75. *Formulaires*, 19 no. 13.

76. *Journaux . . . de Philippe IV*, xvii. See also Nahon 1977, 62.

77. Saige 1881, 219–23, nos. 7, 9.

78. Saige 1881, 221 no. 8.

79. Saige 1881, 221–23 no. 9.

80. Cf., for example, Saige 1881, 225–26 no. 11, 229–31 no. 16, 231 no. 17. Emery 1977, 93–94; Nahon 1977, 60; Saperstein 1986, 30–31.

81. Above chapter 10, text to n. 97.

82. Saperstein 1986, 31.

83. Saige 1881, 217–18 no. 4.

84. Saige 1881, 37.

85. Saige 1881, 36–37.

86. Saige 1881, 226 no. 17.

87. Saige 1881, 229 no. 15.

88. Philippe le Convers: Pegues 1962, 131–38, with additional information now available in Strayer 1980, 22–23, 61, 67, 398, 401.

89. Saige 1881, 37.

90. Above chapter 6, text to nn. 17–18.

91. Jordan 1979b, 43 esp. n. 39.

92. Arbois de Jubainville 1865, VI, nos. 3531–32. Chazan 1973b, 158.

93. From about the mid-1230s until 1253, the count palatine of Champagne expended most of his energy in Navarre, a kingdom that he took possession of from 1234. He did so partly because the kingly title attracted him, and partly because he was at odds with the Capetians in the north; absence from Champagne made the whole situation easier. After 1253, the count's successor spent more time in Champagne; but he was very solicitous of Louis IX, who became his father-in-law.

94. Gerson 1899, 173–261. A Jewish leprosarium, besides the typical Jewish institutions, existed in Provins: Dahan 1980b, 26; Veissière 1973–1974, 52. For the existence of a well-defined Provins jewry, see also *Registres . . . Philippe le Bel*, I, no. 205.

95. In Gerson 1899, 221–41, forty-three localities in the domains of the count of Champagne are said to have possessed Jewish settlements in the Middle Ages. These localities, however, come from the domains of the count at their greatest extent and therefore include towns like Sens which already in 1055 had become a royal town. Using the borders of 1285, the number would fall to about forty. Normandy with few real towns counted a minimum of thirty-eight settlements with Jews; above chapter 3, nn. 70–73. Champagne had more real towns (Provins, Troyes, Reims) with commensurately larger numbers of Jews. It also produced far more lucrative taxation. To anticipate a bit: in the confiscations of 1306, below chapter 12, nn. 74, 82, Champagne produced seven times as much revenue as Normandy. The Norman figure is not quite so comprehensive as the Champenois; Golb 1985, 407. Obviously, too, higher per capita wealth in the mercantile communities of Champagne (cf. Gerson 1899, 248–58) as compared to the largely agricultural communities of Normandy (outside of Rouen) accounts for some of the discrepancy, though Rouen is covered in the Norman figure. An estimate of the population of Champenois Jews at two or three times that of Normandy would be conservative. This would mean four thousand to six thousand Jews in Champagne. See also Guignard 1848–1849, 414 n. 1, on the jewry in Troyes called the *Broce aux juifs* (*Broce* from Lat. *bruscia* (?), "brush" or "undergrowth", perhaps a "thick" population).

96. Piétresson de Saint-Aubin 1920, 86 n. 2, with evidence of, for example, a Jewish mercer.

97. Such as the argument for a close relationship between the fables of Berakyah (possibly an English Jew; Hyams 1974, 285) and those of Marie de France and of theNotes Romance *fabliaux*: HL, XXVII, 494; or between the poetic interludes of Jedaiah ben Abraham Bedersi (Ha-Penini) and the troubadour poems: HL, XXXI, 371–72.

98. Kraus 1968, 151–55, 158.

99. Weinraub 1976.

100. Frappier 1966, 1–31.

101. In general, see Chazan 1973b, 158–60; Gerson 1899, 173–261.

102. For royal tallaging of the Jews of Champagne and concern with usury, see, for example, Saige 1881, 225 no. 11, and Luce 1881, nos. I, X. For references to earlier taxation, above n. 102. See also Gerson 1899, 217 n. 2, 256.

103. Chazan 1973b, 180–81; Darmesteter 1874, 480–81, 485; Darmesteter 1881, 199–247; Gerson 1899, 217–20.

104. Darmesteter 1874, 485 esp. n. 1. Darmesteter speculated that the recent acquisition of Champagne may explain the evident delay of local royal authorities to thwart the breach of jurisdiction.

105. Piétresson de Saint-Aubin 1920, 87.

106. *HL*, XXVII, 475–82; Darmesteter 1874, 482, 483.

107. *HL*, XXVII, 479; Blondheim 1927, 34; Darmesteter 1881, 199–247; Darmesteter 1874, 447, 480.

108. Darmesteter 1874, 443–86. Cf. also Blondheim 1927, 159–61.

109. Darmesterter 1874, 448–49: he translates *rogez* by French, *crainte*. Biblicists use the English words "fear," "sorrow," "trouble," and sometimes "rage." I want to thank Professor Mark Cohen for discussing the elegies with me.

110. Piétresson de Saint-Aubin 1920, 87.

111. In Uzès in eastern Languedoc in 1297, seigneurial officials arrested certain Jews and a Jewess on a blood libel, charging that they had taken a Christian boy, bled him from the neck and collected the blood in a small goblet. There was fear of popular action if they did not act quickly (a jurisdictional dispute with the bishop of Uzès was slowing down the process), but there is no indication that representatives of the crown intervened; cf. Michel 1914, 59–66.

112. Menache 1985, 363; Langmuir 1977, 235–49. Recently (Lourie 1986, 187–220) some doubt has been thrown on why parts of France were without charges of ritual murder in this period. Lourie argues that the impression derives merely from lack of readily available evidence, but there are hints, she suggests, that the south was as given over to fantasies of Jewish perfidy as the north; her "hints" are Iberian. Her conclusion may or may not be true (cf. above n. 111, and Langmuir 1977). The point I am trying to make is that the French crown (unlike, say, the English) did not actively support or prosecute ritual murder accusations—no matter how much evidence of popular accusations eventually comes to light.

113. Grayzel 1933, 34 n. 70.

114. Grayzel 1933, 329 no. XXXII.

115. Grayzel 1933, 139 no. 29.

116. Joinville, chap. X.

117. *Dictionnaire de spiritualité*, IV, cc. 1624–27.

118. Sinanoglou 1973, 490–509.

119. For the obsessive medieval concern for the Holy Innocents, see Raedts 1977, 279–323. Raedts is bringing this information to bear on an analysis of the Children's Crusade of 1212. His cautions about translating the Latin word *puer* as child or boy (pp. 295–300) are excessive with regard to the texts he is studying. To be sure, *puer* could affectionately or demeaningly refer to older

people (cf. modern *garçon* for waiter and recent U.S. southern "boy" for any adult black male). But in his texts *puer* typically signifies "youth," not merely "marginal type."

120. The complication, of course, is that one could impose the miraculous on babies. Many saints did wonders or achieved precocious rationality as infants (or even in the womb): cf. *Golden Legend* for 25 March on John the Baptist and for 16 June on Saint Quiricus. See also Geary 1977, 167.

121. *Golden Legend*, 400 (under the discussion of the Holy Machabees as pre-Passion saints): " . . . the Holy Innocents, in each of whom Christ Himself was slain."

122. For several examples, see above n. 118, Baron 1952–, XI, 164–70; Weill 1907, 270–72. For the phrase *la digne personne*, used in a chronicler's report of the host desecration miracle that Philip accepted, see *HF*, XXI, 133.

123. For a brief evocative picture of Paris in the period of the host desecration accusation, see Champion 1933, 853.

124. Digard 1884–1939, I, no. 441; *HF*, XXI, "Chronique anonyme," 127; XXI, "Chronique anonyme," 132–33; XXII, "De Miraculo hostiae," 32–33; XXIII, Paschal Chronicle of Saint-Denis, 145–46. These and other sources are cited and discussed in Chazan 1973b, 181–82; Menache 1985, 364; Baron 1952–, XI, 168–69.

125. Although one late chronicler gets details wrong (including the sex of the borrower), he verifies the popular memory of the borrower as unsavory. Jews are said to have received the host *a quodam pessimo*; *HF*, XXIII, 145–46.

126. Beside the sources cited above in n. 124, see Michaëlsson 1958, 172; Michaëlsson 1961, 157.

127. *Comptes du Trésor*, no. 267.

128. *HF*, XXII, 33.

129. The allegation of Alphonsus de Spina in the fifteenth century that Philip expelled the Jews because of the host desecration is rejected in Chazan 1973b, 182.

130. Saige 1881, 236 no. 20: "suis nephandis manibus presumpserunt nequiter per-tractare sanctissimum corpus Christi."

131. The bishop of Maguelonne had his residence in Montpellier, but the see was not transferred from Maguelonne to Montpellier officially until the sixteenth century. Hence, it is more proper to speak of Montpellier as a town rather than a city.

132. Jordan 1979b, 72–74, 138–39.

133. Reyerson 1985, 7.

134. Kahn 1889, 263–64, 273–74; Strayer 1980, 53; and below n. 135.

135. Jordan 1979b, 73–74.

136. Reyerson 1985, 44, 64; Reyerson 1982, 122–23; Nahon 1977, 68–69, 71–73. Sometimes it is necessary to argue back from the rich notarial archives of a later period, but there is no reason to doubt that these accurately reflect thirteenth-century realities in a general way; cf. Reyerson 1985, 24, 66, and Kahn 1894, 121.

137. Shatzmiller 1977a, 337–44.

138. Jordan 1979b, 138.
139. Jordan 1979b, 139.
140. Jordan 1979b, 199–200.
141. *HGL*, VI, 881–82, esp. n. 2.
142. Langlois 1887, 407–08 no. 130, 409 no. 135, 411–12 no. 152.
143. Langlois 1887, 413 no. 157.
144. Reyerson 1985, 6; Strayer 1980, 53.
145. Strayer 1980, 106–07, 408; Saperstein 1986, 30.
146. A curious possible cultural borrowing was the use of the word *Thalamus* for the municipal registers. It has been argued that the word is derived from Talmud, in the sense of "big book"; cf. *HL*, XXXI, 739; *Thalamus parvus*, v–vi.
147. Kahn 1889, 260–61, 267–70.
148. Kahn 1894, 121–24.
149. On rates and schedules, see Reyerson 1985, 80–81, and Reyerson 1980, 200–01.
150. Cf. Reyerson 1985, 5–7, 68; Reyerson 1980, 200–01.
151. Nahon 1977, 53.
152. The treaty and its consequences are treated in Jordan 1979b, 197–99; Buisson 1970–1971, 1–19.
153. Strayer 1977, 270.
154. Cf. Strayer 1977, 271.
155. A truce was established in 1297. The formal settlement of the war was delayed until 1303; Strayer 1977, 271.
156. Strayer 1980, 251–55.
157. Strayer 1977, 275.
158. Strayer 1977, 275.
159. Saige 1881, 35.
160. Renna 1973, 675–93; Strayer 1980, 252–53.
161. Strayer 1969, 3–19.
162. Saige 1881, 236 no. 20; Luce 1881, no. VII. Cf. Chazan 1973b, 178; Stow 1981, 175.
163. Saige 1881, 235–36 no. 20. I do not see the text cited here, embedded in an order supporting the Inquisition, as a significant departure from Philip's earlier policies as Chazan does. It merely clarifies those policies. Cf. Chazan 1973b, 177–78, 187–88; and Chazan 1980, 187–88 (with a translation).
164. Saige 1881, 236.
165. For example, at Orléans; Cochard 1895, 71. There is additional material brought together by Chazan, but he regards it as evidence that the crown was content during most of the reign of Philip to wink at moneylending, a conclusion I cannot accept; Chazan 1973b, 163–79.
166. Luce 1881, no. XVII.

Chapter 12

1. Cf. above chapter 9, text to nn. 34–40.

2. Above chapter 11, text to nn. 143–50, and Strayer 1980, 324–37, and more generally, pp. 324–67.

3. Kantorowicz 1957, 249–58.

4. Strayer 1980, 262–79.

5. Saperstein 1986, 31–32; Strayer 1980, 14.

6. Saperstein 1986, 27–38, for the events and theory which follow. See also on the stages of the controversy Touati 1977, 174–84.

7. Saperstein 1986, 32. On seigneurial license to excommunicate, cf. Shatzmiller 1980b, 63–69, and Shatzmiller 1973b, 53 n. 1.

8. Strayer 1980, 153–55.

9. So argued by Chazan 1973b, 174–75, who has analyzed the data brought together by Luce 1881, nos. IV-VI. See also Caro 1920–1924, II, 78.

10. On the career of Charles of Valois, see Petit 1900.

11. Brown 1976, 370–71.

12. The motivation was imputed to Philip IV by a Jewish commentator; see below chapter 13, text to n. 1.

13. Saige 1881, 93. In the notes that follow I have ordinarily provided references to the texts in Saige 1881 or in the *Registres . . . Philippe IV*. It should be pointed out, however, that most of these texts are also available in Luce 1881. In general on the *captio*, cf. Chazan 1973b, 196– 99; Golb 1985, 401–10; Caro 1920–1924, II, 91–99. For a translation of a writ of commission, Chazan 1980, 290.

14. Blumenkranz 1962, 18; Nahon 1962, 68–73, 78–80; Chazan 1973b, 195.

15. Cf. Graetz 1897–1911, VII, 246.

16. Below nn. 28–36.

17. Cf. above chapter 4, text to nn. 80–85; chapter 6, text to nn. 32–34. There seems to be no doubt that the secret was successfully kept from the Jews; cf. Aubenas 1968, 167.

18. Above chapter 4, text to nn. 44, 61.

19. On the nature of the books, see Saige 1881, 99–100; Loeb 1884, 161–96.

20. *Registres . . . Philippe IV*, I, no. 893. Loeb 1887a, 40; Chazan 1973b, 199.

21. *Gascon Rolls*, 347 no. 1233, 488 no. 1670. Cf. Jordan 1976, 47–48; Jordan 1978, 48–49.

22. Above chapter 2, text to n. 32; chapter 4, text to nn. 44, 62–63.

23. Lipman 1981–82/1984, 13.

24. Saige 1881, 93–94.

25. Dossat 1977, 119–20.

26. Saige 1881, 94.

27. Saige 1881, 92–93 n. 2, 243–44 no. 1.

28. Ferran 1903, 184–85.

29. Above chapter 10, text to nn. 53–60.

30. Ferran 1903, 184–85.

31. Saige 1881, 272–80 nos. 1–3, 287–88 no. 7, 290–91 no. 9, 293–302 nos. 1–3, 303–08 nos. 1–2; Mignon 1899, nos. 2165–71.

32. *Registres . . . Philippe IV*, I, no. 1277.

33. Saige 1881, 101.

34. *Registres . . . Philippe IV*, I, nos. 485, 541; Saige 1881, 92 n. 2, 101–02, 308–19 no. LI, 324–25 no. LIII.
35. *Registres . . . Philippe IV*, I, nos. 759, 835, 1310, 2034; Saige 1881, 101, 290–93 nos. 9–10; Regné 1909, 96–100.
36. Saige 1881, 95, 256–58 no. 11. Dossat 1977, 120–21.
37. Noticed and addressed in Menache 1984, 700; Chazan 1973b, 200–01.
38. For the information that follows, *Registres . . . Philippe IV*, I, nos. 2085, 2222, 2225.
39. Saige 1881, 104.
40. Saige 1881, 331–33 no. LVIII.
41. Mignon 1899, nos. 2127, 2175.
42. *Registres . . . Philippe IV*, I, no. 441; Saige 1881, 256–58 no. 11, 260–64 no. 13.
43. Saige 1881, 99.
44. P. de Bonavalle and Jean Barmont in the *bailliage* of Bourges; Raoul Rousselet in the *sénéchaussée* of Cahors-Périgord; Jean Britonis in the *sénéchaussée* of Rouergue. See Mignon 1899, nos. 2135, 2137, 2161–64. See also Dossat 1977, 118–19.
45. Cf. Schwab 1895, 290, 292–94.
46. *Registres . . . Philippe IV*, I, no. 930.
47. *Registres . . . Philippe IV*, I, nos. 1016, 1020–21; Saige 1881, 293–300 nos. 1–2, 303–06 no. 1.
48. On what they did get, see Jordan 1986, 107 n. 60.
49. Mignon 1899, no. 2162; *Registres . . . Philippe IV*, I, no. 1020.
50. *Registres . . . Philippe IV*, I, nos. 441, 473, 930, 1014, 1457–59.
51. *Registres . . . Philippe IV*, I, no. 1907.
52. Mignon 1899, nos. 2140, 2169; Saige 1881, 256–58 no. 11. See also Dossat 1977, 133.
53. Cf. Nolin 1969, 272–75.
54. Mignon 1899, nos. 579, 1382, 1423, 2137, 2141, 2155–56, 2168, 2174, etc.
55. For example, Mignon 1899, nos. 2163–67, 2170, 2173, 2175, 2177, etc.
56. Cf. Chazan 1980, 291–92, for a translation of a directive on collection of debts, 1309.
57. *Registres . . . Philippe IV*, I, no. 843.
58. Cf. Saige 1881, 325–26 no. LIV.
59. Cf. *Registres . . . Philippe IV*, I, no. 1418.
60. Saige 1881, 325–26 no. LIV: "Audita queremonia. . . ."
61. *Registres . . . Philippe IV*, I, no. 893.
62. Saige 1881, 325–26 no. LIV; Luce 1881; nos. LXXXVIII–LXXXIX.
63. *Journaux du Trésor de Philippe IV*, no. 5987; Mignon 1899, nos. 1427, 2160, etc.; *Journaux du Trésor de Charles IV*, nos. 7764, 8462.
64. Many examples are in the roll inventoried in Mignon 1899, nos. 2125–80.
65. *Registres . . . Philippe IV*, I, no. 753.
66. Cf. Mignon 1899, no. 2129.
67. On estimates of the profit, cf. below nn. 71–92.
68. *Journaux du Trésor de Philippe IV*, no. 5874. Cf. Chazan 1973b, 193.
69. *Journaux du Trésor de Philippe IV*, no. 5934.

70. For example, *Journaux du Trésor de Philippe IV*, nos. 5870, 5890.

71. Saige 1881, 104: "Cette mesure violente fut loin de produire les résultats que ses auteurs avaient espérés." Schwarzfuchs 1975, 89: "Le roi ne fut cependant pas satisfait des résultats obtenus." Though Strayer (Strayer 1939, 10 n. 13) early in his career challenged the traditional views, he did not entirely liberate himself from these older views in his later work: Strayer 1980, 154 and n. 48, "The expulsion of the Jews seems to have been fairly profitable."

72. Strayer 1980, 84 n. 43, and 152, on the manipulation of the currency. See also Nahon 1977, 78–79; Dossat 1977, 129; Saige 1881, 103.

73. Above chapter 10, text following n. 76.

74. Strayer 1980, 84 n. 43; Caro 1920–1924, II, 94.

75. Caro 1920–1924, II, 91–92. The steles may have been conceded rather than sold for profit to the chapter of the Sainte-Chapelle of Dijon; Marilier 1954–1958, 173–78. On the history of the cemetery before its desecration, cf. Robert 1883, 282, and Gerson 1882, 224–29.

76. Regné 1910, 68–70; Graboïs 1977, 153; and above chapter 10, text to n. 77.

77. Calculations are based on Regné 1910, 72–76. As usual I have converted to good money. See also Saige 1881, 98.

78. Unfortunately few records have survived to flesh out the matter; Regné 1910, 80–81.

79. The shift from the "relativement calme" sojourn of the Jews in Burgundy to the era of following Capetian policies, including takings, is noticed in Marlier 1954–1958, 171–72. See also Robert 1883, 281–82; Nahon 1970, 23.

80. Cf. Kahn 1891a, 272–73.

81. Normandy: *Registres . . . Philippe IV*, I, no. 308; Mignon 1899, no. 2144. Vermandois: *Registres . . . Philippe IV*, I, no. 317. Sénonais: Chazan 1973b, 197. Orléanais: *Journaux du Trésor de Philippe IV*, nos. 5823, 5914. Touraine: *Journaux du Trésor de Philippe IV*, nos. 5824, 5863, 5934, 5987; Mignon 1899, nos. 1485–86, 1528, 2139–41. Bourges: Mignon 1899, nos. 2135, 2137. Paris: *Journaux du Trésor de Philippe IV*, I, no. 5851; Mignon 1899, nos. 2125, 2127.

82. Strayer 1980, 84 n. 43; Chazan 1973b, 197.

83. Strayer 1980, 84 n. 43.

84. Mignon 1899, no. 2135.

85. Above n. 81.

86. Strayer 1980, 84 n. 43.

87. Auvergne: Mignon 1899, nos. 1423, 2159–60; *Journaux du Trésor de Philippe IV*, no. 5890. Rouergue: Mignon 1899, no. 2164. Cahors-Périgord: Mignon 1899, nos. 2161–62.

88. Mignon 1899, no. 2159.

89. On the population of Touraine, above chapter 4, text to n. 21.

90. But cf. Chazan 1973b, 197, on sizable profits from re-leasing cemeteries in the north or from amortizations from conveying them into mortmain.

91. Cf. above, for example, on Picardy (the *bailliage* of Vermandois). Chapter 10, text to nn. 15–19.

92. Cf. Strayer 1980, 154 n. 48.

93. Cf. *Registres . . . Philippe IV*, I, no. 482.

94. Jordan 1986b, 107 n. 60.
95. *Registres . . . Philippe IV*, I, no. 308.
96. *Registres . . . Philippe IV*, I, no. 1058. Saige 1881, 44.
97. All references to *Registres . . . Philippe IV*, I. Squires: nos. 1014, 1459. Lawyers and judges: nos. 477, 926, 1910 (all mention *magistri*), 485 (judge), 1457 (lawyer). Notaries: nos. 1012, 1016, 1459, 1907. Royal administrators: nos. 542 (sergeant), 560 (valet of sergeant). Physicians: nos. 925, 1005. Merchants: nos. 439, 442, 1013. Artisans: nos. 940, 1020.
98. *Registres . . . Philippe IV*, I, no. 381.
99. Strayer 1980, 56. There is also much data on wages available in Sivéry 1984, 133–50.
100. *Registres . . . Philippe IV*, I, no. 43; Saige 1881, 245–47 no. 3.
101. *Registres . . . Philippe IV*, I, no. 444; Saige 1881, 247–48 no. 4.
102. For example: AD: Loir-et-Cher, G 2500, MS 6 (undated but early fourteenth century): "Expensa pro parva domo quam tenet Johannes Guerini in vico de judearia. primo pro una dicta coopertore et [f]amuli sui pro ponendo unum stilicidium in dicta doma iiij s. ij d. et pro portagio dicti stilicidii et pro pice xj d."
103. *Registres . . . Philippe IV*, I, nos. 514, 604–05, 683–84, 719, 729, 924, 1458–59, 1861; Saige 1881, 249–54 nos. 6, 8–9, 264–65 no. 14, 280–81 no. 4, 286–87 no. 6.

Chapter 13

1. Stow 1984, 60 n. 146. Also Baron 1952–, XI, 217.
2. The quotation and contrary argument are given in Menache 1984, 700; Menache 1985, 365.
3. On the contest with Boniface VIII and its consequences, see Strayer 1980, 262–81. See also Menache 1985, 365, and the religious aura she detects about the treatment of the struggle by the chroniclers.
4. Above chapter 11, text to n. 69.
5. Strayer 1980, 423: "The one thing that his people could not forgive was Philip's financial policy." See also pp. 152–53.
6. Contrary to Menache 1984, 700, where lack of "excitement" is alleged. Cf. also Menache 1987, 223–36.
7. "Continuatio Chronici Girardi de Fracheto," *HF*, XXI, 27; "E Floribus chronicorum . . . auctore Bernardo Guidonis," *HF*, XXI, 716.
8. For example: "Ex anonymo regum Franciae chronico," *HF*, XXII, 19, and "Ex Uticensis monasterii annalibus," *HF*, XXIII, 483. This may be hindsight, of course.
9. Most chroniclers, in fact, do this. See, for example, the emphatic coupling in, "E Chronico anonymi Cadomensis," *HF*, XXII, 25.
10. *Roman de Fauvel*, ll. 999–1002. This text is discussed in Strayer 1980, 290–91.
11. "Excerpta e memoriali historiarum Johannis a Sancto Victore," *HF*, XXI, 647. Assis 1983, 291, 299; Yerushalmi 1970, 322, 334–35; Chazan 1973b, 195–96.

12. Assis 1983, 299–302.

13. "Chronique rimée attribuée à Geffroi de Paris," *HF*, XXII, 118–19. Menache 1984, 701; Saige 1881, 105.

14. Above chapter 11, text to n. 159.

15. Cf. Molard 1893, 573–74.

16. Demographers have developed a number of population pyramids to describe industrial and non-industrial age-sex distributions. It would be difficult to decide on which of these might be close to the profile of Jewish population in 1300. A stable (no-growth) situation might see more than 10% or 15% of the population above age 60, with less than 10% under the age of 4, but this is all guesswork (cf. for a beginner's introduction, Pressat 1985, 179). It is even more risky to guess at the size of the sick population. The Jews of France in 1300 had large numbers of recent poor and forced immigrants, most of whom, I presume, were healthy, but the level of sickness might have been higher than that of the native popoulation. (No such case can be made for voluntary immigrants.) Even if we had figures on the number of inmates of the Jewish institutions for the sick (we have none), these would not provide good indices of the extent of illness, because most sick people remained at home unless there was a perceived need for segregation (leprosy) or for decisive intervention that could be achieved at a hospital. Indeed, some Christian hospital statutes barred entrance to the chronically ill, lest the institutions be transformed into rest homes or nursing homes; see Rubin 1987, 157–58. The number of pregnant women in the Jewish population also cannot be known. A plausible argument is this: if we suppose that mortality before the age of two was high (25%) and that childhood mortality (ages 2–12) was equally high, then no less than about one-third of the women of child-bearing age had to be in some stage of pregnancy in each twelve-month period to sustain a stable population. Cf. Russell 1972, 61 (births spaced approximately every thirty months). Whether the harsh policies of the 1280s and 1290s had led to an increase or decrease in fertility is unknowable; whether in the short term the events of 1306 led to a decline in the number of pregnancies is equally unknowable.

17. They obviously gave them up, for records of auctioning of the property sometimes exist. For example: *Registres . . . Philippe IV*, I, no. 1015. For references to the two institutions cited, see Dahan 1980b, 26.

18. "Excerpta e memoriali historiarum Johannis a Sancto Victore," *HF*, XXI, 647; "Continuatio Chronici Girardi de Fracheto," *HF*, XXI, 27: "praefigens sub poena mortis certum terminum egressionis eisdem." See also the evidence cited by Golb 1985, 404, and Graetz 1897–1911, VII, 245– 46, on the seizure of everything except the clothes they wore.

19. "Excerpta e memoriali historiarum Johannis a Sancto Victore," *HF*, XXI, 647. Also Menache 1984, 700.

20. Assis 1983, 289.

21. Collected or noticed by Renan in *HL*, XXXI, 383–84, 391, 464, 567–68, 594–95, 612, 691, 721. Also *HL*, XXVII, 726.

22. "I will divide them among Jacob, / I will scatter them among Israel."

23. *HL*, XXXI, 391 (translated from the French of Renan).

24. For example, *HL*, XXXI, 383–84.
25. *HL*, XXXI, 567–68, 594–95, 691.
26. *HL*, XXXI, 464, 612, 721. Cf. Graboïs 1977, 156 n. 47.
27. The order of expulsion might not have run in Brittany; Loeb 1887a, 39–40 n. 2; Blumenkranz 1962, 19. But there were no Jews in Brittany (from 1240). Since a Jewish presence seems to have been an almost essential precondition for a principality to accept refugees, there is no reason to believe that Jews in 1306 tried to go to Brittany. See also for brief remarks on the lands of exile, Chazan 1973b, 195.
28. Bégin 1842–1843, 256. More generally, see Baron 1952–, X, 16–20.
29. Blumenkranz 1962, 19–20.
30. Bégin 1842–1843, 261; but cf. Blumenkranz 1962, 19–20.
31. Weill 1966, 288 (it has also been alleged that twelfth-century Jews of the Barrois were expelled in 1186, but this is highly dubious).
32. I will be discussing these localities and several smaller ones (Weissenburg, Wesel, Soultz, etc.) below.
33. Morey 1883, 4–5. It has been suggested occasionally that Jews reached the province earlier in the wake of the exile of Philip Augustus in 1182, but the evidence is not conclusive.
34. Above chapter 1, text to n. 56.
35. Finkelstein 1924; Agus 1965.
36. Mendel 1979, 239–56; Niermeyer 1967, 11–12.
37. Blumenkranz 1962, 20.
38. Doniach 1932, 84–92.
39. Bégin 1842–1843, 249, on Colmar and Weissenburg.
40. The sources are available in *MGH*, *SS*, IX, 746; XVII, 77, 415; XXV, 255, 546, 711. See also Bégin 1842–1843, 257–58.
41. Pirenne 1937, 132. See also Chazan 1980, 199–201, for a translation into English of Thomas's instructions.
42. Weill 1966, 288.
43. Morey 1883, 4–5.
44. Cipolla 1980, 264.
45. With regard to the economy of the Franche-Comté, see Fiétier 1977, 152–61. Fiétier believes that the presence of Jews bespeaks a sophisticated economy in the thirteenth century (p. 159).
46. Morey 1883, 1–2, 4. For the Breton comparison, above chapter 4, text to nn. 91–98.
47. Morey 1883, 2, 4–6.
48. On the matters treated in this paragraph, see Redoutey 1977, 207–31; Loeb 1884, 161–64.
49. Morey 1883, 7–10, 13. Lacking absolute sovereignty in Franche-Comté, Philip evidently did not issue his expulsion order for the province; but cf. Loeb 1884, 161–64.
50. Below chapter 14, n. 84.
51. Below n. 136.

52. The incident is related in the *Historiae memorabiles* of Rudolf von Schlettstadt; Schwartz 1975, 53.
53. Schwartz 1975, 54.
54. Gérard and Liblin 1854, 143–44.
55. Gérard and Liblin 1854, 168–69, 178–79.
56. Schwartz 1975, 54–55.
57. Schwartz 1975, 53.
58. Blumenkranz 1962, 20.
59. Hilgard 1885, 119–20 no. 158.
60. Bégin 1842–1843, 261.
61. Martens 1954, 150 n.2.
62. Weill 1966, 288–89.
63. Strayer 1980, 320.
64. Blumenkranz 1962, 19–20; Martens 1954, 150; Bégin 1842–1843, 261.
65. Blumenkranz 1962, 20; Bégin 1842–1843, 262.
66. Blumenkranz 1962, 20.
67. Blumenkranz 1962, 20–21; Loeb 1887a, 39–40 n. 2. Cf. Marilier 1954–1958, 172.
68. For the data and conclusions in this paragraph, see Blumenkranz 1962, 20–21.
69. Bégin 1842–1843, 261.
70. Gilson 1968, 94.
71. Bégin 1842–1843, 262.
72. Nahon 1976, 37–43, with emendations in Weyl 1976, 71; Weyl 1974, 128 no. 21.
73. Cf. Blumenkranz 1962, 21. The community might have been sustained by intermittent additional immigrants.
74. Baron 1952–, X, 4–16; Loeb 1887a, 39–40 n. 2; Gerson 1884, 236.
75. Calmann 1984, map. p. 24; See also Gasparri 1980, 215–18; Gasparri 1973–1974, 22–24; Bardinet 1880a, 20, 43–44.
76. Calmann 1984, map. p. 24.
77. But cf. below nn. 110–11.
78. Calmann 1984, 22–24; Baratier 1973, 91–96; Portal 1907, 258–324; Bardinet 1880a, 6–7, 9.
79. Cf. Bardinet 1880b, 6–7, 12–15, 19–40.
80. Above chapter 10, text to nn. 20–62.
81. Bardinet 1880a, 6–7.
82. Gross 1969/1897, 2–5.
83. Bardinet 1880a, 6, 8, 10–11; Bardinet 1880b, 1.
84. Dahan 1980b, 21–22; Bardinet 1880a, 8–10. (Or, perhaps, sixty-five.)
85. Blumenkranz 1962, 21.
86. Gross 1969/1897, 607–08.
87. Aubenas 1968, 168; Aubenas and Guénon 1948, 3; Crémieux 1903, 254–68. It may also be a sign of solicitousness toward the Jews that official news was sometimes provided them in Hebrew translations of Latin; cf. *HL*, XXXI, 459–60.
88. Gross 1969/1897, 79–83, 370–80.
89. For example, Aubenas and Guénon 1948, 3.
90. Gross 1969/1897, 78, 368, etc.

91. Evidence will be presented below on several cities and towns of Provence where moneylending was the chief occupation of the Jews: Marseilles, Aix, Trets, Manosque, etc. See also Boulet 1975, 10.

92. Shatzmiller 1984b, 68–70; Shatzmiller 1973b, 12.

93. Shatzmiller 1973a, 327–33, 335–38.

94. On the jurisdiction of the Hospital, Shatzmiller 1973b, 49–54; on the role of the Inquisition, above n. 93.

95. Shatzmiller 1973a, 331; Shatzmiller 1980e, 159–73.

96. Definitive treatments of these matters are contained in Bourrilly 1925, 1–156, and Portal 1907, 1–275. Briefer and more succinct is Baratier 1973, 72–90.

97. Portal 1907, 283–88; Bourrilly 1925, 164–83.

98. Bourrilly 1925, 171–72, 213. A small section of Marseilles, the so-called "Lower Town," was under the jurisdiction of the abbey of Saint-Victor. Another small section, the "Upper Town," fell under the jurisdiction of the bishop. Both sections had independent access to the sea and, therefore, the inhabitants, who made their livings from maritime trade, shared the enthusiasm for the economic boom in Mediterranean commerce that accompanied Louis IX's crusade. Charles purchased the "Upper Town" in 1257; Portal 1907, 316–17. It was not until 1275 that he secured his rights in the "Lower Town"; Bourrilly 1925, 240 n. 2.

99. Portal 1907, 299–303; Bourrilly 1925, 217–23.

100. Portal 1907, 305–24; Bourrilly 1925, 223–40.

101. Grayzel 1933, 302–05, 326–27, 334–35. HGL, VI, 304.

102. Crémieux 1903, 36–47.

103. Crémieux 1903, 27–28; Shatzmiller 1984a, 207.

104. Cf. Shatzmiller 1984a, 207: "A Jewish doctor, who treated a visiting Italian merchant [in Marseilles] with the wrong drugs [in 1261], lost his patient. The doctor had to flee the city, *and the whole Jewish community of the city was in great danger . . .* " (my emphasis).

105. Bourrilly 1925, 463–64, 478.

106. Shatzmiller 1970, 222.

107. Cf. Crémieux 1903, 1–27. With regard to Charles's careful attitude with regard to jurisdiction over the Jews; see Gross 1969/1897, 368.

108. Crémieux 1903, 1–27, gives the data on restrictions, their mitigation and makes the favorable conclusion.

109. For other examples of legislation, municipal and baronial, against social and commercial integration between Christians and Jews in Provence, see Jordan 1976, 42 nn. 47–48.

110. For full discussions of the organization and administration of the tallaging system and its consequent history, see Shatzmiller 1970, 222–30; Coulet 1985a, 439–45.

111. Blumenkranz 1962, 21; Loeb 1887a, 39–40 n. 2; Gerson 1884, 236.

112. Weill 1983, 52; Bégin 1842–1843, 261.

113. Blumenkranz, 1962, 21.

114. Loeb 1887a, 39–40 n. 2. Blumenkranz may overstate the case when he talks

about Jewish settlement in the Comtat-Venaissin being *trop faible* to sustain large numbers of immigrants; Blumenkranz 1962, 21.

115. Drouard 1973–1974, 54–60. The age of the Tarascon community depends on the dating (and interpretation) of a Hebrew inscription; cf. Drouard 1973–1974, 53, and Chabot 1915, 169–70. Dates suggested include 1193, 1196, 1210.

116. Coulet 1978, 79–80. For the later history of the Jews of Aix, see Coulet 1978, 80–95; Blumenkranz 1983, 1–10; Baratier 1961, 216–20; Dahan 1980b, 21–22.

117. Benhaiem 1977, 29; Gross 1969/1897, 86.

118. Crémieux 1903, 28–32.

119. Marseilles: Blumenkranz 1962, 22. Trets: below text following n. 126.

120. Brun 1975, 22; Blumenkranz 1962, 22; Bégin 1842–1843, 261. (Calmann 1984, 21, is in error to say that the Jews were expelled from Provence in 1306.)

121. Bégin 1842–1843, 261.

122. Robert acceded in 1309. The instructions are published in Giraud 1846, II, 67–68.

123. Bardinet 1880a, 7; and above n. 120.

124. One wonders whether the struggle in the tiny hamlet of Gordes over the Jews' right to continue in the moneylending business (Shatzmiller 1979, 351–54) owes something to the presence of immigrants and the scurry to find clients. One might compare the evidence from Trets, below text following n. 126; also Coulet 1985b, 372.

125. Coulet 1983, 153–57.

126. The rich and exciting material on Trets has been brilliantly evoked in Menkès 1971, 277–303, 417–50. All the information and conclusions on Trets that follow in the text have been synthesized from Menkès's discussion.

127. Evidence of the confiscations in Champagne: above chapter 12, n. 74. On the translation of Navarre to Louis, see Leroy 1985, 4, and Strayer 1980, 18.

128. Leroy 1984, 38.

129. Strayer 1980, 18–19; Leroy 1985, 4.

130. Below chapter 14, n. 14.

131. Pons 1984, 215–21 nos. 17, 19–24.

132. Cf. above chapter 12, n. 43.

133. Assis 1983, 298, 305.

134. Hillgarth 1975, 4.

135. Leroy 1986, 16; Leroy 1984, 38.

136. Leroy 1986, 16; Leroy 1984, 38.

137. I am deducing this from the sometimes imprecise statements in Leroy 1986, 16–17.

138. Alternatively, after the exile of 1322 in the return of 1359; see Leroy 1984, 35–39.

139. Cf. Blumenkranz 1962, 23, who argues that the refugee Jews became remarkably well integrated in Navarre!

140. Above chapter 7, text to n. 96; chapter 10, text to n. 99.

141. Assis 1983, 292–94, for the majority of examples that follow.

142. Besides Assis (above n. 141) see *HL*, XXXI, 650.

143. Blumenkranz 1962, 22. Cf. Loeb 1887a, 39–40 n. 2.

144. Saige 1881, 114; Renan in *HL*, XXXI, 403–04.

145. Assis 1983, 297–99, 305.
146. Assis 1983, 299.
147. In general on the reception of the Jews in the Crown of Aragon, Assis 1983, 288–89, 303.
148. Assis 1983, 295–96; Secall i Guëll 1983, 327.
149. Assis 1983, 294–95, 302–04; Blumenkranz 1962, 22.
150. I am extrapolating from the very problematic but suggestive data in Secall i Guëll 1983, 143, 605–07, but in more general terms the author of this work stresses the impact of the French immigration (pp. 327, 330).
151. Cf. Assis 1983, 305–06. Blumenkranz 1962, 22: "le refuge . . . par excellence."
152. Blumenkranz 1962, 22.
153. Assis 1983, 294–95 n. 54, 302.
154. Assis 1983, 299–302, 309; Pons 1984, 223–24 no. 30.
155. Lourie 1986, 187–220. See also Chazan 1980, 126–28, for a similar incident in the environs of Saragossa, 1294.
156. Pons 1984, 226–27 no. 34.
157. Assis 1983, 296.
158. There is no way to achieve a full occupational profile of the immigrants; cf. Assis 1983, 307–08. But on the hostility, see Assis 1983, 296, 308.
159. Assis 1983, 308–09; Chazan 1973b, 198.
160. Assis 1983, 304.
161. Assis 1983, 309–10.
162. Tunisia: Pons 1984, 225–26 no. 33. Besides Palestine, further information might exist for Italy, the islands of the Mediterranean and north African states.
163. Graboïs 1979, 67.

Chapter 14

1. Strayer 1980, 417–19.
2. Wood 1976, 385–87; Strayer 1980, 19.
3. In general, see Artonne 1912.
4. Cf. Baudon de Mony 1897, 12.
5. *Ordonnances*, I, 551–52.
6. *Ordonnances*, I, 553–57; and above chapter 12, text to n. 61. The directive had more or less to be repeated in 1320; Saige 1881, 333–34 no. LIX.
7. For the background to the introduction of the notariate, cf. Carolus- Barré 1963, 428–35. The order is printed in *Ordonnances*, I, 557.
8. *Ordonnances*, I, 557–60.
9. *Ordonnances*, I, 560–67, 573–76.
10. *Ordonnances*, I, 567–73 (supplement to the Burgundians, 17 May 1315), 576–82 (supplements to the Champenois, May 1315), 587–94 (supplements to the Normans, 22 July 1315).
11. *Ordonnances*, I, 580–81 (May 1315). Philip IV had resisted adhering to the

principle *cessante causa* (the cause of the subsidy having ceased, the subsidy must cease); see Strayer 1980, 418–19, and Brown 1972, 567–85.

12. *Ordonnances*, I, 583. No serious scholar has ever denied the financial motivation of the manumission (cf. Dareste de la Chavanne 1858/1976, 221; Sée 1901, 242–44; Bloch 1920, 163–72), but assessing the realized value of the act has been very difficult. Bloch's is the most profound discussion.

13. *Ordonnances*, I, 582, 584–86 (ordinances of 2 July 1315 and 9 July 1315).

14. *Ordonnances*, I, 595–92.

15. Loeb 1887a, 41 n. 1.

16. Saige 1881, 106.

17. Loeb 1887a, 41 n. 1.

18. All references are to the chapter divisions in the edition in *Ordonnances*, I, 595–97. For brief general discussions, see Chazan 1973b, 202–03; Baron 1952–, X, 67–68; and Caro 1920–1924, II, 99–101.

19. Chapter 2.

20. Chapter 12. Chapter 13 addressed questions of redemption of pledges and schedules of payments. Jews could not demand full payment in less than a year, but Christians could discharge their debts sooner to void future interest.

21. Chapters 14, 16.

22. Chapters 12, 15.

23. Chapters 3, 17. The editors of *Ordonnances* associate the provision against disputation with the famous passage in Joinville's *Histoire de saint Louis* (chap. X) which records Louis IX's statement that a Christian layman should use his sword against a Jew who maligns the Christian faith.

24. Chapters 18–20. In chapter 11 the king addressed the question of those Jews who chose to live under the lordship of other seigneurs. Here he repeated old formulas to the effect that barons should not take possession of his Jews or he of theirs.

25. Chapter 4; also Saige 1881, 330–31 no. LVII. Loeb 1887a, 41 n. 1; Barber 1981, 163–65.

26. Chapter 5.

27. Chapters 5–6.

28. Chapter 7.

29. Chapter 8. The agreement specified (chapter 1) that resettlement was to take place in towns that had previously had settlements, not elsewhere. So, synagogues would not have been consecrated in towns that had never known them.

30. Chapter 9.

31. Chapter 10. Loeb 1887a, 41.

32. Baron 1952–, X, 68–70.

33. Assis 1983, 310.

34. Cochard 1895, 109–12; Marilier 1954–1958, 172; Vincent 1930, 299; Gerson 1899, 258.

35. Montpellier and Toulouse: Kahn 1889, 265; Szapiro 1966, 397. Orléans and Dijon: Cochard 1895, 85; Marilier 1954–1958, 174–75.

36. Regné 1910, 87–89.

37. The argument in this paragraph is based on data provided by an ordinance of reform that deals with the problems, dated 1317 (below n. 38).

38. *Ordonnances*, I, 645–47.

39. *Ordonnances*, I, 645–47, chapters 3, 10.

40. *Ordonnances*, I, 645–47, chapters 6–7.

41. *Ordonnances*, I, 645–47, chapter 10.

42. *Ordonnances*, I, 645–47, chapter 5. An ordinance erroneously assigned a date of February 1318 in *Ordonnances*, I, 682–83, is not relevant to a discussion of the Jews of the fourteenth century. It actually dates from February 1218 (o.s.), on which, see above chapter 5, nn. 48–62.

43. The most recent discussion is Tyerman 1984, 15–34.

44. Lucas 1930, 345–77. See also Fourquin 1979, 246–50; Duby 1968, 295.

45. Barber 1981, 146–47; Menache 1985, 366–69; Caro 1920–1924, II, 107–10.

46. Barber 1981, 146–48, 153.

47. References above n. 45, and cf. Guignard 1848–1849, 413–15.

48. Barber 1981, 148–49, 153.

49. On the violence, including the burning of registers, see Assis 1983, 310; Barber 1981, 146, 149–53; Szapiro 1966, 399. On the ecclesiastical investigation of forced baptisms, see Pales-Gobilliard 1977, 99–112; Yerushalmi 1970, 341; Grayzel 1955, 89–120.

50. Barber 1981, 147, 156–57; Jordan 1987a, 454.

51. On all these matters, see Barber 1981, 148, 153–56.

52. *Journaux du Trésor de Charles IV*, no. 3668.

53. Above chapter 9, text to n. 24; also Jordan 1987, 452–54.

54. Above chapter 1, text to nn. 76–77; and chapter 2, text to nn. 77–85.

55. Menache 1985, 369–70; Baron 1952–, XI, 158–64 (with additional material on charges of poisoning); Caro 1920–1924, II, 111–13.

56. Le Grand 1898, 138, 140 n. 5, 141 n. 6; Menache 1985, 369–70.

57. There is much dispute about the number of people burned in Chinon. Estimates range from eight (Graetz) to one hundred sixty (Kaufmann), which seems decidedly high; see for a conspectus of opinions, wherein Kaufmann criticizes Graetz, Kaufmann 1894, 298–301. See also Grimaud 1895–1896, 140, and Grimaud 1889–1891, 140–41.

58. Grimaud 1889–1891, 141; Grimaud 1895–1896, 139–41.

59. *QTur*, nos. 1075, 1077, 1103–05, 1217–18, 1243, 1260, 1262.

60. *QTur*, nos. 1086, 1091–93, 1097, 1270.

61. Grimaud 1895–1896, 139–40.

62. *Journaux du Trésor de Charles IV*, xxiii–xxiv. See also Henneman 1971, 38.

63. Above chapter 4, text following n. 69; and chapter 11, text to n. 168.

64. *Journaux du Trésor de Charles IV*, xxiii–xxiv.

65. Scholars often write that Philip V issued the order and Charles confirmed it; others give varying dates for Charles's order when they attribute it originally to him. A good discussion is in Caro 1920–1924, II, 114.

66. *Vie Saint Jehan-Baptiste*, epilogue, p. 224. Of course, his perception of these difficulties might refer to a period in the year 1322 old style, that is, from Easter 1322 to Easter 1323 much of which postdates the order of expulsion.

67. The *Journaux du Trésor de Charles IV* have an enormous number of references to the fine. They show collections in Normandy, Champagne (the bailliages of Troyes, Meaux, Vitry, Chaumont, and the town of Fismes), the Mâconnais, the *bailliages* of Tours, Bourges, Amiens, Senlis, Orléans, Sens, Vermandois and its borderlands, and in the *sénéchaussées* of Beaucaire and Carcassonne and other regions of Languedoc. Collection in the queen's lands—Samois, Gretz, Flagy, Lorris, Château-Landon, Beaugency, Corbeil, etc.—also contributed to the final tally. Occasionally there are records not of collections per se but of the wages of collectors, such as in the viscounty of Paris and the *sénéchaussée* of Toulouse. Precise references to individual aspects of the collection will be made in subsequent notes.
68. *Journaux du Trésor de Charles IV*, no. 5909.
69. Assis 1983, 311.
70. *Journaux du Trésor de Charles IV*, nos. 3731, 5913.
71. *Journaux du Trésor de Charles IV*, no. 3668 (in the *sénéchaussée* of Carcassonne).
72. *Journaux du Trésor de Charles IV*, no. 4770; and below nn. 74, 75. See also Henneman 1971, 49.
73. *Journaux du Trésor de Charles IV*, nos. 4347 and 4378 (demands for accounting in Languedoc), 6731 (incident in Roquemaure), 9604 (fraud in Tours).
74. Haginus: *Journaux du Trésor de Charles IV*, nos. 2242, 2284, 2605, 2826, 2920. Similar examples: nos. 1685–86, 1909.
75. *Journaux du Trésor de Charles IV*, nos. 4770, 6883. See also Henneman, 82. Occasionally, as during other *captiones* involving mounting arrears, the government temporarily forbad collection of debts; Henneman 1971, 50.
76. Mignon 1899, 373–75 nos. XVIII, XXX. Henneman 1971, 46, 48–49, 174.
77. Dossat 1977, 122; Szapiro 1966, 397–98. On Raymond's role in the earlier *captio*, see Saige 1881, 94, 103, 253, etc.
78. Gerson 1882, 223.
79. Assis 1983, 312; *HL*, XXXI, 450–51.
80. Assis 1983, 312–14.
81. Assis 1983, 313; Bégin 1842–1843, 242. On the narrow definition of forced conversion, see the references above, n. 49.
82. Kohn suggests that there were some exceptional visits by doctors in the next several decades; Kohn 1982b, 17–18. Loeb suggests that Jews at Saint-Denis remained by royal privilege; Loeb 1887a, 52. The Jews of the king of Majorca may not have been successfully expelled from Montpellier; cf. Henneman 1971, 48, 174, for some suggestive, if inconclusive, data.
83. Two of the borderlands immediately enforced the expulsion order. The widow of Philip V the Tall followed her brother-in-law's lead and expelled the Jews from the Franche-Comté. It is believed that Jews filtered back into the county relatively quickly, for since Philip V died without legitimate issue, Capetian influence waned in the Franche-Comté. Evidence shows small numbers of Jews (one or two families even) after 1322 but before 1348 at Baulay, Granges, Montjustin, and Sainte-Marie-en-Chaux. On these matters, see Morey 1883, 9; Caro 1920–1924, II, 115. On the Jews of the Franche-Comté before 1322, see above chapter 13, text to nn. 33, 43, 45–48. The other borderland that followed

the example of the French expulsion was Bar; the count made a considerable profit from the expulsion. Jews did not return to Bar in any numbers until the nineteenth century; Weill 1966, 292–94. On Bar before 1322, above chapter 13, text to nn. 31, 42, 44.

84. No attempt has been made to be comprehensive. For a few indications of the range of problems in various localities on the borderlands of royal France, see Weil 1983, 54–55, 57–58 (taxation and demographic catastrophe in Dauphiné); Coulet 1978, 81 (demographic catastrophe in Aix-en-Provence); Gasparri 1973–1974, 22–23 (similarly in Orange); Esposito 1938, 786–93 (blood libel in Savoy); Gerson 1884, 236 (persecution in Savoy); Bégin 1842–1843, 286–91, 296 (massacres in the Rhineland); Bardinet 1880a, 20 (massacres in the Comtat-Venaissin); Morey 1883, 13–16 (massacres in the Franche-Comté); Crémieux 1930, 49–71, and Crémieux 1931, 43–64 (anti-Jewish riots in Toulon). The Memorial Book of the Jews of Mainz records martyrdoms in two hundred seventy-nine places in 1348 including locations with recent French immigration like the Brabant; Levin 1884, 136.

85. Neubauer 1885, 86–92; Cohn 1970, 131–41.

86. Loeb 1887a, 41; Luce 1878, 362–70; Kohn 1982b, 18.

87. Schwarzfuchs 1957; Kohn 1982b, 5–138.

88. Kohn 1982b, 24–26, 47, 56; Szapiro 1966, 398; Schwarzfuchs 1957, 42–43.

89. Kohn 1982b, 21, 49; Schwarzfuchs 1957, 44; Jusselin 1907, 145–46; Kahn 1889, 265–66, 274–77.

90. Kohn 1982b, 20–21.

91. Kohn 1982b, 7–24, 28, 31, 51–52; Loeb 1887a, 42.

92. Braunstein 1984, 200–09; Paravicini 1984, 210–20.

93. Lehoux 1956, 38–57.

94. Loeb 1887a, 53–54. Cf. Luce 1878, 368–70, and Luce 1890–1893, I, 170–71. See also Schwarzfuchs 1957, 45–48, and Kohn 1982b, 26–27.

95. Schwarzfuchs 1957. Also Kohn 1985, 133–48.

96. Kohn 1982b, 49; Loeb 1887a, 42; Schwarzfuchs 1957, 47.

97. Kohn 1982b, 50–51.

98. Kohn 1982b, 53–54.

99. Kohn 1982b, 50, 53; Stein 1918–1919, 116–20; Stein 1899, 55–59; Cochard 1895, 93–96.

100. On the financial mattters, cf. Kohn 1982b, 44–47, 57.

101. Baron 1952–, X, 168–87. On the massacres in the general political context of peninsular history, see Hillgarth 1976, 400–01; O'Callaghan 1975, 536–37.

102. Kohn 1982b, 57.

103. Cohen 1981, 146–54; Cohen 1980, 325. Cf. Kohn 1982b, 42–43.

104. Kohn 1982b, 59.

105. Quantin 1873, G 124; Kohn 1982b, 57–58, 60–61. Anchel believed that some of those who decided not to leave remained secret Jews; see Anchel 1938, 6; Anchel 1940, 56–58.

106. Kohn 1982b, 59–60.

107. Nordmann 1925, 5, 10, 12–13.

108. Gerson 1884, 237–40; Trevor-Roper 1969, 105–13. A profanation of the host accusation is slightly earlier; Weill 1907, 270–72.
109. Cf. Baldwin 1986, 50–52, 379–80.
110. The dedicatory is printed in Kail 1962, 399–407.

Chapter 15

1. Guenée 1985 is a comprehensive set of studies of late medieval and early modern states and state-building.
2. Cf. Lewis 1954, 105.
3. Jordan, "The Last Tormentor of Christ," 29–30.

References

All manuscript (MS) citations are carefully identified in the notes in the body of the book with the standard abbreviations:

AD: Archives Départementales
AN: Archives Nationales (Paris)
Bibl.: Biblioteca, Bibliothek, Bibliothèque
BN: Bibliothèque Nationale (Paris)

The "List of References" has been prepared with ease of consultation as the principal objective in following up a citation from the notes to a piece of printed material. It therefore consists of an undivided list, winnowed so as to include only works actually cited in the notes. Many other works were in fact consulted; the large majority of these are cited in several articles that I have published that deal with issues treated in or related to this book. I have referred to these articles rather than reprint all the bibliography here. Occasionally I have used a version of a study that may seem strange. Most important, I routinely cite the German edition of Graetz rather than the later English edition/version. I have done so because the English is a travesty. Anyone who reads it must come away with the idea that Graetz was an idiot when, in reality, he was a first-rate and subtle scholar.

Though nowhere cited in the notes, an essential bibliographical aid for works on French Jewry, works that appeared prior to its publication date, is Bernhard Blumenkranz's *Bibliographie des juifs en France* (Paris, 1974).

AASS. Acta sanctorum quotquot toto orbe coluntur. Ed. J. Bolland and others. Antwerp and elsewhere: 1643–.
Abrahams 1932. Abrahams, I. *Jewish Life in the Middle Ages.* London: 1932.
Abulafia 1981. Abulafia, A. "An Eleventh-Century Exchange of Letters between a Christian and a Jew," *Journal of Medieval History*, 7 (1981), 153–74.
Idem 1984. "An Attempt by Gilbert Crispin, Abbot of Westminster, at Rational Argument in the Jewish-Christian Debate," *Studia Monastica*, 26 (1984), 55–74.
Actes du Parlement. Actes du Parlement de Paris. Ed. E. Boutaric. 2 vols. Paris: 1863.
Adgar 1982. Adgar. *Le Gracial.* Ed. P. Kunstmann. Ottawa: 1982.
Adler 1939. Adler, M. *The Jews of Medieval England.* London: 1939.

Agus 1954–1955. Agus, I. "The Rights and Immunities of the Minority," *Jewish Quarterly Review*, n.s. 45 (1954–1955), 120–29.

Idem 1960–1961. "Preconceptions and Stereotypes in Jewish Historiography," *Jewish Quarterly Review*, n.s. 51 (1960–1961), 242–53.

Idem 1965. *Urban Civilization in Pre-Crusade Europe*. New York: 1965.

Idem 1969. *The Heroic Age of Franco-Germany Jewry*. New York: 1969.

Ahsmann 1930. Ahsmann, H. *Le Culte de la sainte Vierge et la littérature française profane du moyen âge*. Utrecht, Nimegen, and Paris: 1930.

Alphonsus de Spina ca. 1471. Alphonsus de Spina. *Fortalitium fidei contra fidei christianae hostes*. Strassburg: Johannes Mentelin, not after 1471.

Alter 1981. Alter, R. *The Art of Biblical Narrative*. New York: 1981.

Alverny 1982. Alverny, M.-T. d'. "Translations and Translators," in *Renaissance and Renewal in the Twelfth Century*. Ed. R. Benson and G. Constable. Cambridge, Mass.:1982.

Ambrose of Milan 1972. Ambrose of Milan. "Jacob and the Happy Life" in *Seven Exegetical Works*. Tr. M. McHugh. Washington, D.C.: 1972.

Anchel 1938. Anchel, R. Notes of a lecture delivered 18 November 1937 before the Société de l'Histoire de Paris in *Bulletin de la Société de l'histoire de Paris et de l'Ile de France*, 65 (1938), 6.

Idem 1940. "The Early History of the Jewish Quarters in Paris," *Jewish Social Studies*, 2 (1940), 45–60.

Anselme 1674a. Anselme, Père. *Histoire de la maison royale de France*. Paris: 1674.

Idem 1674b. *Histoire des grands officiers de la covronne de France*. Paris: 1674.

Arbois de Jubainville 1865. Arbois de Jubainville, M. d'. *Histoire des ducs et comtes de Champagne*. 6 vols. in 7 parts. Paris: 1865.

Archives . . . cartulaires. *Archives de la ville de Montpellier*, III: *Inventaire des cartulaires de Montpellier (980–1789)*. Ed. J. Berthelet. Montpellier: 1901–1907.

Artonne 1912. Artonne, A. *Le Mouvement de 1314 et les chartes provinciales de 1315*. Paris: 1912.

Assis 1983. Assis, Y. "Juifs de France réfugiés en Aragon (XIIIe–XIVe siècles)," *Revue des études juives*, 142 (1983), 284–322.

Aubenas 1968. Aubenas, R. "A Propos du testament d'un juif carcassonnais de 1305: Reflexions et programme de recherches," *Fédération des sociétés académiques et savantes de Languedoc, Pyrenées, Gascogne*, 1968, 165–71.

Aubenas and Guenon 1948. Aubenas, R. and L. Guenon, "Notes sur la condition des juifs d'Hyères au XIVe siècle," *Recueil de mémoires et travaux publiés par la Société d'histoire du droit* (Université de Montpellier), fasc. 1, 1948, 1–3.

Avenel 1878. Avenel G. d'. *Les Evêques et archevêques de Paris*, I. Paris: 1878.

Babylonian Talmud. *The Babylonian Talmud*. Ed. I. Epstein. 35 vols. London: 1948–1952.

Bachrach 1977. Bachrach, B. *Early Medieval Jewish Policy in Western Europe*. Minneapolis: 1977.

Idem 1980. "On the Role of the Jews in the Establishment of the Spanish March (768–814)," in *Hispania Judaica*, I: *History*. Ed. J. Solà-Solé. Barcelona: 1980.

Baldwin 1970. Baldwin, J. *Masters, Princes and Merchants: The Social Views of Peter the Chanter and His Circle*. 2 vols. Princeton: 1970.

Idem 1986. *The Government of Philip Augustus*. Berkeley, Ca.: 1986.

Idem 1988. "The Case of Philip Augustus," *Viator*, 19 (1988), 195–207.

Banitt 1961. Banitt, M. "Fragments d'un glossaire judéo-français du moyen âge," *Revue des études juives*, 120 (1961), 259–96.

Idem 1968. "L'Etude des glossaires bibliques des juifs de France au moyen âge: Méthode et application," *Proceedings of the Israel Academy of Sciences and Humanities*, 2 (1968), 188–210.

Baratier 1961. Baratier, E. *La Démographie provençale du XIIIe au XVIe siècle*. Paris: 1961.

Idem 1973. *Histoire de Marseille*. Toulouse: 1973.

Barber 1981. Barber, M. "The Pastoureaux of 1320," *Journal of Ecclesiastical History*, (1981), 143–66.

Idem 1984. "The Crusade of the Shepherds in 1251," *Proceedings of the Tenth Annual Meeting of the Western Society for French Historical Studies*. Lawrence, Kan.: 1984.

Bardinet 1880a. Bardinet, L. "Condition civile des juifs du Comtat Venaissin pendant le séjour des papes à Avignon," *Revue historique*, 12 (1880), 1–47.

Idem 1880b. "Les Juifs du Comtat Venaissin au moyen âge: Leur rôle économique et intellectuel," *Revue historique*, 14 (1880), 1–60.

Baron 1952– . Baron, S. *A Social and Religious History of the Jews*, 2nd ed. 18 vols. to date. New York: 1952– .

Bartlett 1981. Bartlett, R. "The Impact of Royal Government in the French Ardennes: The Evidence of the 1247 *Enquête*," *Journal of Medieval History*, 7 (1981), 83–96.

Baudon de Mony 1897. Baudon de Mony, C. "La Mort et les funérailles de Philippe le Bel," *Bibliothèque de l'Ecole des Chartes*, 58 (1897), 5–14.

Bautier 1980a. Bautier, R.-H. "Philippe Auguste: La Personnalité du roi," in *La France de Philippe Auguste: Le Temps des mutations*. Paris: 1980.

Idem 1980b. "La Place du règne de Philippe Auguste dans l'histoire de la France médiévale," in *La France de Philippe Auguste: Le Temps des mutations*. Paris: 1980.

Idem 1981. "'Clercs mécaniques' et 'clercs marchands' dans la France du XIIIe siècle," *Académie des Inscriptions et Belles-Lettres: Comptes rendus*, 1981, 209–42.

Beaumanoir 1884–1885.*Oeuvres poétiques de Beaumanoir*. 2 vols. Ed. H. Suchier. Paris: 1884–1885.

Bedos 1980. Bedos, B. "Les Sceaux," in *Art et archéologie des juifs*. Paris: 1980.

Bégin 1842–1843. Bégin, E.-A. "Histoire des juifs dans le nord-est de la France," *Mémoires de l'Académie de Metz*, 24 (1842–1843), part 1, 111–336.

Belperron 1967. Belperron, P. *La Croisade contre les Albigeois*. Paris: 1967.

Beltran and Dahan 1981. Beltran, E. and G. Dahan. "Un Hébraisant à Paris vers 1400: Jacques Legrand," *Archives juives*, 17 (1981), 41–49.

Benhaiem 1977. Benhaiem, D. "Notes sur des décisionnaires médiévaux: Quelques corrections et additions à la *Gallia judaica* d'H. Gross," *Archives juives*, 13 (1977), 29–31.

Benichou 1970. Benichou, L. "Recherches sur la communauté juive de Marseille au XIIIe siècle," *Archives juives*, 7 (1970), 9–11.

Berger 1975. Berger, D. "Christian Heresy and Jewish Polemic in the Twelfth and Thirteenth Centuries," *Harvard Theological Review*, 68 (1975), 287–303.

Idem 1986. "Mission to the Jews and Jewish-Christian Contacts in the Polemical Literature of the High Middle Ages," *American Historical Review*, 91 (1986), 576–91.

Berger 1893. Berger, E. *Saint Louis et Innocent IV*. Paris: 1893.

Bible moralisée. La Bible moralisée illustrée. 4 vols. Ed. A. de Laborde. Paris: 1911–1927.

Bisson 1965. Bisson, T. "Negotiations for Taxes under Alfonse of Poitiers," in *Studies Presented to the International Commission for the History of Representative and Parliamentary Institutions*. Vienna: 1965.

Blanc 1896. Blanc, A. "Les Transformations du Latin *Judaicus*," *Annales du Midi*, 8 (1896), 195–99.

Blanchet 1889. Blanchet, J.-A. "Les Juifs à Pamiers en 1256," *Revue des études juives*, 18 (1889), 139–41.

Bloch 1920. Bloch, M. *Rois et serfs*. Paris: 1920.

Blondheim 1909. Blondheim, D. "Le Glossaire d'Oxford," *Revue des études juives*, 57 (1909), 1–18.

Idem 1926. "Contribution à l'étude de la poésie judéo-française," *Revue des études juives*, 81 (1926), 379–93.

Idem 1927. "Contribution à l'étude de la poésie judéo-française," parts 2 and 3, *Revue des études juives*, 83 (1927), 22–51, 146–62.

Blum 1978. Blum, J. *The End of the Old Order in Rural Europe*. Princeton, N.J.: 1978.

Blumenkranz 1952. Blumenkranz, B. "A Propos du (ou des) *Tractatus contra Iudaeos* de Fulbert de Chartres," *Revue du moyen âge latin*, 8 (1952), 51–54.

Idem 1958–1962. "Quartiers juifs en France (XIIe, XIIIe et XIVe siècles)," *Mélanges de philosophie et de littérature juives*, 3–5 (1958–1962), 77–86.

Idem 1960. *Juifs et chrétiens dans le monde occidental, 430–1096*. Paris and The Hague: 1960.

Idem 1962. "En 1306: Chemins d'un exil," *Evidences*, 13 (1962), 17–23.

Idem 1963. *Les Auteurs chrétiens latins du moyen âge sur les juifs et le judaisme*. Paris and The Hague: 1963.

Idem 1964. "Anti-Jewish Polemics and Legislation in the Middle Ages: Literary Fiction or Reality," *Journal of Jewish Studies*, 15 (1964), 125–40.

Idem 1972. *Histoire des juifs en France*. Toulouse: 1972.

Idem 1973–1974. "Louis IX ou Saint Louis et les juifs," *Archives juives*, 10 (1973–1974), 18–21.

Idem 1974. *Bibliographie des juifs en France*. Paris: 1974.

Idem 1977. *Juifs et chrétiens: Patristique et moyen âge*. London: 1977.

Idem 1978. "Synagogues en France du haut moyen-âge," *Archives juives*, 14 (1978), 37–42.

Idem 1980. "Inventaire archéologique," in *Art et archéologie des juifs*. Paris: 1980.

Idem 1983. "Un Quartier juif au moyen âge: Aix-en-Provence (juillet–septembre 1341)," *Archives juives*, 19 (1983), 1–10.

Blumenkranz and Chatillon 1956. Blumenkranz, B. and J. Châtillon, "De la polémique antijuive à la catéchèse chrétienne: L'Objet, le contenu et les sources d'une anonyme *Altercatio synagogae et ecclesiae* du XIIe siècle," *Recherches de théologie ancienne et médiévale*, 23 (1956), 40–60.

Bordier 1869. Bordier, H.-L. *Philippe de Remi, sire de Beaumanoir.* Paris: 1869.

Borrelli de Serres 1895–1901. Borrelli de Serres, L. *Recherches sur divers services publics du XIIIe au XVIIe siècles.* 3 vols. Paris: 1895–1901.

Borst 1984. Borst, A. *Les Cathares.* Paris: 1984.

Boulet 1975. Boulet, M. Abstract of *La Communauté juive de Salon-de-Provence* (Thèse de 3ème cycle, Université d'Aix-en-Provence). *Archives juives,* 11 (1975), 10.

Bourrilly 1925. Bourrilly, V.-L. *Essai sur l'histoire politique de la commune de Marseille des origines à la victoire de Charles d'Anjou.* Aix-en-Provence: 1925.

Boussard 1938. Boussard, J. *Le Comté d'Anjou sous Henri Plantagenet et ses fils.* Paris: 1938.

Boutaric 1870. Boutaric, E. *Saint Loius et Alfonse de Poitiers.* Paris: 1870.

Bouton 1963. Bouton, A. "Les Juifs dans le Maine," *Bulletin philologique et historique,* 1963, 711–23.

Braunstein 1984. Braunstein, P. "Die französische Wirtschaft am Ende des Mittelalters: ein Uberblick," in *Europa 1400: Die Krise des Spätmittelalters.* Ed. F. Seibt and W. Eberhard. Stuttgart: 1984.

Bréal 1896. Bréal, M. "Judaica," *Annales du Midi,* 8 (1896), 88–91.

Brown 1972. Brown, E. "*Cessante causa* and the Taxes of the Last Capetians: The Political Applications of a Philosophical Maxim," *Studia gratiana* [*Post scripta*], 15 (1972), 565–88.

Idem 1976. "Royal Salvation and Needs of State in Late Capetian France," in *Order and Innovation in the Middle Ages.* Ed. W. Jordan, B. McNab, and T. Ruiz. Princeton: 1976.

Bruel 1867. Bruel, A. "Notes de Vyon d'Hérouval sur les baptisés et les convers et sur les enquêteurs royaux au temps de saint Louis et de ses successeurs (1234–1334)," *Bibliothèque de l'Ecole des Chartes,* 28 (1867), 610–21.

Brun 1975. Brun, G. *Les Juifs du pape à Carpentras.* Carpentras: 1975.

Brundage 1969. Brundage, J. *Medieval Canon Law and the Crusader.* Madison: 1969.

Brunschvicg 1894. Brunschvicg, L. "Les Juifs d'Angers et du pays angevin," *Revue des études juives,* 29 (1894), 229–44.

Bry 1970. Bry, G. *Histoire du Perche.* Paris: 1970.

Buisson, 1970–1971. Buisson, L. "Saint Louis et l'Aquitaine," *Actes de l'Académie nationale des sciences, belles-lettres et arts de Bordeaux,* 4th series, 26 (1970–1971), 1–19.

Calendar of the Plea Rolls of the Exchequer of the Jews. Ed. J. Rigg. 4 vols. London: 1971.

Calmann 1984. Calmann, M. *The Carrière of Carpentras.* Oxford: 1984.

Carmi 1981. Carmi, T. *The Penguin Book of Hebrew Verse.* Harmondsworth: 1981.

Caro 1920–1924. Garo, G. *Sozial und Wirtschaftsgeschichte der Juden.* 2 vols. 1920–1924. Reprint, Hildensheim: 1964.

Carolus-Barré 1963. Carolus-Barré, L. "La Juridiction gracieuse à Paris dans le dernier tiers du XIIIe siècle: L'officialité et le Châtelet," *Le Moyen Age,* 1963, 417–35.

Castellani 1972. Castellani, C. "Le Rôle économique de la communauté juive de Carpentras au debut du XVe siècle," *Annales: Economies, sociétés, civilisations*, 27 (1972), 583–611.

Cathares en Occitanie. *Les Cathares en Occitanie*. Ed. R. Lafont et al. Paris: 1982.

Cazelles 1972. Cazelles, R. *Nouvelle histoire de Paris*. Paris: 1972.

Chabot 1915. Chabot, J.-B. "Note sur l'inscription hébraïque de Saint-Gabriel à Tarascon," *Bulletin archéologique du Comité des travaux historiques et scientifiques*, 1915, 167–70.

Chalande 1906–1909. Chalande, J. "La Rue des juifs à Toulouse aux quinzième, seizième et dix-septième siècles," *Bulletin de la Société archéologique du Midi de la France*, 1906–1909, 367–72.

Champion 1933. Champion, P. "Juifs et lombards à Paris au moyen âge," *Revue de Paris*, 15 (June, 1933), 846–61.

Charles 1913. Charles, R. *The Apocrypha and Pseudepigrapha of the Old Testament*. 2 vols. Oxford: 1913.

Châtillon 1984. Châtillon, J. "La Bible dans les écoles du XIIe siècle," in *Le Moyen Age et la Bible*. Ed. P. Riché and G. Lobrichon. Paris: 1984.

Chazan 1968. Chazan, R. "The Blois Incident of 1171: A Study in Jewish Intercommunal Organization," *Proceedings of the American Academy for Jewish Research*, 36 (1968), 13–31.

Idem 1969. "The Bray Incident of 1192: *Realpolitik* and Folk Slander," *Proceedings of the American Academy for Jewish Research*, 37 (1969), 1–18.

Idem 1970. "The Persecution of 992," *Revue des études juives*, 129 (1970), 217–21.

Idem 1970–1971. "1007–1012: Initial Crisis for Northern-European Jewry," *Proceedings of the American Academy for Jewish Research*, 38–39 (1970– 1971), 101–18.

Idem 1973a. "Archbishop Guy Fulcodi of Narbonne and His Jews," *Revue des études juives*, 132 (1973), 587–94.

Idem 1973b. *Medieval Jewry in Northern France: A Political and Social History*. Baltimore and London: 1973.

Idem 1977. "The Barcelona 'Disputation' of 1263: Church Missionizing and Jewish Response," *Speculum*, 52 (1977), 824–42.

Idem 1980. *Church, State and Jew in the Middle Ages*. New York: 1980.

Idem 1983a. "An Ashkenazic Anti-Christian Treatise," *Journal of Jewish Studies*, 34 (1983), 63–72.

Idem 1983b. "From Friar Paul to Friar Raymond: The Development of Innovative Missionizing Argumentation," *Harvard Theological Review*, 76 (1983), 289–306.

Idem 1984. "The Deeds of the Jewish Community of Cologne," *Journal of Jewish Studies*, 35 (1984), 185–95.

Idem 1987. Review of K. Stow, *The '1007' Anonymous*, *Speculum*, 62 (1987), 728–31.

Chédeville 1968. Chédeville, A. *Liber controversiarum sancti Vincenti Cenomannensis*. Paris: 1968.

Idem 1973. *Chartres et ses campagnes (XIe–XIIIe s.)*. Paris: 1973.

Cheney 1976. Cheney, C. *Innocent III and England*. Stuttgart: 1976.

Chevalier 1871. Chevalier, C.-U.-J., ed. *Cartulaire municipal de la ville de Montélimar*. Montélimar: 1871.

Cholvy 1982. Cholvy, G. *Le Languedoc et le Roussillon*. Roanne and Le Coteau: 1982.

Choueka 1980. Choueka, Y. "Computerized Full-Text Retrieval Systems and Research in the Humanities: The Responsa Project," *Computers and the Humanities*, 14 (1980), 153–69.

Chronica de Mailros. *Chronica de Mailros*. Ed. J. Hay and A. Pringle. Edinburgh: 1835.

Chronicle of Jocelin of Brakelond. *The Chronicle of Jocelin of Brakelond*. Ed. H. Butler. London: 1951 [1949].

Cipolla 1980. Cipolla, C. *Before the Industrial Revolution*. 2nd ed. New York: 1980.

Cochard 1895. Cochard, T. *La Juiverie d'Orléans*. Orléans: 1895 [repr. 1976].

Cohen 1980. Cohen, E. "Patterns of Crime in Fourteenth-Century Paris," *French Historical Studies*, XI (1980), 307–27.

Idem 1981. "Jewish Criminals in Late Fourteenth-Century France," *Zion*, 46 (1981), 146–54.

Cohen 1982. Cohen, J. *The Friars and the Jews*. Ithaca, N.Y.: 1982.

Idem 1983a. "The Jews as Killers of Christ in the Latin Tradition, from Augustine to the Friars," *Traditio*, 39 (1983), 1–27.

Idem 1986. "Scholarship and Intolerance in the Medieval Academy: The Study and Evaluation of Judaism in European Christendom," *American Historical Review*, 91 (19886), 592–613.

Cohen 1983b. Cohen, N. "Two That Are One—Sibling Rivalry in Genesis," *Judaism*, 32 (1983), 331–42.

Cohn 1970. Cohn, N. *The Pursuit of the Millennium*. 2nd ed. New York: 1970.

Comptes du Trésor du Louvre. *Les Comptes du Trésor du Louvre*. Ed. R. Fawtier. Paris: 1930.

Cormier 1944. Cormier, R. *L'Administration municipale de Nevers*. Unpub. (AD: Nièvre, MS 166).

Coulet 1978a. Coulet, N. "Autour d'un quinzain des métiers de la communauté juive d'Aix en 1437," in *Actes de la Table ronde du G. I. S. méditerranée*, Abbaye de Senanque, October 1978.

Idem 1978b. "'Juif intouchable' et interdits alimentaires," in *Exclus et systèmes d'exclusion dans la littérature et la civilisation médiévales*. Aix-en-Provence and Paris: 1978.

Idem 1983. "Reconstruction d'une synagogue à Saint-Rémy de Provence (1352)," *Revue des études juives*, 142 (1983), 153–59.

Idem 1985a. "La Tallia Judeorum en Provence après la peste noire," *Provence historique*, no. 142, 1985, 439–45.

Idem 1985b. "Frontières incertaines: Les Juifs de Provence au moyen-âge," *Provence historique*, no. 142, 1985, 371–76.

Idem 1986. "Les Juifs en Provence au bas moyen-âge: Les Limites d'une marginalité," in *Minorités et marginaux en Espagne et dans le Midi de la France*. Paris: 1986.

Crémieux 1903. Crémieux, A. "Les Juifs de Marseille au moyen-âge," *Revue des études juives*, 46 (1903), 1–47, 246–68.

Idem 1930. "Les Juifs de Toulon au moyen-âge et le massacre du 13 Avril 1348," *Revue des études juives*, 89 (1930), 33–72.

Culi 1977–. Culi, Y. *The Torah Anthology*. Tr. A. Kaplan. New York and Jerusalem: 1977–.

Cyril of Alexandria. "Glaphyrorum in Genesim," in *PG* (q.v.), LXIX.

Dahan 1978. Dahan, G. "Rashi, sujet de la controverse de 1240," *Archives juives*, 14 (1978), 43–54.

Idem 1979. "La Leçon de Guillaume de Bourges: Ses transcriptions de l'hébreu," *Archives juives*, 15 (1979), 23–33.

Idem 1980a. "Les Juifs dans les Miracles de Gautier de Coincy," *Archives juives*, 16 (1980), 41–48, 59–68.

Idem 1980b. "Quartiers juifs et rues des juifs," in *Art et archéologie des juifs en France médiévale*. Ed. B. Blumenkranz. Toulouse: 1980.

Idem 1982. "L'Exégèse de l'histoire de Caïn et Abel du XIIe au XIVe siècle en Occident," *Recherches de théologie ancienne et médiévale*, 49 (1982), 21–89.

Idem 1983. "L'Exégèse de l'histoire de Caïn et Abel du XIIe au XIVe siècle en Occident," (fin), *Recherches de théologie ancienne et médiévale*, 50 (1983), 5–68.

Dareste de la Chavanne 1858. Dareste de la Chavanne, A.-E.-C. *Histoire des classes agricoles*. Paris: 1858 (repr. 1976).

Darmsteter 1872. Darmsteter, A. "Glosses et glossaires hébreux-français du moyen-âge," *Romania*, 1 (1872), 146–76.

Idem 1874. "Deux élégies du Vatican," *Romania*, 3 (1874), 443–86.

Idem 1881. "L'Autodafé de Troyes (24 avril 1288)," *Revue des études juives*, 2 (1881), 199–247.

Davidson 1967. Davidson, G. *A Dictionary of Angels*. New York: 1967.

Davis 1888. Davis, M. *Shetaroth: Hebrew Deeds of English Jews before 1290*. London: 1888.

Delaborde 1882. Delaborde, H. *Oeuvres de Rigord et de Guillaume le Breton*, I. Paris: 1882.

Delisle 1852. Delisle, L. *Cartulaire normand de Philippe-Auguste, Louis VIII, Saint-Louis, et Philippe le Hardi*. Caen: 1852.

Idem 1864. *Recueil de jugements de l'Echiquier de Normandie*. Paris: 1864.

Idem 1877. "Notes sur quelques manuscrits," *Mémoires de la Société de l'histoire de Paris et de l'Ile-de-France*, 4 (1877), 183–238.

Delumeau 1969. Delumeau, J. *Histoire de la Bretagne*. Toulouse: 1969.

Denis 1911. Denis, L.-J. *Archives du Cogner: Série H—Art. 97*. Paris and Le Mans: 1911.

De Roover 1948. De Roover, R. *Money, Banking and Credit in Medieval Bruges*. Cambridge, Mass.: 1948.

Dictionnaire de spiritualité. *Dictionnaire de spiritualité, ascetique et mystique*. 12 vols to date. Paris: 1932–.

Dictionnaire topographique . . . Nièvre. *Dictionnaire topographique de la Nièvre*. Nevers (?): 1865.

Digard 1884–1939. Digard, G. and others. *Les Registres de Boniface VIII*. 4 vols. Paris: 1884–1939.

Dion 1903. Dion, A. de. *Cartulaire de l'abbaye de Porrois*, I. Paris: 1903.

Dobson 1974. Dobson, R. "The Jews of Medieval York and the Massacre of March 1190," *Borthwick Papers*, no. 45. York: 1974.

Doehaerd 1950. Doehaerd, R. "Un Paradoxe géographique: Laon, capitale du vin," *Annales: Economies, sociétés, civilisations,* 5 (1950), 145– 65.

Doniach 1932. Doniach, N. "Le Poème de Benjamin le Scribe sur R. Samson le Martyr," *Revue des études juives,* 93 (1932), 84–92.

Dornic 1960. Dornic, F. *Histoire du Maine.* Paris: 1960.

Idem 1961. *Histoire de l'Anjou.* Paris: 1961.

Dossat 1969. Dossat, Y. "Simon de Montfort," *Cahiers de Fanjeaux,* 4 (1969), 288–98.

Idem 1972. "Patriotisme mérdional du clergé au XIIIe siècle," *Cahiers de Fanjeaux,* 7 (1972), 419–52.

Idem 1977. "Les Juifs à Toulouse: Un démi-siècle d'histoire communautaire," *Cahiers de Fanjeaux,* 12 (1977), 117–39.

Douais 1888. Douais, C. "Le Quartier des juifs à Toulouse au treizième siècle," *Bulletin de la Société archéologique du Midi de la France,* n.s. no. 2 (1888), 118–19.

Idem 1897. "Une Charte de 1252 avec une notule en écriture rabbinique," *Bulletin de la Société archéologique du Midi de la France,* n.s. no. 19 (1897), 42–43.

Driver 1904. Driver, S. *The Book of Genesis.* London: 1904.

Idem 1954. *The Book of Genesis.* New ed. London: 1954.

Dröes 1982. Dröes, F. *De Katharen: Grens van een Cultuur.* Amsterdam: 1982.

Drouard 1973–1974. Drouard, A. "Les Juifs à Tarascon au moyen âge," *Archives juives,* 10 (1973–1974), 53–60.

Duby 1968. Duby, G. *Rural Economy and Country Life in the Medieval West.* Trans. C. Postan. London: 1968.

Durbin and Muir 1981. Durbin, P. and L. Muir. *The "Passion de Semur".* Leeds: 1981.

Durtelle de Saint-Saveur 1957/1935. Durtelle de Saint-Saveur, E. *Histoire de Bretagne.* 2 vols. 4th ed. Rennes: 1957/1935.

Emery 1941. Emery, R. *Heresy and Inquisition in Narbonne.* New York: 1941.

Idem 1959. *The Jews of Perpignan in the Thirteenth Century.* New York: 1959.

Idem 1977. "Le Prêt d'argent juif en Languedoc et Roussillon," *Cahiers de Fanjeaux,* 12 (1977), 85–98.

Emmerson 1981. Emmerson, R. *Antichrist in the Middle Ages: A Study of Medieval Apocalypticism, Art, and Literature.* Seattle: 1981.

Encyclopaedia Judaica. *Encyclopaedia Judaica.* 16 vols. Jerusalem: 1972.

Esposito 1938. Esposito, M. "Un Procès contre les juifs de la Savoie en 1329," *Revue d'histoire écclésiastique,* 34 (1938), 785–801.

Farcy 1985. Farcy, P. de. *Cartulaire de Saint-Victeur au Mans.* Paris: 1895.

Fawtier 1960. Fawtier, R. *The Capetian Kings of France.* L. Butler and R. Adam. London: 1960.

Ferran 1903. Ferran, le chanoine. "Privilèges et franchises des juifs, à Pamiers, au moyen âge," *Bulletin philologique et historique,* 1093, 184–85.

Fiétier 1977. Fiétier, R. *Histoire de la Franche-Comté.* Toulouse: 1977.

Finkelstein 1924. Finkelstein, L. *Jewish Self-Government in the Middle Ages.* New York: 1924.

Flint 1986. Flint, V. "Anti-Jewish Literature and Attitudes in the Twelfth Century," *Journal of Jewish Studies,* 37 (1986), 39–57.

Formulaires. "Formulaire de Jean de Caux," in *Formules des lettres*. Ed. C.-V. Langlois. Paris: 1890–1897.

Fossier 1968. Fossier, R. *La Terre et les hommes en Picardie*. 2 vols. Paris: 1968.

Fournier 1959. Fournier, P.-F. "Origines des baillis de Mâcon," *Bulletin philologique et historique*, 1959, 473–80.

Fournier and Guébin 1959. Fournier, P.-F. and P. Guébin. *Enquêtes administratives d'Alfonse de Poitiers*. Paris: 1959.

Fourquin 1964. Fourquin, G. *Les Campagnes de la région parisienne à la fin du moyen âge*. Paris: 1964.

Idem. 1979. *Histoire économique de l'Occident médiéval*. Paris: 1979.

Franklin 1883. Franklin, A. "Les Armoires des corporations ouvrières de Paris," *Mémoires de la Société de l'histoire de Paris et de l'Ile-de-France*, 10 (1883), 127–78.

Frappier 1966. Frappier, J. "Le *Conte du Graal* est-il une allégorie judéo-chrétienne?" part 2, *Romance Philology*, 20 (1966), 1–31.

Friedenberg 1987. Friedenberg, D. *Medieval Jewish Seals from Europe*. Detroit, Mi.: 1987.

Gaillard 1920–1922. Gaillard, B. "Une Charte inédite du XIIIe siècle en faveur des juifs de Narbonne," *Mémoires de la Société archéologique de Montpellier*, 2nd series, 8 (1920–1922), 102–11.

Gallia christiana. *Gallia christiana in provincias ecclesiasticas distributa*. 16 vols. Paris: 1715–1865.

Garrigues 1981. Garrigues, M. *Le Premier cartulaire de l'abbaye cistercienne de Pontigny*. Paris: 1981.

Gascon Rolls. *Gascon Rolls Preserved in the Public Record Office, 1307–1317*. Ed. Yves Renouard. London: 1962.

Gasparri 1973–1974. Gasparri, F. "Les Juifs d'Orange (1311–1380) d'après les archives notariales," *Archives juives*, 10 (1973–1974), 22–33.

Idem 1980. "La Population d'Orange au XIVe siècle," *Provence historique*, 30 (1980), 215–18.

Gaster 1925–1928. Gaster, M. *Studies and Texts in Folklore, Magic, Mediaeval Romance, Hebrew Apocrypha and Samaritan Archaeology*. 3 vols. London: 1925–1928.

Geary 1977. Geary, P. "Saint Helen of Athyra and the Cathedral of Troyes in the Thirteenth Century," *Journal of Medieval and Renaissance Studies*, 7 (1977), 149–68 and plates.

Geiger 1872. Geiger, A. (?) "Mittelalterliche Siegel," *Jüdische Zeitschrift für Wissenschaft und Leben*, 10 (1872), 281–85.

Gérard and Liblin 1854. Gérard, C. and J. Liblin. *Les Annales et la Chronique des Dominicains de Colmar*. Colmar: 1854.

Gerber 1981. Gerber, H. "Jews and Money-Lending in the Ottoman Empire," *Jewish Quarterly Review*, 72 (1981), 100–18.

Geremek 1976. Geremek, B. *Les Marginaux parisiens aux XIVe et XVe siècle*. Tr. D. Beauvois. Paris: 1976.

Gerson 1882. Gerson, M. "Les Pierres tumulaires hébraïques de Dijon," *Revue des études juives*, 6 (1882), 222–29.

Idem 1884. "Notes sur les juifs des états de la Savoie," *Revue des études juives*, 8 (1884), 235–42.

Idem 1899. "Les Juifs en Champagne," *Mémoires de la Société académique d'agriculture, des sciences, arts et belles-lettres du département de l'Aube*, 63 (1899), 173–261.

Gilchrist 1969. Gilchrist, J. *The Church and Economic Activity in the Middle Ages.* London and elsewhere: 1969.

Gilson 1968. Gilson, J. *Genappe à travers les âges.* Genappe: 1968.

Ginsburger 1927. Ginsburger, M. "L'Empoisonnement des puits et la peste noire," *Revue des études juives*, 84 (1927), 34–36.

Giraud 1846. Giraud, C. *Essai sur l'histoire du droit français au moyen âge.* 2 vols. Paris: 1846.

Glossa ordinaria. PL, CXIII (see below).

Golb, 1966. Golb, N. "New Light on the Persecution of French Jews at the Time of the First Crusade," *Proceedings of the American Academy for Jewish Research*, 34 (1966), 1–63.

Idem 1977. "The Forgotten Jewish History of Medieval Rouen," two parts, *Archaeology*, 30 (1977), 254–64, 314–25.

Idem 1979a. "L'Académie juive de Rouen dans les manuscrits du moyen âge," *Archéologia*, no. 129 (April 1979), 24–31.

Idem 1979b. "Exceptionelle découverte à Rouen: Une école hébraïque du XIIe siècle," *Archéologia*, no. 129 (April 1979), 8–23.

Idem 1985. *Les Juifs de Rouen au moyen âge: Portrait d'une culture oubliée.* Rouen: 1985.

Golden Legend. The Golden Legend of Jacobus de Voragine. Ed. G. Ryan and H. Ripperger. 2 vols. London and elsewhere: 1941.

Golding 1966. Golding, M. "The Juridical Basis of Communal Association in Medieval Rabbinic Legal Thought," *Jewish Social Studies*, 28 (1966), 67–78.

Goodich 1981. Goodich, M. "Contours of Female Piety in Late Medieval Hagiography," *Church History*, 50 (1981), 20–32.

Gouron 1984. Gouron, A. *La Science du droit dans le Midi de la France au moyen âge.* London: 1984.

Graboïs, A. "L'Abbaye de Saint-Denis et les juifs sous l'abbatiat de Suger," *Annales: Economies, sociétés, civilisations*, 24 (1969), 1187–95.

Idem 1970. "Du Crédit juif à Paris au temps de saint Louis," *Revue des études juives*, 129 (1970), 5–22.

Idem 1977. "Les Ecoles de Narbonne au XIIIe siècle," *Cahiers de Fanjeaux*, 12 (1977), 141–57.

Idem 1979. "The Idea of Political Zionism in the 13th and Early 14th Centuries," in *Festschrift Rëuben R. Hecht.* Rev. Eng. ed. Jerusalem: 1979.

Idem 1984. "L'Exegèse rabbinique," in *Le Moyen Age et la Bible.* Ed. P. Riché and G. Lobrichon. Paris: 1984.

Graetz 1897–1911. Graetz, H. *Geschichte der Juden.* 11 vols. in 14 parts. 4th corrected ed. Leipzig: [1897–1911].

Grande Encyclopédie. La Grande Encyclopédie. 31 vols. Paris: 1886–1902.

Grandmaison 1886–1888. Grandmaison, L. de. Note of a communication read before the Société archéologique de la Touraine, 28 March 1888, *Bulletin de la Société archéologique de la Touraine*, 7 (1886–1888), 405.

Idem 1889. "Le Cimetière des juifs à Tours," *Revue des études juives*, 18 (1889), 262–75.

Grayzel 1933. Grayzel, S. *The Church and the Jews in the XIIIth Century.* Philadelphia: 1933.

Idem 1940. "The Avignon Popes and the Jews," *Historica judaica*, 2 (1940), 1–12.

Idem 1955. "The Confession of a Medieval Jewish Convert," *Historia judaica*, 17 (1955), 89–120.

Idem 1967. *Histoire des juifs*, I. Paris: 1967.

Gregory the Great. "Regulae pastoralis Liber," *PL*, LXXVII (see below).Griffé 1973.

Griffé, E. *Le Languedoc cathare au temps de la croisade (1209–1229).* Paris: 1973.

Idem 1980. *Le Languedoc cathare et l'Inquisition (1229–1329).* Paris: 1980.

Grimaud 1889–1891. Grimaud, H. Lecture (27 November 1889) before the Société archéologique de la Touraine (summary), *Bulletin de la Société archéologique de la Touraine*, 8 (1889–1891), 140–41.

Idem 1895–1896. "Le Quartier juif à Chinon au XIVe siècle," *Bulletin de la Société archéologique de la Touraine*, 10 (1895–1896), 137–41.

Gross 1969/1897. Gross, H. *Gallia judaica*, with supplement (S. Schwarzfuchs). Amsterdam: 1969 (orig. 1897).

Guébin and Lyon 1926–1930. Guébin, P. and E. Lyon. *Petri Vallium Sarnaii monachi Hystoria albigensis.* 2 vols. Paris: 1926–1930.

Gueneau n. d. Gueneau, V. "Les Rues de Nevers," *Mémoires de la Société académique du Nivernais*, 28 (n.d.), 122–65.

Guenée 1985. Guenée, B. *States and Rulers in Later Medieval Europe.* Tr. J. Vale. Oxford and New York: 1985.

Guérard 1840. Guérard, B. *Cartulaire de l'abbaye de Saint-Père de Chartres.* 2 vols. Paris: 1840 Guignard 1848–1849.

Guignard, P. "Mandement de Philippe le Long relatif aux juifs de Troyes," *Bibliothèque de l'école de Chartes*, 10 (1848–1849), 413–15.

Guillaume 1893. Guillaume, P. *Chartes de Durbon.* Montreuil-sur-Mer: 1893.

Guillaume de Bourges 1981. Guillaume de Bourges. *Livre des guerres du Seigneur.* Ed. G. Dahan. Paris: 1981.

Gutsch 1928. Gutsch, M. "A Twelfth Century Preacher—Fulk of Neuilly," in *The Crusades and Other Historical Essays.* Ed. L. Paetow. New York: 1928.

Guttmann 1889. Guttmann, J. "Guillaume d'Auvergne et la littérature juive," *Revue des études juives*, 18 (1889), 243–55.

Habermann 1945. Habermann, A. *Sefer Gezerot Ashkenaz ve-Tsarfat.* Jerusalem: 1945.

Hanawalt 1984. Hanawalt, B. "Keepers of the Lights: Late Medieval English Parish Guilds," *Journal of Medieval and Renaissance Studies*, 14 (1984), 21–37.

Häring 1982. Häring, N. "Commentary and Hermeneutics," in *Renaissance and Renewal in the Twelfth Century.* Ed. R. Benson and G. Constable. Cambridge, Mass.: 1982.

Haskins 1955. Haskins, C. *The Renaissance of the Twelfth Century.* Cleveland and New York: 1955.

Henneman 1971. Henneman, J. *Royal Taxation in Fourteenth Century France.* Princeton: 1971.

Herman 1973. Herman, G. "A Note on Medieval Anti-Judaism, as Reflected in the *Chansons de Geste*," *"Annuale medievale*, 14 (1973), 63–73.

HF. *Recueil des historiens des Gaules et de la France*. Ed. M. Bouquet and others. 24 vols. Paris: 1738–1904.

HGL. *Histoire générale de Languedoc*. Ed. J. Vaissète and others. 2nd ed. 16 vols. Toulouse: 1872–1904.

Hilgard 1885. Hilgard, A. *Urkunden zur Geschichte der Stadt Speyer*. Strassbourg: 1885.

Hillgarth 1975. Hillgarth, J. *The Problem of a Catalan Mediterranean Empire, 1229–1327*. Supplement 8: *English Historical Review*. 1975.

Idem 1976. *The Spanish Kingdoms, 1250–1516*. Oxford: 1976.

Himmelfarb 1984. Himmelfarb, M. "R. Moses the Preacher and the Testaments of the Twelve Patriarchs," *AJSreview*, 9 (1984), 55–78.

HL. *Histoire littéraire de la France*. 32 vols. Paris: 1824–1875.

Hrabanus Maurus. "Commentarium in Genesim," *PL*, CVII (see below).

Hucher 1869. Hucher, E. "Charte de Bérengère concernant des juifs," *Revue des sociétés savants*, 4th series, 10 (1869), 464–68.

Hyams 1974. Hyams, P. "The Jewish Minority in Mediaeval England," *Journal of Jewish Studies*, 25 (1974), 270–93.

Intermédiaire des chercheurs et curieux. Communications on *rues des juifs, rues juives*, etc., *L'Intermédiaire des chercheurs et curieux*, 35 (1896), 36 (1897), 37 (1898), 38 (1899).

Inventaire des AD: Cher. Inventaire des Archives Départementales du Cher, série G. Ed. T. Hubert and E. Hubert. Châteauroux: 1893.

Inventaire-Sommaire des AD: Indre. Inventaire-sommaire des Archives Départementales de l'Indre, série A. Ed. E. Hubert. Châteauroux: 1901.

Isidore of Seville. "Quaestiones in Vetus Testamentum," *PL*, LXXXIII (see below).

Jacobs 1889. Jacobs, J. "Une Lettre française d'un juif anglais au XIIIe siècle," *Revue des études juives*, 18 (1889), 256–61.

Idem 1893. *The Jews of Angevin England*. New York and London: 1893.

James 1924. James, M. *The Apocryphal New Testament*. Oxford: 1924.

James and Jessopp 1896. James, M. and A. Jessopp. *The Life and Miracles of St. William of Norwich*. Cambridge: 1896.

Janvier 1850–1852. Janvier, A. "Note sur les juifs," *Bulletin de la Société des antiquaires de Picardie*, 4 (1850–1852), 287–91.

Jarrett 1926. Jarrett, B. *Social Theories of the Middle Ages*. London: 1926.

Jeffrey 1981. Jeffrey, P. "A Bidding Prayer for Reconciliation," *Ephemerides liturgicae*, 95 (1981), 351–56.

Jerusalem Bible. The Jerusalem Bible. Garden City, N.Y.: 1968.

Joinville. Jean de Joinville. *Histoire de saint Louis*. Ed. J. Natalis de Wailly. Paris: 1872.

Jordan 1976. Jordan, W. "Problems of the Meat Market of Béziers, 1240–1247—A Question of Anti-Semitism," *Revue des études juives*, 135 (1976), 31–49.

Idem 1978. "Jews on Top: Women and the Availability of Consumption Loans in Northern France in the Mid-Thirteenth Century," *Journal of Jewish Studies*, 29 (1978), 39–56.

Idem 1979a. "Jewish-Christian Relations in Mid-Thirteenth Century France: An Unpublished *Enquête* from Picardy," *Revue des études juives*, 138 (1979), 47–54.

Idem 1979b. *Louis IX and the Challenge of the Crusade: A Study in Rulership.* Princeton: 1979.

Idem 1979c. "*Stephaton*: The Origin of the Name," *Classical Folia*, 33 (1979), 83–86.

Idem 1981. "Communal Administration in France, 1257–1270: Problems Discovered and Solutions Imposed," *Revue belge de philologie et d'histoire*, 59 (1981), 292–313.

Idem 1982. "Approaches to the Court Scene in the Bond Story: Equity and Mercy or Reason and Nature," *Shakespeare Quarterly*, 33 (1982), 49–59.

Idem 1983. "An Aspect of Credit in Picardy in the 1240s: The Deterioration of Jewish-Christian Financial Relations," *Revue des études juives*, 142 (1983), 141–52.

Idem 1984. "A Jewish Atelier for Illuminated Manuscripts at Aimens?," *Weiner Jahrbuch für Kunstgeschichte*, 37 (1984), 155–56.

Idem 1986a. "Christian Excommunication of the Jews in the Middle Ages: A Restatement of the Issues," *Jewish History*, 1 (1986), 31–38.

Idem 1986b. *From Servitude to Freedom: Manumission in the Sénonais in the Thirteenth Century.* Philadelphia: 1986.

Idem 1987a. "Pastoureaux," in the *Dictionary of the Middle Ages.* Ed. J. Strayer. Vol. 9. New York: 1987.

Idem 1987b. "A travers le regard des enfants," *Provence historique*, 1987, 531–43.

Idem 1987c. "The Last Tormentor of Christ," *Jewish Quarterly Review*, 78 (1987), 21–47.

Idem 1988a. "The Case of Saint Louis," *Viator*, 19 (1988), 209–17.

Idem 1988b. "Women and Credit in the Middle Ages: Problems and Directions," *Journal of European Economic History*, 17 (1988), 33–62.

Josse 1882. Josse, H. "Histoire de la ville de Bray-sur-Somme," *Mémoires de la Société des antiquaires de Picardie*, third series, 7 (1882), 185–587.

Joubert 1854. Joubert, Abbé. "Portail de l'église cathédrale d'Angers: Inscriptions hébraïques, traduites par M. l'abbé Delacroix, du Séminaire de Versailles," *Mémoires de la Société d'agriculture, sciences et arts d'Angers*, second series, 5 (1854), 129–32.

Journaux du Trésor de Charles IV. Les *Journaux du Trésor de Charles IV le Bel.* Ed. J. Viard. Paris: 1917.

Journaux du Trésor de Philippe IV. Les *Journaux du Trésor de Philippe IV le Bel.* Ed. J. Viard. Paris: 1940.

Jusselin 1907a. Jusselin, M. "Documents financières concernant les mesures prises par Alphonse de Poitiers contre les juifs (1268– 1269)," *Bibliothèque de l'Ecole des chartes*, 68 (1907), 130–49.

Idem 1907b. "Projet d'ordonnance concernant la situation des juifs sous Jean II le Bon," *Revue des études juives*, 54 (1907), 142–46.

Kahn 1889. Kahn, S. "Documents inédits sur les juifs de Montpellier," *Revue des études juives*, 19 (1889), 259–81.

Idem 1891a. "Documents inédits sur les juifs de Montpellier au moyen âge," *Revue des études juives*, 22 (1891), 264–79.

Idem 1891b. "Documents inédits sur les juifs de Montpellier au moyen âge," *Revue des études juives*, 23 (1891), 265–78.

Idem 1894. "Documents inédits sur les juifs de Montpellier au moyen âge," *Revue des études juives*, (1894), 118–41.

Idem 1912. "Les Juifs de Posquières et de Saint-Gilles au moyen âge," *Mémoires de l'Académie de Nimes*, 1912 (part 3), 1–22.

Kail 1962. Kail, A. "Note sur un passage de *La Vengeance Jhesucrist* d'Eustache Marcadé," *Revue des études juives*, 121 (1962), 399–407.

Kanarfogel 1986. Kanarfogel, E. "The '*Aliyah* of 'Three Hundred Rabbis' in 1211: Tosafist Attitudes Toward Settling in the Land of Israel," *Jewish Quarterly Review*, 76 (1986) 191–215.

Kantorowicz 1957. Kantorowicz, E. *The King's Two Bodies: A Study in Medieval Political Theology*. Princeton: 1957.

Katz 1937. Katz, S. *The Jews in the Visigothic and Frankish Kingdoms of Spain and Gaul*. Cambridge, Mass.: 1937.

Kaufmann 1889. Kaufmann, D. "Les Juifs et la Bible de l'abbé Etienne de Cîteaux," *Revue des études juives*, 18 (1889), 131–33.

Idem 1894. "R. Eliézer b. Joseph et le martyre de Chinon," *Revue des études juives*, 29 (1894), 298–301.

Kee 1983. Kee, H. "The Socio-Cultural Setting of Joseph and Aseneth," *New Testament Studies*, 29 (1983), 394–413.

Kirschenbaum 1985. Kirschenbaum, A. "Jewish and Christian Theories of Usury in the Middle Ages," *Jewish Quarterly Review*, 75 (1985), 270–89.

Kisch 1938. Kisch, G. "The 'Jewish Law of Concealment'," *Historia judaica*, 1 (1938), 3–30.

Idem 1970. *The Jews in Medieval Germany: A Study of their Legal and Social Status*. 2nd ed. New York: 1970.

Knowles 1962. Knowles, D. *The Evolution of Medieval Thought*. New York: 1962.

Koenig 1955–. Koenig, F. *Les Miracles de Nostre Dame par Gautier de Coinci*. Geneva and Lille: 1955–.

Kohn 1982a. Kohn, R. "Fortunes et genres de vies des juifs De Dijon à la fin du XIVe siècle," *Annales de Bourgogne*, 54 (1982), 171–92.

Idem 1982b. "Les Juifs de la France du Nord à travers les archives du Parlement de Paris (1359?-1394)," *Revue des études juives*, 141 (1982), 5–138.

Idem 1983. "Le Statut forain: Marchands étrangers, lombards et juifs en France royale et en Bourgogne (seconde moitié du XIVe siècle)," *Revue historique de droit français et étranger*, 1983, 7–24.

Idem 1985. "Royal Power and Rabbinical Authority in 14th Century France," in *Approaches to Judaism in Medieval Times*, II. Ed. D. Blumenthal.[Brown Judaic Studies, no. 57] Chico, Ca.: 1985.

Kraus 1968. Kraus, H. "Christian-Jewish Disputation in a 13th Century Lancet at the Cathedral of Troyes," *Gazette des Beaux-Arts*, 72 (1968), 151–58.

Kriegel 1979. Kriegel, M. *Les Juifs à la fin du moyen âge*. Paris: 1979.

Kukenheim Ezn 1963. Kukenheim Ezn, L. "*Judeo-gallica* ou *Gallo-judaica*," *Neophilologus*, 47 (1963), 89–107.

Kunstmann 1981. Kunstmann, P. *Treize miracles de Notre-Dame*. Ottawa: 1981.

Labarge 1970. Labarge, M. "Saint Louis et les juifs," in *Siècle de saint Louis*. Paris: 1970.

La Borderie 1896–1914. La Borderie, A. de. *Histoire de Bretagne*. 6 vols. Rennes and Paris: 1896–1814.

Lacave La Plagne Barris 1899. Lacave La Plagne Barris, C. de. *Cartulaires du chapitre de l'église métropolitaine Sainte-Marie d'Auch*. Paris and Auch: 1899.

Lafont 1974. Lafont, R. *La Revendication occitane*. Paris: 1974.

Lalore 1875. Lalore, C. *Collection des principaux cartulaires du diocèse de Troyes*. 7 vols. Paris and Troyes: 1875.

Lambert 1976. Lambert, M. *Medieval Heresy*. New York: 1976.

Landau 1973. Landau, L. "Aspects et problèmes spécifiques de l'histoire des juifs en France," *Revue d'histoire de l'église de France*, 59 (1973), 229–50.

Langholm 1984. Langholm, O. *The Aristotelian Analysis of Usury*. Bergen and elsewhere: 1984.

Langlois 1887. Langlois, C.-V. *Le Règne de Philippe III le Hardi*. Paris: 1887.

Idem 1888. *Textes relatifs à l'histoire de Parlement*. Paris: 1888.

Langmuir 1960. Langmuir, G. "'Judei nostri' and Capetian Legislation," *Traditio*, 16 (1960), 203–39.

Idem 1971. "Anti-Judaism as the Necessary Preparation for Anti-Semitism," *Viator*, 2 (1971), 383–90.

Idem 1972. "Knights's Tale of Young Hugh of Lincoln," *Speculum*, 47 (1972), 459–82.

Idem 1977. "L'Absence d'accusation de meurtre rituel à l'ouest du Rhône," in *Juifs et judaïsme de Languedoc, XIIIe siècle-début XIVe siècle*. Toulouse: 1977.

Idem 1980. "*Tanquam servi*: The Change in Jewish Status in French Law about 1200," in *Les Juifs dans l'histoire de France, premier Colloque international de Haifa*. Leiden: 1980.

Idem 1984. "Thomas of Monmouth: Detector of Ritual Murder," *Speculum*, 59 (1984), 820–46.

Idem 1985. "Historiographic Crucifixion," in *Les Juifs au regard de l'histoire: Mélanges en l'honneur de Bernhard Blumenkranz*. Paris: 1985.

Idem 1986. "Comment," *American Historical Review*, 91 (1986), 614–24.

La Serve 1838. La Serve, F. "Les Juifs à Lyon," *Revue du Lyonnais*, 7 (1938).

Lasker 1977. Lasker, D. *Jewish Philosophical Polemics against Christianity in the Middle Ages*. New York: 1977.

Lauer 1924. Lauer, C. "R. Meir Halévy und der Streit um das Grossrabbinat in Frankreich," *Jahrbuch der Jüdisch-Literarischen Gesellschaft*," 16 (1924), 1–42.

Layettes. Layettes du Trésor des chartes. 5 vols. Ed. A. Teulet and others. Paris: 1863–1909.

Lazar 1967. Lazar, M. "Enseignement et spectacle: La 'Disputatio' comme 'scène à faire' dans le drame religieux du moyen âge," *Scripta hierosolymitana*, 19 (1967), 126–51.

Lazard 1887. Lazard, L. "Les Revenus tirés des juifs de France dans le domaine royal (XIIIe siècle)," *Revue des études juives*, 15 (1887), 233–61.

Idem 1888. "Les Juifs de Touraine," *Revue des études juives*, 17 (1888), 210–34.

Leclercq 1982. Leclercq, J. *The Love of Learning and the Desire for God: A Study of Monastic Culture*. Tr. C. Misrahi. New York: 1982.

Legeay 1889–1890. Legeay, F. "Note sur les juifs au Mans," *Bulletin de la Société d'agriculture, sciences et arts de la Sarthe*, second series, 24 (2889–1890), 211–20.

Le Goff 1986. Le Goff, J. *La Bourse et la vie: Economie et religion au moyen âge*. Paris: 1986.

Le Grand 1898. Le Grand, L. "Les Maisons-Dieu et léproseries du diocèse de Paris au milieu du XIVe siècle," *Mémoires de la Société de l'histoire de Paris et de l'Ile-de-France*, 25 (1898), 47–178.

Lehoux 1956. Lehoux, F. "Le Duc de Berri, les juifs et les lombards," *Revue historique*, 215 (1956), 38–57.

Leidenger n.d. Leidenger, G. *Miniaturen aus Handschriften der Kgl. Hof-und Staatsbibliothek in München*, V. Munich: n.d.

Lejeune 1979. Lejeune, R. *Littérature et société occitane au moyen âge*. Liege: 1979.

Lepage 1865. Lepage, H. *Les Archives de Nancy*. 4 vols. Nancy: 1865.

Lépinois 1854–1858. Lépinois, E. de. *Histoire de Chartres*. 2 vols. Chartres: 1854–1858.

Léroquais 1924. Léroquais, V. *Les Sacramentaires et les missels manuscrits, Planches*. Paris: 1924.

Leroy 1984. Leroy, B. "Entre deux mondes politiques: les juifs du royaume de Navarre," *Archives juives*, 20 (1984), 35–39.

Idem 1985. *The Jews of Navarre in the Late Middle Ages*. Tr. J. Green. Jerusalem: 1985.

Idem 1986 = Leroy 1984, republished in *Revue historique*, no. 557, jan.-mar. 1986, pp. 29–37.

Le Roy Ladurie 1962. Le Roy Ladurie, E. *Histoire du Languedoc*. Paris: 1962.

Idem 1976. *Montaillou, village occitan, de 1294 à 1324*. Paris: 1976.

Idem 1979. *Montaillou: The Promised Land of Error*. Tr. B. Bray. New York: 1979.

Lespinasse 1909–1914. Lespinasse, R. de. *Le Nivernais et les comtes de Nevers*. 3 vols. Paris: 1909–1914.

Lespinasse and Bonnardot 1879. Lespinasse, R. de and F. Bonnardot. *Le Livre des métiers d'Etienne Boileau*. Paris: 1879.

Levin 1884. Levin. "Localités illustrés par le martyre des juifs en 1096 et 1349," *Revue des études juives*, 8 (1884), 134–37.

Levine 1986. Levine, R. "Why Praise Jews: Satire and History in the Middle Ages," *Journal of Medieval History*, 12 (1986), 291–96.

Lévy 1889. Lévy, E. "Un Document sur les juifs du Barrois en 1321–23," *Revue des études juives*, 19 (1889), 246–58.

Levy 1964. Levy, R. *Trésor de la langue des juifs français au moyen âge*. Austin: 1964.

Lewis, 1985. Lewis, A(ndrew). "Fourteen Charters of Robert I of Dreux (1152–1188)," *Traditio*, 41 (1985), 145–79.

Lewis 1974. Lewis, A(rchibald). "The Formation of Territorial States in Southern France and Catalonia 1050–1270 AD," in *Mélanges Roger Aubenas*. Montpellier: 1974.

Idem 1976. "Northern European Sea Power and the Staits of Gibraltar, 1031–1350 AD," in *Order and Innovation in the Middle Ages*. Ed. W. Jordan, B. McNab, and T. Ruiz. Princeton: 1976.

Idem 1980. "Patterns of Economic Development in Southern France 1050–1271 AD," *Studies in Medieval and Renaissance History*, n.s., 3 (1980), 57–83.

Lewis 1954. Lewis, W. *The Splendid Century: Life in the France of Louis XIV*. New York: 1954.

Lewy 1955. Lewy, I. *The Growth of the Pentateuch*. New York: 1955.

Liebeschütz 1959. Liebeschütz, H. "The Crusading Movement in Its Bearing on the Christian Attitude towards Jewry," *Journal of Jewish Study*, 10 (1959), 97–112.

Idem 1983. *Synagoga und Ecclesia*. Heidelberg: 1983.

Lipman 1967. Lipman, V. *The Jews of Medieval Norwich*. London: 1967.

Idem 1981–82/1984. "Jews and Castles in Medieval England," *Transactions of the Jewish Historical Society of England*, 28 (1981–82, publ. 1984), 1–19.

Little 1971. Little, L. "Pride Goes before Avarice: Social Change and the Vices in Latin Christendom," *American Historical Review*, 76 (1971), 16–49.

Idem 1978. *Religious Poverty and the Profit Economy in Medieval Europe*. Ithaca, N.Y.: 1978.

Loeb 1882. Loeb, I. "Pierres tumulaires à Macon," *Revue des études juives*, 5 (1882), 104–06.

Idem 1884. "Deux livres de commerce du commencement du XIVe siècle," *Revue des études juives*, 8 (1884), 161–96.

Idem 1887a. "Les Expulsions des juifs de France au XIVe siècle," in *Jubelschrift zum siebzigsten Geburtstage des Prof. Dr. H. Graetz*.Breslau: 1887.

Idem 1887b. "Expulsion des juifs de Salins et Bracon," *Revue des études juives*, 15 (1887), 298–301.

Idem 1888. "Les Négociants juifs à Marseille au milieu du XIIIe siècle," *Revue des études juives*, 16 (1888), 73–83.

Longnon 1877. Longnon, A. *Rôle des fiefs du comté de Champagne: Texte*. Paris: 1877.

Longperier 1859. Longperier, A. de. "Sceaux à legende bilingue, hébraïque et française," *Bulletin de la Société nationale des antiquaires*, 1859, 164–66.

Idem 1872. "Notice sur quelques sceaux juifs bilingues," *Comptes-rendus des séances de l'Académie des Inscriptions et Belles-Lettres*, third series, 1 (1872), 234–42.

Idem 1874. "Inscriptions de la France," second part, *Journal des savants*, 1874. pp. 646–73.

Lot and Fawtier 1932. Lot, F. and R. Fawtier. *Le Premier budget de la monarchie française*. Paris: 1932.

Lourie 1986. Lourie, E. "A Plot Which Failed? The Case of the Corpse Found in the Jewish *Call* of Barcelona (1301)," *Mediterranean Historical Review*, 1 (1986), 187–220.

Lucas 1930. Lucas, H. "The Great European Famine of 1315, 1316, and 1317," *Speculum*, 5 (1930), 343–77.

Luce 1878. Luce, S. "Les Juifs sous Charles V et le fonds hébraïque du Trésor des chartes, en 1372," *Revue historique*, 7 (1878), 362–70.

Idem 1881. "Catalogue des documents du Trésor des chartes relatifs aux juifs sous le règne de Philippe le Bel," *Revue des études juives*, 2 (1881), 15–72.

Idem 1890–1893. *La France pendant la Guerre de Cent ans*. 2 vols. Paris: 1890–1893.

Maccoby 1982. Maccoby, H. *Judaism on Trial: Jewish-Christian Disputations in the Middle Ages*. Rutherford, N.J., and elsewhere: 1982.

Macler 1906. Macler, F. "Inscription hébraïque de Musée de Bourges," *Revue des études juives*, 52 (1906), 221–23.

Madaule 1967. Madaule, J. *The Albigensian Crusade*. Tr. B. Wall. New York: 1967.

Malvezin 1875. Malvezin, T. *Histoire des juifs à Bordeaux*. Bordeaux: 1875.

Mann 1926. Mann, J. "Une Source de l'histoire juive au XIIIe siècle: La Lettre polémique de Jacob b. Elie à Pablo Christiani," *Revue des études juives*, 82 (1926), 363–78.

Idem 1930. "Obadya, prosélyte normand converti au judaïsme, et sa meguilla," *Revue des études juives*, 89 (1930), 244–59.

Idem 1931–1935. *Texts and Studies in Jewish History and Literature*. 2 vols. Cincinnati, Oh.: 1931–1935.

Manselli 1977. Manselli, R. "La Polémique contre les juifs dans la polémique antihérétique," *Cahiers de Fanjeaux*, 12 (1977), 251–67.

Marchegay 1883. Marchegay, P. "Douze chartes originales et inédites en langue vulgaire du centre et de l'ouest de la France, 1238–1299," *Bibliothèque de l'Ecole des Chartes*, 44 (1883), 284–300.

Marcus 1980. Marcus, I. "The Politics and Ethics of Pietism in Judaism: The *Hasidim* of Medieval Germany," *Journal of Religious Studies*, 8 (1980), 227–58.

Idem 1981. *Piety and Society: The Jewish Pietists of Medieval Germany*. Leiden: 1981.

Idem 1982. "From Politics to Martyrdom: Shifting Paradigms in the Hebrew Narratives of the 1096 Crusade Riots," *Prooftexts*, 2 (1982), 40–52.

Idem 1986. "Hierarchies, Religious Boundaries and Jewish Spirituality in Medieval Germany," *Jewish History*, 1 (1986), 7–26.

Marcus 1938. Marcus, J. *The Jew in the Medieval World*. Cincinnati, Oh.: 1938.

Marilier 1954–1958. Marilier, J. "Les Etablissements juifs à Dijon au début du XIVe siècle," *Mémoires de la Commission des antiquaires de la Côte d'Or*, 24 (1954–1958), 171–78.

Martène and Durand 1724–1733. Martène, E. and U. Durand. *Veterum scriptorum et monumentorum historicorum, dogmaticorum, moralium: Amplissima collectio*. 9 vols. Paris: 1724–1733.

Martens 1954. Martens, M. *L'Administration du domaine ducal en Brabant au moyen âge* (Mémoires de l'Académie royale de Belgique, Classe des lettres, vol. 48). Brussels: 1954.

Matthew Paris 1872–1873. Matthew Paris. *Chronica majora*. 7 vols. Ed. H. Luard. London: 1872–1873.

Menache 1984. Menache, S. "Philippe le Bel—genèse d'une image," *Revue belge de philologie et d'histoire*, 62 (1984), 689–702.

Idem 1985. "Faith, Myth, and Politics—The Stereotype of the Jews and their Expulsion from England and France," *Jewish Quarterly Review*, 75 (1985), 351–74.

Idem 1987. "The King, The Church and the Jews," *Journal of Medieval History*, 13 (1987), 223–36.

Mendel 1979. Mendel, P. "Les Juifs à Metz," *Annales de l'Est*, 1979, pp. 239–56.

Menkes 1971. Menkes, F. "Une Communauté juive en Provence au XIVe siècle: étude d'un groupe social," 2 parts, *Le Moyen âge*, 77 (1971), 277–303, 417–50.

Méras 1967. Méras, M. "Une Prétendue persecution de juifs à Moissac sous l'abbatiat de Durand de Brédon," *Annales du Midi*, 79 (1967), 317–19.

Merlet and Jarry 1896. Merlet, L. and L. Jarry. *Cartulaire de l'abbaye de la Madeleine de Châteaudun*. Châteaudun: 1896.

Mestayer 1975. Mestayer, M. "Ruelle des juifs à Douai," *Archives juives*, II (1975), 55.

Métais 1893–1904. Métais, C. *Cartulaire de l'abbaye cardinale de la Trinité de Vendôme*, 5 vols. Paris: 1893–1904.

Meyer 1875–1879. Meyer, P. *La Chanson de la Croisade contre les Albigeois*. 2 vols. Paris: 1875–1879.

MGH. *Monumenta Germaniae historica*
　　Sub-series: *SS* = *Scriptores*
　　　　　　Quellen zur Geistesgeschichte

Michaëlsson 1951. Le Michaëlsson, K. *Le Livre de la taille de Paris, l'an 1313* (Acta Universitatis Gothoburgensis, vol. 57). Göteborg: 1951.

Idem 1958. *Le Livre de la taille de Paris, l'an 1296* (Acta Universitatis Gothoburgensis, vol. 64). Göteborg: 1958.

Idem 1961. *Le Livre de la taille de Paris, l'an 1297* (Acta Universitatis Gothoburgensis, vol. 67). Göteborg: 1961.

Michel 1910. Michel, R. *L'Administration royale dans la sénéchaussée de Beaucaire au temps de saint Louis*. Paris: 1910.

Idem 1914. "Une accusation de meurtre rituel contre les juifs d'Uzès en 1297," *Bibliothèque de l'Ecole des Chartes*, 75 (1914), 59–66.

Mignon 1899. Mignon, *Inventaire d'anciens comptes royaux*, I. Ed. C.-V. Langlois. Paris: 1899.

Miracle de saint Nicolas. *Miracle de saint Nicolas et d'un juif.* Ed. O. Jodogne. Geneva: 1982.

Molard 1893. Molard, F. "Inscription hébraïque trouvée dans la Tour de l'Horloge, durant les dernières réparations," *Bulletin de la Société des sciences naturelles et historiques du département de l'Yonne*, 47 (1893), 537–74.

Moliner 1883. Moliner, A. "Enquête sur un meurtre imputé aux juifs de Valréas," *Le Cabinet historique*, 29 (1883), 121–33.

Idem 1894–1900. *Correspondance administrative d'Alfonse de Poitiers*. Paris: 1894–1900.

Mollat and Wolff 1973. Mollat, M. and P. Wolff. *The Popular Revolutions of the Late Middle Ages*. Tr. A. Lytton-Sells. London: 1973.

Moore 1974. Moore, R. "St. Bernard's Mission to Languedoc in 1145," *Bulletin of the Institute of Historical Research*, 47 (1974), 1–10.

Idem 1985. *The Origins of European Dissent*. New York: 1985.

Idem 1987. *The Formation of a Persecuting Society*. Oxford: 1987.

Morey 1883. Morey, J. "Les Juifs en Franche-Comté au XIVe siècle," *Revue des études juives*, 7 (1883), 1–39.

Mousset 1950. Mousset, J. *Saint Louis*. Tours: 1950.

Musset 1902. Musset, G. "Note" on the Jews of La Rochelle in the Middle Ages, *Bulletin philologique et historique*, 1902, p. 149.

Nahon 1962. Nahon, G. "Contribution à l'histoire de juifs en France sous Philippe le Bel, à propos d'une publication recente," *Revue des études juives*, 121 (1962), 59–80.

Idem 1966. "Les Juifs dans les domaines d'Alfonse de Poitiers, 1241–1271," *Revue des études juives*, 125 (1966), 167–211.

Idem 1969. "Le Crédit et les juifs dans la France du XIIIe siècle," *Annales: Economies, sociétés, civilisations*, 24 (1969), 1121–48.

Idem 1970. "Les Ordonnances de saint Louis sur les juifs," *Les Nouveaux cahiers*, 6 (1970), 18–35.

Idem 1975a. "Documents sur les juifs de Normandie médiévale au Public Record Office de Londres," *Archives juives*, 11 (1975), 3–10.

Idem 1975b. "Pour une géographie administrative des juifs dans la France de saint Louis," *Revue historique*, no. 516 (1975), 305–44.

Idem 1976. "Rapport sur les inscriptions hérbaïques médiévales de l'Alsace et de la Lorraine, avec le texte des inscriptions inédites de Nancy," *Archives juives*, 12 (1976), 37–43.

Idem 1977. "Condition fiscale et économique des juifs," *Cahiers de Fanjeaux*, 12 (1977), 51–84.

Neubauer 1885. Neubauer, A. "Documents sur Avignon," *Revue des études juives*, 10 (1885), 79–97.

Newman 1937. Newman, W. *Le Domaine royal sous les premiers Capétiens (987–1180)*. Paris: 1937.

Niermeyer 1967. Niermeyer, J. *"Judaeorum sequaces*: Joodse kooplieden en Christelijke kooplieden—Bijdrage tot de onstaansgeschiedenis van de Lotharingse burgerij (elfde eeuw)," *Mededelingen der Koninklijke Nederlanse Akademie van Wetenschappen, Afd. Letterkunde*, new series, 30 (1967), 171–84.

Nolin 1969. Nolin, E. "Découverte d'un 'trésor' à Arnay-sous-Vitteaux au XIVe s.," *Annales de Bourgogne*, 41 (1969), 272–75.

Noonan 1957. Noonan, J. *The Scholastic Analysis of Usury*. Cambridge, Mass.: 1957.

Nordmann 1925. Nordmann, A. "Histoire des juifs à Genève," *Revue des études juives*, 80 (1925), 1–41.

Nortier and Baldwin 1980. Nortier, M. and J. Baldwin, "Contributions à l'étude des finances de Philippe Auguste," *Bibliothèque de l'Ecole des chartes*, 138 (1980), 5–33.

Noth 1972. Noth, M. *A History of Pentateuchal Traditions*. Tr. B. Anderson. Englewood Cliffs, N.J.: 1972.

Oberman 1981. Oberman, H. *The Roots of Anti-Semitism in the Age of Renaissance and Reformation*. Tr. J. Porter. Philadelphia: 1981.

O'Brien 1968. O'Brien J. "Jews and Cathari in Medieval France," *Comparative Studies in Society and History*, 10 (1968), 215–20.

O'Callaghan 1975. O'Callaghan, J. *A History of Medieval Spain*. Ithaca, N.Y.: 1975.

Oden 1983. Oden, R. "Jacob as Father, Husband and Nephew: Kinship Studies and the Patriarchal Narratives," *Journal of Biblical Literature*, 102 (1983), 189–205.

OEillet des Murs 1856. OEillet des Murs, M. *Histoire des comtes du Perche*. Nogent-le-Rotrou: 1856.

Omont 1905. Omont, H. "Documents nouveaux sur la Grande Confrérie Notre-Dame aux prêtres et bourgeois," *Mémoires de la Société de l'histoire de Paris et de l'Ile de France*, 32 (1905), 1–88.

Ordonnances. Ordonnances des rois de France de la troisième race. 21 vols. Ed. E.-J. Laurière and others. Paris: 1723–1849.

Orr 1915. Orr, J. *Les Oeuvres de Guiot de Provins*. Manchester: 1915.

Pales-Gobilliard 1977. Pales-Gobilliard, A. "L'Inquisition et les juifs: le Cas de Jacques Fournier," *Cahiers de Fanjeaux*, 12 (1977), 97–114.

Palmer 1982. Palmer, R. *The County Courts of Medieval England, 1150–1350*. Princeton: 1982.

Idem 1985. "The Origins of Property in England," *Law and History Review*, 3 (1985), 1–50, 375–96.

Papi 1977. Papi, M. "Studi e problemi sull' antigiudaismo medievale," *Archivio storico italiano*, 135 (1977), 141–64.

Paravicini 1984. Paravicini, W. "Die Krise der französischen Gesellschaft im Zeitalter des Hundertjährigen Krieges," in *Europa 1400: Die Krise des Spätmittelalters*. Ed. F. Seibt and W. Eberhard. Stuttgart: 1984.

Parkes 1938a. Parkes, J. "Christian Influence on the Status of the Jews in Europe," *Historia judaica*, 1 (1938), 31–38.

Idem 1938b. *The Jew in the Medieval Community: A Study of His Political and Economic Situation*. London: 1938.

Paterson 1986. Paterson, L. "Tournaments and Knightly Sports in Twelfth-and Thirteenth-Century Occitania," *Medium Aevum*, 55 (1986), 72–79.

Pegues 1962. Pegues, F. *The Lawyers of the Last Capetians*. Princeton: 1962.

Petit 1900. Petit, J. *Charles de Valois (1270–1325)*. Paris: 1900.

Petit-Dutaillis 1894. Petit-Dutaillis, C. *Etude sur la vie et le règne de Louis VIII (1187–1226)*. Paris: 1894.

Petrus Riga. Petrus Riga. *Aurora*. 2 vols. Ed. P. Beichner. Notre Dame, Ind.: 1965.

Pflaum 1930. Pflaum, H. "Les scènes de juifs dans la littérature dramatique du moyen-âge," *Revue des études juives*, 89 (1930), 111–34.

Idem 1934. "Der allegorische Streit zwischen Synagoge und Kirche in der europäischen Dichtung des Mittelalters," *Archivum Romanicum*, 18 (1934), 243–340.

PG. Patrilogiae cursus completus, series graeca. Comp. J.-P. Migne. Paris: 1857–1889.

Piétresson de Saint-Aubin 1920. Piétresson de Saint-Aubin, P. "Document inédit relatif aux juifs de Troyes," *Le Moyen âge*, 31 (1920), 84–87.

Pirenne 1937. Pirenne, H. *Economic and Social History of Medieval Europe*. Tr. I. Clegg. New York: 1937.

Pitt-Rivers 1977. Pitt-Rivers, J. *The Fate of Shechem or the Politics of Sex: Essays in the Anthropology of the Mediterranean*. Cambridge: 1977.

PL. Patrilogiae cursus completus, series latina. Comp. J.-P. Migne. Paris: 1844–1864.

Poliakov 1965. Poliakov, L. *The History of Anti-Semitism, I: From the Time of Christ to the Court Jews*. Tr. R. Howard. New York: 1965.

Idem 1967. *Les Banquiers juifs et le Saint-siège du XIIIe au XVIIe siècle*. Paris: 1967.

Pollock and Maitland 1968. Pollock, F. and F. Maitland. *The History of English Law before the Time of Edward I*. 2 vols. Cambridge: 1968.

Pons 1984. Pons, A. *Los Judios del reino de Mallorca durante los siglos XIII y XIV*, I. Palma de Mallorca: 1984.

Poole 1951. Poole, A. *From Domesday Book to Magna Carta*. Oxford: 1951.

Poquet 1857. Poquet, Abbé. *Les Miracles de la sainte Vierge*. Paris: 1857.

Portal 1907. Portal, F. *La République marseillaise du XIII siècle, 1200–1263*. Marseille: 1907.

Powicke 1953. Powicke, M. *The Thirteenth Century*. London: 1953.

Idem 1960. *The Loss of Normandy*. Manchester: 1960.

Pressat 1985. Pressat, R. *The Dictionary of Demography*. Ed. C. Wilson. Oxford: 1985.

Prestwich 1980. Prestwich, M. *The Three Edwards*. New York: 1980.

Prévot 1975. Prévot, P. *Histoire du ghetto d'Avignon: A travers la carrière des juifs d'Avignon*. Avignon: 1975.

Prud'homme 1835. Prud'homme, E. "Die Judengasse (La Rue des juifs): Chronique strasbourgeois (1349)," *Revue d'Alsace*, 2 (1835), 36–42.

Purcell 1975. Purcell, M. *Papal Crusading Policy, 1244–1291*. Leyden: 1975.

QBit. *Queremoniae biterrensium 1247*, in *HF*, XXIV, 319–84.

QCar. *Queremoniae carcassonensium 1247*, in *HF*, XXIV, 296–319.

QCen. *Queremoniae cenomannorum et andegavorum 1247*, in *HF*, XXIV, 73–93.

QNor. *Queremoniae normannorum 1247*, in *HF*, XXIV, 1–72.

QTur. *Queremoniae turonum, santonum, et pictavorum 1247*, in *HF*, XXIV, 94–252.

Quantin 1873. Quantin, M. *Recueil de pièces pour faire suite au Cartulaire général de l'Yonne*. Auxerre and Paris: 1873.

Rabinowitz 1938. Rabinowitz, L. *The Social Life of the Jews of Northern France in the XII-XIV Centuries*. London: 1938.

Idem 1940. "The Herem Ha-Yishub and the Merchant Guild in Goslar," *Historia judaica*, 2 (1940), 13–19.

Raedts 1977. Raedts, P. "The Children's Crusade of 1212," *Journal of Medieval History*, 3 (1977), 279–323.

Ramban 1971. Ramban (Rabbi Moses ben Nachman/Nachmanides). *Commentary on the Torah: Genesis*. Tr. C. Chavel. New York: 1971.

Ramette 1971. Ramette, Y. "L'Inscription hébraique de Lozère retrouvée." *Revue des études juives*, 130 (1971), 463–64.

Rashi 1905. Rashi (Rabbi Solomon ben Isaac). *Kommentar des Salomo B. Isak über den Pentateuch [al Torah]*. Ed. A. Berliner. Frankfurt-am-Main: 1905.

Rauh 1979. Rauh, H. *Das Bild des Antichrist im Mittelalter: Von Tyconius zum Deutschen Symbolismus*. 2nd ed. Münster: 1979.

Reallexikon. *Reallexikon für Antike und Christentum*. Stuttgart: 1950–.

Réau 1955–1959. Réau, L. *Iconographie de l'art chrétien*, 3 vols. in 6 parts. Paris: 1955–1959.

Recueil des actes de Philippe Auguste. *Recueil des actes de Philippe Auguste*. 4 vols. Eds. H.-F. Delaborde and others. Paris: 1916– 1979.

Recueil des statuts. *Recueil des statuts, ordonnances et réglements synodaux de l'archidiocèse de Sens*. Sens: 1854.

Redoutey 1977. Redoutey, J.-P. "Philippe le Bel et la Franche-Comté," in *Provinces et états dans la France de l'Est* (Cahiers de l'Association interuniversitaire de l'Est, no. 19, 1977), pp. 207–31.

Registres . . . Philippe IV. *Registres du Trésor des chartes*, I: *Règne de Philippe le Bel*. Ed. R. Fawtier. Paris: 1958.

Regné 1908. Regné. J. "Etude sur la condition des juifs de Narbonne du Ve au XIVe siècle," *Revue des études juives*, 55 (1908), 1–36, 221–43.

Idem 1909. "Etude sur la condition des juifs de Narbonne du Ve au XIVe siecle," *Revue des études juives*, 58 (1909), 75–105, 200–25.

Idem 1910. "Etude sur la condition des juifs de Narbonne du Ve au XIVe siècle," *Revue des études juives*, 59 (1910), 58–89.

Rembaum 1982. Rembaum, J. "The Talmud and the Popes: Reflections on the Talmud Trials of the 1240s," *Viator*, 13 (1982), 203–21.

Remy 1881. Remy, A. *Histoire de Châtillon-sur-Marne.* Reims: 1881.

Renna 1973. Renna, T. "Kingship in the *Disputatio inter clericum et militem*," *Speculum*, 48 (1973), 675–93.

Reyerson 1980. Reyerson, K. "Les Opérations de crédit dans la coutume et dans la vie des affaires à Montpellier au moyen âge: Le Problème de l'usure," in *Diritto comune e diritti locali nella storia dell'Europa.* Varenna: 1980.

Idem 1982. "Medieval Silks in Montpellier: The Silk Market ca. 1250–ca. 1350," *Journal of European Economic History*, 11 (1982), 117–40.

Idem 1985. *Business, Banking and Finance in Medieval Montpellier.* Toronto: 1935.

Richard 1983. Richard, J. *Saint Louis: Roi d'une France féodale, soutien de la Terre Sainte.* Paris: 1983.

Richards 1977. Richards, P. *The Medieval Leper and His Northern Heir.* Cambridge and Totowa: 1977.

Richardson 1960. Richardson, H. *English Jewry under the Angevin Kings.* London: 1960.

Riquet 1976. Riquet, M. "Saint Louis roi de France et les juifs," in *Septième centenaire de la mort de saint Louis.* Paris: 1976.

Robert 1881. Robert, U. "Catalogue d'actes relatifs aux juifs pendant le moyen âge," *Revue des études juives*, 3 (1881), 211–24.

Idem 1883. "Chartes relatives aux juifs de Dijon," *Revue des études juives*, 7 (1883), 281–83.

Roblin 1952a. Roblin, M. "Les Cimetières juifs de Paris au moyen âge," *Fédération des sociétés historiques et archéologiques de Paris et de l'Ile-de-France: Mémoires*, 4 (1952), 7–19.

Idem 1952b. *Les Juifs de Paris.* Paris: 1952.

Roman de Fauvel. Le Roman de Fauvel. Ed. A Langfors. Paris: 1914–1919.

Romano 1977. Romano, D. "La Transmission des sciences arabes par les juifs en Languedoc," *Cahiers de Fanjeaux*, 12 (1977), 363–86.

Roquebert 1970. Roquebert, M. *L'Epopée cathare, 1198–1212: L'Invasion.* Toulouse: 1970.

Rosenthal 1960. Rosenthal, E. "Anti-Christian Polemic in Medieval Bible Commentaires," *Journal of Jewish Studies*, 11 (1960), 115–35.

Rosenthal 1956/1957. Rosenthal, J. "The Talmud on Trial," *Jewish Quarterly Review*, new series, 47 (1956/1957), 58–76, 145–69.

Idem 1957. "Prolegomena to a Critical Edition of *Milhamot Adonai* of Jacob Ben Reuben," *Proceedings of the American Academy for Jewish Research*, 26 (1957), 127–37.

Roth 1932. Roth, C. "The Jews in the Middle Ages," in *The Cambridge Medieval History*, VII. Cambridge: 1932.

Idem 1941. *A History of the Jews in England.* Oxford: 1941.

Idem 1964. *A History of the Jews in England.* 3rd ed. Oxford: 1964.

Rotuli de oblatis. Rotuli de oblatis et finibus. Ed. T. Hardy. London: 1835.

Rotuli litterarum patentium. Rotuli litterarum patentium. Ed. T. Hardy. London: 1835.

Rubin 1987. Rubin, M. *Charity and Community in Medieval Cambridge.* Cambridge: 1987.

Russell 1984. Russell, J(effrey). *Lucifer: The Devil in the Middle Ages.* Ithaca and London: 1984.

Russell 1972. Russell, J(osiah). "Population in Europe 500–1500," in *Fontana Economic History of Europe*, I: *The Middle Ages.* Ed. C. Cipolla. London: 1972.

Saige 1881. Saige, G. *Les Juifs du Languedoc antérieurement au XIVe siècle.* Paris: 1881.

Saillant 1934. Saillant, L. *Au pays du Maine.* 2nd ed. Le Mans: 1934.

Salzman 1968. Salzman, L. *Edward I.* London: 1968.

Saperstein 1986. Saperstein, M. "The Conflict over the Rashba's Herem on Philosophical Study: A Political Perspective," *Jewish History*, 1 (1986), 27–38.

Sarachek 1968. Sarachek, J. *The Doctrine of the Messiah in Medieval Jewish Literature.* 2nd ed. New York: 1968.

Schiff 1982. Schiff, E. *From Stereotype to Metaphor: The Jew in Contemporary Drama.* Albany, N.Y.: 1982.

Schmidt 1983. Schmidt, C. *Histoire et doctrine des cathares.* Bayonne, N.J.: 1983.

Schrire 1966. Schrire, T. *Hebrew Amulets: Their Decipherment and Interpretation.* London: 1966.

Schwab 1884. Schwab, M. "Inscription juive du musée de Saint-Germain," *Revue des études juives*, 8 (1884), 137–38.

Idem 1887. "Trois inscriptions hébraïques de Mantes," *Revue des études juives*, 15 (1887), 295–98.

Idem 1895. "Notes de comptabilité juive du XIIIe et du XIVe siècle," *Revue des études juives*, 30 (1895), 289–94.

Idem 1897. "Inscriptions hébraïques en France du XIIe au XVe siècle," *Bulletin archéologique du Comité des travaux historiques et scientifiques*, 1897, pp. 178–217.

Idem 1904. "Rapport sur les inscriptions hébraïques en France," *Nouvelles archives des missions scientifiques et littéraires*, 12 (1904), 143–402.

Idem 1909. "Une Epitaphe juive trouvée à Paris," *Bulletin de la Société de l'histoire de Paris et de l'Ile de France*, 36 (1909), 113–16.

Schwartz 1975. Schwartz, J. "Juifs d'Alsace vers 1300," *Archives juives*, 11 (1975), 53–55.

Schwarzfuchs 1957. Schwarzfuchs, S. *Etudes sur l'origine et le développement du rabbinat au moyen âge.* Paris: 1957.

Idem 1966. "De la condition des juifs de France aux XIIe et XIIIe siècles," *Revue des études juives*, 125 (1966), 221–32.

Idem 1975. *Les Juifs de France.* Paris: 1975.

Schweitzer 1971. Schweitzer, F. *A History of the Jews since the First Century AD.* New York: 1971.

Secall i Güell, 1983. Secall i Güell, G. *Les Jueries médiévals tarragonines.* Valls: 1983.

Sée 1901. Sée, H. *Les Classes rurales et le régime domanial en France au moyen âge.* Paris: 1901.

Sefer ha-Yashar. Sefer ha-Yashar or the Book of Jasher. Salt Lake City: 1887 (repr. 1965).

Septimus 1979. Septimus, B. "Piety and Power in Thirteenth-Century Catalonia," in *Studies in Medieval Jewish History and Literature*. Ed. I. Twersky. Cambridge, Mass. and London: 1979.

Shahar 1977. Shahar, S. "Ecrits cathares et commentaires d'Abraham Abulafia sur le 'Livre de la création': Images et idées communes," *Cahiers de Fanjeaux*, 12 (1977), 345–62.

Shatzmiller 1970. Shatzmiller, J. "La Perception de la Tallia judeorum en Provence au milieu du XIVe siècle," *Annales du Midi*, 82 (1970), 221–36.

Idem 1973a. "L'Inquisition et les juifs de Provence au XIIIe s.," *Provence historique*, 23 (1973), 327–38.

Idem 1973b. *Recherches sur la communauté juive de Manosque*. Paris: 1973.

Idem 1977a. "Contacts et échanges entre savants juifs et chrétiens à Montpellier vers 1300," *Cahiers de Fanjeaux*, 12 (1977), 377–44.

Idem 1977b. "'Tumultus et rumor in sinagoga': An Aspect of Social Life of Provencal Jews in the Middle Ages," *AJSreview* (1977), 227–55.

Idem 1977–1978. "Calendar of the Plea Rolls," *Jewish Quarterly Review*, new series, 68 (1977–1978), 173–76.

Idem 1979. "En Provence médiévale: Les Juifs de Gordes (Vaucluse) (1312)," *Revue des études juives*, 138 (1979), 351–54.

Idem 1980a. "Les Ecoles dans la littérature rabbinique," in *Art et archéologie des juifs en France médiévale*. Ed. B. Blumenkranz. Toulouse: 1980.

Idem 1980b. "L'Excommunication, la communauté juive et les autorités tempo- relles au moyen-âge," in *Les Juifs dans l'histoire de France*. Ed. M. Yardeni. Lei- den: 1980.

Idem 1980c. "Paulus Christiani: Un Aspect de son activité anti-juive," in *Hommage à Georges Vajda*. Ed. G. Nahon and C. Touati. Louvain: 1980.

Idem 1980d. "Structures communautaires juives à Marseille: Une Confirmation," *Provence historique*, 30 (1980), 218–19.

Idem 1980e. "Researches on Anti-Semitism in the Middle Ages: An Accusation of Jews Profaning the Cross," in *Studies in the History of the Jewish People and the Land of Israel*. Haifa: 1980.

Idem 1981. "Converts and Judaizers in the Early Fourteenth Century," *Harvard Theological Review*, 74 (9181), 63–78.

Idem 1982a. Doctors and Medical Practice in Germany around the Year 1200: The Evidence of *Sefer Hasidim*," *Journal of Jewish Studies*, 33 (1982), 583–93.

Idem 1928b. "Onomastique juive du Languedoc: Le Nom Halafta," *Archives juives*, 18 (1982), 24.

Idem 1982–1983. "In Search of the 'Book of Figures': Medicine and Astrology in Montpellier at the Turn of the Fourteenth Century," *AJSreview*, 7–8 (1982–1983), 383–407.

Idem 1983a. "Doctors and Medical Practices in Germany around the Year 1200: The Evidence of *Sefer Asaph*," *Proceedings of the American Academy of Jewish Research*, 50 (1983), 149–64.

Idem 1983b. "Terminologie politique en hébreu médiéval: Jalons pour un glos- saire," *Revue des études juives*, 142 (1983), 133–40.

Idem 1984a. "Doctors' Fees and their Medical Responsibility," in *Sources of Social History: Private Acts of the Late Middle Ages*.Ed. P. Brezzi and E. Lee. Toronto: 1984.

Idem 1984b. "Droit féodal et legislation rabbinique: La Cuisson du pain chez les juifs du moyen âge," in *Manger et boire au moyen âge*. Nice: 1984.

Shereshevsky 1968–1969. Shereshevsky, E. "Hebrew Traditions in Peter Comestor's *Historia Scholastica*, I *Genesis*," *Jewish Quarterly Review*, new series, 59 (1968–1969), 268–89.

Shohet 1931. Shohet, D. *The Jewish Court in the Middle Ages*. New York: 1931.

Siberry 1985. Siberry, E. *Criticism of Crusading, 1095–1274*. Oxford: 1985.

Sigal 1977. Sigal, P. *The Emergence of Contemporary Judaism*, II. Pittsburgh: 1967. 1977.

Sinanoglou 1973. Sinanoglou, L. "The Christ Child as Sacrifice," *Speculum*, 48 (1973), 490–509.

Sirat 1966. Sirat, C. "Une Formule divinatoire latine dans deux manuscrits hébreux," *Revue des études juives*, 125 (1966), 391–94.

Sivéry 1983a. Sivéry, G. *Saint Louis et son siècle*. Paris: 1983.

Idem 1983b. "Le Mécontentement dans le royaume de France et les Enquêtes de saint Louis," *Revue historique*, no. 545 (Jan.-Mar. 1983), 3–24.

Idem 1984. *L'Economie du royaume de France au siècle de saint Louis*. Lille: 1984.

Smalley 1952. Smalley, B. *The Study of the Bible in the Middle Ages*. Oxford: 1952.

Idem 1983. *The Study of the Bible in the Middle Ages*. 3rd ed. Oxford: 1983.

Smyser 1937. Smyser, H. *The Pseudo-Turpin*. Cambridge, Mass.: 1937.

Souchet 1867–1873. Souchet, J.-B. *Histoire du diocèse et de la ville de Chartres*. 4 vols. Chartres: 1867–1873.

Soultrait 1873. Soultrait, J. *Inventaire des titres de Nevers*. Nevers: 1873.

Southern 1953. Southern, R. *The Making of the Middle Ages*. New Haven: 1953.

Stacey 1988. Stacey, R. "1240–60: A Watershed in Anglo-Jewish Relations?," *Bulletin of the Institute of Historical Research*, 61 (1988), 135–50.

Stein 1899. Stein, H. "Les Juifs de Montereau au moyen âge," *Annales de la Société historique du Gâtinais*, 17 (1899), 54–61.

Idem 1918–1919. "Les Juifs de Montereau au moyen-âge (nouveaux documents)," *Annales de la Société historique du Gâtinais*, 34 (1918– 1919), 116–20.

Stein 1955. Stein, S. "The Development of the Jewish Law on Interest from the Biblical Period to the Expulsion of the Jews from England,"*Historia judaica*, 17 (1955), 3–40.

Idem 1959. "A Disputation on Moneylending between Jews and Gentiles in Me'ir b. Simeon's Milhemeth Miswah (Narbonne, 13th Cent.)," *Journal of Jewish Studies*, 10 (1959), 45–61.

Stengers 1950. Stengers, J. *Les Juifs dans le Pays-Bas au moyen âge* (Académie royale de Belge, Classe des Lettres, Mémoires, 45). Brussels: 1950.

Stow 1977. Stow, K. *Catholic Thought and Papal Jewry Policy, 1555–1593*. New York: 1977.

Idem 1981. "Papal and Royal Attitudes toward Jewish Lending in the Thirteenth Century," *AJSreview*, 6 (1981), 161–83.

Idem 1984. *The '1007 Anonymous' and Papal Sovereignty*. Cincinnati, Oh.: 1984.

Straus 1942. Straus, R. "The 'Jewish Hat' as an Aspect of Social History," *Jewish Social Studies*, 4 (1942), 59–72.

Strayer 1932. Strayer, J. *The Administration of Normandy under Saint Louis*. Cambridge, Mass.: 1932.

Idem 1953. "The Crusade Against Aragon," *Speculum*, 28 (1953), 102–13.

Idem 1969. "France: The Holy Land, the Chosen People, and the Most Christian King," in *Action and Conviction in Early Modern Europe*. Ed. T. Rabb and J. Seigel. Princeton: 1969.

Idem 1970. *On the Medieval Origins of the Modern State*. Princeton: 1970.

Idem 1971a. *The Albigensian Crusades*. New York: 1971.

Idem 1971b. *Medieval Statecraft and the Perspectives of History*. Ed. J. Benton and T. Bisson. Princeton: 1971.

Idem 1977. "The Costs and Profits of War: The Anglo-French Conflict of 1294–1303," in *The Medieval City*. Ed. H. Miskimin and others. New Haven: 1977.

Idem 1980. *The Reign of Philip the Fair*. Princeton: 1980.

Strayer and Taylor 1939. Strayer, J. and C. Taylor. *Studies in Early French Taxation*. Cambridge: 1939.

Stroumsa 1983. Stroumsa, G. "Form(s) of God: Some Notes on Metatron and Christ," *Harvard Theological Review*, 76 (1983), 269–88.

Stubbs 1876. Stubbs, W. *The Historical Works of Master Ralph de Diceto*. 2 vols. London: 1876.

Study of Judaism. The Study of Judaism: Bibliographical Essays. New York: 1972.

Sumption 1978. Sumption, J. *The Albigensian Crusade*. London and Boston. 1978.

Synan 1965. Synan, E. *The Popes and the Jews in the Middle Ages*. New York and London: 1965.

Szapiro 1966. Szapiro, E. "Les Cimetières juifs de Toulouse au moyen âge," *Revue des études juives*, 125 (1966), 395–99.

Talmage 1967. Talmage, F. "R. David Kimhi as Polemicist," *Hebrew Union College Annual*, 38 (1967), 213–35.

Idem 1975. *Disputation and Dialogue: Readings in the Jewish Christian Encounter*. New York: 1975.

Idem 1987. Review of N. Golb, *Les Juifs de Rouen*, in *American Historical Review*, 92 (1987), 648.

Tardif 1881–1903. Tardif, E.-J. *Coutumiers de Normandie*. 2 vols. in 3 parts. Rouen and Paris: 1881–1903.

Temko 1954. Temko, A. "The Burning of the Talmud in Paris. Date: 1242," *Commentary*, 17 (1954), 446–55.

Idem 1955. "The Dark Age of Medieval Jewry: Persecution, Expulsion, the End of the Paris Synagogue," *Commentary*, 20 (1955), 228–39.

Idem 1959. "The Four Holy Communities: The Jewries of Medieval Provence," *Commentary*, 27 (1959), 223–42.

Thalamus parvus. Thalamus parvus: Le Petit Thalamus. Montpellier: 1836.

Thibault 1933. Thibault, F. "La Condition des personnes en France du IXe siècle au mouvement communal," *Revue historique de droit français et étranger*, 1933, pp. 424–77, 696–722.

Thillier and Jarry 1906. Thillier, J. and E. Jarry. *Cartulaire de Sainte-Croix d'Orleans*. Paris: 1906.

Thomas 1885. Thomas, A. "Les Juifs et la rue Joutx-Aigues, à Toulouse," *Annales du Midi*, 7 (1885), 439–42.

Thouzellier 1973. Thouzellier, C. *Livre des deux principes*. Paris: 1973.

Idem 1977. *Rituel cathare*. Paris: 1977.

Timbal 1950. Timbal, P. *Un conflit d'annexion au moyen âge: l'application de la coutume de Paris au pays d'Albigeois*. Toulouse: 1950.

Toch 1982. Toch, M. "Geld und Kredit in einer spätmittelalterlichen Landschaft: zu einem unbeachteten hebräischen Schuldenregister aus Niederbayern (1329–1332)," *Deutsches Archiv*, 38 (1982), 499–50.

Touati 1977. Touati, C. "Les Deux conflicts autour de Maimonide et des études philosophiques," *Cahiers de Fanjeaux*, 12 (1977), 173–84.

Touitou 1984. Touitou, E. "La Rénaissance du 12e siècle et l'exégèse biblique de Rashbam," *Archives juives*, 20 (1984), 3–12.

Idem 1985. "Quelques aspects de l'exégèse biblique juive en France médiévale," *Archives juives*, 21 (1985), 35–39.

Idem 1986. "Exégèse et polémique en France médièvale." *Archives juives* 22 (1986), 51–53.

Toynbee 1929. Toynbee, M. S. *Louis of Toulouse*. Manchester: 1929.

Trachtenberg 1939. Trachtenberg, J. *Jewish Magic and Superstition*. New York: 1939.

Idem 1944. *The Devil and the Jews*. New Haven and London: 1944.

Treharne 1971. Treharne, R. *The Baronial Plan of Reform, 1258–1263*. Manchester: 1971.

Trevor-Roper, 1969. Trevor-Roper, H. *The European Witch-Craze*. New York: 1969.

Tyerman 1984. Tyerman, C. "Philip V of France, the Assemblies of 1319–20 and the Crusade," *Bulletin of the Institute of Historical Research*, 57 (1984), 15–34.

Urbach 1955. Urbach, E. *Ba'alei Ha-Tosafot*. Jerusalem: 1955.

Veissière 1973–1974. Veissière, M. "Pour une meilleure connaissance des juifs à Provins au moyen âge," *Archives juives*, 10 (1973–1974), 52.

Vidal 1887, Vidal, P. "Les Juifs des anciens comtés de Roussillon et de Cerdagne," *Revue des études juives*, 15 (1887), 19–55.

Idem 1888. "Les Juifs des anciens comtés de Roussillon et de Cerdagne," *Revue des études juives*, 16 (1888), 1–23, 170–203.

Vie Saint Jehan-Baptiste. *Vie Saint Jehan-Baptiste: A Critical Edition of an Old French Poem of the Early Fourteenth Century*. Ed. R. Gieber. Tübingen: 1978.

Villand 1982. Villand, R. "Toponymes juifs de la Manche," *Archives juives*, 18 (1982), 55–59.

Vincent 1930. Vincent, Dr. "Les Juifs du Poitou, au bas moyen âge," *Revue d'histoire économique et sociale*, 18 (1930), 265–313.

Von Rad 1961. Von Rad, G. *Genesis: A Commentary*. Tr. J. Marks. Philadelphia: 1961.

Wacholder 1960–1961. Wacholder, B. "Cases of Proselytizing in the Tosafist Responsa," *Jewish Quarterly Review*, new series, 51 (1960–1961), 288–315.

Wakefield 1974. Wakefield, W. *Heresy, Crusade and Inquisition in Southern France, 110–1250.* London: 1974.

Wechsler 1975. Wechsler, J. "A Change in the Iconography of the Song of Songs in 12th and 13th Century Latin Bibles," in *Texts and Responses: Studies Presented to Nahum N. Glatzer.* Ed. M. Fishbane and P. Flohr. Leiden: 1975.

Weill 1966. Weill, G. "Les Juifs dans le Barrois et la Meuse du moyen âge à nos jours," *Revue des études juives,* 125 (1966), 287–301.

Idem 1983. "La Pierre écrite: Epitaphe hébraïque de la tombe juive de Serres et les juifs du Serrois," *Revue des études juives,* 142 (1983), 21–72.

Weill 1907. Weill, J. "Un Juif brulé a Metz vers 1385 pour profanation d'hostie," *Revue des études juives,* 53 (1907), 270–72.

Weinberg 1924. Weinberg, M. "Untersuchungen über das Wesen des Memorbuches," *Jahrbuch der Jüdisch-Literarischen Gesellschaft,* 16 (1924), 253–320.

Weinraub 1976. Weinraub, E. *Chrétien's Jewish Grail: A New Investigation of the Imagery and Significance of Chrétien de Troyes's Grail Episode Based upon Medieval Hebraic Sources.* Chapel Hill, N.C.: 1976.

Weiss 1888/1889. Weiss, I. "The Study of the Talmud in the Thirteenth Century," *Jewish Quarterly Review,* I (1888/1889), 289–313.

Werblowsky 1960. Werblowsky, R. "Crispin's Disputation," *Journal of Jewish Studies,* II (1960), 69–77.

Weyl 1974. Weyl, R. "Les Inscriptions hébraïques des musées de Strasbourg," *Cahiers alsaciens d'archéologie, d'art et d'histoire,* 1974, pp. 123–41.

Idem 1976. "Corrections," *Archives juives,* 12 (1976), 71.

Wifall 1983. Wifall, W. "The Tribes of Yahweh: A Synchronic Study with a Diachronic Title," *Zeitschrift für die Altestamentliche Wissenschaft,* 95 (1983), 197–209.

Wolff 1967. Wolff, P. *Histoire du Languedoc.* Toulouse: 1967.

Wood 1966. Wood, C. *The French Apanages and the Capetian Monarchy, 1224–1328.* Cambridge, Mass.: 1966.

Idem 1976. "Queens, Queans, and Kingship: An Inquiry into Theories of Royal Legitimacy in Late Medieval England and France," in *Order and Innovation in the Middle Ages: Essays in Honor of Joseph R. Strayer.* Ed. W. Jordan, B. McNab and T. Ruiz. Princeton: 1976.

Yerushalmi 1970. Yerushalmi, Y. "The Inquisition and the Jews of France in the Time of Bernard Gui," *Harvard Theological Review,* 63 (1970), 317–76.

Zimmer 1976. Zimmer, E. "Medieval Jewry in Northern France," *Jewish Quarterly Review,* 66 (1976), 176–80.

Zuckerman 1972. Zuckerman, A. *A Jewish Princedom in Feudal France, 768–900,* New York: 1972.

Index

French towns with initial *Le* or *La* are indexed under "L". Place names and institutions preceded by Saint or Sainte will be found under "S"; but individual saints, kings and popes are listed under their given names. Where the endnotes provide information supplementary to that available in the text, or where they include discussions of controversial opinions, references have been furnished in the index.

readmission/resettlement of Jews in France
(after 1198) 37–47; (after 1315) 240–43,
323 n. 29; (after 1359) 248
rex christianissimus 68, 250–51, 256
Rhineland 218, 220, 222–23, 326 n. 84; massacres 11–12; 19–20, 22, 51
ribaldi (in Albigensian Crusade) 122
Richard I the Lionhearted 35, 40, 66
Richard of Paris (*or* of Pontoise) 18–19
Richard of Saint-Victor 14; *Benjamin minor*
264 n. 45
Richardson, H., views of 54, 64, 275 n. 79
Rigord 9–10, 23, 26, 28, 31, 33–34, 37–38,
43–44
riots, anti-Jewish 249–50, 326 n. 84
ritual humiliation 304 n. 66; *osculum pedum*
232
ritual murder 17–19, 136–37, 146–47, 153, 191,
219, 222, 226, 265 nn. 74, 76, 296 n. 44,
310 n. 112. *See also* blood libel
Robert de Curçon 68, 73, 77, 79–81, 280 n.
78
Robert Gaugin 265 n. 72
Robert of Anjou 230
Robert of Auxerre 40, 44, 283 n. 48
Robert of Bury 18
Robert of Dreux 99
Robert of Torigni 18
Robert Poulain 81
Roblin, M., views of 9
Rodez 289 n. 5
Rodulfus Cointe 294 n. 15
Roman de Fauvel 316 n. 10
Roquemaure 247
Roth, C., views of 16
rouelle. See sign of infamy
Rouen 51, 53–54, 212, 275–76 n. 83
Rouergue 211
Rousillon 232, 235
royal domain 3–4; Jews (1180) 23–24;
guard of churches 111–12. *See also* Ile de
France
Rudolf von Schlettstadt 319 n. 52
Rudolph I 219

Saige, G., views of 122–23, 165, 168–69, 187,
205, 209, 235
Saint-Antonin of Pamiers 167–68, 204
Saint-Cyr of Nevers 186
Saint-Denis 6, 34, 325 n. 82

Saint-Etienne of Nevers 185
Saint-Etienne of Toulouse 172
Saint-Florentin, abbey of 162
Saint-Gilles 205, 210; council (1209) 293 n.
93
Saint-Jean-d'Angély 105
Saint-Jean-sur-Tourbe 286 n. 10
Saint-Loup of Champagne 88
Saint-Maixent 234
Saint-Maximin 231
Saint-Malo 281 n. 95
Saint-Martin of Tours 80
Saint-Pol 69, 286 n. 10
Saint-Pourçain 234
Saint-Quentin 156
Saint-Remy-de-Provence 231
Saint-Yved of Braine 37
Sainte-Chapelle, Dijon 315 n. 75
Sainte-Chapelle, Paris 161
Sainte-Marie-en-Chaux 325–26 n. 83
Sainte-Menehould 286 n. 10
Sainte-Scholasse-sur-Sarthe 54–55
Sainte-Suzanne 286 n. 10
"saints (children)" 17, 311 n. 120. *See also*
William of Norwich; Harold of
Gloucester; Richard of Paris; etc.
Saperstein, M., views of 201
Saragossa 322 n. 155
Saulnières 281 n. 95
Saumur 59–60
Savari de Mauléon 289 n. 8
Savoy 224, 229, 231, 326 n. 84
Schwarzfuchs, S., views of 209, 248–49
scola. See synagogue
seals and sealing, Jewish 42, 62–64, 74, 96;
in Brittany 71. *See also* bonds
Sées 54
Segré 59
seisin, *see* jurisdiction
Senlis 43
Sens and Sénonais 6, 32, 43, 53, 211
serfs, manumission 240. *See also* Jews, anal-
ogy with serfs
Sermaize 156
Serres 229
servants of Jews, restrictions 68, 135
sexual relations, restrictions 24, 182
Sézanne 213
Shakespeare 46
Shatzmiller, J., views 226

University of Pennsylvania Press
MIDDLE AGES SERIES
EDWARD PETERS, GENERAL EDITOR

Edward Peters, ed. *Christian Society and the Crusades, 1198–1229*. Sources in Translation, including The Capture of Damietta by Oliver of Paderborn. 1971

Edward Peters, ed. *The First Crusade: The Chronicle of Fulcher of Chartres and Other Source Materials*. 1971

Katherine Fischer Drew, trans. *The Burgundian Code: The Book of Constitutions or Law of Gundobad and Additional Enactments*. 1972

G. G. Coulton. *From St. Francis to Dante: Translations from the Chronicle of the Franciscan Salimbene (1221–1288)*. 1972

Alan C. Kors and Edward Peters, eds. *Witchcraft in Europe, 1110–1700: A Documentary History*. 1972

Richard C. Dales. *The Scientific Achievement of the Middle Ages*. 1973

Katherine Fischer Drew, trans. *The Lombard Laws*. 1973

Edward Peters, ed. *Monks, Bishops, and Pagans: Christian Culture in Gaul and Italy, 500–700*. 1975

Jeanne Krochalis and Edward Peters, ed. and trans. *The World of Piers Plowman*. 1975

Julius Goebel, Jr. *Felony and Misdemeanor: A Study in the History of Criminal Law*. 1976

Susan Mosher Stuard, ed. *Women in Medieval Society*. 1976

Clifford Peterson. *Saint Erkenwald*. 1977

Robert Somerville and Kenneth Pennington, eds. *Law, Church, and Society: Essays in Honor of Stephan Kuttner*. 1977

Donald E. Queller. *The Fourth Crusade: The Conquest of Constantinople, 1201–1204*. 1977

Pierre Riché (Jo Ann McNamara, trans.). *Daily Life in the World of Charlemagne*. 1978

Edward Peters, ed. *Heresy and Authority in Medieval Europe*. 1980

Suzanne Fonay Wemple. *Women in Frankish Society: Marriage and the Cloister, 500–900*. 1981

Edward Peters. *The Magician, the Witch, and the Law*. 1982

Barbara H. Rosenwein. *Rhinoceros Bound: Cluny in the Tenth Century*. 1982

Steven D. Sargent, ed. and trans. *On the Threshold of Exact Science: Selected Writings of Anneliese Maier on Late Medieval Natural Philosophy*. 1982

Benedicta Ward. *Miracles and the Medieval Mind: Theory, Record, and Event, 1000–1215*. 1982

Harry Turtledove, trans. *The Chronicle of Theophanes: An English Translation of* anni mundi *6095–6305 (A.D. 602–813)*. 1982

Leonard Cantor, ed. *The English Medieval Landscape*. 1982

Charles T. Davis. *Dante's Italy and Other Essays*. 1984

George T. Dennis, trans. *Maurice's Strategikon: Handbook of Byzantine Military Strategy.* 1984

Thomas F. X. Noble. *The Republic of St. Peter: The Birth of the Papal State, 680–825.* 1984

Kenneth Pennington. *Pope and Bishops: The Papal Monarchy in the Twelfth and Thirteenth Centuries.* 1984

Patrick J. Geary. *Aristocracy in Provence: The Rhône Basin at the Dawn of the Carolingian Age.* 1985

C. Stephen Jaeger. *The Origins of Courtliness: Civilizing Trends and the Formation of Courtly Ideals, 939–2210.* 1985

J. N. Hillgarth, ed. *Christianity and Paganism, 350–750: The Conversion of Western Europe.* 1986

William Chester Jordan. *From Servitude to Freedom: Manumission in the Sénonais in the Thirteenth Century.* 1986

James William Brodman. *Ransoming Captives in Crusader Spain: The Order of Merced on the Christian-Islamic Frontier.* 1986

Frank Tobin. *Meister Eckhart: Thought and Language.* 1986

Daniel Bornstein, trans. *Dino Compagni's Chronicle of Florence.* 1986

James M. Powell. *Anatomy of a Crusade, 1213–1221.* 1986

Jonathan Riley-Smith. *The First Crusade and the Idea of Crusading.* 1986

Susan Mosher Stuard, ed. *Women in Medieval History and Historiography.* 1987

Avril Henry, ed. *The Mirour of Mans Saluacioune.* 1987

María Rosa Menocal. *The Arabic Role in Medieval Literary History.* 1987

Margaret J. Ehrhart. *The Judgment of the Trojan Prince Paris in Medieval Literature.* 1987

Betsy Bowden. *Chaucer Aloud: The Varieties of Textual Interpretation.* 1987

Felipe Fernández-Armesto. *Before Columbus: Exploration and Colonization from the Mediterranean to the Atlantic, 1229–1492.* 1987

Michael Resler, trans. *EREC by Hartmann von Aue.* 1987

A. J. Minnis. *Medieval Theory of Authorship.* 1988

Uta-Renate Blumenthal. *The Investiture Controversy: Church and Monarchy from the Ninth to the Twelfth Century.* 1988

Robert Hollander. *Boccaccio's Last Fiction: "Il Corbaccio."* 1988

Ralph Turner. *Men Raised from the Dust: Administrative Service and Upward Mobility in Angevin England.* 1988

David Anderson. *Before the Knight's Tale: Imitation of Classical Epic in Boccaccio's "Teseida."* 1988

Charlotte A. Newman. *The Anglo-Norman Nobility in the Reign of Henry I: The Second Generation.* 1988

Joseph F. O'Callaghan. *The Cortes of Castile-León, 1188–1350.* 1988

William D. Paden. *The Voice of the Trobairitz: Essays on the Women Troubadours.* 1989

William Chester Jordan. *The French Monarchy and the Jews: From Philip Augustus to the Last Capetians.* 1989

Edward B. Irving, Jr. *Rereading "Beowulf."* 1989

David Burr. *Olivi and Franciscan Poverty: The Origins of the "Usus Pauper" Controversy.* 1989

Willene B. Clark and Meradith McMunn, eds. *Beasts and Birds of the Middle Ages: The Bestiary and Its Legacy.* 1989